HILL COUNTRY BALL

HILL COUNTRY BALL

DEPRESSION-ERA BASEBALL IN THE TEXAS GERMAN BELT

RICHARD W. BUTLER JR.

FOREWORD BY JEREMY AFFELDT

TEXAS TECH UNIVERSITY PRESS

This book is typeset in Adobe Caslon Pro. The paper used in this book meets the minimum requirements of ANSI/NISO Z39.48–1992 (R1997). ♾

Designed by Hannah Gaskamp
Cover design by Hannah Gaskamp
Cover photos, clockwise from bottom left: Boerne White Sox player Henry Fabra (courtesy of Patrick Heath Public Library, Boerne, Texas), Boerne White Sox player Edgar Bergmann (courtesy of Betsy Sueltenfuss Bergmann), Kerrville All-Stars player Freddy Dimery (courtesy of Clifton Fifer Jr.), and Boerne White Sox player Bruno Dedecker (courtesy of Patrick Heath Public Library, Boerne, Texas).

Library of Congress Cataloging-in-Publication Data on file

ISBN: 978–1-68283–315–5 (paperback)
ISBN: 978–1-68283–316–2 (ebook)

Texas Tech University Press
Box 41037
Lubbock, Texas 79409–1037 USA
800.832.4042
ttup@ttu.edu
www.ttupress.org

For Maggie

Remember the days of old; consider the generations long past. Ask your father, and he will tell you, your elders, and they will explain it to you.

DEUTERONOMY 32:7

The lines have fallen for me in pleasant places; indeed, I have a beautiful inheritance.

PSALM 16:6

CONTENTS

ILLUSTRATIONS

TABLES

FOREWORD

When I won my first World Series, I celebrated with my team on the mound and looked around at 40,000 fans. The lights were blazing and cameras were flashing as the weight of history lifted off our shoulders. But as the champagne dried and the headlines faded, what I carried with me wasn't the scoreboard or the statistics—it was a quiet memory of my first game on a dusty diamond in a small town, where my mom and dad sat in a folding chair behind home plate and the only cheers came from neighbors and friends.

Reading *Hill Country Ball* brought me back to those roots, to a time when baseball wasn't about million-dollar contracts or ESPN highlight reels, but about pride, community, and connection. Richard Butler has captured a part of America that many have forgotten—or maybe never knew existed. His stories of Depression-era "town ball" in the Texas Hill Country reminded me of what baseball really is at its core: not a sport, but a language: a way for people to express hope, belonging, resilience, and joy.

In these pages, you'll meet men who pitched after working 10 hours on a ranch, who played for the honor of their hometown—not a paycheck. You'll feel the dirt under their cleats, the sting of a fastball missed, and the elation of a game well played in front of a modest crowd that cared deeply. This was baseball not as spectacle, but as sacred tradition.

As someone who's played in packed stadiums and lifted the World Series trophy three times, I can tell you: greatness isn't just measured in rings. It's found in the grit of a shortstop in Boerne booting a grounder but showing up again next Sunday. It's in the laughter after a postgame dance on the bridge in Comfort. It's in the courage of a Black team in Kerrville playing for dignity when few were watching.

I tip my cap to the men and women who kept the game alive in the Hill Country during the hardest of times—and to Richard Butler for telling their story with such care. Whether you're a lifelong fan or simply curious about the spirit of small-town America, this book reminds us that baseball was, and always will be, the people's game.

Let's play ball.

JEREMY AFFELDT
THREE-TIME WORLD SERIES CHAMPION

PREFACE

I first felt the appeal of Hill Country baseball while I was spending time inside the local jail. Before you jump to any conclusions, let me explain.

Just after I moved to the Hill Country, I visited the Old Jail Museum in Boerne, Texas. Paul Barwick, special projects director for the City of Boerne, is a kind gentleman who gives tours of the museum on Saturday mornings. Apart from the old jail cells, the museum displays numerous artifacts illustrating the history of Boerne and Kendall County. Just inside the door, I noticed a large photograph of the Boerne White Sox from many years ago. Mr. Barwick saw my interest and struck up a conversation. Little did I know where that would lead.

When I inquired about the history of the Boerne White Sox, whose players were beaming back at me from the museum wall, Mr. Barwick responded that the Patrick Heath Public Library in Boerne had a file on the team. When I ventured to the library, Robin Stauber, adult services librarian, kindly allowed me to review the historic file. Upon opening it, I was fascinated by more photographs of White Sox players as well as newspaper articles from 1934 and 1935.

For a fan of baseball history, the visit to the Old Jail Museum and the examination of the library file struck a chord, starting me on a quest in pursuit of an untold story from a bygone era. As I began to research newspaper articles from that time, I realized that the story was much larger than just the Boerne White Sox. It was the story of baseball in the Hill Country, which served to strengthen communities that were suffering the economic hardships of the Depression. But it was also part of a larger story fashioned by the nature of baseball itself.

Baseball is the quintessential American game because it demands accountability. Unlike most team sports, it requires discrete performances on every pitch, if not every play. While there is some teamwork in baseball (as on a 6–4–3 double play), most of the game's outcomes depend on how one or two players perform the basic skills of baseball: pitching, hitting, baserunning, and fielding. As a result, baseball is at its heart a lonely game. Indeed, nothing is lonelier than a shortstop booting an easy groundball or a batter striking out with the bases loaded. The pitcher is perhaps the loneliest player of all—standing on the mound in the middle of the diamond, he cannot escape the ire of fans after a batter smacks a hanging curveball over the fence. Like no other sport, baseball puts individual successes or failures on display for all to see. Just ask Boston Red Sox first baseman Bill Buckner, who infamously let a groundball through his legs in the 1986 World Series, culminating a miraculous comeback by the New York Mets and tainting Buckner's otherwise storied career.

Strangely, the strife in baseball is also what makes it so appealing. A fan struggling to make ends meet can relate to a pitcher unable to find the strike zone. A young boy coming of age finds inspiration in a weak-hitting utility infielder trying to find a niche on his club. An elderly fan facing his own mortality roots for an aging veteran trying desperately to hang on for one more season in the big leagues.

Because it so well reflects our human aspirations, and our frequent failures to realize them, baseball is a microcosm of society. It has been said that "[w]hoever wants to know the heart and mind of America had better learn baseball."[1] This is true because baseball mirrors the culture in which it is played. The rough-and-tumble of the Deadball Era mirrored American life in the first two decades of the twentieth century, which in many ways was still grounded in the Wild West. In a telling transition, Babe Ruth's home runs perfectly encapsulated the Roaring Twenties, reflecting both a changing game and a changing nation. The move of the New York Giants and Brooklyn Dodgers to California in 1958 symbolized the nation's population shift westward. In the following decade, the Houston Astrodome was built—the first indoor baseball stadium. Shortly after, aging but cherished ballparks in Philadelphia, Pittsburgh, St. Louis, and Cincinnati were replaced with sterile, multipurpose stadiums. Both developments in the tumultuous 1960s and early 1970s marked the push for urban renewal and the modernization of America.

All the same, baseball does not merely embody the time and place in which it is played. When everything is torn asunder in dark days, baseball often provides us with a sense of belonging. Why? Because baseball reminds us of a simpler time. Baseball began as a rural game played in pastures across the country. Its bucolic origins allow for no adherence to a clock. A game lasts as long as it takes to record 27 outs without pressure to conform to external measures. This alluring simplicity connects us to a common past that may be more imagined than real, but it is the imagination that stirs our soul.

Mindful of the way that baseball both mirrors and shapes the environment in which it is played, we can examine town baseball in the Hill Country, which featured a distinctly German spin in its early years. German settlers in the Hill Country brought with them their love for competition and physical fitness. They also enjoyed social activities in *Vereine,* the plural of the German word, *Verein,* which means a club, association, or union, such as a singing club or a bowling club.

In the late nineteenth century, German settlers took to baseball quickly, making it their own by turning it into a community-wide event on Sunday afternoons. Thus, Germans assimilated baseball into their culture by making the sport a new kind of *Verein*—a melding of German and American culture that was uniquely Texan. Once Germans embraced baseball, teams sprang up in every town in the Hill Country. Baseball joined the cadence of the summer like the shrill buzzing of cicadas on a scorching afternoon.

During the Depression, the region's bond with baseball became even stronger as the game served as a critical means of fostering community connections when times were tough. The commonality of German ancestry and the isolation of the Hill Country, along with the communal appeal of baseball, provided a buffer against the worst aspects of economic privation.

As we shall see, however, Germans were not the only ones in the region to bond through baseball. Kerrville had the largest Black population in the Hill Country. Like Black people throughout Texas and the South, they suffered the brutal racism of the Jim Crow era. Despite this, Kerrville fielded a prominent Black baseball team that thrived even during the Depression, often playing talented Black teams from San Antonio and occasionally against White teams. Best known as the All-Stars, the team engendered pride and unity in the Kerrville Black community, especially on Juneteenth, when baseball was always the featured entertainment. Tragically, Jim Crow racism meant that local newspapers paid little attention to Black baseball teams (and indeed to the entire Black community). As a result, there is a dearth of newspaper coverage from which we can glean their story. Nevertheless, the information we do have reveals that, even more so than White teams in the Hill Country, the All-Stars played a paramount role in coalescing their community during the Depression years and beyond.

Before beginning our exploration of Hill Country baseball, we must address our characterization of it as "town ball." In their fine book, *Baseball: The People's Game*, Harold Seymour and Dorothy Seymour Mills provided a diagram of the "house of baseball," which illustrates the hierarchy of baseball before World War II.[2] This hierarchy includes "town teams," slotted below semiprofessional teams and organized baseball (i.e., major leagues and minor leagues). But since a few Hill Country players were paid, what is the difference between town teams and semiprofessional teams? How many players must be paid for a team to be considered semiprofessional rather than a town team?

Baseball in the Hill Country was played by players primarily representing their hometown. After the Hill Country League (HCL) was formed in 1930, teams in the Hill Country consisted of 15 players who were required to live in the town or the county where the team was located. The only exception was that the HCL did allow a team to enlist not more than two paid players, who were often pitchers. In contrast, the Mountain League, formed in 1933, prohibited paid players, thus restricting rosters to local players. However, even where paid players were permitted in the HCL, not all teams hired "outside" players. Fredericksburg, for example, prided itself on fielding a club without "ringers."

Seymour and Mills recognized that it was not unusual for town teams to include a few paid players.[3] Although the line between a town team and a semiprofessional team is admittedly fuzzy, a paid player or two does not make a team semiprofessional. Instead, our assessment of Hill Country baseball must rest on a more nuanced basis.

In this case, the key factor is that Hill Country ballplayers were typically motivated by pride in their hometown and their love of baseball rather than money. Nearly all players toiled on a gratis basis for their hometown team, many playing for five or more years and some playing for more than 20 years. Since they were carrying the name of the town on the front of their uniforms, these men were heroes to their townsfolk. Town team fans wanted to cheer for their local heroes. A fan in Comfort reflected these sentiments well in 1926:

> And the reason I enjoy our games here [Comfort] is not far to seek. Furthermore the very thing I like most about the Comfort game is the thing some of the boys feel most apologetic about. I mean just this and nothing more, that it is our team and not a bunch of hired men from Santone [San Antonio] or some other place. If we had the wealth of Croesus we might buy a crack team that would make the bozos over in Fredericksburg afraid to play us. Kerrville might well tremble at the mention of our name. Boerne might die of envy on the spot. But what credit would all that be to Comfort? It would be just a confession that we were such rotten ballplayers up here in the finest little town in Texas that the only way we could get a team together would be to buy one.[4]

In other words, unlike semipro teams, there was no point in winning if their team won only because they paid outside players. Fans took pride in their hometown team. They could do so only if the team consisted of family members, friends, and neighbors (with only a few exceptions) so that the honor of the town was on the line every game.

Moreover, ethnic ties (and in the case of Kerrville's Black team, racial bonds) underscored the intimate relationship between the ballclubs and their communities. Town teams played a role in embellishing the close-knit feel of their communities. This role was not affected by a few players receiving modest sums. For these reasons, we consider Hill Country baseball clubs in the Depression era to be "town teams" within the "house of baseball" hierarchy proffered by Harold Seymour and Dorothy Seymour Mills.

Having completed the obligatory preface, we can now explore the story of the men who played town ball in the Hill Country during the Depression. My prayer is that their aspirations and struggles will not be forgotten.

Figure 1. Boerne White Sox player Bruno Dedecker with catcher, circa 1915. (Courtesy of Patrick Heath Public Library, Boerne, Texas.)

AUTHOR'S NOTE

At the outset, we must address two items for the benefit of the reader. First, the names of the Hill Country ballplayers were taken from box scores and newspaper articles. Even in newspaper reports, however, many players were identified by their surnames only. Where given names are known or otherwise noted, we use them but, in some cases, only surnames can be used to refer to players.

Second, in Appendices A–F, we have compiled individual and team statistics from available box scores for three Hill Country League seasons (1930–32) and three Mountain League seasons (1933–1935). However, due to the paucity of information on earned runs in box scores, earned run average (ERA), a common pitching statistic, could not be compiled. As an alternative, we have assembled pitching statistics using total run average (TRA) based on *total* runs allowed by a pitcher (both earned and unearned). Because a pitcher can be victimized by errors, TRA is not as useful as ERA[1] but it does allow us to compare the relative performances of pitchers. Throughout the book, we will occasionally refer to TRA when discussing pitchers.

For more detailed information on the individual and team statistics assembled from box scores and their limitations, see the Notes on Team Statistics Compiled from Box Scores following the acknowledgments.

HILL COUNTRY BALL

CHAPTER 1

A BORROWING FROM THE NEW WORLD: 1867–1899

Among many enduring consequences, the Civil War had the salutary effect of spreading baseball across Texas and the South. According to historians, Confederate soldiers likely learned the game as prisoners of war in the North or while guarding Union prisoners at Confederate prisons.[1]

Although it is a myth that Abner Doubleday "invented" baseball, he may have played a role in bringing baseball to Texas after the Civil War. In his military career, Doubleday served as the sub-assistant commissioner of the Freedmen's Bureau for Galveston County in 1867.[2] In that capacity, he has been credited with organizing the first baseball game in Texas at Galveston on February 22, 1867. Although no solid evidence supports this claim,[3] the first baseball clubs in Texas organized in Galveston about this time:

> Texans returning from the war or occupying Union troops might well have brought the game with them to the busy seaport. The ease with which baseball migrated offered a clear sign of its vitality. Thousands of soldiers of both armies encountered the game for the first time, took to its excitement, introduced it to their home communities, and in the process greatly enhanced the game's popularity. Since most German and Czech immigrants caught their first glimpse of Texas in Galveston, they might well have caught their first glimpse of baseball there as well.[4]

As baseball spread west from Galveston, it soon became popular in the Texas Hill Country. To appreciate how the game took root in the Hill Country, we must first understand the people who settled there, their cultures and fault lines, and how they lived, worked, worshipped, and met together as a community. The

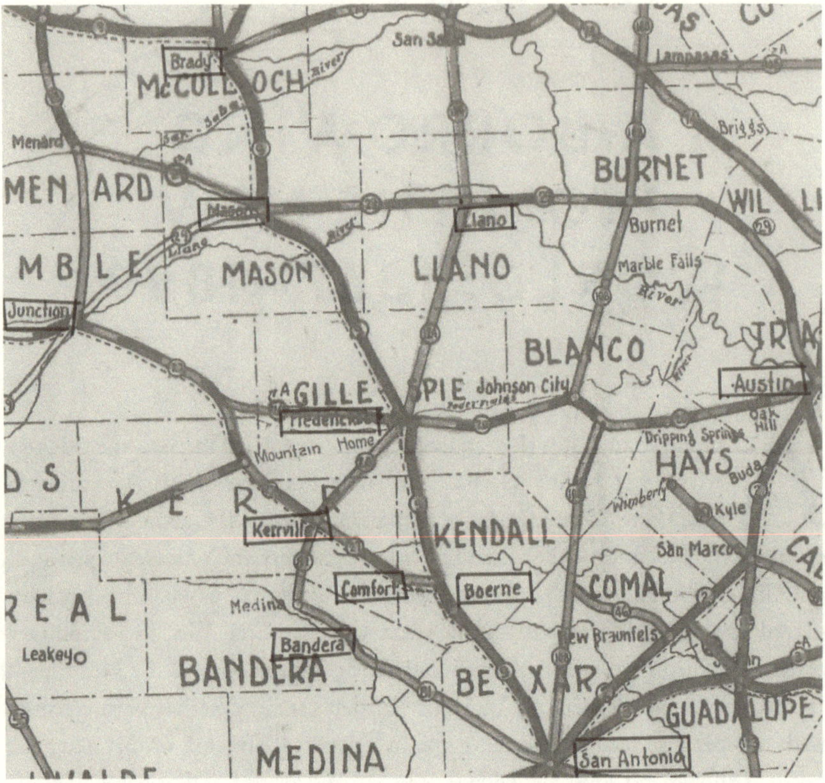

Figure 2. The Texas Hill Country as shown on a 1929 state highway map.

cultural milieu of the Hill Country determined how the early settlers came to enjoy the game of baseball.

The Hill Country, shown on the map above, is the area of south-central Texas west and southwest of Austin and northwest of San Antonio—a region known for its karst topography, where rugged hills of limestone or granite dominate the terrain. These hills "were not pushed up like mountains but instead were left in place as erosion carved out valleys between them."[5] In geographic terms, the Hill Country consists of the eastern edge of the Edwards Plateau and the Llano Uplift. The Balcones Escarpment separates the Edwards Plateau from the lower elevations to the east and south, including San Antonio and the coastal plain of Texas.

Some have called the Hill Country the "sweet spot" of Texas.[6] Hills featuring rocky outcroppings that overlook vales of live oak and Ashe juniper trees—Texans call them cedars—make for an appealing landscape. Indeed, the Hill Country "is known for its beautiful displays of spring wildflowers, scenic vistas, clear and cool streams, and quaint small towns."[7] Others have romanticized the Hill Country as "a magic kingdom, a Xanadu, a place different from the rest of the world,"[8] thanks to its rugged hills and dry, clean air.

The Hill Country was settled primarily by Germans. Between 1844 and 1860, twenty thousand Germans emigrated to Texas,[9] most of them finding their way to the beguiling highlands of the Hill Country.[10] Many came under the auspices of the Adelsverein, a society organized in Germany in 1842 to promote and support mass German immigration to Texas.[11] The area where a large influx of Germans settled in Texas, from Galveston west to the Hill Country, is sometimes referred to as the "Texas German Belt."[12] Since German settlement largely created the cultural backdrop for the development of baseball in the Hill Country during the late nineteenth and early twentieth centuries, we will examine the patterns of German immigration.

Germans first settled the Hill Country in New Braunfels, then established a second settlement in Fredericksburg in 1846.[13] Unlike many immigrants to America, Germans did not migrate to the Hill Country to evade religious oppression (although their Lutheran or Catholic faith remained of paramount importance to them). Instead, many left Germany to escape the political and economic upheaval occurring there in the 1830s and 1840s.[14] German immigrants also "followed their longing for new opportunities, . . . and the desire to escape the over-crowded homeland."[15] Later, many Germans fled from the political repression that followed the failed German revolution in 1848.[16]

While German immigrants were united by their common heritage, their backgrounds varied. Some were members of the working class seeking a better life for their family, others were idealistic university students hoping to forge a utopian community, and still others were intellectuals devoted to letters and the finer things in life.[17] These differences, together with the challenges of their new environment, influenced the nature of various Hill Country communities for many years, and still do today.

As one of the first German settlements, Fredericksburg endured some early hardships but thrived as a center of German immigration from which other settlements in the region were launched.[18] Indeed, Fredericksburg, patterned after German villages along the Rhine with one long, wide main street,[19] became a cornerstone of German Texan economic and cultural life. Fredericksburg's central location in the Hill Country proved advantageous, especially in the early years. Fredericksburg was located on one of the main roads to the Rio Grande Valley opened by the federal government after the Mexican War ended in 1848.[20] In addition, the town lay on the Upper Emigrant Road used by pioneers heading west to California.[21] Since Fredericksburg was the last stop for sojourners to purchase supplies before heading to El Paso, local shopkeepers prospered during the gold rush.[22] Soon Fredericksburg grew into a thriving town, helped by the construction of nearby Fort Martin Scott, which expanded markets for local merchants.[23]

Fredericksburg clung tightly to German culture and traditions including the German language. It was not until after 1900 that "purely English-speaking" teachers were hired by Fredericksburg's public schools.[24] As the town grew near the end of the nineteenth century, the first electric-light company arrived in 1896 while train service by the San Antonio, Fredericksburg and Northern Railway began in 1913.[25] By 1930, Fredericksburg was developing a reputation as a resort center.[26] Despite these changes, Fredericksburg remained a mainstay of German Texan culture. Even today, Gillespie County, where Fredericksburg is located, "continues to be recognized for its cultural identity and observance of a lifestyle based on long-established traditions."[27]

Kerrville began as a German settlement but later remade itself into a cattle town.[28] At first a shingle-makers camp and then the home of a grist and lumber mill founded by German settlers, Kerrville became an important cattle drive station thanks to its location at the junction of the Old Trail, coming from Bandera south of Kerrville, and the Matamoros Trail, coming from San Antonio and Boerne to the southeast.[29] These trails merged at Kerrville to become the Western Trail which sent cattle to Dodge City, displacing the Chisholm Trail as the major route to northern cattle markets.[30] Although the cattle drives did not last long, they made a lasting impression, branding Kerrville with a cattlemen identity that remains in place.[31] Reflecting this identity, Kerrville hosts a museum originally called the Cowboy Artists of America Museum, now named the Museum of Western Art. Today, Kerrville is known as "the Heart of the Hills."[32]

Like Fredericksburg and Kerrville, Boerne was a German town but unlike the other two, it became so simply because it was located in a predominantly German region, not because it was a planned community.[33] The first settlement in the early 1850s was a small utopian community, which disbanded within a year or two.[34] However, what is now Boerne was located on the route from San Antonio to Fredericksburg, Kerrville, and other communities.[35] As a result, it was not long before speculators (including Anglos such as English surveyor John James) purchased land in what is now Boerne, hoping to cash in on a prime location. In contrast to planned German settlements in the Hill Country, Boerne was "a straight up commercial development."[36]

Boerne did not blossom immediately, taking decades to develop into a permanent settlement.[37] In 1861, George Wilkins Kendall, for whom Kendall County is named, moved to a ranch outside Boerne where he raised Merino sheep. He is considered "the father of the Texas sheep industry."[38] Thanks to Kendall's innovations, the sheep ranching industry flourished in the Hill Country.[39] Ranchers raising sheep for wool and raising goats for mohair became significant economic drivers in the Hill Country, especially during the otherwise lean Depression years, as we shall see later. George Wilkins Kendall is but one example of the entrepreneurial spirit that motivated early settlers in Boerne—a spirit that remains today.

Comfort was known as a settlement of German freethinkers,[40] resulting in no churches being built in Comfort until 1892.[41] The Civil War served as a fault line that ran through Comfort and the Hill Country, forcing Germans to take sides on the pivotal issues of slavery and secession in their adopted country. Whether they were Lutheran, Catholic, or freethinkers, many Hill Country Germans opposed both slavery and secession, though not always to the same degree, and many remained sympathetic, if not loyal, to the Union.[42] However, Unionism was "more widespread in the Hill Country than was abolitionism."[43] After leaving the political turmoil of Germany just 15 years before, many pro-Union Germans simply wanted to maintain the stability and security of the status quo.[44]

Comfort was a stronghold of pro-Union sentiment.[45] In 1862, a group of 68 armed loyalists, mostly German, headed south toward Mexico, avoiding conscription into Confederate military service and planning ultimately to meet up with the Union Army. However, 28 of them were killed by the Confederate Army—some were executed after capture—in a clash near the Nueces River, later known as the "Massacre on the Nueces."[46] Four months later, seven other loyalists who had escaped the massacre were killed by the Confederates when trying to cross the Rio Grande, raising the death toll to 35.

After the end of the Civil War, the remains of the 35 dead loyalists—the Confederates had left their bodies unburied—were interred under an obelisk in Comfort under the German words, *Treue der Union* (True to the Union).[47] The obelisk is the only monument to Union dead in a Confederate state.[48] Over the years, Comfort residents retained their free-spirited principles, resisting the establishment of formal governmental structure. Comfort remains an unincorporated community today.[49]

In contrast to other communities in the Hill Country, Bandera was not settled by Germans.[50] Rather, Bandera's first residents were Upper Silesian sawmill workers recruited from a Polish colony in Karnes County.[51] Like Kerrville, Bandera began as a shingle-makers camp before the sawmills came to town. Later, Bandera

Figure 3. Treue der Union Monument in Comfort.

became a cattle-trail town when it served as the starting point for the Old Trail going north to Kerrville and beyond.[52] In recognition of its renown as a cattle town, Bandera is known as the "Cowboy Capital of the World."[53]

Other towns in the Hill Country north of Fredericksburg were originally settled by Germans, but the settlement of these places did not occur until later due to their remoteness as well as clashes between Native Americans and settlers. In 1842, the Republic of Texas issued a land grant of more than three million acres north and west of the future site of Fredericksburg to Harry Francis Fisher, Burchard Miller, and Joseph Baker. This grant, known as the Fisher-Miller Land Grant, was sold in 1845 to the Adelsverein, the German society responsible for sending thousands of German immigrants to Texas.[54] Since the Fisher-Miller Land Grant was far from the other German settlements and settlers had little protection from attacks by Comanches, most German immigrants did not venture beyond New Braunfels and Fredericksburg.[55]

In 1847, John Meusebach, a leader of the German settlers, negotiated a treaty with the Comanches to allow German settlers to live within the Fisher-Miller Land Grant.[56] Following the treaty, five small German settlements were populated along the Llano River but only one, Castell, survived. According to historians, "most of the immigrants who were deeded land in the Fisher-Miller Land Grant never occupied their holdings because they were so far from the base settlements"[57] of New Braunfels and Fredericksburg. In addition, the fear of attacks by Native Americans within that area remained a concern despite the treaty. As a result, German settlements in the towns of Llano, Brady, and Mason—all within the Fisher-Miller Land Grant—did not take hold until 25 years later after Native American tribes were moved to reservations.[58] The remoteness of Llano, Brady, and Mason from southern Hill Country towns such as Boerne, Comfort, Kerrville, and Bandera would later play a key role in the story of Hill Country baseball.

Wherever they settled in Texas, German immigrants clung tightly to their language and culture in their new land, resisting assimilation. The German language was spoken in school, church, and at home while literary societies, music societies, athletic associations, and other clubs preserved German cultural identity.[59]

At the same time, Germans inevitably integrated certain aspects of their new land into their daily lives in Texas, "replacing what it lost from not being in close contact with the old world by liberal borrowings from the new world—refurbished with a German accent."[60]

Baseball became one of those "borrowings from the new world." While baseball was purely an American game unknown to continental Europeans, the German culture transplanted to America was well suited to the sport. Germans were energetic and exuberant people who loved "organized fun." Clubs, associations, societies, and fairs were "important traditions which the German Texan retained by making them into something Texan and American."[61]

Germans often organized social and recreational activities by establishing a club, known in German as a *Verein.* For example, Boerne had a singing club (*Gesangverein*), a bowling club (*Turnverein*), and a shooting club (*Schuetzenverein*).[62] Similar to other activities, baseball had its "origins in the German penchant for coming together in clubs (or *Vereines*) for social activity."[63] Even though German immigrants brought no history of bat and ball games with them (unlike English immigrants who played rounders and cricket), baseball became popular because "Germans were . . . preoccupied with physical

Figure 4. Boerne White Sox player Henry Fabra, circa 1915. (Courtesy of Patrick Heath Public Library, Boerne, Texas.)

training and fitness, and baseball was just a facet of their obsession with physical well-being."[64]

Two decades after the Civil War, German immigrants in south-central Texas "began a love affair with baseball."[65] German children took to the new game, establishing a foundation for its growth. Children began playing baseball in school and after church on Sunday. As young boys matured, the "spirit of competition carried over into adulthood, though still on an informal basis prior to the turn of the century."[66]

In the late nineteenth century, baseball developed as a community event that offered players and fans a respite from their labors in a hardscrabble environment. Baseball was played in pastures where sheep or cattle often roamed among bluebonnets. Women prepared lunch baskets and lemonade as games attracted many from miles around.[67] A Sunday baseball game against another town was indeed a momentous occasion. Since bragging rights were on the line, it was not uncommon for town teams to hire an outsider, usually a pitcher, as a "ringer."

As baseball grew in popularity, town teams arose throughout the Hill Country. One of the earliest recorded organized baseball games in the Hill Country took place in 1891. A team from Kerrville traveled to Bandera to take on the local nine. Bandera's team was sponsored by Judge Charles Montague and "enthusiastically boosted" by Judge Hugh Duffy.[68] Mrs. Charles Montague made uniforms for the team. Despite the vigorous local support, Bandera suffered an ignominious defeat, 94–0.[69] Catcher Anton Pyka was the only Bandera player to connect the bat with the ball, reaching third base but failing to score.[70] Perhaps fittingly, the name of the Bandera shortstop was Loss Carmichael.[71] Consistent with Kerrville's reputation as a mecca for those seeking the healing power of the Hill Country's climate, the captain of the Kerrville team was referred to as a "health-seeker by the name of Barrett."[72]

From these desultory "match" games, town teams playing a more regular schedule sprang up in Fredericksburg, Llano, Boerne, Kerrville, Comfort, and other Hill Country towns. In the first two decades of the twentieth century, town baseball evolved from makeshift teams playing occasional, albeit well-attended, contests to organized ballclubs playing Sunday afternoons from April to September. In fields far and wide, town baseball became a staple of Hill Country life, as we shall explore in chapter 3.

CHAPTER 2

BASEBALL IS NO HIGHBROW GAME: 1900–1929

After the turn of the century, ballclubs formed in nearly every Hill Country town, providing enough opponents that teams could schedule games for most Sundays throughout the spring and summer. The earliest photographs of town teams depict rosters of doughty ballplayers, eager for their chance to shine on the diamond against newfound foes from nearby burgs.

Despite deep roots in their local communities, many, but not all, of the Hill Country teams took their nicknames from major-league teams, especially the most successful teams in baseball's Deadball Era.[1] The Fredericksburg team played as early as 1910, based on the first known photograph of it (see fig. 5). Fredericksburg adopted the nickname of the New York Giants, manager John McGraw's scrappy team that won the 1905 World Series and won National League pennants in 1911, 1912, 1913, and 1917. Even in their early years, Fredericksburg was a superb club, briefly including a future major-league star. Before he began his 12-year career as an outfielder with the Chicago White Sox and Cleveland Indians, Austin native Bibb Falk played a few games for Fredericksburg in 1918.[2]

Similarly, the earliest photograph of the Boerne team (see fig. 7) dates from 1912.[3] Boerne adopted the moniker of the Chicago White Sox, who were dubbed the "hitless Wonders" after their surprising victory over the cross-town Cubs in the 1906 World Series. The White Sox later defeated McGraw's Giants in the 1917 World Series.

The photographs on pp. 15–16 show an Old English "B" on Boerne's uniforms, like the Old English "D" still used today by the Detroit Tigers. In later years, the Boerne team adopted the distinctive "Sox" logo of the Chicago White Sox as their own, placing on their uniforms a large "S" with a smaller "o" in the top loop of the "S" and a smaller "x" in the bottom loop.[4]

Figure 5. 1910 Fredericksburg Giants. Top row: (L–R) Lawrence Krauskopf, third base; George Bershaw, manager; Alfred Schandua, right field. Middle row (L–R): Johnnie Mueller, second base; Louis Mart, first base; Arthur Sellers, center field; Felix Schmidt, second base; Lucian Wright, shortstop. Bottom row (L–R): V. A. Cottle, pitcher; Otto Feuge, catcher; Gus Hartmann, catcher; Emil Wahrmund, pitcher and outfielder. (Courtesy of Enderlin Collection, Gillespie County Historical Society, Fredericksburg, Texas.)

Figure 6. Fredericksburg Giants, late 1920s. The names of the Fredericksburg players in this photograph have not survived. (Courtesy of Gillespie County Historical Society, Fredericksburg, Texas.)

Figure 7. Boerne White Sox, 1912. Top row (L–R): Henry Fabra, Louis Guthrie, Ross Nowlin, Harry McFarland, McCall (first name unknown), Louis Gueldner, Edgar Offer. Bottom row (L–R): Hilmar Fabra, Fred Loe, Pat Ebensberger, Willie Janensch. (Courtesy of Patrick Heath Public Library, Boerne, Texas.)

Figure 8. Boerne White Sox, 1914. Top row (L–R): Henry Fabra, Max Theis, Fred Loe, Harry Chittenden, George "Speed Ball" Wedge, Charlie Saunders, scorekeeper Sidney Levyson. Bottom row (L–R): Calvin North, Bruno Dedecker, Arthur Fabra, manager Charles Wedge, Herbert Wedge, Franklin Lewis. Seated on the ground: mascot Ernst Adler. (Courtesy of Patrick Heath Public Library, Boerne, Texas.)

Figure 9. Boerne White Sox, 1914. (L–R): Ross Nowlin, Arthur Fabra, Bruno Dedecker, Otto Schwarz, Gene Adams, Leonard Seideman, Paul Seideman, Henry Fabra, Charlie Saunders, Fred Lowe, "Fueldner" (an Army base pitcher, probably Louis Gueldner, see fig. 7), and unknown player. (Courtesy of Patrick Heath Public Library, Boerne, Texas.)

Comfort's baseball origins can be traced to an even earlier time than that of Fredericksburg and Boerne. A letter to the editor of the *Comfort News* on May 13, 1904, implored residents to form a baseball team since "there are plenty of young men around Comfort, especially among the farmers who would make splendid players, and there are any number of fine sites for a baseball grounds."[5] The first mention of an actual baseball game is found in 1908:

> The COMFORT BASEBALL CLUB met the SISTERDALE JUNIORS on the home diamond Sunday afternoon and defeated them by the score of 41 to 13. The score was too lopsided to create any excitement, but it proved interesting enough to keep a good size crowd of spectators on the grounds through the game.[6]

The first known photograph of the Comfort team was taken in 1922.[7] By that time, the team was known as the Broncos—unlike Fredericksburg, Boerne, and Kerrville, the local squad did not assume the nickname of a major-league team.

Figure 10. Comfort Broncos, 1922. Standing: Ernst Doebbler, manager; Bill Steves, umpire; James Saylor, scorekeeper. Top row (L–R): Walter Stahmann, Chester Faltin, F. M. "Pat" Faust, Bob Davenport, Guy Reese. Middle row (L–R): Joe Pankratz, J. E. "Skid" Skidmore, Del "Shotgun" Burney, Buck Nowlin. Bottom row (L–R): Chester Karger, Udo Letz. (Courtesy of Comfort Heritage Foundation, Inc., Comfort, Texas.)

Figure 11. Kerrville Athletics, circa 1912. The names of the players have not survived. (Reprinted courtesy of Joe Herring Jr., Kerrville, Texas.)

Figure 12. Kerrville Athletics, 1925. Top row (L–R): Bob Barry, pitcher; J. B. Remschel, center fielder; W. Jacobie, utility player; William Burns, pitcher; E. Schwethelm, manager. Middle row (L–R): Sam Amberson, shortstop; Emmett Henke, right fielder; Herbert Holchak, captain and third baseman; Eugene Butt, scorekeeper; William Saenger, pitcher. Bottom row (L–R): Edwin McCarthy, catcher; Louis Wilson, first baseman; Charlie Kuesel, second baseman; Cecil Robinsen, left fielder; Ellis (first name unknown), utility player. Team mascot Charlie Morris sits in front. When this photograph was published on March 17, 1984, in the *Kerrville Mountain Sun*, the article noted the following regarding William Saenger in 1925: "Saenger was the 19 year old ace of the pitching staff with a one-hitter to his credit and held the strong San Antonio independent team to five hits." (Reprinted courtesy of *The Kerrville Daily Times*, Kerrville, Texas, as successor to the *Kerrville Mountain Sun.*)

The Kerrville Athletics began play not later than 1912 when the first surviving photograph, shown above, was taken. Kerrville regularly fielded a team by 1917.[8] Like Fredericksburg and Boerne, Kerrville chose the nickname of a successful major-league club, the Philadelphia Athletics, who won the World Series in 1910, 1911, and 1913. However, the team would later be known briefly as the Tourists, reflecting Kerrville's attraction to vacationers, and then the Braves—at the time the nickname of Boston's National League club.

The Kerrville Athletics met with early success. One example of Kerrville's prowess is that, according to the *Kerrville Mountain Sun,* the 1925 Athletics outscored their opponents, 40–12.[9] The Kerrville club enjoyed a spirited rivalry with the Fredericksburg Giants, which lasted many years. Whether they played in Kerrville or Fredericksburg, these games attracted large contingents of both home fans and those who traveled to support their clubs in "hostile" territory.

While Bandera's first venture into baseball did not fare well (the 94–0 loss to Kerrville), Bandera persevered, regularly fielding a team not later than 1925, based on a team photograph from that year.[10] However, Bandera's early years in town baseball reveal a team with a pugilistic bent. In one game in Hondo (30 miles south of Bandera), Frank Montague Sr., the son of Judge Charles Montague,[11] blasted a home run that broke a second story window in a nearby building. When the building owner came to the diamond to complain, "Coach Judge," as the players called Charles Montague, "started to take a poke at him," resulting in a brawl described as "a good fist fight [which] was much more fun than baseball to these hillbillies from Bandera in those days."[12]

On another occasion, when Bandera hosted Boerne, a fight broke out over an umpire's call. After the game, Coach Charles Montague and his team arrived at his front porch with bloody noses and swollen lips. Montague's wife, Laura, then discovered that the uniforms she had so lovingly made were now "nothing but tatters and rags hanging from the bruised and battered frames of the players."[13] Mrs. Montague flew into a rage. Coach Montague's grandson, Frank Montague Jr., later reported that "[w]hat happened next with this Pennsylvania Dutch gal's temper flying—her husband, the eminent Judge and Coach and the entire team catching the brunt of this wrath—cannot be printed here."[14]

Farther north in the Hill Country, Llano also produced a town team at an early stage. In 1913, Llano was playing a regular slate of games, including a game against Marble Falls.[15] The following year, L. C. Callaway, owner of the Llano ballpark at the time, moved it to the site known as the "picnic grounds" (later part of Robinson State Park),[16] where it would be more convenient for baseball and other events during an Independence Day celebration.[17] In 1916, the Llano club divided into south Llano and north Llano teams to play a January game in preparation for the upcoming summer season.[18] The *Llano News* explained the appeal of baseball to young men, even in remote areas like the Hill Country:

> Although there is still frost in the air and several freezes are yet to be registered in the Llano country before winter is over, the boys have been playing the great American game among themselves for several weeks. Baseball has a grip on the heart strings of the American boy which no other game can secure.

> They play football a few months in the fall, basket ball occasionally, and probably a little tennis or track. But they begin playing America's National game early after Christmas, and they never tire wielding the bat and do not stop until they are forced to do so by the cold weather of the late fall. Baseball is no highbrow game, but it is the game of the masses and it is the only game that can draw two million people out every year to witness it. It is the American game, and the Llano boys are going to furnish the Llano fans of this city with thrills such as a certain Ty Cobb furnishes the fans of every big league city. The Llano boys like the boys of every other town in America, had rather be another Ty Cobb than to be president.[19]

In Texas, as elsewhere in the nation, town baseball was a propitious development fulfilling several social needs in rural areas such as the Hill Country. A town baseball team "helped refresh the often parched social landscape of rural America,"[20] while providing "a lively diversion that interrupted the dullness of daily routine and the deep quiet of bucolic life."[21] Moreover, small-town residents were naturally attracted to baseball games with nearby towns because they "used baseball games to sublimate temptation to open warfare against neighboring towns."[22] As town teams began to play regularly, baseball became more than mere recreation. A town's team became a "cohesive agent in the community," providing an outward expression of local pride and establishing a close bond between teams and their residents.[23]

In a column in the *Comfort News* in 1926, John C. Petrie articulated the love of many Hill Country fans for town baseball on Sunday afternoons:

> I have only one complaint to register and that is against the present popular custom of having only one Sunday in a week. If the parsons would get together and devote two days a week to the interests of the Lord and baseball, I at least would be strongly in favor of it. That would give the pious ones two days to go to Church and the rest of us two games instead of one.[24]

The surging popularity of baseball is best shown by its prominent role in county fairs and Independence Day celebrations. The annual Gillespie County Fair in Fredericksburg and the Kendall County Fair in Boerne always included ball games, often doubleheaders, that attracted raucous crowds. The Fourth of July was perhaps even more compelling. As Harold Seymour and Dorothy Seymour

Figure 13. Boerne White Sox players, circa 1915. A note on the photograph states that it depicts the three Wedge brothers. Observe the horse-drawn carriage next to the automobile. (Courtesy of Patrick Heath Public Library, Boerne, Texas.)

Mills noted in *Baseball: The People's Game*, "[a] game between town teams ranked with parades, patriotic orations, and firecrackers as a Fourth of July must."[25] Town teams often played a doubleheader on the Fourth of July in addition to their regular schedule of Sunday games, which occasionally resulted in teams playing three games in two days.

Baseball, like everything else in the Hill Country, remained distinctly German. In fact, as late as 1930, nearly 90 percent of Gillespie County residents were descendants of original German settlers.[26] Numerous ballplayers reflected the German heritage of the Hill Country. As we shall see, most teams boasted a plethora of German names on their roster—Bergmann, Uecker, Pfeiffer, Klaerner, Schneider, Langerhans, Kutzer, Pankratz, Nagel, Saenger, Toler, and many others. Mostly Germans played on the Fredericksburg, Boerne, and Comfort clubs; fewer German names appeared on other rosters, reflecting the lesser influence of Germans in the settlement and development of those communities. Nonetheless, German influence prevailed.

Apart from the dominance of German culture, we must keep in mind that the Hill Country was sparsely populated. Even the larger towns were relatively small. In 1930, Kerrville was the largest Hill Country town with a population of 4,546. Fredericksburg was next with 2,246 residents. Llano's population was 2,124. Boerne had a population of 1,117, while Bandera had only 580 residents.[27]

Because the Hill Country had a singularly "small town" feel, baseball was a family affair. For example, the Fredericksburg Giants often boasted four Klaerners on their roster[28] while the Boerne White Sox relied upon the Uecker[29] brothers (Albert, Edwin, Johnny, and Tuddy) and the Bergmann brothers (Edgar and Walter) as mainstays. Two brothers, Joe Pankratz and Ernst "Skeeter" Pankratz,[30] starred for the Comfort Broncos for many years. Later, their younger brother August, known as "Manny," also played for Comfort.[31]

The Hill Country was also home to the Deike Brothers, an all-brother independent team from Hye, a small town between Fredericksburg and Johnson City.[32] In 1935, the Deike Brothers famously played another all-brother team from Waukegan, Illinois, in Wichita, Kansas, losing, 11–5.[33] It is worth noting here that the Deike Brothers team in the 1920s briefly included a lanky player named Lyndon Johnson—the future president was "a darn good first baseman" who "could hit pretty well."[34]

True to their culture, Germans differed in their approach to playing baseball and other sports on the Sabbath. Unlike the Puritan tradition of the Northeast, the Lutheran and Catholic faith of most Hill Country Germans did not proscribe recreational activities on Sunday, such as games, dances, and beer drinking.[35] In other parts of the nation, baseball on the Sabbath was banned by so-called blue laws, even in major-league cities like Boston and Philadelphia until 1929[36] and 1934, respectively.[37] Germans never recognized such constraints. Instead, baseball games in the Hill Country were held on Sunday afternoons, just like other social and recreational activities.

Figure 14. Boerne White Sox, 1920s. Top row (L–R): Arthur Schoenig, Arthur Pfeiffer, Clarence Holekamp, Egon Bremer, Vincent Phillip, Gus Wendler, and Tom Dugosh. Bottom row (L–R): Herbert Dienger, Anton Leidl, Anton Bergmann, Melvin Insall, and Edwin Stendenbach. Front: Rudy Leidl. This photo in the Dietert Historical Archives of the Patrick Heath Public Library identifies only seven men in the top row even though eight are shown. Perhaps archivists identified only the uniformed players in the top row, leaving out the name of the gentleman at the far left. (Courtesy of Patrick Heath Public Library.)

Town teams in Fredericksburg, Llano, Boerne, Kerrville, Comfort, and Bandera flourished during the Roaring Twenties. Between World War I and the Depression, incipient rivalries developed into full-blown feuds in the Hill Country.

One of those rivalries may have started, or perhaps just intensified, over a dispute between Fredericksburg and Llano regarding the use of the spitball. Thanks to a lengthy diatribe in the *Llano News* by Llano manager L. C. Callaway, we have his side of the controversy. According to Callaway, 18 Llano players and some fans traveled in a Pullman truck to Fredericksburg for a Sunday afternoon ball game in 1921. The Llano contingent ate lunch at Alfred Schaefer's hotel and were later joined by 150 more Llano supporters in downtown Fredericksburg, which "looked like the streets of Llano on a busy day, with the exception of a few stray sheep that would stroll by."[38]

During the pre-game warm-up, Fredericksburg's player-manager, a well-known spitball artist named Lee, inquired whether Llano players would use rosin on the ball. Callaway replied that if Lee used the "slippery elm" on the ball—spitball pitchers often chewed slippery elm bark to enhance the effect of their saliva on the pitch—Llano players would rosin the ball to dry off the "slobber." Lee refused to pitch unless he could throw his unhindered spitball, producing a letter "from someone in San Antonio by the name of McNutt" purporting to show Lee's spitball was permitted.[39] In response, Callaway pulled out his copy of the baseball rules showing that spitballs were illegal since the major leagues banned them in 1920.[40] A heated argument ensued. When Fredericksburg refused to play unless Lee could use his spitball and Llano refused to accede to this demand, the game was canceled just before game time, sending home the disappointed crowd.

Callaway complained that Fredericksburg failed to pay the customary travel expense of $20 to the visitors, referring to the Giants as "a bunch of crooked quiters [*sic*]."[41] Callaway also issued a warning to other town teams:

> My advice to any manager contemplating a game with the Fredericksburg Giants is, you better forget it. And if it weighs too heavily on their minds and they can't make up their minds not to go, just get you a dull razor and cut their throats as it will be better than going over there and let that bunch of crooks beg out.[42]

The *Fredericksburg Standard* reported only that the game with Llano was called off because "the managers of the respective teams could not agree on certain matters."[43] As we shall see in later chapters, Fredericksburg and Llano enjoyed a spirited rivalry in the Hill Country League in the 1930s, but the fervor between the clubs may have originated with this spitball dispute a decade earlier.

On the economic front, the prosperity during the Roaring Twenties did not last. The nation's economy came to a screeching halt with the stock market crash in October 1929, resulting in the Great Depression, which lasted for nearly a decade. The nation suffered a significant increase in poverty: the national unemployment rate increased from 3.2 percent in 1929 to 24.9 percent just four years later.[44]

Even in the early 1930s, the Hill Country remained isolated from other regions due to bad roads and rough terrain.[45] As the Depression deepened, life became more precarious on the ranches of the Hill Country. Fredericksburg grocer Erwin Woerner quipped at the time, "'people were poor but did not know it."[46] On the other hand, the remoteness of the Hill Country and the bonds of common German ancestry that facilitated trade and bartering with merchants cushioned the harshest aspects of the Depression.[47]

Figure 15. Fredericksburg Giants, circa 1927. Back row, standing (L–R): Felix Saenger (manager), Eugene "Gene" Fuller, Clarence "Pepper" Probst, Al Hollmig, Elias "Red" Klaerner, Lawrence "Freddy" Peter, Ernst "Spike" Nagel. Center row, seated (L–R): Edgar Klett, Robert Klett, Felix Hahn, Emil Juenke, Udo Henke, Hugo Klaerner. Front, on the ground (L–R): Paul Knopp, Milton Durst. (Photo courtesy of Enderlin Collection, Gillespie County Historical Society, Fredericksburg, Texas.)

During the Depression years—indeed until the second half of the twentieth century—baseball was the dominant sport in the Hill Country and Texas at large.[48] For example, it was typical for San Antonio sports editors to dedicate a full page covering all eight major-league games of the previous day. Stars like Babe Ruth, Lou Gehrig, Jimmie Foxx, and Lefty Grove, to name only a few, captured the imagination of young and old fans alike.

The passion for baseball was even greater at the local level. In a challenging time in the Hill Country, baseball was a "mania," a social event that was "part athletic contest and part community picnic."[49] Baseball served as a galvanizing force, weaving critical threads into the social fabric of the Hill Country: "Baseball was more than entertainment. It was a respite from tough times. It helped a generation of isolated Hill Country folk endure the Great Depression. Baseball was the peoples' game [*sic*]."[50]

Before we move on to town baseball during the Depression, we turn to the stories of two legendary pitchers, each with enduring ties to the Hill Country.

CHAPTER 3

RUBE AND OL' DIZ

A Tragic Ending and an Auspicious Start

During the town ball era, the Hill Country served briefly as the home of two larger-than-life Hall of Fame pitchers—one after his major-league career ended and the other before it began. Rube Waddell came to Boerne in 1913, seeking unsuccessfully to stave off the progression of the serious illness that took his life. More than a decade later, teenager Dizzy Dean made his way to San Antonio, honing his fastball while hurling for Fort Sam Houston and moonlighting for Hill Country town teams. Rube and Dizzy possessed unconventional personalities that endeared them to fans even more so than their dominance on the mound. Both still enjoy mythical status among baseball fans today.

AILING RUBE WADDELL SEEKS RESPITE IN THE HILL COUNTRY

Apart from its visual beauty, the Hill Country became known for its appealing climate, resulting in a reputation for recuperative powers, which sparked a connection with Rube Waddell. A strapping farm boy, Rube was a daunting left-handed pitcher when he began his professional career in Louisville in 1897.[1] His blazing fastball and swooping curve terrified hitters, but managers soon learned Rube was eccentric, to say the least. Among other peculiarities, Rube would sometimes turn cartwheels and walk on his hands back to the dugout at the end of an inning, puzzling his teammates but delighting the fans.[2]

After Rube's exasperating behavior wore out the patience of major-league ballclubs in Louisville, Pittsburgh, and Chicago, Connie Mack traded for Rube in 1902 to play for his Philadelphia Athletics. Unlike others, Mack was able to harness Rube's unmistakable talent. Rube compiled a 24–7 record in 1902—the first of four consecutive 20-win seasons and the first of six consecutive seasons in which he led the American League in strikeouts.[3] In 1904 Rube set the major-league strikeout record with 349 whiffs[4]—a record that stood for more than a half-century until broken by Sandy Koufax in 1965. For these achievements, Waddell was elected to the Hall of Fame in 1946.[5]

After his major-league career ended when he lost the zip on his fastball, Rube lived in Hickman, Kentucky, a Mississippi River town. He resided on a farm owned by Joe Cantillon, owner of the Minneapolis Millers, the minor league team for which Rube was then pitching. In January 1913 Rube helped the citizens of Hickman fight a major flood by piling sandbags while standing in the freezing river, causing him to develop a severe case of pneumonia.[6] He recovered, but two months later, Rube suffered a relapse after another flood required more sandbagging.[7] Not one to take care of himself, Rube could not shake his illness this time. This is where the Hill Country comes into Rube's story.

At that time, Boerne's dry climate and salubrious air made it a magnet for those suffering from lung afflictions. Many lung patients traveled to sanitariums in Boerne, including Saint Mary's Sanitarium. Fortuitously, Rube's sister Margaret and her husband, Frederick Austin, lived on a ranch near Boerne. Cantillon, again serving as Rube's benefactor, paid for his train trip to Boerne, where he was met by Margaret and Frederick, who cared for him in hopes of thwarting the progression of his disease.[8]

Margaret and her husband did everything they could, but Rube's phthisic condition continued to worsen. They admitted him to a sanitarium in San Antonio for treatment in March 1914. When former teammates visited Rube later that month, he had become so frail and gaunt that they did not recognize him.[9] Rube died on April 1, 1914, and was buried in Mission Burial Park South in San Antonio.[10] Rube's grave was signified only by a small wooden marker but in 1921, his former manager, Connie Mack, raised funds to pay for a more fitting memorial—a granite monument standing slightly more than six feet high, the same height as Rube.[11] Baseball fans still pay homage to Rube Waddell today by visiting his San Antonio grave, more than a century after his untimely death.

TEENAGER DIZZY DEAN LAUNCHES HIS CAREER

Dizzy Dean is best known for winning 30 games and leading the 1934 St. Louis Cardinals, nicknamed the "Gashouse Gang," to the World Series title. But he first began to pitch in organized ball while at Fort Sam Houston in San Antonio. Over many years, the *Comfort News* reported that in 1925, Dizzy Dean also pitched as a teenager for the Comfort Broncos, playing under the alias "Van Biber."[12]

The first *Comfort News* article was published on October 2, 1958, featuring a photograph of two Comfort players. The photograph had been discovered by H. P. Schwethelm, who was told that one of the players was Dizzy Dean and that he had pitched for Comfort using "Van Biber" as an assumed name.[13]

Figure 16. Rube Waddell. (Public domain.)

Based on that clue, the *Comfort News* discovered four games in 1925 in which "Van Biber" appeared—one game pitching against Comfort, then three games pitching for the Broncos.[14]

Nearly 20 years later, the *Comfort News* published another article in 1977 in which Richard "Buck" Nowlin, a catcher for the Broncos in the 1920s, remembered catching Dizzy Dean in two ball games.[15] Nowlin did not mention the "Van Biber" alias but, regarding Dean, he commented that "he had a lot of smoke" and "he was easy to catch because he had great control.'"[16]

Others have corroborated the story of Dean pitching for the Broncos. Gerhard Petermann—a beloved Comfort schoolteacher, principal, superintendent, and coach—recalled in 1977 that he saw Dizzy Dean pitch for the Broncos in one game in the late 1920s.[17]

Joe Pankratz, a prominent player for the Broncos from the 1920s through the 1940s, told his daughters about Dean playing for Comfort. Dean made quite an impression on Pankratz. He told his daughters that Dizzy Dean rode a motorcycle to the games. When he arrived, he enjoyed taking the motorcycle for a spin around the diamond.[18]

Given these newspaper reports and recollections by multiple players and observers, we will examine in detail the 1925 games in which "Van Biber" pitched to assess whether this was Dizzy Dean pitching under an alias. "Van Biber" began his foray into the Hill Country by hurling two games for Fort Sam Houston, first in Comfort, then in Kerrville. In the first game on April 5, 1925, "Van Biber" limited the Broncos to four hits, shutting them out, 2–0, at Faltin Field.[19] The *Comfort News* reported that "the pitching of Van Biber was too much for the local boys, who have not yet acquired their batting eyes."[20]

The following Sunday, "Van Biber" started for Fort Sam Houston when the club traveled to Kerrville.[21] "Van Biber" pitched brilliantly, allowing just five hits, striking out 20 batters and issuing just one walk.[22] He enjoyed a fine day at the plate as well, smacking two hits and scoring a run. Despite his heroics, "Van Biber" and Fort Sam Houston required 10 innings to prevail, 3–2.[23] The account of the game in the *Kerrville Mountain Sun* referred once to "the Van person" so if this was a pseudonym, perhaps it was not completely unknown to his opponents.

In nineteen innings of work against Comfort and Kerrville, "Van Biber" yielded only nine hits and two runs. After these splendid outings, the Broncos enlisted "Van Biber" to pitch for them. As a result, on April 26, "Van Biber" started for the Broncos against the Fredericksburg Giants at Comfort's Faltin Field.[24]

The Broncos opened the scoring with Joe Pankratz's two-run homer in the first but "Van Biber" could not hold the Giants, who scored three runs in the second—all unearned after a two-out error. Fredericksburg added single runs against "Van Biber" in the fourth and sixth to take a 5–2 lead. Comfort rallied but fell short, 5–4, handing "Van Biber" the loss.[25] "Van Biber" struck out 10 but walked five and allowed nine hits (eight singles and a triple).[26] Fredericksburg's Al Hollmig, who would later serve as a player-manager for the hometown Giants, earned the complete game victory.

Fredericksburg returned to Comfort for a rematch between "Van Biber" and Hollmig on May 17. "Van Biber" dominated the Giants this time, "applying a nice coat of whitewash"[27] by hurling a one-hit shutout and striking out ten.[28] The game was scoreless until the eighth, when Comfort scored three runs on two hits and two Fredericksburg errors to secure a 3–0 victory.[29]

In his final appearance for Comfort the following Sunday, "Van Biber" and the Broncos traveled to San Antonio where they played a "morning and afternoon" doubleheader against the San Antonio Aztecs. According to the *Comfort News*, "the long trip from Comfort, coupled with the intense heat, left the Bronchos [*sic*] listless."[30] After the Aztecs rolled over the Broncos, 10–1, in the morning game, "Van Biber" started the afternoon game. Perhaps it was the heat or the Aztecs may have just been a strong club, but "the offerings of Van Biber afforded the Aztecs some fine batting practice."[31] "Van Biber" was rocked by the Aztecs, yielding eight runs before he was mercifully relieved in the fourth inning.[32] Carlock, the Broncos' reliever, held the Aztecs scoreless for the rest of the game but the damage had been done. Comfort lost, 8–0.

This loss ended the brief sojourn of "Van Biber" into Comfort baseball. "Van Biber" had defeated Comfort and Kerrville while pitching for Fort Sam Houston. After Comfort recruited him, "Van Biber" won one of three starts for the Broncos.

So, did Dizzy Dean pitch as "Van Biber" in 1925? There are several additional details we must consider. First, there was an actual pitcher named Van Biber on the Fort Sam Houston ballclub in 1925.[33] We know this because in early June 1925, the actual Van Biber left the US Army and Fort Sam Houston when he signed a professional baseball contract with the Cleveland Indians who assigned him to a Three-I League team in Decatur, Illinois.[34] Dizzy Dean, however, did not leave Fort Sam Houston until 1929 when he left the army. As a result, Dean could have pitched for Comfort as "Van Biber" only if he used the name as a pseudonym while the real Van Biber stayed on post at Fort Sam Houston.

Second, there is the timing of Dizzy Dean's arrival at Fort Sam Houston. Dizzy's father, Monroe Dean, was an itinerant laborer who traveled where he could find work. The Dean family (Dizzy, his father, and his younger brother, Paul) moved from Arkansas to Oklahoma in the early 1920s. At some point, the Deans came to live near Fort Sam Houston in San Antonio. The biography of Dizzy Dean published by the Society for American Baseball Research states that as the Deans "made their way through Texas looking for work, they came upon Fort Sam Houston, near San Antonio."[35] No date is provided for their arrival, but it is certainly before Dean enlisted in the army in 1926. However, two other biographers of Dizzy Dean, Vince Staten and Robert Gregory, conclude that Dean did not arrive at Fort Sam Houston until 1926.[36] Both state that in the spring of 1926, Dean pitched high school baseball as a 16-year-old in Oklahoma, where his family lived until he enlisted in the army.[37] If Staten and Gregory are correct, Dean was living in Oklahoma in 1925 and could not have pitched at that time as "Van Biber" or under any other assumed name.

Third, Dean was only 15 years old in 1925. According to his biographers, he did not enlist in the army until 1926. If that is true, then Dean pitched as "Van Biber" in 1925 only if his family moved near Fort Sam Houston when his father was looking for work, and the Fort Sam Houston ballclub, after discovering his pitching prowess, decided to start him as "Van Biber" for a few games even though he had not yet joined the army. This may seem unlikely, but it is possible since Dizzy Dean's prodigious talent at a young age and his effusive personality are well known. He never lacked confidence.

We must also remember that Dizzy Dean was an elusive character, and many contradictions lie in the path of any biographer. In fact, his biographers do not agree on some basic facts about Dean's life before he came to Fort Sam Houston.[38]

We also should not discount the recollections of players like Buck Nowlin and Joe Pankratz, among other players to be sure, who recalled Dean pitching for the Broncos. Indeed, Nowlin remembered catching two games for Dean. Gerhard Petermann, a respected educator in Comfort, observed at least one of the games pitched by Dean. Nowlin, Pankratz, and Petermann were stolid men of integrity, not given to exaggeration or puffery.

Moreover, apart from the question of Dean pitching as "Van Biber," there is no doubt that Dean did pitch for Hill Country town teams. Since the Fort Sam Houston team played games on Mondays, Hill Country clubs often hired army pitchers for their Sunday games. In fact, Dean's biographers found that he did pitch for several Hill Country town teams during his time at Fort Sam Houston (1927–1928), including a game in which he pitched for New Braunfels against Seguin under the alias "Schultz."[39] For his mound work, Dean earned $10 and a pound of barbecue ribs.[40] Dean also pitched Castroville to a doubleheader sweep, although it is not clear when.[41] More importantly, Gregory concluded that he "pitched for or against such towns as Comfort, Boerne, Kerrville, Fredericksburg, D'Hanis, Hondo, Frio, Medina, Sabinal, Utopia, and Uvalde."[42] One of those games occurred in 1927 when Dean pitched in relief for the Twelfth Field Artillery team, saving a 4–0 victory over Boerne at the Kendall County Fairgrounds and showing "more curves and speed [than] ever seen in these parts."[43]

Dean clearly pitched in the Hill Country, both for and against town teams while he was at Fort Sam Houston. Several firsthand recollections of Comfort players and other observers specifically recall Dean pitching for the Broncos."[44]

Figure 17. Dizzy Dean as a teenage pitcher for the San Antonio Public Service Company. (Printed under Shutterstock Editorial License.)

However, apart from the "Van Biber" games in 1925, we have not found any games in which Dean played for Comfort under his real name, or either of the aliases, "Van Biber" or "Schultz." Perhaps Dean played under a different assumed name.

In any event, we do know that after pitching for Fort Sam Houston in 1927 and 1928, Dean left the army in 1929 to pitch for the San Antonio Public Service

Company team. During his time with that squad, he was discovered by a scout who signed him to a contract with the Houston Buffaloes of the AAA Texas League,[45] a minor league club of the St. Louis Cardinals. After a stint with the Buffaloes, Dean debuted in the major leagues in 1930, winning his only appearance for St. Louis, before sticking in the majors for good in 1932, fashioning an 18–15 record.[46] Dean went 20–18 for the Cardinals in 1933, then ascended to stardom by winning 30 games as the star pitcher for the 1934 World Series champions.[47] Dean won 28 games in 1935 and 24 games in 1936, cementing his place in baseball lore. Dean was elected to the National Baseball Hall of Fame in 1953.[48] Later, he became known to a new generation of fans in the sixties when he served as the color commentator on ABC's Game of the Week broadcast.

Whether or not Dizzy Dean pitched as "Van Biber" as a 15-year-old in 1925, he did, at a minimum, blossom on Hill Country mounds. It was there that Dizzy polished his teenage skills pitching for and against town teams before maturing into a legendary pitcher destined for Cooperstown.

CHAPTER 4

FREDERICKSBURG CAN BE JUSTLY PROUD

Hill Country League, 1930

Between 1910 and 1929, town teams played regularly in the Hill Country but did so without the benefit of a formal league. Teams playing "independent" ball could schedule compelling games with rival towns, which attracted large crowds. But teams sometimes found it hard to find opponents within a convenient distance, forcing them to face ballclubs that neither interested their local fans nor provided a competitive game.[1] A lack of uniform rules among clubs was also a concern. The popularity of baseball demanded more from town teams. Thus, by 1930, town teams desired the structure and stability that could be provided only by forming a league of like-minded squads.

Given the stock market crash in October 1929, it may be surprising that town teams would consider the formation of their first baseball league in the following spring. However, the ripples of the Depression caused by the market crash were slow to reach the isolated Hill Country. In the winter of 1929–30, for example, local retailers in Kerrville were more concerned about the threat posed by chain stores. In February, 36 Kerrville merchants formed a unit of the Merchants' Minute Men, a national organization aimed at protecting local businesses from an influx of chain stores.[2]

In the meantime, Hill Country residents were excited by the prospect of country singer-songwriter Jimmie Rodgers performing at Schwethelm's Theater in Comfort on March 2.[3] Rodgers was then the nation's most popular recording artist, known as the "Blue Yodeler" for his yodeling style. Rodgers would later be regarded as the "Father of Country Music," but in 1930 he was already suffering from tuberculosis, which would eventually cause his demise in 1937. Like Rube Waddell 15 years earlier, Rodgers moved to the Hill Country in 1929 for health reasons, building a house in Kerrville to take advantage of the dry and mild air.[4]

Figure 18. Former Jimmie Rodgers home in Kerrville today. (Author photo.)

He called his home the "Blue Yodeler's Paradise."[5] At the time of his concert in Comfort, Hill Country residents considered him to be one of their own.

About the same time as Rodgers's concert in Comfort, Kerrville sportswriter Bob Bennett spearheaded the effort to create the Hill Country League in early 1930.[6] The inaugural HCL consisted of the Boerne White Sox, Comfort Broncos, Fredericksburg Giants, Kerrville Tourists, Llano Cowboys, and Mason Mavericks. Boerne, Kerrville, and Comfort occupied the southern part of the Hill Country. Fredericksburg was centrally located, while Llano and Mason were located north of Fredericksburg.[7] The clubs elected Bennett as HCL president.[8]

The HCL followed a 26-game schedule beginning April 6 and ending September 14.[9] The first- and second-place teams would play a best-of-three series for the championship. The league set uniform admission prices at 40 cents for adults and 15 cents for children,[10] prices that would later be reduced as the Depression took hold. Umpires would be hired by the home team. The league limited rosters to 15 players and adopted a rule that a club could have no more than two paid players to limit the number of ringers.[11] All unpaid players were required to reside in the same county as the team's location.

Figure 19. Jimmie Rodgers in Texas attire. (Jimmie Rodgers in Texas Attire by WestCoast DRIP is licensed under CC BY-SA 4.0, https://creativecommons.org/licenses/by-sa/4.0/?ref=openverse. No changes were made to the image. Source: Creative Commons.)

Town teams were not industrial clubs formed by businessmen who stocked them with their employees. Instead, players came from all walks of life—from ranch hands, butchers, and blacksmiths to store clerks and bookkeepers. The only qualification (besides residency) was a player's proficiency on the diamond. Tryouts were held in the spring for players hoping to play for the team, although most squads could count on a cadre of veteran ballplayers who returned each spring. Occasionally, a player home from college for the summer would latch on to a team roster as well. Since the ballplayers were considered hometown heroes by local fans, unpaid players often played for their hometown teams for many years, sometimes more than 10 years. A number of these players would later become civic and business leaders in their communities.[12]

Of the few paid players permitted by the HCL, some were known to move from team to team, sometimes in the middle of the season. Most often, they were pitchers. For example, Bryan "Zip" Myler, a former pitcher for Fort Sam Houston, pitched for Boerne in 1930, then started the 1931 season in Comfort before skipping town to play for Kerrville for the remainder of that season. Similarly, southpaw Haskell Archer started the 1933 season with Kerrville but left midseason for Comfort. In 1935, Archer toiled for the Legion Cubs, a new entry in the Mountain League. But perhaps the most peripatetic of all was the University of Texas pitching star Vernon Taylor who, in 1932, made one start for Kerrville then jumped ship to the Brady Turks. After the regular season concluded without Brady making the postseason, Llano retained Taylor's services for the championship series with Mason. Llano's enticement of Taylor paid off when he won two games of the series, giving the Cowboys the 1932 HCL championship.[13] But these were exceptions to the general rule. By limiting paid players to no more than two per team, the HCL intended to protect the integrity of the league's town teams.

One of baseball's appealing attributes is the common use of player nicknames. Rabbit Maranville, Shoeless Joe Jackson, Wahoo Sam Crawford, Goose Goslin, and Socks Seybold were just a few of the exotic names of many major leaguers in the early twentieth century. Ballplayers in the Hill Country do not disappoint us in this regard. A perusal of team rosters revealed players with colorful sobriquets such as Skeeter Pankratz, Smokey Klaerner, Chink Taylor, Goat Gardner, Zip Myler, Pepper Probst, Cheese Bremer, Flop Harris, Jelly Harris, Lefty Draper, Slim Esbeck, and Chicken Henke—all talented players. Nicknames also evolved to reflect what was happening in major-league baseball. For example, after Dizzy Dean and his brother Paul "Daffy" Dean led the St. Louis Cardinals to the 1934 World Series title, brothers Elias Klaerner and Phillip Klaerner became known by Fredericksburg fans as "Dizzy" and "Daffy," respectively.[14]

Another amusing, and long-forgotten, aspect of town teams was that the ballclubs typically had mascots. The mascots were young boys, often the sons of team officers, managers, or players. For example, Ernst Adler, young son of Boerne White Sox President H. O. Adler, served as the mascot for the White Sox. Early photographs of the Boerne White Sox, Fredericksburg Giants, Kerrville Athletics, and Llano Cowboys all show a mascot sitting in the foreground.[15] A mascot served not only as the batboy but also as team factotum, performing whatever duties were required on the diamond.

Players traveled to away games by automobile. Sometimes they were accompanied by wives or girlfriends with a picnic basket full of food and beverages for the trip. Other times, the team crowded as many players as they could into one vehicle. It was not unusual for Sunday drivers in the Hill Country to come upon a group of uniformed ballplayers huddled by the side of the road while they fixed a flat tire. Of course, vehicles were not plentiful during the Depression, so teams often implored their fans who owned automobiles to allow a player or two to hitch a ride to the game.

Town teams did not have the kind of owners we usually associate with professional baseball. Rather, most clubs were governed by a board of directors, usually manned by prominent local businessmen who loved baseball and hoped to procure goodwill for their own enterprises. A club's board of directors elected officers, such as a president, secretary, and treasurer. The board of directors usually named one of its members as the business manager and hired the field manager for the team. Each club elected league representatives, typically two per team, who served as the board of directors of the league.

Boerne enjoyed the most stable club management. Both president H. O. Adler, a retail merchant, and business manager Udo Harz, a Boerne businessman, served the White Sox for many years in the 1920s and 1930s.[16] In contrast, Kerrville's board of directors rotated business managers, appointing a different director to serve in that capacity each year from 1930 through 1933.[17] Occasionally, the results on the diamond directly affected team management. For example, after a dismal 1934 season when the Braves finished in last place with a 2–13 record, all of Kerrville's directors resigned, necessitating the election of a new board before the 1935 season.[18]

The Fredericksburg Giants followed a different corporate model.[19] The Gillespie County Fair Association sponsored the Giants. As sponsor, the fair association appointed the team manager in January or February of each year while players voted to elect the team captain. According to the Giants' constitution, the team's "ruling body" consisted of the Fair Association Sports Committee, the team manager, the team captain, and one team member selected by the manager and captain. The manager also served as the vice president of the team.

The Giants' bylaws provided for allocation of funds at season's end after the deduction of operational expenses. The team deposited one-third of any surplus into a fund to pay for team uniforms and one-fourth into a "benefit fund" to improve their diamond at Fair Park and purchase equipment. The remaining surplus funds were given to players as gifts at the conclusion of the season in amounts determined by the manager, captain, and a team representative. As a result, although Fredericksburg could claim that the team did not "pay" any of its players, the stars of the club could reasonably expect to receive a small sum at season's end.

Before the 1930 season began, the formation of the HCL generated much optimism for all clubs. Excitement for the new league ran even higher after Kerrville hosted its first major-league exhibition game on March 19 when the New York Giants and Chicago White Sox traveled to town from their San Antonio spring training grounds. Most of the players fielded that day by the Giants and White Sox were backup or part-time players, but they were nonetheless major leaguers.

Before a crowd of 1,500 fans—the largest crowd ever at the Kerrville ballpark—the White Sox edged the Giants, 9–6, led by left fielder Dave Harris, who smashed two home runs.[20] The Giants scored four runs in the first inning on home runs by players identified in newspaper accounts as Rees (probably outfielder Andy Reese) and Fisher.[21] The White Sox duplicated the feat in the bottom of the first, scoring four tallies on home runs by Harris and starting pitcher Ed Walsh (son of Hall of Fame White Sox pitcher Ed Walsh). The second clout of Harris and a home run by a player identified as Blackerby[22] handed the win to the Sox.[23] Proceeds from the game went to the emergency relief fund of the Kerrville American Legion Post.[24]

Buoyed by this taste of major-league baseball, fans embraced the HCL. In anticipation of this new chapter in Hill Country baseball, groundskeepers raked the stones from dirt infields and scythed weeds from outfield grass to prepare diamonds for the league debut. As Fredericksburg prepared to host Kerrville for its first game, the *Fredericksburg Standard* called it "[t]he most auspicious opening day in the Fredericksburg Giants ballclub history."[25]

Thanks to donations by local businessmen, the Giants purchased new uniforms to mark the coming season. The uniforms featured black and orange colors patterned after their major-league namesake, the New York Giants—silver-gray with

Figure 20. Comfort Broncos, 1930. Top row (L–R): Edgar Scheele, utility outfielder; Walter Kutzer, utility infielder; Carl King, second base; Paul Weiss, outfielder; Gus Wendler, outfielder; Robert Lindner, outfielder; Christie Lindemann, pitcher; Ernst Doebbler, manager; Chester Karger, scorekeeper. Bottom row (L–R): F. M. "Pat" Faust, league umpire; Skeeter Pankratz, third base; Felix Meyer, catcher; Morris Goforth, first base; Joe Pankratz, shortstop; Sid Wright Sr., utility infielder; Leonard Maddox, pitcher; Harold Krauter, pitcher. (Courtesy of Comfort Heritage Foundation, Inc., Comfort, Texas.)

black braid trimmings and an orange, Old English "F" on the chest, matched with black socks featuring two narrow stripes and black caps with a small orange "F."[26]

As for the other clubs, "[e]veryone in the Hill Country is highly interested in the new project and enthusiasm is running high in all of the towns of the league territory."[27] The *Comfort News* joined the chorus, commenting that the league was an "important step forward" and that "more local interest will be shown this season than was the case in the past."[28]

Fredericksburg was a veteran club managed by player-manager Al Hollmig,[29] who was a fearsome hitter. Second baseman Paul Knopp and third baseman Lawrence Peter starred on the infield while Milton Durst excelled in center field. Veteran pitcher Clarence "Pepper" Probst led the mound corps, but 22-year-old right-hander Hugo Klaerner was expected to challenge for the top spot. No one doubted that the Giants, long a powerhouse in Hill Country baseball, would compete for the HCL title.

Since Llano is 38 miles north of Fredericksburg, the Cowboys were less known to fans in Boerne, Comfort, and Kerrville but they would soon be powered by a former major leaguer—32-year-old C. L. "Chink" Taylor, a native of Burnet, Texas, who played eight games for the Chicago Cubs in 1925.[30] After his brief appearance in the majors, Taylor toiled in the minor leagues for four years, playing in 1929 with the Chattanooga Lookouts and the Houston Buffaloes. After that season, Houston shipped him to the Omaha Packers of the Class A Western League, but Omaha released him in May 1930. Taylor returned to Burnet, then came to Llano to play for the Cowboys and opened a filling station.[31] In addition to Taylor, right fielder Huldie Mather and shortstop M. A. Reed powered Llano's offense, while strikeout artist Lefty Draper anchored the mound. Outfielder Cecil Hutto occasionally toed the rubber as well.

Boerne's pitching staff featured two veterans, Zip Myler, a former army base pitcher, and Tommy Dugosh. Second baseman Rudy Leidl[32] sparked the White Sox offense from the leadoff spot, while third baseman Egon "Cheese" Bremer and right fielder Albert Uecker swung powerful bats. Longtime manager Ed Kaiser piloted the Sox.

Wood Thornberry, a right-handed pitcher with "blinding speed and a nice assortment of curves,"[33] was expected to pace the Kerrville Tourists. Andy Andrews, a former Schreiner Institute athlete and a "veritable box of pepper,"[34] served as Thornberry's battery mate. Third baseman Louie Wootton, shortstop Bob Coleman, and first baseman Clergy Hollimon[35] pounded the fences for the team. Al Holchak, a former Kerrville player, skippered the club.

Like Fredericksburg, the Comfort Broncos fielded an experienced club. Brothers Joe and Skeeter Pankratz teamed up on the infield while swinging potent bats. Speedy outfielder Walter Kutzer kept opposing pitchers off balance while catcher Felix Meyer was a dangerous hitter. The Broncos expected a strong season from Leonard Maddox, a veteran pitcher who formerly pitched for Kerrville.[36]

Right-hander Roswell "Rod" Sanders was a standout pitcher for the Mason Mavericks. Outfielder-first baseman Pat Hatch was a strong hitter who could also pitch, but some observers questioned whether the supporting cast behind Sanders and Hatch would measure up to the other clubs.

On Opening Day, Fredericksburg and Kerrville, rivals for many years, met at Fair Park in Fredericksburg amid much pomp and circumstance.[37] Before the game, the Seven Yellow Jackets Orchestra serenaded fans. League president

Bob Bennett then delivered remarks and Fredericksburg Mayor Joe Stein threw out the first pitch.[38] Both teams featured strong hurlers—Pepper Probst for the Giants and Wood Thornberry for the Tourists—so fans anticipated a close game. Down 3–2 in the fourth, the Giants scored two unearned runs on an error by second baseman Saenger.[39] Probst held the Tourists scoreless the rest of the way, striking out the last batter in the ninth with runners on second and third, to preserve the Giants' victory, 4–3. Fredericksburg third baseman Lawrence Peter rapped three extra-base hits (two doubles and a triple) while Tourists shortstop Bob Coleman contributed three hits.

Elsewhere, Comfort catcher Felix Meyer belted four hits, including a double and a triple, while left fielder Robert Lindner added a double among three hits to lead the Broncos to an 11–8 win over Boerne.[40] White Sox catcher Walter Kalisky tallied four hits while first baseman Clarence Holekamp slapped three singles for the White Sox.

In Mason, the Mavericks managed only five hits off Llano pitcher Cecil Hutto and struck out 10 times, but they eked out a 5–3 victory, thanks to four runs in the fourth inning.[41] Hutto crushed a double and triple in the Cowboys' losing effort. Mason hurler Rod Sanders struck out 14 batters and gave up seven hits, earning the victory.

The HCL was off and running. Early in the season, however, the Kerrville Tourists endured several unexpected challenges. On April 27, Kerrville's ace pitcher, Wood Thornberry—known to fans as the "Duke of Thornberry"—squared off with Llano's slim southpaw, Lefty Draper, at Llano's Robinson State Park. It was a tight game; the clubs were tied, 2–2, in the bottom of the ninth when Kerrville catcher Andy Andrews averted defeat for the Tourists thanks to his knowledge of the local ground rules. With two outs and Paul McLeod on base at first, John Pinckney, the Llano leadoff hitter, slammed a line drive over third base that rolled into a cluster of parked cars. By the time left fielder Baker retrieved the ball, the runner had crossed the plate, apparently sending Kerrville home in defeat. However, Andrews "leaped and shrieked and continued to do so until Umpire Gray sent Pinckney back to second and McLeod back to third on a ground rule limiting runners to two bases in case the ball should happen to strike automobiles parking around the playing field."[42] Saved by the ground rule, Thornberry retired the next hitter, sending the game into extra innings.

Thornberry and Draper mowed down their opposition for six more innings; Thornberry struck out 23 batters while Draper fanned 18. At the end of 15 innings, the umpire called the game on account of darkness. As a result, the outstanding hurling of both Thornberry and Draper went for naught in a 2–2 tie. The *Kerrville Mountain Sun* noted: "Another round or so might have been played, but the players were sagging at the heels and Umpire Gray, who had been charged by both sides with acute astigmatism at various times during the festivities, did not care to risk life or limb further. Consequently, at the end of the 15th inning, he called it a draw."[43]

A week later, Kerrville traveled to Comfort where they ran into a buzzsaw in the form of minor league pitcher Frank Watt, who pitched in the Texas League from 1925 through 1929 for San Antonio, Fort Worth, and Houston.[44] Watt dominated the Kerrville batters, striking out 10 and shutting them out, 4–0. The *Kerrville Mountain Sun* commented that Watt had "too much candlepower for the Hill Country League."[45]

Kerrville protested the game, perhaps on grounds that Watt was still under a professional contract in violation of league restrictions on "outside" players. Although Watt did not pitch in the minors in 1930, he ended up pitching for the Philadelphia Phillies in 1931, fashioning a 5–5 record with a 4.84 ERA. Even though Watt never played professionally after 1931, he was clearly a pitcher of near-major-league quality when he shut out the Tourists in 1930. The league's response to the protest is unclear, but no record of the game being replayed could be found. However, Watt did not pitch again in the 1930 HCL season, which suggests that the league did take some remedial action.

Later in May, the Tourists encountered yet another obstacle, this time of the natural variety. On May 18, Kerrville was scheduled to travel to Boerne to meet the White Sox at the Kendall County Fairgrounds. However, the Guadalupe River flooded after 2.58 inches of rain, resulting in the drowning of a 13-year-old boy.[46] The flood imperiled the Tourists' trip to Boerne, necessitating some ingenuity. When Kerrville players and fans reached the turgid river, "they overcame the difficulty by 'cooning it' across the Southern Pacific Railway bridge and were transported to Boerne by cars sent from that point."[47]

Kerrville's travails were rewarded with a 4–3 victory over the host White Sox, improving their season record to 3–3. The Tourists then shut out Mason, 1–0, on May 25,[48] but Thornberry suffered a tough loss, 3–2, to Mason on June 1.[49] In that game, Mason scored the eventual winning run in the seventh inning when Mavericks pitcher Rod Sanders reached first on an error and then scored after Thornberry threw three successive wild pitches.[50] It was Mason's first victory since the Opening Day win against Llano.

For unknown reasons, the "Duke of Thornberry" did not appear on the mound for Kerrville after the June 1 loss. We can only speculate, but perhaps the 15 innings Thornberry pitched in the tie game on April 27 resulted in a sore arm that eventually ended his season. But the Tourists did not sit idly. They brought on board former Boerne infielder Anton "Tony" Leidl to play third base. Brother of Boerne second baseman Rudy Leidl, Anton started the season as Boerne's shortstop but left the club for Kerrville. Leidl was known as a "consistent performer afield [who] wields a powerful war club when he once gets his stride."[51] The Tourists were making a push for the pennant.

While Kerrville encountered some early trials, Llano took charge of the league. After losing the opening game to Mason, the Cowboys defeated Fredericksburg twice. The first win on April 13 resulted from the heroics of shortstop M. A. Reed. Down 7–6 with two outs in the ninth, the Cowboys rallied against Giants pitcher Hugo Klaerner, tying the score when Reed tripled and scored on a fielding error by Giants second baseman Paul Knopp. Then in the bottom of the 11th inning, Reed singled—his third hit of the game—to drive in the decisive run in an 8–7 victory.[52] Llano prevailed despite committing five errors—all on the infield—exposing the porous fielding that would occasionally plague the Cowboys.

On May 4, the Cowboys traveled to Fair Park in Fredericksburg for the second meeting with the Giants. Both teams knocked their opponent's starting pitcher out of the game. Hugo Klaerner relieved Pepper Probst after the Cowboys built a 5–0 lead in the fifth inning, but the Giants rallied for four runs in the eighth inning. After Llano's Lefty Draper relieved Cecil Hutto in that frame, the Cowboys held on to win, 6–4.[53]

Draper then pitched consecutive three-hit shutouts against Comfort—the first a 3–0 victory on May 11[54] and the second a 2–0 gem on May 25.[55] The next Sunday, Draper continued his stellar mound work and Chink Taylor homered to trounce Boerne, 8–2, in front of Llano's largest crowd of the season.[56] The Cowboys now boasted a 6–2 record—good enough for first place and an early lead in the pennant chase.[57]

Fredericksburg struggled, losing to Boerne, 5–3, on May 25, after a White Sox rally started with a controversial play. The Giants were leading 3–2 in the bottom of the eighth when White Sox catcher Walter Kalisky stepped to the plate to lead off the inning against Giants pitcher Hugo Klaerner:

> Kalisky, the Boerne receiver, who had been unable to do anything with Klaerner's low curve ball, ran up at least three or more steps out of the batter's box and hit a hard drive directly back at the pitcher, hitting the latter in the belt. This brought forth a vigorous protest from the Giants' manager, Schuch, who declared that the hit was an illegally batted ball and that the batter under the rules was out. Umpire Nickels would not

> allow the objection and ordered that play be resumed. Whereupon, the Giants manager asked the umpire to announce that the game was played under protest. The blow seemed to have unnerved Klaerner considerably.[58]

Following this hubbub, Kalisky was sacrificed to second base. After White Sox left fielder Harry Schweppe walked, right fielder Edgar Harz drove in Kalisky with a single, tying the score at 3–3. Pitcher Tommy Dugosh then laid down a perfect squeeze bunt along the third base line to score Schweppe. Rudy Leidl drilled a double to deep center field, scoring Harz with an insurance run. Dugosh held the Giants scoreless in the ninth to capture the 5–3 victory.

The league disallowed the Giants' protest of the game. The *Fredericksburg Standard* sharply criticized the league's decision, pointing out that Boerne had failed to mark off the batter's box as required by baseball rules. The newspaper concluded that Fredericksburg's protest was well founded, warning that "if the club directors of the league continue to countenance such open violations, we are almost certain that the venture will crash on the rocks before long, all of which we certainly hope will never come about."[59] Fredericksburg's objections to the denial of the protest would not be the last dispute over league decisions in Hill Country baseball.

After the distressing loss to Boerne, the woes of the Giants continued the following Sunday. Host Comfort knocked Pepper Probst out of the game in the sixth inning while the Giants could not solve the offerings of Broncos starter Leonard Maddox, who scattered six hits in a 3–1 win.[60] Comfort right fielder Robert Lindner smacked two hits and made a game-saving catch in the ninth inning.[61] The two consecutive losses dropped the Giants to a 5–4 mark.

Like Fredericksburg, Boerne was also plagued by inconsistency. Although they earned tough wins over Llano and Fredericksburg, Boerne could not keep up with Llano, thanks to two one-run losses to Kerrville, both times to Tourists starter Wood Thornberry—3–2 in 10 innings on April 13 and 4–3 on May 18—the game in which the Tourists were forced to negotiate the flooded Guadalupe River to reach the Kendall County Fairgrounds in Boerne. After their loss to Llano, 8–2, on June 1, the White Sox dropped to .500 at 4–4.

Kerrville remained in the hunt at 4–4, but losing the services of star hurler Wood Thornberry, probably due to a sore arm, was a blow. Southpaw Tommy Swayze replaced Thornberry on the mound, but he lost his first four starts, dropping the Tourists out of contention.

Comfort won three of its first five games but then lost three in a row, two to Llano (Lefty Draper's two shutouts) and a 6–1 loss to Fredericksburg on May 18 when Pepper Probst returned to the mound for the Giants, holding the Broncos to six hits.[62] Two weeks later, the Broncos recovered to grab the 3–1 win from Fredericksburg on their home diamond, giving the Broncos a 4–5 record and keeping their pennant hopes alive.[63]

Mason, after defeating Llano on Opening Day, lost six in a row. The losses included a 10–1 shellacking by Llano in front of a large crowd at Mason on May 18.[64] In that game, the Mavericks committed seven errors while Llano's offensive assault forced Mason starter Rod Sanders out of the game in the sixth inning. The Mavericks ended the losing streak on June 1 by edging Kerrville, 3–2, in Wood Thornberry's last appearance for the Tourists, but Mason remained in the cellar with a 2–6 record.[65] (The June 5 standings for the HCL are shown in Table 1.)[66]

Table 1. HCL Standings, June 5, 1930

	W	L	GB	Pct.
Llano	6	2	---	.750
Fredericksburg	5	4	1½	.556
Boerne	4	4	2	.500
Kerrville	4	4	2	.500
Comfort	4	5	2½	.444
Mason	2	6	4	.250

As the Texas heat began to swelter, making the sunbaked infields hard as rock, Hill Country denizens wondered whether any club could mount a challenge to Llano. Fredericksburg answered the call by proceeding to win seven in a row behind Hugo Klaerner and his younger brother, Chester "Smokey" Klaerner,[67] who returned to Fredericksburg for the summer after starring as a Rice Institute[68] hurler. The wins included a hard-fought 3–2 victory over Llano on June 29. In that game, Hugo Klaerner limited the Cowboys to four hits, while striking out 10 and contributing two hits to the cause.[69]

Boerne split a doubleheader with Kerrville on July 4, shortly after the Kerrville nine had returned to their original nickname, the "Athletics," as part of a club reorganization.[70] For the first game, Kerrville "imported" Chester Klaerner from Fredericksburg.[71] Klaerner and Zip Myler battled to a 1–1 standoff through 10 innings before the White Sox scored two runs in the top of the 11th inning to secure the 3–1 victory. Despite limiting the White Sox to three hits, Klaerner took the loss in his only appearance for the renamed Athletics.[72] Kerrville salvaged the nightcap, 4–3, behind Tommy Swayze who fanned 11 in his first win after four losses.[73]

Boerne disrupted Fredericksburg's winning streak with a 6–1 victory on July 20, when Zip Myler stymied the Giants, limiting them to five singles and striking out ten, handing Hugo Klaerner the loss. Fredericksburg rebounded at Comfort the next week, raising their record to 13–5, when Chester Klaerner and Leonard Maddox hooked up in a pitcher's duel. Tied 1–1 after nine innings, the Giants scored two runs in the top of the 10th, when Lawrence Peter doubled to drive in the go-ahead run and Chester Klaerner singled him in. Klaerner held the Broncos in the bottom of the 10th to secure a well-deserved win, 3–1.[74]

Except for the loss to the Giants, Llano also kept winning, taking six of seven games, including a 20–4 humiliation of Mason on July 4.[75] As of July 27, the Cowboys, now 13–3, remained one game ahead of the Giants (13–5) although they were two games ahead in the loss column.[76]

Boerne climbed into the pennant race by winning seven of nine games, sparked by the addition of shortstop Charlie English on June 22. English played for the Fifteenth Field Artillery team at Fort Sam Houston but moonlighted with various clubs.[77] When English joined Boerne, his powerful bat solidified the attack as they surged to challenge Fredericksburg and Llano for the flag.

However, Boerne lost ground on July 27, when Llano defeated the White Sox, 6–3. Llano left fielder Huldie Mather belted four hits to lead the Cowboys to the win when Boerne pitcher Zip Myler could not replicate his outstanding outing against the Giants the week before. Lefty Draper scattered six hits while striking out seven for Llano. Boerne dropped to 11–7, three games behind Llano.

Kerrville, Comfort, and Mason shuffled along. Kerrville crushed Mason, 10–0, on July 27, when Kerrville southpaw Tommy Swayze limited the Mavericks to three hits and fanned 11.[78] The Athletics were now only 6–10, but that was good enough for fourth place.

Comfort was comfortably in fifth place at 5–12. After managing a 5–6 record with an extra-inning 8–7 victory over Kerrville on June 29,[79] the Broncos lost six in a row. Each loss came at the hands of Fredericksburg and Llano, including a bizarre ending at Fredericksburg on July 13. Comfort's hurler, Lefty Marberger, kept pace with Hugo Klaerner as they both shut out their opposition through 10 innings. In the top of the 11th, the Broncos broke through for five runs off Klaerner—three runs on a homer by Skeeter Pankratz when his line drive danced between Giants center fielder Milton Durst and left fielder Emil "Chicken" Henke. Then after a single by Felix Meyer, Marberger knocked a base hit to center that took a bad hop over Durst, allowing Marberger to cruise around the bases for the second home run in the inning, giving Comfort a 5–0 lead. The Giants rallied against a tired Marberger, scoring three runs, two on a triple by Durst. Leonard Maddox relieved Marberger only to be greeted by Edgar Klett's two-run home run blast, tying the score, 5–5. After Maddox recorded the second out of the inning, Hugo Klaerner tripled. Paul Knopp's single scored Klaerner to consummate the six-run rally, breaking the hearts of the Broncos, 6–5.[80]

Last-place Mason, after breaking a six-game losing streak by defeating Kerrville, 3–2, on June 1,[81] proceeded to lose six more in a row until the Mavericks managed to edge Kerrville again, 5–4, on July 20.[82] In securing the victory, Mason took advantage of six Kerrville errors. They scored four runs in the top of the ninth for the deciding margin. Kerrville pitcher Tommy Swayze took the loss despite giving up just six hits. But Kerrville got revenge when Swayze shut out the Mavericks on three hits the following Sunday, 10–0,[83] leaving Mason firmly ensconced in the basement with a 3–14 record.

When fourth-place Kerrville hosted Llano on August 3, the Athletics stood at 6–10 and were in a slide, having lost seven of their last nine games, while the Cowboys (13–3) were enjoying a five-game winning streak. As a result, Hill Country fans were stunned when Kerrville swept a doubleheader from Llano that afternoon: "The Kerrville Athletics astonished the natives, amazed the visitors and surprised themselves Sunday afternoon by dusting off the Llano Lambs, Hill Country League leaders, in a doubleheader. The competition was keen throughout the afternoon and the final statistics were 3 to 1 and 4 to 3."[84]

In the opening game, Kerrville pitcher Tommy Swayze struck out 11 and held the Cowboys to four hits, the only run scoring on a solo homer by Chink Taylor.[85] Llano's ace, Lefty Draper, took the 3–1 loss. In the second game, Anton Leidl[86] moved from second base to the mound, scattering six hits and striking out seven, to take the 4–3 win for Kerrville after the Athletics rallied for three runs in the sixth inning against Llano's backup pitcher, Cecil Hutto.[87]

In Fredericksburg, Boerne squeezed by the Giants, 5–3, in 10 innings.[88] White Sox pitcher Zip Myler allowed seven hits while striking out 13. Boerne scored the winning runs in the 10th on a two-run triple by H. Johnston, a former army base star who was added to the White Sox roster as a "utility infielder."

The unexpected doubleheader loss by Llano, coupled with Boerne's victory over Fredericksburg, tightened the pennant race considerably. Llano (13–5) now held just a one-half game advantage over Fredericksburg (13–6) and a mere one-and-one-half game lead over Boerne (12–7). Suddenly, it was a three-team race with six weeks left in the season, as shown by the standings on August 3 (see Table 2).[89]

Table 2. HCL Standings, August 3, 1930

	W	L	GB	Pct.
Llano	13	5	---	.722
Fredericksburg	13	6	½	.684
Boerne	12	7	1½	.632
Kerrville	8	10	5	.444
Comfort	7	12	6½	.368
Mason	3	16	10½	.158

After Llano cruised to a 7–2 win over Mason on August 10[90] and Fredericksburg stopped Kerrville, 5–1, on the same day,[91] the Giants traveled to Llano with first place on the line on August 17. Lefty Draper and Hugo Klaerner, the starters for Llano and Fredericksburg, respectively, were among the best pitchers in the league, but neither had his best stuff in this game. In the fifth inning, Llano scored seven runs on six hits and two errors, taking a 9–5 lead and knocking Klaerner out of the game in favor of his younger brother, Chester "Smokey" Klaerner. But the Giants, down 9–7, rallied for five runs in the top of the ninth on three errors by the Cowboys, a pair of stolen bases, two singles and a long triple by first baseman-manager Al Hollmig to win, 12–10.[92] Fredericksburg (14–6) moved one-half game ahead of the Cowboys (13–6). For the first time since the third week of the season, Llano no longer held the top rung in the standings.

The three league leaders sailed through their games on August 24. Behind the hurling of brothers Chester and Hugo Klaerner, Fredericksburg handed Kerrville its third straight loss, 13–2,[93] while Llano outslugged Mason, 15–6.[94] Boerne whitewashed Comfort, 12–0,[95] led by the hot hitting of young shortstop Charlie English, who slammed three hits for the second game in a row.[96]

The convincing wins by Fredericksburg (16–6) and Llano (15–6) set up a rematch between the clubs for the following Sunday. For reasons that are not clear, Llano started a new pitcher, Harry White, rather than regular Lefty Draper or occasional starter Cecil Hutto. Playing on Llano's home diamond in Robinson State Park,[97] the game started quietly as neither club could score through three innings. The Cowboys scored first in the bottom of the fourth on a fielder's choice when the Giants failed to complete a double play with the bases loaded. Harry White then held the Giants scoreless until the eighth inning when Hugo Klaerner singled in a run, leveling the score at 1–1. However, trouble started to brew in the bottom of the eighth. The home plate umpire, hired by Llano as the home team, initially made some ball-strike calls questioned by the Giants. According to the *Fredericksburg Standard*: "White was up. Ball one strike two. Another right down the middle, 'Ball two' says the ump. Another right over, [catcher Udo] Henke tossed the ball to third thinking it was a strikeout. 'Ball three' yells the ump. Then another pitch straight over, White swung and singled to right."[98]

After a sacrifice bunt, John Pinckney singled, sending White to third. The next batter hit a line drive that bounced past Giants left fielder Elias Klaerner, scoring White. Pinckney was also waved around third on the play, trying to score a crucial insurance run as Klaerner's throw came to the plate. Even though "the ball appeared to have beat him by several feet," the umpire ruled Pinckney safe at home, giving the Cowboys a 3–1 lead. The Giants protested the call to no avail, causing player-manager Al Hollmig to remove his players from the diamond, resulting in a 9–0 forfeit.[99]

Fans and players alike milled around the diamond in the aftermath of the forfeit which, according to the *Fredericksburg Standard*, elicited some ethnic aspersions:

> The stands emptied slowly and the large crowd surged on the playing field. It was a miracle that no trouble ensued as the crowd was in a bad mood and a mere ball game could have caused possibly the loss of life. To one whose mother can proudly wear a service pin with five stars on it, due to the fact that five of her seven sons served for their country during the horrible world war, it was an insult to hear Llano fans tell the Fredericksburg contingent to go back to their "Dutch Kingdom." That we were Germans, American born was about all that could be held up against "friendly neighbors." Good sportsmanship and fair play appear to be sadly missing.[100]

In contrast to the *Fredericksburg Standard*, the *Llano News* reported merely that Fredericksburg walked off the field when the team "contended that the umpire had made a bad decision."[101] Despite the grumbling on the diamond, the *Llano News* commended the sportsmanship in the HCL, making no mention of the ill feelings after the forfeit but encouraging the clubs "to see that harmony prevails and sportsmanship is classed above victories and losses."[102]

The forfeit left Fredericksburg (16–7) one-half game behind the Cowboys (16–6) with three games to play. Fortunately for the Giants, they played last-place Mason in all three games (including a doubleheader on September 7) while

Llano's schedule included a doubleheader at Boerne the following Sunday. The White Sox were in third but at 15–8 after stomping Kerrville 16–9,[103] they remained in contention. As a result, the White Sox would be no pushover for Llano.

As expected, Fredericksburg swept the doubleheader from Mason on September 7. Pepper Probst, with the benefit of four double plays, mowed down the Mavericks, 6–2, in the opener. Despite injuring his arm while playing center field in the opening game, Hugo Klaerner managed to pitch the Giants to victory in the second game, 7–6, thanks to home runs by his cousin, center fielder Elias Klaerner, and Pepper Probst, playing left field in the nightcap.[104] The win clinched a berth for the Giants in the championship series with one week remaining in the season.

All eyes turned to the Kendall County Fairgrounds[105] in Boerne where the White Sox hosted Llano for a doubleheader. Left fielder Albert Uecker paced the White Sox in the first game by smashing two doubles and scoring three runs to lead Boerne to victory, 7–3.[106] White Sox hurler Zip Myler allowed 11 hits but yielded only three runs.

As the teams took the field for the second game (a seven-inning game by agreement), the White Sox (16–8) were just one-half game behind the Cowboys (16–7) for the second place slot in the championship series. If the White Sox won both the nightcap and their final game at Comfort on September 14, the worst they could do would be to tie for second place with Llano. If that occurred, Boerne and Llano would meet in a playoff game for the right to meet Fredericksburg for the league title.

Like the Giants–Cowboys game a week earlier, the nightcap was fraught with controversy. After Llano scored six runs off Zip Myler, forcing his departure in the second inning, Boerne called on Hargrove, a pitcher for the San Antonio club of the Texas League, to the mound. Llano immediately protested the game, objecting to the use of Hargrove, who was apparently still under a minor league contract.[107] However, it all became moot when the Cowboys scored two more runs off Hargrove in the third inning and Cowboys ace starter Lefty Draper held on for an 8–6 win.[108]

Llano's win meant that if they defeated Kerrville on September 14, they would finish second and meet Fredericksburg in the championship series. If Llano lost to the Athletics and Boerne prevailed at Comfort, then things got complicated because the White Sox would end the season one-half game behind the Cowboys. If that happened, Kerrville and Llano would then be required to make up the 15-inning tie game on April 27.[109] If Llano lost the makeup game, Boerne and

Llano would then finish tied for second place, resulting in a playoff game for second place between the White Sox and the Cowboys.

With all that in mind, Boerne took care of business in Comfort on September 14, scoring five runs in the first inning and pounding the Broncos, 17–2. Comfort was missing Skeeter Pankratz, a key player who was out with a broken arm, and several other players.[110] However, Llano did not falter in Kerrville, winning in workmanlike fashion, 5–1, behind new pitcher Harry White who struck out 15 and scattered six hits. Llano's win secured second place and the opportunity to play Fredericksburg in the championship series. In a game winding up the season, Hugo Klaerner pitched Fredericksburg to a 5–2 victory at Mason, striking out 13.

(The final HCL standings for 1930 are shown in Table 3.)[111]

Table 3. HCL Final Standings, 1930

	W	L	GB	Pct.
Fredericksburg	19	7	---	.731
Llano	18	7	½	.720
Boerne	17	9	2	.654
Kerrville	10	15	8½	.400
Comfort	8	18	11	.308
Mason	5	21	14	.192

To prepare for the championship series, the HCL directors met in Fredericksburg on September 16. Normally, such a business meeting is a tranquil affair. But this meeting was characterized as "rollicking" and "stormy" because Boerne lodged a protest, claiming that Llano's Chink Taylor was a member of the Omaha club in the Western League while playing in the Hill Country League in violation of league rules, making him an ineligible player.[112] Boerne was attempting to dislodge Llano from second place, and a slot in the championship series, by claiming that Llano should forfeit all games in which Taylor appeared—nearly all of their regular season games. According to the *Kerrville Mountain Sun*, "[p]rotests and charges of bad sportsmanship flew thick and fast."[113] By a majority vote, however, the league directors rejected the protest. Despite the acrimony, the directors eventually moved on to perform the coin flip for the series. Llano won, giving the Cowboys home-field advantage for the first and third games.

The first game of the best-of-three championship series between Fredericksburg and Llano on September 21 drew "perhaps the largest crowd ever gathered" at Robinson State Park, attracting fans from Fredericksburg as well as other Hill Country towns.[114]

Llano pounded out 12 hits, scoring eight runs after four innings and knocking Giants ace Hugo Klaerner out of the game. After the onslaught, Cowboys starter Harry White cruised to the win, 9–2.[115] Chink Taylor stroked three hits including a double and scored three runs to lead the Cowboys' attack.

The teams traveled to Fair Park in Fredericksburg for the second game. A Llano triumph would garner the championship for the Cowboys. With the Giants' back against the wall after Hugo Klaerner's poor outing in the first game, player-manager Al Hollmig gave himself the nod as the starting pitcher.

The game was played in drizzling rain, but the hopes of Giants fans were even more dampened when Llano roughed up Hollmig for eight runs, building up a 10–3 lead after seven innings. Despite the wet conditions, Fredericksburg stormed back, scoring five runs in the bottom of the eighth to pull within two runs, 10–8, and knocking out Harry White, whose lack of control—he walked seven batters in the game—contributed to the rally. In relief, Hugo Klaerner held the Cowboys scoreless in the top of the ninth. In the bottom of the inning, the Cowboys called upon untested relief pitcher Cross to save the game. Cross had pitched only one-and-one-third innings in the regular season. The Giants feasted on his offerings, combining three hits with three walks to score three runs.[116] Capped by Hugo Klaerner's game-winning single, the Giants stunned the Cowboys, 11–10.[117] Despite their collapse, Llano pitchers White and Cross did not shoulder the entire blame for Llano's loss—the Cowboys committed eight errors in the game.

Fredericksburg's shocking comeback left a single game to decide the championship. Originally, the game was scheduled to be played in Llano on October 5, but heavy rain canceled the game, sending the final game back to Fredericksburg on October 12.[118]

Rain affected the championship game as well, resulting in several delays, but the Giants started where they left off two weeks earlier against Harry White, scoring seven runs in the first four innings for a 7–1 lead. Hugo Klaerner kept the Cowboys at bay, although he needed relief help in the eighth inning from Marvin Deike—one of the famous Deike Brothers—to secure the win, 11–6,[119] gaining the inaugural Hill Country League championship for Fredericksburg. The Giants belted 16 hits, including three each by left fielder Emil Henke, first baseman-manager Al Hollmig, and catcher Felix Hahn.

For their title, the Giants received an 18-inch silver loving cup furnished by W. H. Schaefer of the Central Drug Company in Fredericksburg, while each player received watch fobs with miniature gold-filled baseballs presented by A. G. Spalding Company of San Antonio.[120]

The *Fredericksburg Standard* lauded the 1930 HCL season as "a far greater success than first estimated,"[121] noting the high level of enthusiasm in every town. The league treasurer reported income of $312.00 and expenses of only $12.50, allowing the league to distribute the net earnings of $299.50 equally to each club.[122] However, the *Fredericksburg Standard* noted that unlike the Giants, who fielded only local athletes, some clubs may have needed those funds to recoup payments to "outside" players:

> Since the roster of the Giants is made up entirely of home boys, who play without salary or remuneration of any kind, Fredericksburg can be justly proud of their record, which can not be equaled anywhere in this section. . . . Many of the other clubs found it necessary to hire or use outside players, who have had considerable experience, professionally or otherwise, which necessitated great sums of money in order they be able to compete with the class of baseball put forth by the Giants.[123]

Speaking of finances, the close of the 1930 season allows us to peek into the finances of town teams, thanks to a surviving ledger of the Boerne White Sox.[124] As one might expect, town teams incurred myriad expenses during the season. For the 1930 White Sox, these included payments for groundskeeping (from $2.50 to $8.00 for labor periodically performed, plus $41 for sand on the diamond), umpires (typically two umpires at $5 each per game), bats (nine bats for $13.50), balls ($16.65), bases ($8.88), advertising for games in the local newspaper ($5 per month), and the league entrance fee ($50).

The largest sums, however, were listed in the ledger as game expenses (e.g., "Expense—Comfort Game"). These sums ranged from $40 to $62 per game. The ledger does not describe the nature of these expenses, but they could have included a fee paid to visiting teams for travel expenses and reimbursement of Boerne players for the cost of meals and gasoline for away games. Interestingly, related to the fateful doubleheader against Llano on September 7 that knocked the White Sox out of the championship series, the ledger does show a "Llano doubleheader expense" of $77.50 for payments to five players, including "outside" pitcher, Hargrove ($25), a former professional minor leaguer, and Boerne's ace pitcher, Zip Myler ($15)—large sums in those days. Other than this doubleheader with Llano, the White Sox ledger does not specifically show any payments to players in 1930. However, the ledger entry does invite the question how Boerne could pay five players for the Llano doubleheader in compliance with league rules limiting paid players to two. Total 1930 expenses for the White Sox amounted to $1,498.69.

Most of the revenues of town teams came from gate receipts. The 1930 White Sox gate receipts ranged from $58 for a game with Comfort on August 24 to $209 for the crucial doubleheader against Llano on September 7. The White Sox received total revenues of $1,686.82 in 1930, ending the season in the black. However, the ledger also reflects that the White Sox needed voluntary donations to make ends meet. The White Sox received two cash donations, denoted in the ledger as "collections by committee." These two "collections" totaled $367.50. In addition, the White Sox may have "passed a hat" around the large crowd attending the September 7 doubleheader with Llano since the ledger indicates "donations" of $30.50 were received. But for these voluntary collections and donations amounting to $398, the White Sox would have suffered a net loss for the year.

Regarding the season on the diamond, Appendix A contains the 1930 statistics for each team in the Hill Country League.[125] The *Fredericksburg Standard* published the batting averages for the 1930 Giants championship team (see Table 4).[126]

Table 4. Fredericksburg Giants Hitting Statistics, 1930

Player	G	AB	H	AVG.
M. Deike	3	6	3	.500
Kott	3	11	4	.364
Hollmig	31	105	38	.362
Peter	26	87	28	.322
H. Klaerner	25	74	23	.311
C. Klaerner	7	17	5	.294
Klett	27	102	30	.294
Fuller	28	108	31	.287
Durst	25	98	27	.275
Probst	12	31	8	.258
Knopp	29	120	30	.250
E. Henke	25	90	21	.233
E. Klaerner	18	53	12	.227
L. Deike	8	22	5	.226
U. Henke	26	97	21	.216
F. Hahn	20	62	12	.193

Langerhans	1	2	0	.000
W. Hollmig	0	0	0	.000
Totals	31*	1085	298	.275

* The Giants played twenty-six games in the HCL regular season and three in the Championship Series. The total of thirty-one games includes two exhibition games during the Gillespie County Fair. Fredericksburg's season statistics in Appendix A reflect only the twenty-six regular season games.

E. E. Martin, official scorer for the Llano Cowboys, named an all-star team for the 1930 HCL season based on the votes of the league's official scorers (see Table 5).[127]

Table 5. HCL All-Star Team, 1930

Position	Player	Team
Catcher	Udo Henke	Fredericksburg
	Oran Lewis	Llano
First Base	Jack Holloway	Llano
Second Base	Rudy Leidl	Boerne
Shortstop	M. A. Reed	Llano
Third Base	Cheese Bremer	Boerne
Left Field	Chink Taylor	Llano
Center Field	Milton Durst	Fredericksburg
Right Field	Huldie Mather	Llano
Pitcher	Lefty Draper	Llano
	Hugo Klaerner	Fredericksburg
	Zip Myler	Boerne
Manager	Chink Taylor	Llano

Player-manager Al Hollmig and young star Hugo Klaerner led Fredericksburg to the title. Based on the season statistics published in the *Fredericksburg Standard*,[128] Hollmig hit .362 while Klaerner hit .311 and fashioned a 10–4 mark on the mound, striking out 135 batters in 110 2/3 innings. Pepper Probst went 6–2 as the second starter behind Klaerner. Llano hit .300 as a team,[129] led by former major leaguer Chink Taylor who hit .457 with 18 extra-base hits in just 20 games. Outfielder Huldie Mather hit .414 while leading the league with five triples. The Cowboys led the league with

Figure 21. Boerne White Sox players Harry Schweppe and Harry Phillip. (Courtesy of Tom Phillip.)

47 stolen bases (13 by Taylor). Pitcher Lefty Draper tallied a 12–3 mark in 15 starts.

Third baseman Egon "Cheese" Bremer topped Boerne with a .357 average, but Charlie English boosted the White Sox when he joined the club at shortstop in

June, finishing with a .328 average. Zip Myler spun a 13–5 record in 21 games (17 starts) for the White Sox. First baseman Clergy Hollimon was Kerrville's best hitter, batting .329 with five extra-base hits. Wood Thornberry (3–4) pitched well early in the season but pitched in only eight games before he was sidelined, likely by a sore arm. After leaving Boerne, Anton Leidl bolstered Kerrville at both shortstop and on the mound. Leidl hit .292 and went 3–3 in six starts.

Joe Pankratz starred for Comfort, hitting .300 and slugging .450 while playing both shortstop and second base. Gus Wendler hit .298, alternating middle infield positions with Pankratz. Pitcher Leonard Maddox disappointed, giving up 61 runs in 86 innings for a 4–7 record. As expected, pitcher Rod Sanders was the bright spot for Mason, but he managed only a 3–9 mark with a 5.46 TRA[130] for the last-place Mavericks. As a team, the Mavericks hit a paltry .177, scoring only 51 runs in the 16 games for which box scores exist.

The first year of the Hill Country League was a promising start for the new organization despite a contentious forfeit by Fredericksburg and an occasional kerfuffle along the way. The season began with much fanfare and ended with a thrilling three-game championship series. In between those milestones, Hill Country fans enjoyed a pennant race among Fredericksburg, Llano, and Boerne as well as an occasional upset by second-division clubs. The passions of the inaugural season did not go unnoticed. As the curtain of the Depression descended across the nation, baseball would serve as a unifying force in the Hill Country, increasing the ferocity of inter-town rivalries while at the same time bolstering the common ties among German-dominated communities.

CHAPTER 5

MR. FAULT FINDER

Comfort, 1930

While the Hill Country's newspapers generally supported, and even explicitly promoted, their town teams, the relationship between newspapers and town teams was not always harmonious. The best example of a rocky relationship occurred early in the 1930 season when a newspaper editorial provoked a squabble between the *Comfort News* and the hometown Broncos.[1]

After Comfort lost at home to Boerne, 12–4, on April 27, 1930, the *Comfort News* published an editorial excoriating the Broncos' uninspired play, sparking spirited responses from two players. The May 1 editorial chastened the Broncos, especially for the team's loose fielding:

> A capacity crowd turned out to greet the Broncos on their second appearance on the home lot. White Sox supporters came up from Boerne in droves and were well repaid for their efforts. For they had the pleasure of seeing the Sox give a very able exhibition of fielding and hitting; in short they played a bang up game of baseball which showed up especially well against the short comings of the Broncos. Lack of hits when hits meant runs and errors on the part of the Broncos infield when errors meant runs—for the Sox and too easy a take-off by [Broncos pitcher] Maddox put the Broncos at a disadvantage they could not overcome later in the game.
>
> We doubt whether the Broncos will continue to receive such support as they did Sunday, if the management persists in its policy to keep older and more experienced players on the bench while the fledgelings [*sic*] continue to mess up plays; and send batters up to the plate, seemingly instructed to "look the first pitch over," and all to the advantage of the pitcher, for he certainly always grooved the first one for the Broncos to look at.[2]

In reply, the *Comfort News* received two letters to the editor—one from an anonymous player and the other from Broncos captain, Joe Pankratz. The newspaper published both responses in the May 8 edition. Under the headline, "Cussing the Editor," the anonymous player exhorted the *Comfort News* to support the Broncos as the hometown team:

> Have a heart, Mrs. Editor, have a heart. In last week's *News* you said some unkind things about the Comfort Broncos. That about experience of players sitting on the bench while young kids mess up the plays wasn't very complimentary; I'll say it wasn't. And that about us probably losing the support of the fans wasn't very encouraging. Naturally it takes a lot of practice and tryouts and shifting of players to make a good team out of any bunch of ball tossers and that is just what we are trying to make.
>
> The home paper should root for the home town team, not knock it, don't be like that. We now have a percentage of 600 and are tied with one other team for first place. I think that's pretty hot. I'd like to see some of our grandstand critics get in the game and beat it.
>
> We are going to be away for two Sundays, but when we get back, come on down and give us the glad hand and let out a few lusty yells for the Broncos. We extend you a special invitation.
>
> A Bronco[3]

Under the headline, "Takes Exception to our Editorial," captain Joe Pankratz also responded on May 8 to the editorial, explaining to "Mister Fault Finder" that fielding is never perfect:

> In reply to your article of last week concerning our team I want to state that it is quite easy to play a game from the grandstand but it is entirely a different story to get out on the field. Now as to having experienced players on the bench, I don't know of any, I think if there are any they are in the game at all time. As to fielding "Mister Fault Finder" have you ever seen a team that was perfect at all times? No that team hasn't played ball yet. Yes we played a very loose game in every way here on the 27 of April, but a game of an entirely different tune Sunday, it would have been a game without fault if it hadn't been for an error myself, yes it was a very easy ball to catch but I just didn't catch it so I guess that ruined the game from your point of view.

The captain went on to remind the newspaper that the unpaid ballplayers were playing only for the glory of Comfort:

> Now as to criticizing my ballplayers as is done from one game to another. Have you ever stopped to think that these boys are playing for the fun of the game, and the glory of the town. They are giving at least two days of their time a week to try and get in shape to play and if any of them were perfect they most certainly would not be playing in this league. These boys don't get a cent for the time they are spending to advertise and add glory to the name of Comfort, which "Mister Fault Finder" they will do before the season is over.
>
> Do you think that your personal criticism is helping the boys any or advertising the town. With a paid player it is entirely different he deserves criticism like this, but I think that a player that plays for the glory of the game and the town does not deserve it. And as to our attendance I think that a fan that is for Comfort in victory will be for Comfort in defeat. The fan that wants to see Comfort beat will be there, and so will the critic. See you all next Sunday.
>
> Joe Pankratz[4]

The contentious editorial aroused the Comfort ballclub in its next game on May 4—a snappy 4–0 win over Kerrville in which former minor league pitcher Frank Watt hurled a four-hit shutout and the Broncos committed only one error (coincidentally, by Joe Pankratz).[5] In the same edition as the two responses, the *Comfort News* published a second editorial praising the Broncos for their shutout win and encouraging fans to attend ball games:

> We are sorry to see our predictions in regard to the attendance at ball games come so near to fulfillment last Sunday. Those fans who stayed away because the Boerne–Comfort game of the Sunday before resulted so disastrously for the Broncos just missed seeing one of the best games that has ever been turned in by a Comfort team. The Broncos were up on their toes from the beginning to the end of the game, and if our critical editorial of last week had anything to do with this display of aggressiveness, we hope that this editorial lamenting the lack of attendance last Sunday will have the same effect on the patrons; for in the final analysis it must be admitted that it takes cash customers as well as ballplayers to have a team in the League.[6]

However, after the Broncos lost to Llano, 3–0, the next Sunday, the newspaper returned to its critical posture in yet another editorial:

> The two articles in last week's issue of the News taking exception to our "fault finding" editorial of the preceding week, have failed utterly in disturbing our sense of complacency, nor do we feel that we have been guilty of anything calling for a rebuke. We took the precaution before we published our editorial, of showing it to one of the steadiest and most valuable players on the Comfort team, and were told that, "it was good as far as it went, but not strong enough," the criticism directed at the management, we heard voiced at different times and by different groups, about town, and that it was timely, was made evident by the brand of baseball we were regaled with on Sunday the 4th ult. And as for the Captain's supposition that the error committed by him spoiling the game for us, is an error in itself, for in the first place it did not change the out come [*sic*] of the game, and secondly it was not entirely unexpected. We expect to continue to support the Broncos with cash donations, admission price to games, and publicity in our columns, and we'll tell the world about them when they are going good and we'll offer constructive criticism, when they are not so good.
>
> The game with Llano on Sunday bore out our criticism directed at the tyros.[7]

After Comfort shut out Kerrville on May 4, the Broncos held a 3–2 record, achieving a measure of vindication following the initial editorial. However, the shutout loss to Llano on May 11 began a three-game skid. As it turned out, the May 4 victory over Kerrville represented the high-water mark for the Broncos, who later lost 10 of their last 11 games in the season to finish in fifth place with an 8–18 mark. At the close of the season, the Broncos could do nothing but wait until 1931 to prove the *Comfort News* wrong.

CHAPTER 6

THIS SIDE OF BELL MOUNTAIN

Hill Country League, 1931

Thanks to George Wilkins Kendall, the pioneer for whom Kendall County is named and the "father of the Texas sheep industry,"[1] the Hill Country, a region well suited to grazing, grew into a center for raising sheep and Angora goats, producing wool and mohair, respectively. By the 1930s, Texas was producing 80 percent of the world's mohair,[2] and much of that was produced in the Hill Country. In the spring of 1931, prices were down[3] as the stock market crash in October 1929 began to spread through the economy. In January 1931, the Texas Wool and Mohair Warehouse Association recommended to its members that all mohair be consigned to the National Wool Marketing Corporation to achieve higher prices by consolidating the state's mohair (seven million pounds) in cooperatives free from competition with private dealers.[4] Kerrville's Schreiner Wool and Mohair Commission Company, led by A. C. Schreiner, was one of the state's largest wool and mohair brokers. In fact, Kerrville became known as the "Mohair Capital of the World."[5]

As the Depression set in, many in the Hill Country earned some much-needed cash by trapping during the winter months. Most of the furs were fox, ringtail, skunk, opossum, and civet, but raccoon furs brought the highest prices—as much as three dollars per pelt.[6] Kerrville accounted for 25,000 furs in the winter of 1931, although this number was down by one-third from the previous year due to a decline in prices.[7]

While the isolation of the Hill Country made the region less vulnerable to the stock market crash than other parts of the country, residents of the Hill Country were not immune from the Depression's financial pressures, which caused some unemployed laborers to become desperate. In February 1931, Walter Price, a 36-year-old farmhand with five children, was arrested after he attempted to extort $3,000 from Louis A. Schreiner, a Kerrville banker and brother of A. C.

Schreiner.[8] Price wrote a letter to Schreiner demanding the money for "laborers out of work," threatening his life if he failed to comply.[9] Price was arrested when he picked up a decoy package left by police.[10] Law enforcement officials noted that the plot was similar to other extortion attempts aimed at wealthy businessmen in San Antonio.[11]

The Depression was also beginning to affect Hill Country baseball. While the 1930 season was successful, the Hill Country League suffered two key losses shortly before the 1931 season began. First, at a league meeting in Fredericksburg on March 18, 1931, Llano chose not to field a team, withdrawing from the league.[12] Llano apparently took such action "on account of objection to playing regulations."[13] The nature of Llano's concern is not clear, but the regulations seem to have resulted in a shortage of players for the club. The league directors then voted to replace Llano with the Junction Firemen. Like Mason, Junction is a town in the northwestern portion of the Hill Country.[14] Once the vote to admit Junction was completed, the league suffered the second blow when "the Boerne representatives voiced strong sentiment against the increased mileage their club would be compelled to travel to fulfill their schedule."[15] Boerne then announced it would withdraw from the league.

After Boerne's decision to withdraw, Bandera—also represented at the meeting—was given an opportunity to join the league in place of Boerne, but Bandera declined "as a matter of courtesy or rather sympathy for the Boerne club."[16] At that point, Llano's representatives, still in attendance at the meeting, were invited to rejoin the league but they also demurred. The league then accepted a bid by Pontotoc, an unincorporated town with a population around 300 located 20 miles northwest of Llano in Mason County, completing the restructuring of the HCL.[17] Many of the former Llano players joined the nearby Pontotoc club—known as the Pirates—including top players such as outfielder Huldie Mather, catcher Paul McLeod, shortstop M. A. Reed, and pitcher Lefty Draper.

Thus, in one fell swoop, the Hill Country League lost Llano and Boerne, two of its three best teams. Llano was replaced by Junction while Boerne was replaced by Pontotoc. Mason, Junction, and Pontotoc were northern teams while Fredericksburg was in the heart of the Hill Country. Only Kerrville and Comfort remained as southern teams. Boerne's withdrawal due to concerns over travel expenses was the first indication that the Depression would not spare Hill Country baseball.[18] Boerne would play an independent schedule in 1931, but several White Sox players chose to play for HCL clubs in 1931.

Although Fredericksburg was now a notch above all other teams in the league, the Giants received unsettling news before the season began when their young star, Hugo Klaerner, left Fredericksburg to pitch for the Kerrville club due to unspecified "differences with Giants management."[19] To shore up their pitching corps in the absence of Klaerner, the Giants enlisted Rod Sanders, Mason's top pitcher in 1930, and, as a backup, Chester "Smokey" Klaerner, Hugo's younger brother, who pitched well at the end of the 1930 season. However, as in 1930, Chester would not be available until after the Rice Institute baseball team completed its spring season.[20] Felix Saenger, who managed the Giants beginning in 1924, returned to his familiar role in 1931.[21] Al Hollmig manned first base but relinquished the managerial duties to Saenger. The Giants also announced that prices of 40 cents for admission of adults and 15 cents for children would remain in effect for 1931.[22]

With Boerne gone and Pontotoc perhaps not as strong as Llano had been the previous season, Kerrville—now known as the Braves after using "Tourists" and "Athletics" as nicknames in 1930—hoped to climb the ladder with Hugo Klaerner on the mound. The Braves returned sluggers Clergy Hollimon at first base and Anton Leidl at shortstop. Reflecting their new nickname, the Braves sported new uniforms. The *Kerrville Mountain Sun*, employing insensitive language common at the time, reported that the uniforms bore "the likeness of a mean-looking Indian."[23] Former minor leaguer Dick Bischofhausen was named player-manager.[24]

Comfort would require a greater leap to move into contention after finishing 10 games under .500 (8–18) in 1930, but the Broncos returned a solid core of players including brothers Joe Pankratz at shortstop and Skeeter Pankratz at third base in addition to first baseman Morris Goforth and catcher Felix Meyer. Mason simply hoped for signs of improvement, aspiring to climb out of the cellar. Without Rod Sanders, the Mavericks needed pitching help. Pat Hatch was their second-best pitcher in 1930, but he gave up more than one run per inning. The prospects for the Junction Firemen,[25] the newest club, were difficult to gauge until play began but the Firemen recruited heavily from the Junction high school baseball team.

As expected, Fredericksburg showed their mettle early, crushing Kerrville, 10–2, on April 5—a game in which several of Kerrville's regulars were not in the lineup due to an unspecified "misunderstanding."[26] The Giants followed their opening win by crushing Junction, 14–4, on April 12,[27] but the Giants stumbled badly the next Sunday, losing to a surprising Mason club, 9–3.[28] In that game, the Mavericks managed only seven hits, but the Giants, normally a sound fielding club, committed eleven errors—three each by new shortstop Ernst Nagel and second baseman Paul Knopp. At the plate, the Giants accounted for only four hits against Mason's starting pitcher, Pat Hatch, who showed vast improvement over his 1930 mound performance. But the Giants righted the ship quickly, reeling off three consecutive wins (over Junction, Kerrville, and Comfort) to grab first place with a 5–1 mark on May 17. Other teams muddled along. Kerrville lost three of its first five games while Comfort was even at 3–3.

Despite having some of the best Llano players from the 1930 season, Pontotoc was inconsistent. The Pirates dropped the opening game at Comfort, 4–1, even though Lefty Draper struck out 14.[29] The following week, Pontotoc's home opener against Kerrville was delayed briefly while "a fretful rattlesnake in center field" was "dispatched with a bat."[30] Draper then stymied the Braves, scattering 11 hits in a 3–2 victory—the Pirates' first win in the Hill Country League.

Pontotoc's win did not turn the corner for the Pirates as they struggled to a 3–3 record through May 10. The town of Pontotoc turned out to be too small to support a ballclub in the HCL. The *Fredericksburg Standard* noted that "it is generally understood that, due to the size of its town [Pontotoc] and attendance at the games, the Pirates' finances were greatly strained by necessary and incidental expenses incurred to carry out their schedule."[31] As a result, on May 15, the league directors voted to readmit Llano in place of Pontotoc.[32] The roster of Llano's revitalized team included the best Pontotoc players plus some former Llano players, causing the *Kerrville Mountain Sun* to conclude that the Cowboys would be "one of the stronger clubs in the Hill loop."[33] Apart from the impact of Llano's return on the diamond, many recognized that having Llano rejoin the league "will mean better gate receipts for all other club members."[34]

Llano assumed the 3–3 record of Pontotoc. The Cowboys did not have a promising start as a reconstituted team. On May 17, Lefty Draper pitched effectively but Kerrville's Hugo Klaerner shut out the Cowboys, 2–0, striking out 12 and allowing only five hits.[35] Llano, now 3–4, found itself in fifth place, well behind their biggest rival, the league-leading Giants (5–1).[36]

However, Llano bounced back the following week to edge the host Giants in a wild slugfest, 15–13.[37] After getting whitewashed by Hugo Klaerner the week before, the Cowboys knocked the Giants newest pitcher, Rod Sanders, out of the game in the first inning by scoring seven runs, although the Giants responded with six runs of their own in the bottom of the inning. Llano added eight more runs over the next five innings, rapping a total of 20 hits. Although Fredericksburg had only nine hits, Llano's nine errors—poor fielding remained a thorn in the Cowboys' side—kept the game close. Cowboys third baseman John

Pinckney committed four of the errors, but he also smacked three hits, including a double and a home run. Llano player-manager Chink Taylor, shortstop M. A. Reed, and right fielder Huldie Mather also contributed three hits each. A new pitcher stepped up for Llano. Earl Van Huss, a "towering righthander,"[38] relieved starter McDonald[39] in the third inning, limiting the Giants to four runs over six-and-two-thirds innings, to earn the win.

After their critical triumph over Fredericksburg, Llano recorded three more victories, including a 6–2 win over the Giants, 6–2, on June 7, when Van Huss stopped the Giants who committed six errors.[40] The win moved the Cowboys (6–4) within one-half game of Fredericksburg (6–3). Fredericksburg's loss also allowed Kerrville (6–3) to tie the Giants for first place when Hugo Klaerner won three games in a row for Kerrville—two over Mason and one against Junction—after his shutout of Llano on May 17. Luring Klaerner away from the Giants was paying off handsomely for the Braves.

Comfort was also improving. Former Boerne pitcher Zip Myler was now hurling for the Broncos. Former Boerne second baseman Rudy Leidl also joined the club, adding a solid leadoff hitter to the lineup. After losing three in a row, including a heartbreaking 2–1 loss in 12 innings to Fredericksburg,[41] the Broncos embarked on a four-game winning streak.

Comfort first edged Mason, 5–4, on June 7, ending their losing streak. The Broncos then swept a doubleheader with Kerrville on June 14. In the lid-lifter, Myler defeated Hugo Klaerner, striking out 12 and holding the Giants to five hits, while Goforth smacked three hits for a 6–1 win.[42] In the nightcap, Gaffney, an "angular school boy from San Antonio,"[43] took the mound for the Broncos, shutting out the Giants on four hits while third baseman Cheese Bremer—another former Boerne player now toiling for Comfort after Boerne's withdrawal from the HCL—accounted for three hits, including a double, to lead the Braves to a 6–1 victory.[44] Anton Leidl took the loss for the Braves.

In the second game, the Broncos and the Braves nearly came to blows in the fourth inning when two Kerrville players were thrown out at the plate—one in a rundown and one when Hugo Klaerner attempted to steal home. Klaerner "apparently made good his steal of home by coming in standing up; but he was called out on the field and play was held up for at least 20 minutes."[45] The game resumed with a new umpire even though, according to the *Kerrville Mountain Sun,* the league rules required the game to be forfeited when play had been delayed for three minutes.[46]

After their sweep of the Braves, Comfort defeated Llano, 4–1, the following Sunday.[47] Zip Myler scattered eight hits while Broncos left fielder Felix Meyer belted three hits, ending Llano's four-game winning streak. Kerrville recovered from their two losses to Comfort by trouncing Junction, 9–2. Hugo Klaerner dominated the Firemen on the mound while Ben Grantham rapped two hits after moving from catcher to second base.[48]

As a result, on June 21, three clubs—Llano, Kerrville, and Comfort—were all tied for second place with 7–5 records, two games behind Fredericksburg at 9–3.[49] Mason trailed at 4–8 while Junction languished in the cellar at 2–10. Early in the season, it looked like Fredericksburg would dominate the league, but now there were three teams nipping at the Giants' heels (see Table 6).[50]

Table 6. HCL Standings, June 21, 1931

	W	L	GB	Pct.
Fredericksburg	9	3	---	.750
Llano	7	5	2	.583
Kerrville	7	5	2	.583
Comfort	7	5	2	.583
Mason	4	8	5	.333
Junction	2	10	7	.167

The next month proved fatal for Kerrville. After a rainout on June 28, the Braves lost four in a row, including a doubleheader loss at Llano on Saturday, July 4. Kerrville lost the first game, 7–6, in 11 innings.[51] The Braves were leading, 5–3, with two outs in the ninth inning and nobody on base, but Llano second baseman John Pinckney reached on an error by Kerrville third baseman Louie Wootton, then stole second. Kerrville intentionally walked player-manager Chink Taylor, a dangerous hitter. Braves left fielder Baker then dropped an easy fly ball, allowing Pinckney to score and Taylor to advance to third. Taylor promptly stole home to tie the score, 5–5, sending the game to extra innings. The teams traded runs in the 10th. In the bottom of the 11th inning, Pinckney singled. Taylor then singled over second, but the hit eluded Braves center fielder William Saenger,[52] rolling past him and allowing Pinckney to score the winning run all the way from first base, for a 6–5 Llano win. After suffering this crushing defeat, Kerrville lost the nightcap of the twin bill, 16–3, when Hugo Klaerner faltered badly.[53]

The next day, Sunday, July 5, the Braves lost at Fredericksburg when Giants pitcher Chester "Smokey" Klaerner prevailed over his older brother, Hugo, by a 5–4 score to hand the Braves their third loss in two days. Chester led a Giants rally in the seventh inning by drilling a three-run triple off Hugo to tie the game at 4–4, then scored the go-ahead run on a fielder's choice. The only consolation for Kerrville was that the Braves made a triple play in the seventh inning. With Al Hollmig and Elias Klaerner on second and third with no outs, Edgar Klett drove a liner into center. Braves center fielder William Saenger raced in, nearly making a shoestring catch but trapping the ball, paralyzing the runners. Saenger then fired the ball to second to catch Elias Klaerner off the bag. Second baseman Staudt threw to third to do the same to Hollmig. Klett then attempted to stretch his single into a double but was tagged out at second for the third out on the play.

Following its three disastrous losses over the Independence Day weekend, Kerrville filed a protest with the league, alleging "rowdyism and umpiring irregularities" in the July 4 dual loss at Llano—likely involving the heartbreaking 7–6 loss in the first game rather than the one-sided loss in the second game.[54] When the protest was rejected, Kerrville considered withdrawing from the league.[55] Cooler heads prevailed, however, because on Monday, July 20, Kerrville's board of directors voted to stay in the league and play out the season.[56]

Like Kerrville, Comfort collapsed in July. The Broncos played Fredericksburg four times that month, so they had a chance to gain ground on the league leaders, but they lost all four, including a doubleheader sweep on July 4. The final game between the clubs on July 26 was emblematic of the Broncos' slide. Comfort starter Dugosh (probably Tommy Dugosh, who pitched for Boerne in 1930) lasted only until the second inning, allowing five runs. Zip Myler relieved him but could not stem the Giants' offense, giving up six more runs, resulting in an 11–8 loss.[57] With this triumph, the Giants prevailed in all six games with Comfort this season. The only Comfort win during the month came on July 5 when the Broncos romped over last-place Junction, 10–1.[58]

Meanwhile, Fredericksburg and Llano kept winning. The Giants and Cowboys would meet twice in three weeks, starting in Fredericksburg. Heading into this game, Fredericksburg had won eight in a row while Llano was on a four-game winning streak. The Cowboys (11–5) were two-and-one-half games behind Fredericksburg (14–3), but Llano had won the two prior meetings with the Giants.

On July 19, Cowboys starter Earl Van Huss shut down the vaunted Giants offense and contributed two hits while Llano struck for four runs against Fredericksburg starter Rod Sanders, winning 4–1.[59] Two weeks later in Llano, Fredericksburg's Chester Klaerner outdueled Van Huss, 3–1,[60] fooling hitters with his curveball and yielding just three hits. Fredericksburg catcher Felix Hahn drove in the winning runs with a two-run double in the eighth inning. The split of the two games kept Fredericksburg in first place by two-and-one-half games. (The August 2 standings for the HCL are shown in Table 7.)[61]

Table 7. HCL Standings, August 2, 1931

	W	L	GB	Pct.
Fredericksburg	16	4	---	.800
Llano	13	6	2½	.684
Kerrville	9	9	6	.500
Comfort	8	10	7	.444
Mason	6	12	9	.333
Junction	4	15	11½	.211

With their hot July, Llano was now firmly in second place, three-and-one-half games ahead of third-place Kerrville. Llano delivered a knockout punch to the Braves' playoff hopes by taking both ends of a doubleheader on August 16. In the opener, Earl Van Huss pitched a gem, winning 7–2.[62] He allowed only four hits while Llano first baseman Archie Peel—a hard-hitting addition to the Cowboys in 1931—smashed three safeties. Right fielder Huldie Mather and catcher Paul McLeod also contributed three hits each. Kerrville starter Anton Leidl was victimized by six errors behind him. The nightcap proved to be another heartbreaker for Kerrville. The Braves started Zip Myler, who had jumped midseason from Comfort to Kerrville—his third club in two years. Myler was terrific, allowing just three Llano hits, but the Cowboys scored two runs in the first inning on a throwing error by Braves catcher Michaels, giving Llano all the scoring they would need for a 2–1 victory.[63] Lefty Draper stymied the Braves, gaining the win for the Cowboys.

Kerrville rebounded to stun Fredericksburg, 1–0, on August 23 when Anton Leidl hurled a two-hit shutout, but it was too late for the Braves. With three weeks left in the season, third-place Kerrville (10–12) was already eliminated from contention for a playoff spot, six games behind second-place Llano (16–6).

Comfort continued its downward spiral in August, losing three games to Mason by lopsided scores (9–1, 9–4, and 6–2.)[64] By the end of August, Comfort had lost six consecutive games. With a 6–2 victory over the Broncos on August 30, Mason (9–13) edged past Comfort (8–13) into fourth place.[65]

About this time, Hugo Klaerner returned from Kerrville to his hometown Giants in mid-August, apparently forgiving his earlier complaints about Fredericksburg's management. He played a few games at third base with Rod Sanders on the mound but in the second game of a doubleheader on August 16, Hugo started and defeated Junction, 6–2.[66]

With the championship series set between Fredericksburg and Llano—a rematch of the 1930 series—the last two weeks of the HCL season were anticlimactic. Comfort's painful second half ended on an eight-game losing streak, while Kerrville—despite the loss of Hugo Klaerner when he returned to the Giants—won its last three games, including a doubleheader sweep of the Broncos on September 6.[67] In the initial game, hurler Anton Leidl banged out two doubles and a single while striking out 13 Broncos for an 8–5 win.[68] In the second contest, Zip Myler tamed the Broncos, his former club, striking out seven, while catcher Michaels smashed a home run and two singles, to give the Braves a 9–3 triumph.

Mason won two of its last three games, including a satisfying triumph over Fredericksburg on September 13. In that game, the Giants started 20-year-old Phillip Klaerner, brother of Elias Klaerner and cousin of Hugo and Chester, because Rod Sanders was given the week off and Hugo Klaerner suffered from an infected index finger. Although a solid ballplayer, Phillip Klaerner was not as experienced on the mound as his cousins Hugo or Chester. Mason scored four runs off Klaerner in the first inning, winning, 8–4.[69] Mavericks third baseman Dannheim knocked out three hits including a triple.

Junction finished last in its first season in the league, but the Firemen upset Llano, 6–5, on August 30. Several key Llano players were absent from the game—catcher Paul McLeod had an infected toe, starting pitcher Earl Van Huss was sidelined by a bruised wrist, left fielder Corbett Brewer was ill, and player-manager Chink Taylor was scouting teams for Llano's future games in the Austin American Cup, a tournament for amateur clubs.[70] Nevertheless, Junction's win gave their fans a glimmer of hope for the future. After falling behind, 4–0, in the second inning, the Firemen stormed back to score six runs, aided by McWright's two hits and his catches in center field that "saved the game for the Firemen on three different occasions."[71] (The final HCL standings for 1931 are shown in Table 8.)[72]

Table 8. HCL Final Standings, 1931

	W	L	GB	Pct.
Fredericksburg	20	6	---	.769
Llano	16	7	2½	.696
Kerrville	13	12	6½	.520
Mason	10	14	9	.417
Comfort	8	15	10½	.348
Junction	6	19	13½	.240

The Giants finished well ahead of the Cowboys in the regular season, but that was deceiving because Llano assumed the 3–3 record of Pontotoc when Llano replaced the Pirates after six games. Since rejoining the league, Llano engineered a 13–4 record, on par with the Giants' 20–6 pace. However, Hugo Klaerner's return bolstered the Giants as they approached the championship series.

The *Fredericksburg Standard* anticipated a stirring series between the hometown team and the "Cowpunchers" from Llano, but opined that after the Giants led the league all season, "the championship will stay on this side of Bell Mountain," a mountain located 15 miles northeast of Fredericksburg between the two towns.[73]

Both clubs featured a strong lineup but based on season batting averages published in the *Fredericksburg Standard*, Llano had the edge at the plate. The Cowboys featured four hitters who batted over .350 for the season: first baseman Archie Peel (.451), right fielder Huldie Mather (.367), left fielder Corbett Brewer (.366), and player-manager Chink Taylor (.350).[74] Fredericksburg had only one .350 hitter—pitcher Rod Sanders (.356)—although first baseman Al Hollmig (.333) was considered their best hitter.[75] Fredericksburg listed three highly capable pitchers on their postseason roster: Hugo Klaerner, Sanders, and Chester Klaerner. As in 1930, Lefty Draper was not available to the Cowboys for the championship series (perhaps because he returned to school). Llano's other starter, Earl Van Huss, was an accomplished hurler, but the Giants possessed more depth on the mound. Left fielder Riddle was the only other player on Llano's roster who was ready to pitch if needed.

For the first game of the best-of-three series, Llano traveled to Fair Park in Fredericksburg on September 20. League president W. K. Larrimore threw out the first pitch in "ideal baseball weather" in front of a large crowd.[76] The Giants turned to their prodigal son, Hugo Klaerner, who had pitched them to the 1930 crown, while Llano started Earl Van Huss, the only true pitcher on the postseason roster. Despite the superior moundsmen on both clubs, the game turned out to be a brawl.

Fredericksburg started off with a bang, scoring three runs in the bottom of the first inning, when Paul Knopp smacked a two-run home run and Milton Durst singled in another run after Al Hollmig tripled. Llano responded with a run in the second on a single by catcher Paul McLeod and another run on a solo home run by shortstop M. A. Reed in the third. The Cowboys grabbed the lead, 4–3, in the fourth when Archie Peel singled, Corbett Brewer doubled him home, and an error by center fielder Milton Durst scored Brewer.

Llano continued the barrage in the fifth inning. After singles by John Pinckney and Taylor, Peel doubled them in and scored on another error by Durst. Brewer then doubled, sending Hugo Klaerner to the showers in favor of Rod Sanders who allowed another run on a single by Harold Collings.[77] Now leading 8–3, the Cowboys added a run in the sixth on Reed's triple and an error by Giants third baseman Lawrence Peter. In the eighth, Van Huss helped his own cause, driving in two more runs with a double to extend the lead to 11–3.

Van Huss tired in the bottom of the eighth. With two outs and a runner on first, he walked two batters. After Emil "Chicken" Henke doubled home two runs, Van Huss issued two more bases on balls to force in a run. Hollmig then crushed a double, clearing the bases and scoring the sixth run of the inning, bringing the Giants within two runs, 11–9. However, Durst, up for the second time in the inning, grounded out to third to end the threat.

The Cowboys responded in the top of the ninth. Sanders walked Van Huss then Reed singled—his fifth hit of the game. After John Pinckney was safe on a sacrifice bunt when no one covered first base, Sanders walked Taylor to force in a run. After a popout, Peel lined a double over first, driving in three runs. Sanders retired the next two batters, but not before Llano had added four insurance runs. Van Huss retired the Giants in order in the bottom of the ninth, forging a 15–9 victory.[78]

The Cowboys stroked 21 hits, five each by Reed (a home run, a triple, and three singles) and Peel (two doubles and three singles). Fredericksburg scored nine runs on just nine hits, thanks to six walks by Van Huss, but in the field the Giants committed six errors, several of which were costly. For the second game of the series, Fredericksburg made the trek to Llano. Despite his poor showing in the first game, Hugo Klaerner got the call for the Giants. Van Huss returned to the mound for Llano. This time, both pitchers were sharp.

Llano scrounged a run across in the third. With two outs, second baseman John Pinckney walked and stole second. Chink Taylor singled him home for a 1–0 lead. The Giants performed a similar feat in the fourth when shortstop Paul Knopp singled, stole second, and scored on a single by Al Hollmig, tying the score, 1–1. In the top of the fifth, Hugo Klaerner committed a baserunning "boner," killing a scoring opportunity. With two outs, Klaerner advanced from second base to third on a slow roller to first. Thinking the batter had been retired for the third out, Klaerner left the bag, heading to the dugout. However, Llano first baseman Archie Peel fumbled the throw at first, making the batter safe. Seeing Klaerner drift off the bag, Peel raced all the way from first base to tag Klaerner out, ending the inning.[79]

After Klaerner's faux pas ended Fredericksburg's chances in the fifth, neither team scored until the eighth inning. After one out, Llano's Reed singled. One out later, Taylor walked, bringing cleanup hitter Mather to the plate. Mather blasted a three-run home run to center field to give the Cowboys a 4–1 lead.

But the Giants were not done against Van Huss. In the top of the ninth, catcher Felix Hahn walked and third baseman Lawrence Peter singled. Hugo Klaerner hit a grounder for a fielder's choice, second to short. Klaerner then stole second, knocking the ball out of shortstop Reed's hands, allowing Hahn to score from third. Emil Henke singled to right, but right fielder Mather threw out Klaerner at the plate. Henke stole second and advanced to third when catcher Paul McLeod's throw sailed into center field. Van Huss then walked Knopp to put the tying runs on base and the go-ahead run at the plate with two outs. Veteran Udo Henke pinch hit for young second baseman Ernst Nagel, but he hit a weak grounder to Van Huss who tagged him out, giving Llano a nail-biting 4–2 victory that secured the 1931 HCL championship. To the dismay of Giants fans, the HCL title did not remain on the south side of Bell Mountain.[80]

Llano's championship hardware was similar to the trophies received by Fredericksburg in 1930. The team was awarded a "silver loving cup" by W. H. Schaefer, the Fredericksburg druggist who was "one of the most ardent fans of the Hill Country."[81] Mr. Schaefer presented the cup to the Cowboys at the Llano Luncheon Club on October 7.[82] Individual Llano players received championship trophies with gold baseballs from the A. G. Spalding Company.[83]

The Llano Cowboys did not stop with the HCL title. On Sunday, October 4, Llano defeated the Maxwell Catfish in a lopsided doubleheader, winning 14–0 and 20–2, to grab the Austin American Cup, a crown for the winners of an amateur baseball tournament in Central Texas. Huldie Mather homered in both games while Llano pitcher Harry White shut out Maxwell on two hits in the first game, and Earl Van Huss allowed only four hits in the nightcap. With their HCL crown and the Austin American Cup, the Cowboys could now claim to be not only the best team in the Hill Country but also the top club in Central Texas.

There were many outstanding players in the HCL in 1931, as reflected in the statistics shown in Appendix B. Champion Llano featured several sluggers.[84] Player-manager Chink Taylor hit .364 while leading the team in runs (18), home runs (three), and extra-base hits (nine) to fashion a .691 slugging percentage. Right fielder Huldie Mather hit .355, leading the team with 27 hits and five triples. But first baseman Archie Peel put up the most incredible numbers even though he missed a few games. Peel hit .478 with a slugging percentage of .804

Figure 22. Llano Cowboys, 1930s. The only players positively identified in the photo are Corbett Brewer, standing far right, and his brother, Ernest Brewer, sitting far right. (Courtesy of Sam Oatman.)

(three doubles, three triples, and two home runs in 13 games). Earl Van Huss owned a stingy TRA[85] of 2.89 while winning 10 of 12 decisions.

Fredericksburg's hitters scored more than six runs per game.[86] Al Hollmig hit .346, leading the team with 28 hits while playing first base. Left fielder Edgar Klett hit only .250 but scored 22 runs and stroked 11 extra-base hits, including a league-leading seven triples, for a .500 slugging percentage. Part-time second baseman Gene Fuller hit .424 on 14 hits and five extra-base hits in just eight games. Pitcher Rod Sanders admirably filled the primary starting position left vacant by Hugo Klaerner's departure for Kerrville. Sanders was 13–3 in 16 starts with a TRA of 3.85 and 118 strikeouts in 131 innings. Hugo's younger brother, Chester, was even more impressive with a 5–1 mark and a TRA of 3.06.

Kerrville faded but still finished above .500 at 13–12. Before returning to Fredericksburg late in the season, Hugo Klaerner managed a 6–5 record with a TRA of 3.71 and 106 strikeouts in 114 innings. Anton Leidl, the former Boerne infielder, boosted the Braves' offense by leading the Braves in hits (24), runs (20), doubles (six), and slugging percentage (.494). When not manning center field, Leidl started eight games on the mound for a 4–4 record with a TRA of 4.43. Catcher Ben Grantham contributed a .307 batting average with five extra-base hits. Nelson Davis replaced Dick Bischofhausen as manager midway through the season.

Mason improved from 5–21 to 10–14 in 1931. Outfielder Pat Hatch stepped up to lead the team with 17 hits and five extra-base hits, including two home runs, for a productive line of .361/.596 (batting average/slugging percentage). Hatch also filled the gap left by pitcher Rod Sanders' moving to the Fredericksburg club in 1931. He started seven games, winning three despite a TRA of 5.82. The Mavericks might have improved even more but former Llano pitcher Lefty Draper slumped in 1931, losing all five of his starts with a TRA of 4.42.

Comfort won just eight games in the HCL for the second year in a row to finish fifth at 8–15. Shortstop Joe Pankratz emerged as the team's star, hitting .313 and leading the team in steals with four. Second baseman Rudy Leidl triggered the offense as the leadoff hitter, scoring 12 runs in the 14 games for which box scores were found. Right fielder-third baseman Cheese Bremer played only part-time, but he hit .375 with a slugging percentage of .750 thanks to three doubles and three triples in only 24 at-bats. Pitcher Zip Myler proved dependable with a TRA of 3.19 but he could manage only a 3–4 mark. Tommy Dugosh, another former Boerne player, and Haufler were no answer on the mound, both going 0–2 in two starts while giving up more than one run per inning. The young pitcher from San Antonio, Gaffney, pitched a shutout for the Broncos on June 14 but for reasons unknown, he never appeared again.

Junction's first year in the league was not a success. The Firemen won only six games (6–19), batting just .200 as a team while yielding more than eight runs per game. Pitcher-second baseman "Goat" Gardner was a bright spot, hitting four triples while making eight starts on the mound, winning two for a 2–6 record. His TRA of 6.72 was high but it was by far the best on the club. Third baseman Camp was the only regular with a batting average above .300 (he hit .306), although part-time shortstop Ratliff had a slash line of .346/.538 (batting average/slugging percentage) in seven games. Clearly, there was room for Junction's young players to improve in 1932.

In 1931, the HCL survived the loss of both Boerne and Comfort, adding clubs from Pontotoc and Junction. The HCL then skillfully navigated Pontotoc's demise by quickly replacing the Pirates with Llano, restoring the Cowboys to the HCL and assuring a vigorous pennant race between Fredericksburg and the Cowboys—the two best teams in the league. The championship series—a grudge match between Fredericksburg and Llano—left no doubt that Llano deserved the title.

Kerrville and Mason both showed marked improvement in 1931. Their fans hoped that the Mavericks and the Braves could take the next step in 1932 by challenging the top dogs—Llano and Fredericksburg. Comfort fans were surely disappointed with another fifth-place finish. Junction ended in the cellar, but the Firemen were a young team. With a year of experience under their belt, they looked forward to 1932.

After withdrawing from the HCL before the season, Boerne played an independent schedule outside the spotlight, taking on a variety of teams, both town teams and industrial teams. On August 2, Edwin Uecker pitched the White Sox to a 5–2 win over the Dixie Spirits of the San Antonio Industrial League, contributing three hits of his own.[87] Two weeks later, the White Sox upended the Piggly-Wiggly Grocers, a San Antonio industrial team, 8–6, earning their 12th win of the season.[88] Edgar Bergmann picked up the win in relief, allowing just one hit in two-and-two-thirds innings.

At the Kendall County Fair, the White Sox shut out the Waring Eagles, 12–0, on August 28, then were whitewashed the following day, 15–0, by Fredericksburg on an open day in the Giants' league schedule.[89] On September 13, outfielder Albert Uecker smashed a triple and three singles while his brother, Edwin Uecker, shut out the Friedrich All-Stars of the San Antonio Winter League, 4–0.[90]

While the White Sox thrived in their return to independent play, their exit from the league diminished the competition for the HCL's two playoff berths. After Llano was readmitted to the league in May, it soon became clear that Fredericksburg and Llano would return to the championship series. To its credit, the Hill Country League survived the Pontotoc debacle when Llano seamlessly took over the Pirates franchise. By the end of 1931, however, there were storm clouds brewing as the Depression deepened.

CHAPTER 7

DANCING ON THE BRIDGE

Comfort

In the Hill Country, family, friends, and fans gathered on sultry Sunday afternoons to enjoy a game on the diamond. During tough times, baseball was more than just a form of entertainment—baseball fostered a sense of community. The Comfort Broncos exemplified the close ties between Hill Country ballclubs and their towns.

Local businesses often sponsored the Broncos, bearing the expense of uniforms and equipment for the players while gaining publicity and patronage. The sponsorships both created and reflected the strong connection between the team and the community. Sponsors of the Comfort team over the years included Bruno's Curve, Comfort State Bank, Bohnert Grocery, Comfort Hatchery, Handy Andy Store, Holekamp Store, Ingenhuett Store, Molter Grain & Implement Company, the Rathskeller, Stieler Motor, Tom Beaty's Liquor Store, Twin Gables, Schwethelm's, West's Barbershop, Schaetter & Lindner Funeral Home, Log Cabin (owned by player Joe Pankratz), and Comfort Meat Market.[1]

In 1914, Comfort made plans to build a low-water bridge over the Guadalupe River east of town. Later, the bridge, called the Comfort High Street Bridge, became a postgame gathering place. After battling on the diamond at Faltin Field on Eighth Street,[2] the players, their families and friends, as well as fans, would travel the short distance to the bridge and gather along the banks to enjoy a picnic while players rehashed the game. Most memorable, however, were the dances on the bridge, when players and their wives or girlfriends danced "until the wee hours of the night."[3]

In later years, music blared on the car radios. After the sun went down, headlights would shine on the bridge, where many danced under the stars on balmy summer nights. These idyllic scenes would be remembered by players and family members long after the Broncos faded into history.

Figure 23. Comfort ballplayers. (L–R): Christie Lindemann, Joe Pankratz, Morris Goforth, and Skeeter Pankratz. (Courtesy of Shirley Pankratz Solis.)

Although the Broncos played during Prohibition (1920–1933), the ban on alcohol did not deter supporters of the team:

> By now Comfort had a bridge, the car and also prohibition. The latter was of some significance to the baseball team at Comfort. Anyone that was a great fan of baseball supported this local talent. Simply by handing a bottle of beer to the players, regardless if they won or lost.
>
> These supporters were not of the professional bootleggers league, they represented the average family man, who was steadfast in his work, who believed in community sports. They liked beer, made it and gave it to friends and family. The tradition was part of the baseball social status for a long time. By contributing a drink, a strong bond was forged that helped the Broncos in their many ups and downs.[4]

Family members and supporters even accompanied the team on their long treks to play clubs in the northern part of the Hill Country:

> If the Broncos traveled to Mason or Junction, they probably had to leave before the rooster crowed, and came home in the wee hours of the morning . . .
>
> As Mamie Lindemann [wife of player Christie Lindemann] said in her interview, "It was always hot and dusty but we followed the team. We did not have any money to spare, so lunches were packed, drinks for the whole day were included. There were no concession stands." For the next two decades the wives that traveled with the ballplayers put in long hours the day before a game. Remember the whole family went along.[5]

Baseball was a diversion from the daily effects of the Depression. But it also became a social outlet and, for team sponsors, a commercial platform. Baseball in the Hill Country established enduring connections, not just between the team and the community, but among town residents, creating a sense of solidarity in tough times.

CHAPTER 8

OUTSIDE MEN

Hill Country League, 1932

Early in 1932, the Hill Country was rocked by the news that both of Fredericksburg's banks, Citizens Bank and the Bank of Fredericksburg, closed their doors on February 19. Reflecting the familial affection among Germans in the Hill Country, Kerrville banker Louis A. Schreiner—the target of the foiled extortion attempt in 1931—came to the rescue, bringing to Fredericksburg a "considerable amount of cash" to provide businessmen with banking services while the local banks were closed.[1] Fredericksburg responded quickly to the bank closings. By immediately planning the formation of a new bank, "the people of Fredericksburg met the situation with the same fortitude as did their forbears, that sturdy band of German immigrants who in 1846 established a pioneer settlement in the Hill Country."[2]

The new bank, the Fredericksburg National Bank, opened on April 5, less than two months after the bank closings.[3] However, by then, the bank failure had exacted a human toll not limited to the bank's scorned depositors. Albert Koennecke, president of the now defunct Bank of Fredericksburg, slashed his wrists and stabbed himself in the chest but survived when he was found at home by sheriff Alfred Klaerner (father of Hugo and Chester Klaerner) after Koennecke failed to appear at the bank.[4] Before lapsing into unconsciousness, Koennecke told the sheriff that the closing of the bank "preyed on his mind so much that he was unable to stand the strain any longer."[5] Koennecke and three other bank employees were later charged with accepting deposits knowing that the bank was insolvent.[6]

The Hill Country also suffered a natural blow later in 1932. Heavy rains began in Kerrville and Comfort on Thursday, June 30.[7] By the next afternoon, the Guadalupe River rose rapidly, overflowing its banks and washing away 40 houses in Kerrville.[8] Four people drowned in the raging waters. Two of the victims, Mike Odell and Charles Greenleaf, drowned while trying to save a 17-year-old boy trapped in a cypress tree, surrounded by the river.[9] The boy was finally rescued but not before he spent 22 hours in the tree.[10] The other two victims, Ida Stieler, the assistant postmistress at Comfort, and William Bronson, a resident of Austin, were passengers in an automobile between Kerrville and Comfort. They drowned when a "wall of water" swept the vehicle into the river.[11] The flood caused up to $500,000 in property damage.[12]

On the baseball front, Hill Country teams continued to face pressure to reduce travel expenses as the Depression worsened. Like Boerne one year earlier, the Comfort Broncos withdrew from the HCL after the 1931 season. After Junction replaced Boerne in 1931, Comfort had been required to journey to three distant Hill Country towns (Llano, Mason, and Junction), straining the team's coffers. In addition, Comfort is only 15 miles from Boerne (both towns are in Kendall County) so when Boerne withdrew after the 1930 season, Comfort lost a natural rival, which undoubtedly diminished fan interest. The Broncos' lack of success on the diamond may have been a factor as well since they finished with records of 8–18 in 1930 and 8–15 in 1931.[13]

Like Boerne, Comfort played the 1932 season as an independent team after withdrawal from the HCL. The *Comfort News* announced that the 1932 team would consist entirely of local boys who "will play for the love of the game" without "high-salaried outsiders."[14] Unlike in prior years, the Broncos would not solicit financial support from local businessmen but instead would rely solely on gate receipts to cover team expenses.

Since they were natural intra-county rivals, Comfort and Boerne scheduled games with each other in 1932 as well as other independent teams from towns such as Bandera and Alamo Heights.[15] On May 14, Comfort defeated Alamo Heights, 6–2, for their fifth win in a row.[16] Later in the season, however, Boerne shut out the Broncos, 7–0, for the team's third consecutive win over Comfort.[17]

After Comfort withdrew from the HCL in April, the league acted swiftly to replace the Broncos, adding the Brady Turks,[18] another northern team, for the 1932 season. In fact, Brady was 29 miles farther north than Mason. Fredericksburg and Kerrville were now the only circuit teams not located in the northern tier of the Hill Country. The HCL also changed its playoff system. Instead of the top two teams playing for the championship, the season would be divided into halves with the winners of each half qualifying for the championship series.

As teams prepared for the 1932 HCL season, six key players were getting minor league tryouts: Llano first baseman Archie Peel (who hit .451 in 1931)[19] with Dallas of the Texas League, Kerrville catcher Ben Grantham (who hit

Figure 24. Boerne White Sox, 1932. Top row (L–R): Business manager Udo Harz, Anton Bergmann, manager Clarence Holekamp, Arthur Schulze, Johnny Uecker, Gus Milton Wendler, Walter Bergmann, Clarence Bourgeois, president H. O. Adler. Bottom row (L–R): Prof. C. C. Roedus, Harry Schweppe, Gus Pfeiffer, Edgar Bergmann, Harry Phillip, Ernst Nagel, John Bergmann, Dusty Leidl. (Courtesy of Patrick Heath Public Library, Boerne, Texas.)

.367) with San Antonio of the Texas League, Kerrville pitcher Anton Leidl with Memphis of the Southern League,[20] Fredericksburg utility infielder Karl Kott with Houston of the Texas League,[21] and Fredericksburg pitchers Hugo Klaerner and Rod Sanders in the St. Louis Cardinals system.[22] While these tryouts resulted in some uncertainty for spring rosters, they demonstrated that in just two years, the HCL was already establishing its reputation as a league with considerable talent.

Apart from Archie Peel, Llano returned the same roster as the previous season, including the Cowboys' ace pitcher, Earl Van Huss, but Fredericksburg initially faced a mound shortage due to the absence of Hugo Klaerner and Rod Sanders, who were now pursuing minor league ball.[23] Shortly before the season started, the Giants welcomed back veteran pitcher Pepper Probst to bolster their staff.[24] Fortunately for the Giants, Hugo Klaerner returned in early April after his brief stay with the Houston Buffaloes of the Texas League did not work out.[25]

With Hugo's return, Fredericksburg's roster now included five members of the Klaerner family with the addition of 17-year-old Alfons, who could pitch and play the outfield. Alfons joined Hugo and Chester Klaerner, a star pitcher for Rice Institute coming into his own; Elias Klaerner, a 22-year-old hard-hitting outfielder; and Phillip Klaerner, a 20-year-old pitcher who played third base when not on the mound. Chester and Alfons were Hugo's younger brothers. Elias and Phillip were brothers, and cousins to Hugo, Chester, and Alfons. The five Klaerners constituted one-third of the Giants' roster.

The *Fredericksburg Standard* touted the Giants' prospects for 1932. First baseman Al Hollmig was "the terror of opposing pitchers and the guy who has broken up more games in the Hill Country by his long distance clouts than any two men in the league."[26] Right fielder Elias Klaerner was "a great fly shagger and a long distance hitter."[27] Left fielder Edgar Klett was "probably the fastest man in the league" whose "stick work is of a high order."[28] The *Standard* concluded that with these players as a nucleus, "the outlook for a winning team are [*sic*] much brighter than at first expected."[29]

Kerrville also sought pitching help, adding a former major-league pitcher, 41-year-old Scott Perry.[30] Right-hander Perry won 20 games for the Philadelphia Athletics in 1918 but slipped to 4–17 in 1919 and 11–25 in 1920 before retiring after the 1921 season at age 30. Did Perry still wield effective pitches 11 years after he last pitched in the majors? The Braves would soon find out.

In addition, the Braves added two solid players who played for Comfort in 1931—brothers Joe and Skeeter Pankratz. According to newspaper reports, the Pankratz brothers were eligible to play for the Braves because their family residence was located just across the county line in Kerr County, thus not violating the rule requiring non-paid players to reside in the same county as the team.[31] After the Kerrville board of directors reelected Nelson Davis as their manager for the 1932 season,[32] the Braves were poised to challenge Fredericksburg and Llano for the HCL title.

Mason was determined to continue its steady improvement. In 1930, the Mavericks finished last (5–16), but they improved to fourth place (10–14) in 1931. Mason added an exceptional starting right-handed pitcher, Harvey Hardy,[33] in hopes of moving into contention.

Junction, now known as the Mountaineers,[34] could have no illusions about the team's prospects for improving on their last-place finish (6–19) since most of the club still consisted of high school players.[35] As the newest club in the league, Brady was untested.

Before the 1932 season began, Fredericksburg announced that, like in Comfort, admission prices would be reduced from 40 cents to 25 cents for adults while prices for children would remain 15 cents. Town teams were now beginning to feel the effects of the Depression on their gate revenues.

For the third consecutive season, Fredericksburg and Kerrville, those "ancient foes," met on the opening Sunday.[36] The *Fredericksburg Standard* captured Kerrville's hopes for the new season in a manner reflecting the stereotypes of Native Americans in the Jim Crow era:

> For more than a month, Manager Nelson Davis and his Braves have been laboring on the banks of the Guadalupe hammering their war clubs into shape and praying that their victory over the Giants might be their reward. New war chiefs were induced to wear the Brave war paint and the reports coming from the camp forcast [*sic*] a real battle.[37]

The usual pomp and circumstance began the festivities at Fair Park. Giants president Felix Stehling offered a short address before the Fredericksburg Concert Band entertained the fans. League president Bob Bennett then threw out the first pitch and the 1932 season was underway.

Kerrville's experiment with former major leaguer Scott Perry did not last long. Fredericksburg pounded Perry for 16 hits as they bounced the Braves, 10–1.[38] Kerrville would need to look elsewhere to shore up their pitching staff. Hugo Klaerner cruised to the win, allowing just three hits and striking out 12. Shortstop Gus Wendler knocked out four hits in his Fredericksburg debut.[39]

In the other opening games on April 3, Llano upended the Brady Turks, newcomers to the league, 5–2, behind Chink Taylor's three-run home run while Mason shut out Junction, 8–0.[40]

Mason surprised the league early, winning six of its first seven games, including two victories over Fredericksburg. The Mavericks found their rhythm behind new pitcher Harvey Hardy and the hitting of center fielder Pat Hatch, third baseman Hoffman, and shortstop L. Brown. In the first game against the Giants on May 1, Harvey Hardy outclassed Hugo Klaerner, spinning a 4–0 shutout of the Giants.[41] After this game, Hugo Klaerner departed for El Paso to pitch in the Texas-Arizona League, depriving the Giants of the leading pitcher in the league.[42] On May 8, the Mavericks bombed three Giants pitchers—Pepper Probst, Alfons Klaerner, and Paul Knopp, normally an infielder—in a 12–7 romp.[43]

About this time, hard-hitting Al Hollmig left the Giants when he moved to San Antonio, prompting the *Fredericksburg Standard* to lament his loss: "Every real fan in Fredericksburg regrets big Al's departure. Always a credit to the game, he played for the love of sport. He was admired by the players of opposing teams as well as by every one of his teammates. His all-around playing and batting punch will be sorely missed."[44]

Mason's only loss in the first seven games came against Llano, 16–15, in extra innings on April 10.[45] Thanks to cold winds that "made the fielding of balls hit into the air almost impossible,"[46] the clubs smashed 40 hits while Mason made eight fielding miscues. Even so, Harvey Hardy and Mason led, 15–8, heading to the bottom of the ninth, then Hardy collapsed, coughing up seven runs to the Cowboys in the ninth inning, capped by Huldie Mather's two-out, two-run home run. In the 10th, Lefty Draper smacked a game-winning single to hand Hardy the loss. But for this stunning rally by Llano, Mason would have been undefeated after seven games.

Llano also kept pace by winning six of its first seven games, losing only to Fredericksburg, 5–2, on April 24. Fredericksburg stumbled out of the gate, winning just three of its first seven, losing twice to Mason and even losing to the (mostly) high school players of Junction, 16–9, on April 17 when the Mountaineers rallied from a 9–3 deficit to pound the offerings of Pepper Probst and Hugo Klaerner for 13 unanswered runs.[47] Goodman, a high school pitcher from London, Texas, struck out 14 Giants en route to the victory.[48] Junction right fielder Goat Gardner led the attack, banging out four hits, including a home run.[49]

Fredericksburg stopped a three-game losing streak on May 22 when the Giants edged Brady, 8–7. Edgar Klett beat out an infield single with the bases loaded to gain the winning margin in the bottom of the ninth inning.[50] But the following Sunday, the Giants dropped to 4–5 for the season, losing a rematch with Brady, 12–3, when the Turks stroked 16 hits off three Fredericksburg pitchers (Pepper Probst, Phillip Klaerner, and Alfons Klaerner).[51] Four Brady hitters—Goat Gardner (who left Junction to play for the Turks), Samuelson, Pearson, and Archer—each notched three hits. At this low point in the season, Colonel Alf Petsch, who managed the Giants 15 years earlier, hosted a barbecue picnic for the team. The *Fredericksburg Standard* applauded the gesture, noting that "[t]o honor a team when it is winning is of course a fine thing, but to extend such a courtesy when the team has been in more or less of a slump is doubly appreciated."[52]

In Kerrville, after Scott Perry was rocked in the opening game against Fredericksburg, the Braves tried several pitchers, including well-traveled Zip Myler, who ended the 1931 season with Kerrville after pitching for Boerne in 1930 and then Comfort in the first half of 1931. Myler won his first two starts to right the ship, but inconsistency on the mound plagued the Braves for the remainder of the season. Junction and Brady fought to keep out of the cellar, both starting the season by losing six of their first seven games.

On May 22, Kerrville turned to newly recruited University of Texas pitching star Vernon Taylor, a sophomore who had pitched the Longhorns to the Southwest Conference championship earlier that year.[53] Behind Taylor, Kerrville stung Mason, 8–6, despite committing five errors.[54] Taylor limited the Mavericks to six hits while helping his own cause by slapping three singles. The loss dropped the Mavericks (6–2) one game behind Llano (7–1) at the top of the standings. The next Sunday, Llano traveled to Mason, where the Mavericks sought to avenge their 16–15 loss to the Cowboys on April 10. Down 4–3 in the bottom of the ninth, Mason rallied. After Schmidt doubled, he scored on a fielder's choice to tie the game. Dannheim then rapped a pinch-hit single and, after advancing with two outs, scored on a throwing error by Llano third baseman Fritz Bounds to snatch a 5–4 win, elevating the Mavericks (7–2) back into a first-place tie with Llano (7–2).[55]

Needing a win the next week to keep pace with Mason, Llano suffered a controversial loss. Before their contest with Brady on June 5, the Cowboys learned that the Turks enticed pitcher Vernon Taylor away from Kerrville, probably with the lure of some cash. Some in the Hill Country were unhappy with Brady's move. The *Fredericksburg Standard* complained:

> We are not trying to throw a wet blanket on either Kerrville's on [*sic*] Brady's ambitions but to our way of thinking, the idea of importing a player to bolster the team for a crucial game is contrary to the regulations of the league rules. We are referring to the case of Vernon Taylor, star slab artist of the Texas Longhorns. Two weeks ago, he was on the mound for the Braves when they defeated the Mason Mavericks. Next Sunday he is slated to pitch for Brady when they meet the Llano Cowboys. And what other team will pay the price for his services in the future?
>
> If the league directors permit such tactics to continue they might just as well burn their constitution and bylaws and throw player privileges wide open to all comers.[56]

Despite the criticism, Taylor allowed just six hits, as Brady rallied from a 3–0 deficit to upset the Cowboys, 9–3.[57] Brady center fielder Samuelson drove in three runs on four hits including a double. Lefty Draper (now back with Llano after pitching for Mason in 1931) took the loss after giving up six runs in the sixth inning. One week later, Fredericksburg edged Mason, 8–7,[58] when Hugo Klaerner returned from a brief stint with El Paso in the Texas-Arizona League to outlast Mason's Harvey Hardy despite taking a line drive on the third finger of his pitching hand in the fifth inning. Klaerner's injury reduced his effectiveness, allowing the Mavericks to rally from a 6–0 deficit, but Hugo's single in the seventh—his third hit of the game—drove in two runs to nab the victory. Hugo's cousin, right fielder Elias Klaerner, also knocked out three hits. Mason's loss dropped the Mavericks (9–3) into a first-place tie with Llano (9–3).

The Mavericks traveled to Llano on June 26 for the final game of the first half. The winner would be crowned the first-half pennant winner, assuring a berth in the championship series at the conclusion of the regular season. Both teams started their aces—Hardy for Mason, Van Huss for Llano.

In a seesaw contest, the clubs were tied, 4–4, after eight innings. To that point, Llano outhit Mason, 13–5, but seven Llano errors—more of those pesky fielding deficiencies for Llano—kept the Mavericks in the game. With two outs in the top of the ninth and Mason runners on second and third, Cowboys shortstop M. A. Reed fielded a grounder but threw wildly to first. Reed's error, the eighth by Llano, allowed both runners to score for a 6–4 Mason lead. However, Llano did not go quietly in the bottom of the ninth. With two outs, player-manager Chink Taylor doubled off Hardy and Huldie Mather singled Taylor in. Hardy then settled down, inducing slugger Archie Peel, who had returned from his minor league tryout, to ground out, preserving the 6–5 win for Mason and securing the first-half pennant for the surging Mavericks.[59] (Table 9 shows the final first-half standings for 1932.)[60]

Table 9. HCL First-Half Standings, 1932

	W	L	GB	Pct.
Mason	10	3	---	.769
Llano	9	4	1	.692
Fredericksburg	8	5	2	.615
Kerrville	6	7	4	.462
Brady	5	8	5	.385
Junction	1	12	9	.077

Although Fredericksburg fell short, finishing two games behind Mason, the Giants closed out the first half with a four-game winning streak highlighted by a 22–0 victory over Junction on June 26.[61] In that romp, Fredericksburg took advantage of nine Junction errors while winning pitcher Chester Klaerner knocked out four hits and Edgar Klett hit two triples. The Giants hoped to build on that streak in the second half of the season.

The league took notice that after starting 1–6, the Brady Turks showed much improvement, winning four of its next six games thanks in part to their "outside man" on the mound, Vernon Taylor. Their first half included a win over Fredericksburg, 12–3, on May 29. In that contest, Archer[62] stopped the Giants on seven hits while four Turks pounded three hits each (Samuelson, Gardner, Pearson, and Archer).[63] The following Sunday, Taylor was back on the mound, limiting Llano to just six hits while center fielder Samuelson continued his white-hot hitting, smacking four hits to lead Brady over the Cowboys, 9–3.[64] With the slate wiped clean for the second half, the Turks were optimistic they could ascend to the top of the league.

Fredericksburg compiled the highest team batting average in the first half with a .299 mark.[65] Hugo Klaerner (.517), Edgar Klett (.484), and Al Hollmig (.364) were the Giants' top batsmen. Other team batting averages were: Llano (.281), Mason (.268), Kerrville (.254), Junction (.232), and Brady (.226). Despite some lapses, Llano was the top fielding club with a .934 fielding percentage, followed by Mason (.932), Kerrville (.905), Brady (.901), Fredericksburg (.897), and Junction (.864).[66] It was not uncommon to see games where both teams committed three or more errors.

While first-half winner Mason was assured of a berth in the championship series, Llano and Fredericksburg were both on the hot seat. Only one playoff slot was left—the second-half pennant. Fredericksburg and Llano were the only clubs that played in the HCL championship series in 1930 and 1931 but now one of them would be left out of the playoff picture. Indeed, it was possible that neither would return to the title series.

As Hill Country fans contemplated the second half of the season, Kerrville suffered the devastating flood of the Guadalupe River on June 30 and July 1 described earlier. Two days later, Kerrville's game with Brady was canceled when the Brady players were not able to negotiate the impassable roads around Kerrville.[67] However, the next day, Kerrville managed to proceed with an Independence Day doubleheader against first-half winner Mason.[68] Zip Myler and Rod Sanders heartened the Kerrville fans by pitching the Braves to a sweep. Myler twirled a three-hit shutout in the first game for a 4–0 victory. Sanders held the Mavericks to six hits in the nightcap, winning 4–2.[69] Sanders came to the Braves following an unsuccessful minor league tryout[70] after starring for Mason in 1930 and Fredericksburg in 1931. The flood prevented the *Kerrville Mountain Sun* from reporting on other league games "on account of disrupted communications with the outside world."[71]

While Mason was off to a rocky start in the second half, Llano won its first three games, including a July 4 doubleheader sweep of an enervated Junction club.[72] Fredericksburg defeated Junction, 6–1, on July 3[73] then split a July 4 doubleheader with Brady. The first game featured two outstanding college pitchers, Fredericksburg's Chester "Smokey" Klaerner and Brady's Vernon Taylor. Klaerner threw two no-hitters for Rice Institute in 1932, ending the season with an 8–2 record for the Owls, while Taylor was the top pitcher for the University of Texas conference champions.[74] In the July 4 contest, Klaerner held the Turks to six hits but was victimized by five Giants errors. Taylor allowed eight hits but cruised to a 5–1 victory in the opener.[75] Both hurlers struck out nine. In the seven-inning nightcap, Taylor pitched two-thirds of an inning in relief, but it was too late. Hugo Klaerner pitched the Giants to a 6–4 win.[76]

The following Sunday, Fredericksburg (2–1) traveled to Llano (3–0) for the initial second-half showdown between the clubs. The Klaerner brothers led the Giants to a 4–0 win—Chester Klaerner pitched a five-hit shutout while Hugo Klaerner, playing center field, tripled and singled, scoring two runs.[77] Fredericksburg, Llano, and improving Brady were now tied for first place with 3–1 marks.

On Wednesday, July 13, Llano took time out from its league schedule to play an exhibition game against Kerrville to raise funds for victims of the recent flood. The *Llano News* encouraged Llano residents to attend the game:

> Remember, in this instance you are not only going to see a good ball game, but will be making your contribution to a people who are badly in need of financial assistance, many of whom lost homes and all household goods in the recent flood that caused such a great amount of loss to life and property in our sister town.
>
> If you are unable to see this game, then look up the gate keeper or the manager of either the Llano or Kerrville clubs and make a donation of the amount of the admittance fee. Kerrville needs your assistance in these trying days after a disaster such as has seldom been experienced in a Hill Country town.[78]

When league clubs returned to the pennant race the following Sunday, the fortunes of the Giants and the Cowboys began to diverge. After the Giants crushed Kerrville, 11–1, on July 17, Fredericksburg promptly lost their next two. On July 24, Brady's Vernon Taylor whitewashed the Giants, 4–0, to improve Brady's mark to 4–2.[79] The following Sunday, Llano romped over the Giants, 11–4.[80] In that game, the Cowboys scored five runs in the first inning against Chester Klaerner, building an insurmountable 9–0 lead in the fourth inning.

Llano shortstop Red Brown knocked out three hits, including a triple, while Earl Van Huss tamed the Giants' bats.

After two consecutive losses, Fredericksburg, now 4–3, traveled to Mason the next Sunday, hoping to get their season back on track. Instead, their hearts were broken in a dogfight between Hugo Klaerner and Harvey Hardy. The Giants led, 3–2, in the eighth inning when Mason's Schmidt singled. Evans, the next batter, drilled a sharp grounder over first base but right fielder Chester Klaerner "lost sight of the ball after it hit some rubbish near the huge Pecan tree on the right field foul line."[81] Before Klaerner could retrieve the ball from the trash pile, Schmidt scored the tying run.

The Giants squeezed a run across in the top of the ninth, but the Mavericks again rallied. After an error and Harvey Hardy's single put runners on first and third, the Giants intentionally walked Mason's leadoff hitter, Pat Hatch, to load the bases, creating a force play at every base. Nobles' looping base hit scored the tying run, moving Hardy to third. Hugo Klaerner then uncorked a pitch that eluded catcher Felix Hahn. Hardy attempted to score the winning run while Hahn fired the ball to Klaerner, who was covering the plate. Even though Klaerner "had his knee between the runner and home plate as Hardy slid in, [umpire] Larrimore ruled the runner safe and the game was won by Mason,"[82] handing the Giants their third loss in a row. The *Fredericksburg Standard* bemoaned both the field conditions (i.e., the rubbish under the pecan tree that cost the Giants a run) and the umpiring by the crew hired by Mason in the Giants' 5–4 loss, commenting that the league needed "outside and disinterested umpires."[83]

Fredericksburg was now tied with Kerrville for third place at 4–4.[84] With just four games remaining, the Giants were nearly eliminated from contention for the second-half flag. At the same time, Llano fashioned four consecutive wins, including the 11–4 pasting of the Giants on July 31. As of August 7, Llano (7–1) stood atop the standings while Brady (6–2) had risen to second by winning three in a row. The streak began with Vernon Taylor's 4–0 shutout of Fredericksburg on July 24,[85] followed by a 12–1 rout of Mason and a 9–2 victory over Junction.

Llano took care of business, downing Kerrville, 6–1, on August 14,[86] while Brady was rained out at Mason, setting up critical games between Llano and Brady in successive weeks. On August 21, the Cowboys (8–1) traveled to Brady (6–2), where the visitors edged the Turks, 2–1, in a classic face-off between Llano's Earl Van Huss and Brady's Vernon Taylor. Chink Taylor scored what turned out to be the decisive run on three errors. On Taylor's groundball, Miller, Brady's shortstop, threw wildly to first, allowing Taylor to advance to second. Vernon Taylor tried to catch Chink Taylor off the bag but threw errantly into center field as Chink proceeded to third, rounding the bag for home. Brady center fielder, Spec Smith, then fired home wildly to the plate, enabling Chink to score.[87]

The following week in Llano, Van Huss and Taylor squared off again. Llano (9–1) could eliminate Brady (6–3) from contention for the second-half pennant with a victory. Llano built a 4–0 lead, scoring single runs in four of the first five innings. The Turks rallied in the sixth, combining three hits and a walk with four Llano errors to score four runs, tying the game at 4–4. Both pitchers stiffened, neither team scoring until the bottom of the ninth when player-manager Chink Taylor stroked a two-out single to the outfield, scoring Red Brown from third base with the winning run for a 5–4 victory. By earning the second-half title,[88] Llano qualified to play for the league championship for the third consecutive year.

Fredericksburg failed to make the championship series for the first time in three years. Brady continued to surge in the second half thanks to the Turks' "outside man," Vernon Taylor, but fell short in the end. Taylor hit a lusty .346 in addition to his mound efforts while Turks' player-manager Luke Vogel hit .323 with a .452 slugging percentage.

In the final week of the regular season, Llano topped Fredericksburg, 7–2, while Mason blanked Kerrville, 6–0, to leap over the Braves into fourth place.[89] Hoping to record its first win of the second half, Junction was rained out at Brady.[90] (The HCL's final second-half standings are shown in Table 10.)[91]

Table 10. HCL Second-Half Standings, 1932

	W	L	GB	Pct.
Llano	11	1	---	.917
Brady	6	4	4	.600
Fredericksburg	6	5	4½	.545
Mason	5	6	5½	.455
Kerrville	5	7	6	.417
Junction	0	10	10	.000

Although Mason stumbled to a 5–6 mark in the second half, the first-half pennant assured them of a spot against Llano in the best-of-three championship series. Since Brady did not make the championship series, Llano recruited the Turks' star pitcher, Vernon Taylor, for the series.[92] After the University of Texas pitcher started one game for Kerrville before joining Brady in early June, Llano became Taylor's third HCL club in 1932. It is not clear why the HCL permitted this postseason addition to the Cowboys roster when Taylor did not play at all for Llano during the regular season, but it was a boon to the Cowboys, who were riding an eight-game winning streak as they started the series.

Despite the addition of Taylor, Llano tabbed their regular season ace, Earl Van Huss, as their starter in the first game on September 11. Mason countered with a pitcher named "Bradley" rather than the Mavericks' regular starter, Harvey Hardy. According to the *Llano News*, "Bradley" was actually "Flop" Harris, a star southpaw from Texon, a semipro team, playing under an assumed name.[93] In addition, Mason tapped Brady player-manager Luke Vogel to play center field in the series. As a result, three players were new to their teams for the championship series. These "outside men"—Taylor for Llano, Harris and Vogel for Mason—would figure prominently in deciding the HCL title.

For the opening game, Llano traveled to Mason, where "scores of cars filled with people" from Llano came to support the Cowboys.[94] The series began after league president Bob Bennett threw out the ceremonial first pitch. Llano struck in the first inning, when player-manager Chink Taylor doubled after leadoff hitter M. A. Reed singled and stole second. Mason responded in the fourth when two singles and a walk loaded the bases. After a lineout, "[Mason runner] Kygar was safe at first and Schmidt scored when [Llano catcher Paul] McLeod dropped the ball after tagging the runner out."[95] A fly out and strikeout ended the inning, but the game was now tied, 1–1.

Llano scored with two outs in the sixth inning when Chink Taylor doubled again and scored on Huldie Mather's single. Mason answered in the bottom of the inning. Mason left fielder Hoffman walked and advanced to third on a single by Vogel. Hoffman scored when Latham's grounder was thrown away by Cowboys third baseman Red Bounds. Vernon Taylor, making his first series appearance on the mound, relieved Van Huss. Latham stole second and went to third when Vogel scored on Kygar's grounder to the right of Llano second baseman Pinckney, who had no choice but to make the out unassisted at first base. Llano catcher McLeod then picked off Latham at third and Taylor induced a groundout to end the inning, but Mason was now ahead, 3–2.

Harris beaned Bounds in the head in the seventh inning, forcing the batter to leave the game, but Llano did not score. In the top of the ninth, Llano right fielder Huldie Mather opened with a single. After a grounder by "Spot" Falk[96] forced Mather out at second, Falk took second on a balk by Harris, then stole third base. However, Harris struck out McLeod and Pinckney popped out to end the game, a 3–2 victory for Mason.[97] The *Fredericksburg Standard* commented that Mason's additions of Flop Harris and Luke Vogel gave them "the better deal" despite Llano's addition of Vernon Taylor.[98]

On September 18, the series moved to Llano, where, despite the comments of the *Fredericksburg Standard* on the ability of Flop Harris (playing as "Bradley"), Mason began the game with Harvey Hardy, their primary starter during the season. Instead of Van Huss, Llano chose to start their new addition, Vernon Taylor. The game attracted 500 fans to Llano's diamond at Robinson State Park, making "ground rules necessary on balls hit into the cars in right field."[99]

Llano jumped on Hardy early, scoring three runs in the first inning on three hits, two stolen bases, and an error. Mason plated a run in the third without benefit of a hit on two walks, a sacrifice, and a fielder's choice, but the Mavericks would score no more as Taylor allowed only six hits. Llano knocked out 13 hits against Hardy and stole seven bases for a dominant victory, 8–1.[100] Player-manager Chink Taylor had three hits, including a double, while Huldie Mather drove in three runs on a double and single. The series was now knotted at one game apiece, sending the clubs back to Mason for the decisive game.

Before the third game, the Cowboys were honored by the Plaza Café in Llano for winning the second-half title. The festivities included a meal and brief speeches by nearly everyone present, including the players, although player-manager Chink Taylor deferred his comments until after the final game of the series. E. E. Martin, club secretary, offered an interesting tidbit regarding the league's decision to allow Mason to add two players (Harris and Vogel) to its playoff roster while Llano added only one (Vernon Taylor). According to Martin, the league did this "to make the games as even as possible."[101]

On September 25, rain in Mason canceled the scheduled game, forcing players and fans alike to wait another week to decide the championship.[102] After Hardy's loss in the second game, Mason turned again to Flop Harris, winner of the first game, playing this time as "F. H. Bradley,"[103] while Llano returned to Earl Van Huss. The Cowboys anticipated that 100 cars would travel from Llano to Mason for the final game, producing "the largest crowd that ever witnessed an athletical [*sic*] contest of any nature" in Mason.[104]

Mason led the final game, 2–1, when Llano exploded in the fifth inning. First baseman Collings opened with a walk and M. A. Reed followed with a high pop up, which Mason first baseman Schmidt dropped for an error. Red Brown singled to load the bases. Harris walked powerful hitter, Chink Taylor, forcing in a run and tying the game at 2–2. Huldie Mather then blasted a double, scoring two runs and sending Taylor to third. Harris sent Taylor home on a wild pitch. After a strikeout, catcher Paul McLeod singled, scoring Mather with the fifth run of the inning for a 6–2 lead.

The Cowboys scored two more runs in the seventh and four more in the eighth, knocking Harris out of the box, meaning that Flop Harris had flopped. Mason brought left fielder Hoffman in to pitch in relief, but he allowed four more runs in the ninth as Llano cruised to a 16–5 victory, gaining its second consecutive championship in convincing fashion.[105] Vernon Taylor relieved Van Huss in the second inning to earn the win. Three Cowboys each rapped three hits—Mather (a double and two singles, four runs scored), Red Brown (a double and two singles, three runs scored), and left fielder Spot Falk (three singles, one run scored). As the league champion in 1931 and 1932, Llano stood tall in Hill Country baseball.

The league reported receipts of $673.55 for the three-game championship series. After deducting expenses, the league doled out the net revenues to Llano ($227.27), Mason ($151.51), Fredericksburg ($50.50), Brady ($31.56), and Junction ($18.94).[106]

Llano's dominance in 1932 is demonstrated by the fact that the Cowboys scored nearly eight runs per game, outscoring their opponents by 92 runs in the 23 games for which box scores were found—an average differential of four runs per game. (See Appendix C for statistics for the 1932 season.) The Cowboys' attack was again powered by player-manager Chink Taylor, who led the team in batting average (.430), runs (38), hits (40), extra-base hits (13), and stolen bases (29). His slugging percentage (.613) was second only to that of part-time shortstop Red Brown (.659) who did not join the team until early July. Right fielder Huldie Mather posted another superb season (.385/.527—batting average/slugging percentage) while catcher Paul McLeod enjoyed a healthy rise in his batting average from .227 in 1931 to .333 in 1932. On the mound, steady Earl Van Huss produced a 13–4 record in 17 starts.

Despite a weak offense, which resulted in a team batting average of only .230, Mason's hot first half earned them a berth in the championship series, where they fell short after winning the first game against Llano. Center fielder-pitcher Pat Hatch topped the team in runs (14) while hitting .275. Shortstop L. Brown hit .283, the best on the Mavericks among full-time players, while third baseman-outfielder Hoffman hit .276. Outfielder Josefson hit .321 but for unknown reasons did not play after June 12. Pitcher Harvey Hardy performed well, posting an 8–5 record in 14 starts with a TRA of 4.92, but backup pitcher Hatch finished 0–3 with a TRA of 9.64.

Fredericksburg dropped to an overall 14–10 record in 1932, despite Hugo Klaerner's return to the Giants' fold. Klaerner hit .372, second best on the club, but on the mound, he suffered a higher-than-expected TRA of 4.74 resulting in a 6–4 record. His brother, Chester "Smokey" Klaerner, logged an impressive TRA of 2.87 for a 5–3 record. Hugo and Chester's younger brother, Alfons Klaerner, made his Giants debut on the mound in 1932, pitching six-and-one-third innings with no record while their cousin, Phillip Klaerner, recorded a 2–1 mark in 18 1/3 innings.

Left fielder Edgar Klett blossomed into a fearsome power hitter, registering a Babe Ruth–like slugging percentage of .788 to lead the league. In addition to slugging percentage, Klett paced the team in hits (45), batting average (.455), runs (21, tied with Hugo Klaerner), doubles (seven), triples (10), home runs (two), and stolen bases (six). Right fielder Elias Klaerner (.350) and pitcher Chester Klaerner (.370) also swung hot bats. Although Fredericksburg was disappointed not to play in the championship series, the Giants' core of solid players would remain intact for 1933.

Brady's first season in the HCL was promising. After a 5–6 record in the first half, the Turks challenged Llano for the second-half crown. Luring strikeout artist Vernon Taylor[107] away from Kerrville after one start for the Braves turned Brady's fortunes around. For the season, Taylor posted an 8–5 record[108] while hitting .346. Player-manager Luke Vogel topped the club with 14 runs and 20 hits (four of which were doubles) while manning the catcher's gear and occasionally playing centerfield. The Turks' other regulars, center fielder Samuelson (.262), first baseman Pearson (.286), left fielder Prewitt (.245), and third baseman H. Jones (.267), were all dependable ballplayers.

For Kerrville, the 1932 season was a struggle as they fell below .500 with a season record of 11–14. Although the Braves benefited from taking on star infielders Joe and Skeeter Pankratz, who played for Kerrville after Comfort withdrew from the HCL for the 1932 season, the Braves could find no consistency, partly due to a revolving cast of ballplayers. Only four players (Grantham, Staudt, J. Pankratz and S. Pankratz) played 20 or more games for the Braves. A total of 44 players appeared for the Braves—an astounding number considering that rosters were limited to 15 players. There were 16 Kerrville players who appeared in just a single game.

Several Kerrville players emerged from the crowd. Outfielder Louie Wootton hit .304. Third baseman Joe Pankratz hit .257 while stealing eight bases. Beaver hit .318 while playing a solid second base. Shortstop Skeeter Pankratz hit only .221 but tied for the team lead in doubles with four. First baseman Currie hit .414 but did not play in the second half of the season. Catcher Ben Grantham led the team with 28 hits, hitting .272 with both power (four doubles and two triples) and speed (six stolen bases).

Junction could not improve on its 6–19 mark in 1931. The Mountaineers fell to an overall record of 1–22, losing their last 20 games. There were few bright spots for the hapless club. In the 15 games for which box scores were found, Junction was outscored by their opponents, 165–58—an average differential of more than six runs per game. Between June 19 and July 10, the Mountaineers were shut out five games in a row. Two weeks after ending their shutout string in a 16–3 loss to Llano, the Mountaineers were humiliated by Kerrville, 25–6, when they committed 10 errors.[109] Despite their poor record, several Junction players could knock the ball around the diamond—outfielder Goat Gardner (.361), first baseman Buster (.329), and shortstop Blackburn (.352) hit over .300.[110] High school pitcher Goodman fared poorly. In the seven starts for which box scores were found, he managed only a 1–6 record with an elevated TRA of 11.71. As a team, their pitching staff gave up an average of 11 runs per game. Clearly, Junction had nowhere to go but up in 1933.

The Hill Country League achieved a milestone in 1932. For the first time—but not the last—one of the league's former players ascended to the major leagues. Charlie English, a shortstop who played for the Fifteenth Field Artillery club at Fort Sam Houston, began playing for the Boerne White Sox in June 1930, sparking Boerne's run at the HCL pennant. English, batting in the cleanup spot for the White Sox, hit .328 in 67 at-bats with a .463 slugging percentage. (See Appendix A for 1930 statistics.)

In 1931, English embarked on his professional career at Florence of the Class D Palmetto League.[111] The next year, English hit .340 with a .555 slugging percentage while playing mostly third base at Muskogee/Hutchison, a Class C team in the Western Association.[112] The Chicago White Sox rewarded his offensive production in Muskogee/Hutchison with a midseason call-up. English played 24 games, mostly at third base, hitting .318.[113] The 1932 season turned out to be his high-water mark in the majors.

He appeared briefly with the White Sox in 1933 at second base (he went four for nine in three games with two doubles) but then remained in the minors for the next three seasons even though he never hit below .300. He appeared briefly for the New York Giants at second base in 1936 (six games, one plate appearance) and mostly at third base in 17 games for the Cincinnati Reds in 1937 (63 plate appearances, .238 batting average).[114] After that, English played in the minors for more than 10 years, ending his professional career at the age of 39 in 1949.[115] He also served as a player-manager at the end of his career in 1947 and 1949.[116]

The rapid rise of English from the HCL in 1930 to the Chicago White Sox in 1932 not only instilled pride among Hill Country ballclubs. It also increased the interest of professional scouts in local ballplayers. It would not be long before two other Hill Country veterans advanced from the local diamonds to the major leagues.

As the chill air stilled the bats for the winter of 1932–33, Hill Country baseball fans gathered around the proverbial "hot stove" to trade jibes and boasts about the upcoming season. They would soon learn that major changes were coming to the HCL in 1933.

Like Boerne in 1930 and Comfort in 1931, Kerrville wanted to reduce its time and expense for travel. The Braves ended the 1932 season in the red.[117] Perhaps the fans tired of the dizzying rotation of players in and out of the Braves' dugout during the season, resulting in lower attendance. At the same time, the trips to the four distant Hill Country teams in Llano, Mason, Brady, and Junction in 1932 simply became too expensive for the Braves.[118] Fred C. Toler, secretary of the Kerrville club, explained to the *Fredericksburg Standard*:

> These road trips . . . are usually about 80 miles each way, in the present case, and must be made on the average of twice each month during the playing season. The present financial condition of our club necessitates our making drastic reductions in expenses or else passing out of existence. This we do not propose to do and therefore a more compact circuit is the logical conclusion.[119]

These concerns came to a head at the annual league meeting in Mason on February 9, 1933, where Kerrville proposed to divide the HCL into two circuits, one for northern teams and one for southern teams.[120] Before the meeting, representatives of the ballclubs in Boerne and Comfort had assured Kerrville that they would rejoin the HCL under such an arrangement. Indeed, Comfort was financially motivated to rejoin a league with its nearest rivals since the Broncos experienced lower attendance as an independent club in 1932.[121]

In addition to Boerne and Comfort, Bandera, an independent club, committed to joining the southern circuit proposed by Kerrville. Besides three teams, Kerrville was seeking two San Antonio clubs to fill out the proposed southern circuit.

Despite Kerrville's efforts to salvage the HCL by expanding to two circuits, league officers rejected Kerrville's plan,[122] resulting in Kerrville's withdrawal from the HCL.[123] The wave of the Great Depression had now crested and fallen on the league, which lost its third southern Hill Country team in three years.

Kerrville moved quickly to declare its intent to form a new baseball league of southern teams, tentatively labeled as the "Heart o' the Hills Baseball League."[124] A meeting of the prospective ballclubs took place in Comfort on February 17, 1933, where plans for the fledgling league were finalized.[125] As a result, the Hill Country would have a second baseball league in 1933. It was a pivotal moment in Hill Country baseball.

H. O. Adler, a Boerne businessman and president of the White Sox, was elected league president.[126] In the optimism of the February 17 meeting, the league founders could not have foreseen that, two years later, Adler's reign would conclude with an upheaval that shook Hill Country baseball to its core.

CHAPTER 9

H. O. ADLER

Merchant and Baseball Impresario

A respected businessman and civic leader, H. O. Adler served as president of the Boerne White Sox for many years. His unrivaled reputation and management skills led to his election as president of the Mountain League in 1933. Overcoming personal tragedies, Adler exemplified the resilience and fortitude of Hill Country residents.

Henry Oscar Adler was born on November 11, 1882, in Boerne, the youngest of six children of Fritz Adler and Juliana (Noeckel) Adler, who both had emigrated from Germany to Texas in the 1850s. Fritz Adler was a blacksmith who worked at a shop at the corner of Main Street and Newton Street in Boerne.[1] While only 20 years old and still living at home, H. O., as he was now known, opened a general mercantile store in 1902, constructing a one-story wooden building at 236 S. Main Street.[2] Eight years later, H. O. married Ethel Lee Tommins. H. O. and Ethel had four children: Belmont, Dorothy, Vernon, and Glenn. In 1911, Adler replaced the wooden structure with a two-story stone building at the same location to house his incipient family and the growing business which became a general store and grocery.[3] The Adler family lived on the second floor while operating the store below, which was advertised as "A Store of a Million Articles."[4]

H. O. and Ethel suffered a tragedy in the general store on August 24, 1926. On that day, their oldest son, Belmont, 15 years old, was helping in the store. With two others, he was using a hand elevator to move a load of sugar from the basement to the first floor when a rope broke, causing the load to fall, crushing him to death. Belmont was a popular high school student. His funeral was "[o]ne of the largest funerals ever held in Boerne" since "[p]ractically all the citizens of Southern Kendall County attended."[5] H. O.'s travails did not end with Belmont's death. Three years later, Ethel, whose health deteriorated after the loss of her son, died of lymphangitis at the age of 42 on September 17, 1929, leaving H. O. with three children still at home.

Figure 25. Boerne White Sox triumvirate. (L–R): H. O. Adler, president; Ed Kaiser, manager; Udo Harz, business manager. (Courtesy of Tom Phillip.)

It is not known exactly when H. O. became involved with the management of the Boerne White Sox, but it was likely in the early 1920s. With business manager Udo Harz, a local businessman, Adler guided the White Sox whether they played independently, in the Hill Country League, or in the Mountain League.

Figure 26. H. O. Adler Building at 236 South Main Street, built in 1911. (Courtesy of Betsy Bergmann Sueltenfuss.)

When the White Sox joined in forming the Mountain League in 1933, league directors selected the experienced Adler as league president. He served in that capacity until 1935.[6]

Baseball was not Adler's only passion. He was a leader of St. Helena's Episcopal Church in Boerne, where he was superintendent of Sunday schools for 25 years.[7] He also served as the first president of the Kendall County Fair Association.[8] But scouting was his "first love."[9] H. O. led the Boerne Boy Scouts for more than 30 years, receiving the high honor of the Boy Scouts' Silver Beaver Award.[10] When he died on July 10, 1954, he was remembered for "a life of community service."[11]

Adler's building was a prominent part of Boerne in the early twentieth century and remains so today. In 1969, the building was purchased by Edgar Bergmann, the former White Sox pitcher, where Bergmann and, later, his son Randy, operated Bergmann Lumber Company for many years.[12] Today, the building houses Tusculum Brewing Company. The structure stands as a testament to the abiding spirit of H. O. Adler, who built a legacy in Boerne through business, baseball, and the Boy Scouts despite the heartbreak of losing first his young son in a terrible accident and then his grieving wife three years later.

CHAPTER 10

BY THE MARGIN OF A FROG'S EYEBROW

Mountain League, 1933

Due to the quick formation of a new Fredericksburg bank to replace the two that closed, banks in the Hill Country were in reasonably sound financial condition as baseball season approached in 1933. However, closings in other states raised the specter of a run on financial institutions, which caused Texas Governor Miriam Ferguson, known to Texans as "Ma" Ferguson, to impose a five-day banking moratorium on March 3.[1] In response, bankers and businessmen in Kerrville formulated a plan to use scrip while the banks were closed, but the US Department of Treasury nixed the move.[2] Before the Texas moratorium expired, newly inaugurated President Franklin Roosevelt proclaimed a nationwide bank "holiday" for a short period to stem any financial panic.[3]

As wool and mohair prices ebbed in the Depression, ranchers and farmers welcomed oil exploration in the Hill Country. Oil was booming in East Texas after discovery of the East Texas Oil Field in 1930, leading some to explore the Hill Country for oil. For the right to drill, wildcatters made annual rental payments of 25 to 50 cents per acre.[4] Although some expected the Hill Country to harbor large reservoirs, prospectors ultimately found that the region's limestone bedrock was not conducive to the formation of oil. But in the early 1930s, wildcatters provided precious revenues to some landowners.

While the reality of the Depression had clearly sunk in, some Germans in the Hill Country remained obstinate, sometimes in amusing ways. For example, in Fredericksburg, Lions Club members grew exasperated with talk of the Depression popping up at their meetings. As a result, members found an innovative way to avoid repeated references to "the Depression"—they conducted their meetings in German! According to the *Fredericksburg Standard*, the German term for the Depression is a mouthful: *Diezurzeitherrschendeschreckendegeldknappheit*.

Hence, Lions Club members expressed confidence that no one would dare to employ this byzantine expression in ordinary conversation.[5]

In Boerne, the mayor and other civic leaders conveyed their confidence in the future, despite the Depression, by issuing a proclamation that "a glorious new day is about to dawn" and urging all Boerne residents to fly the American flag "until after the emergency."[6] The proclamation further declared: "God is in his Heaven, . . . the government at Washington still lives, . . . the American people cannot be beaten, and we beg EVERY CITIZEN to greet his fellow with a SMILE, and to be all for BOERNE, and for America."[7]

Against this backdrop, the second baseball circuit in the Hill Country took shape by April 1933. The nascent league, formed after Kerrville withdrew from the HCL, was officially named the Mountain League, discarding the original title of "Heart o' the Hills League." Since the city of Kerrville was known to many as the "Heart of the Hills,"[8] it is likely that the other towns found this label too parochial for a league much broader in scope than Kerrville alone. In any event, the newly christened Mountain League prepared to begin play with five clubs—former HCL members Kerrville, Boerne, and Comfort, along with previously independent Bandera and a San Antonio club, Alamo Heights.[9]

At the same time, the HCL added another northern Hill Country team, San Saba (located 32 miles north of Llano), to replace Kerrville. The HCL now consisted of five northern teams (Brady, Junction, Llano, Mason, and San Saba)[10] plus centrally located Fredericksburg.[11] Essentially, the Mountain League and the Hill Country League represented a geographic divide—the new Mountain League featured southern teams while the HCL had evolved into a northern league. Early in the spring, there was talk of a championship series between the winners of the upstart Mountain League and the HCL.[12]

The Mountain League rekindled rivalries among Kerrville, Boerne, and Comfort while adding nearby Bandera. The *Kerrville Daily Times* reported that "[i]nterest in the new amateur loop is intense among Hill Country fans, with strong delegations from cities concerned announcing intentions of 'stepping out' to see Sunday's games."[13] Even in Fredericksburg, which remained in the HCL, it was recognized that the Mountain League was generating much interest and that "huge crowds are expected to attend the opening games."[14]

As in the HCL, Mountain League games were played on Sunday afternoons, although teams also scheduled games on the Fourth of July. Admission prices were generally 25 cents,[15] lower than admission prices in the initial seasons of the HCL, reflecting the harsh economic times. The Mountain League also banned all paid players, requiring teams to draw their players only from their "immediate trade territory."[16] This change not only saved clubs money. It may have also been made in response to several instances when the use of "ringers" in the HCL might have been seen as abusive, such as college star Vernon Taylor pitching for Llano in the 1932 championship series after pitching for Kerrville and Brady in the regular season. The Mountain League also banned doubleheaders, unlike the HCL, and set the league fee paid by each team at $25, half as much as the HCL's $50 fee.[17]

Under the league schedule, each team would play 18 games, the season starting April 2 and ending August 27.[18] Since there were five teams in the league, a "balanced" schedule would have either played a 16-game schedule (each team playing the other four teams four times) or a 20-game schedule (each team playing the other teams five times). According to the 18-game schedule, each team was scheduled to play two teams four times each and the remaining two teams five times each. It is unknown why the league did not choose a "balanced" approach, but the league may have wanted to end the regular season before September 1.

As an independent team for the last two years, the Boerne White Sox were in transition. Twin brothers Albert and Edwin Uecker—Albert was an outfielder-pitcher, while Edwin was primarily a pitcher—were veteran anchors of the club, but they were beginning to slow down. They would soon pass the mantle to their younger brother, Johnny Uecker.[19] Though he was only 27 years old, player-manager Clarence Holekamp—the regular first baseman in prior years—would appear only sporadically in 1933 before becoming a full-time manager in succeeding years.[20] At the same time, 20-year-old pitcher Edgar Bergmann was emerging as a star on the mound. Shortstop Gus Pfeiffer, first baseman Gus Wendler, second baseman Rudy Leidl,[21] center fielder Clarence Bourgeois, right fielder Harry Schweppe, and catcher Harry Phillip rounded out a strong core of players as the White Sox entered Mountain League play.

Kerrville fielded a solid ballclub led by third baseman-pitcher Louie Wootton, first baseman Clergy Hollimon, catcher Ben Grantham, and right fielder Staudt. The Braves added southpaw pitcher Haskell Archer to replace Zip Myler and Rod Sanders, both of whom did not return to Kerrville. Having finished with a disappointing 11–14 record last season, new manager E. M. Hughes hoped the Braves would challenge for the Mountain League flag.[22]

Comfort had not fared well in the HCL, foundering with records of 8–18 in 1930 and 8–15 in 1931 before their withdrawal and independent play in 1932. However, this year, the Broncos boasted a dependable lineup featuring the Pankratz brothers—middle infielder Joe Pankratz and third baseman Skeeter

Figure 27. Boerne players. Back row (L–R): Gus Pfeiffer, Johnny Leidl (younger brother of Anton and Rudy), Harry Schweppe, Johnny Uecker. In front: Harry Phillip. (Courtesy of Tom Phillip.)

Pankratz—who returned to Comfort after their stint with Kerrville in 1932. Joining them was shortstop Ernst Nagel, a former Fredericksburg infielder. To make room for Nagel, Joe Pankratz moved from shortstop to second base. Center fielder-catcher Felix Meyer and first baseman Morris Goforth were staunch players as well. Pitching was the only question mark. Christie Lindemann manned the starting role to begin the season.

As a San Antonio club, the Alamo Heights Firemen were not well known to baseball fans in the Hill Country, but they played both Comfort and Boerne in 1932, Comfort winning, 8–3, in extra innings on July 10 and Boerne prevailing, 11–4, on September 18.[23] In 1933, player-manager Jim Riley led a revamped team—the team was sometimes referred to as the "Rileymen." The Firemen featured first baseman Riley and right fielder Feille, both power hitters, along with Jelly Harris, a speedy catcher, and Clark Nealon, a reliable pitcher.

Bandera, the smallest of the towns in the Mountain League, likely saw the new league as a step up in competition from the team's independent days. Wood Thornberry, the "Duke of Thornberry" who struck out 23 in 15 innings for Kerrville in the infamous 2–2 tie in 1930, would start the season as their mound ace. Second baseman F. Hamilton, outfielder Billings, and shortstop Bob Mansfield rounded out the top ballplayers for the Cowboys.

The clubs readied for the maiden season of the Mountain League. Before the first league game, Comfort spruced up the diamond at Faltin Field:[24]

> Considerable work has been done on the diamond and ballpark this week, assuring the players an excellent playing field, and fans comfortable and clean seats. The fence has been repaired, at the ballclub's expense and it is hoped that all who are interested in seeing a good ballgame will pay the small admission price at the gate and help the home club with their presence as well as from a financial standpoint.[25]

On the opening Sunday, Comfort flexed its muscles at Bandera, overpowering the Cowboys, 19–4. Catcher Felix Meyer led the offense with three hits while Joe Pankratz, Skeeter Pankratz, Ernst Nagel, West, Morris Goforth, and Christie Lindemann each stroked two hits.[26] Lindemann scattered nine hits for the easy win.

In Boerne, Mayor R. L. Hickman threw the ceremonial first pitch to Kendall County Sheriff Edward Bierschwale to celebrate the start of the season at the Kendall County Fairgrounds. Following the festivities, Boerne shortstop Gus Pfeiffer smacked four hits as the Sox edged Kerrville, 9–6. Edgar Bergmann pitched the complete game victory, scattering 11 hits.[27]

After having an off day to start the season, Alamo Heights defeated Bandera, 6–2, on April 9,[28] but suffered a loss when they traveled to Kerrville the following Sunday. In that contest, both clubs pushed across two runs in the second inning before Braves starter Haskell Archer and Firemen twirler Clark Nealon found their rhythm, holding their opposition scoreless until Kerrville scored in the bottom of the ninth. Braves right fielder Jake Goss led off the inning with a single. After a pop out, Archer helped his own cause with a single and shortstop Staudt walked to load the bases. Braves center fielder Monk Warren stepped to the plate and hit a chopper that landed in "no man's land" between the pitcher, catcher, and third baseman. Goss scampered across the plate with the winning run for a 3–2 Kerrville victory.[29]

After the heartbreaking loss to Kerrville, the Firemen caught fire behind the solid hitting of manager-first baseman Jim Riley and right fielder Feille. They edged Boerne, 6–5, on April 23,[30] then smashed Comfort, 11–5, the following Sunday.[31] Despite five Alamo Heights errors in the Comfort game, pitcher Clark Nealon earned the win, contributing three hits to the cause, while Riley blasted a home run. Like the Firemen, the Broncos had 11 hits, three by right fielder Paul Weiss, but the *Comfort News* reported that "poor baserunning" was their undoing.[32] After an off day on May 7, Alamo Heights won their third consecutive game, routing the visitors from Bandera, 13–0.[33]

On May 21, when the Firemen hosted Kerrville, the Braves hoped to repeat their earlier victory. With a win, the Braves, now 3–2 in the season, would tie the Firemen (4–1) for first place. However, Alamo Heights left fielder Turner led off the game with a home run off Kerrville starter Haskell Archer. After an error, right fielder Feille launched another home run, giving the Firemen a 3–0 lead after just three batters. The Firemen cruised to their fourth win in a row, 6–3. Clark Nealon scattered eight hits to garner the victory, moving the Firemen, now 5–1, into first place by two games over Kerrville and Comfort, both 3–3.

At this point in the season, Alamo Heights added a promising young pitcher to the roster. Southpaw Charley Suche just graduated from high school and signed a professional contract with the Cleveland Indians, but the contract provided he would first complete his education—he planned to enroll at Baylor University in the fall.[34] As a result, Alamo Heights grabbed Suche for the Mountain League season, immediately sending him to the mound against Boerne on May 28. Suche pitched brilliantly in his first start, striking out seven White Sox hitters and giving up just seven hits in a 4–1 win.[35] Alamo Heights knocked out Boerne starter Newton with three runs in the third inning. Edgar Bergmann relieved Newton but the damage was already done, given Suche's fancy twirling. Alamo Heights shortstop Johnny Niemic, a former Notre Dame gridiron star playing in his last game with the Firemen, stroked a double and a triple while Riley added two hits to lead the Firemen to their fifth consecutive win, raising their record to 6–1.[36]

Comfort, a hard-hitting club led by the Pankratz brothers, was the only challenger to Alamo Heights early in the season. After the Broncos stomped host Bandera, 19–4, in the opening game,[37] Comfort met Boerne in the Broncos' home opener a week later. Christie Lindemann coughed up five runs in the first three innings, but then settled down, holding the White Sox in check and allowing the Broncos to rally. The Broncos chipped away but still trailed, 5–3, heading to the bottom of the ninth. Boerne pitcher Edwin Uecker allowed consecutive singles by Christie Lindemann, Skeeter Pankratz, and West to load the bases with none out. Edgar Bergmann relieved Uecker but hit Morris Goforth with a pitch and walked Meyer to tie the game. Ernst Nagel then slapped a "Texas Leaguer" into the outfield to send the Broncos home triumphant, 6–5.[38]

After a league off day on April 16,[39] the Broncos stumbled the following week, losing to Kerrville, 14–7, after starting pitcher Christie Lindemann was shelled by the Braves, failing to survive the second inning. Lindemann's poor outing may have resulted from a 40-minute rain delay just after the game started, which turned the diamond into a muddy pit, but that did little to assuage Comfort's disappointment with the loss.[40]

On April 30, Alamo Heights spanked Comfort, 11–5, despite committing five errors.[41] Lindemann was again knocked out of the game, this time in the third inning.[42] Clearly, the Broncos needed pitching help to match their potent offense. Comfort turned to its best player, Joe Pankratz, to overcome their mound woes, moving him from second base to the mound, perhaps because he had pitched well in an exhibition game against Richter Bakery, winning, 3–2, on April 16.[43] The strategy paid off immediately when the Broncos trounced Bandera, 13–4, on May 7.[44] Pankratz went the distance while outfielder-first baseman Arthur Bergmann smacked three hits and four other players—left fielder Walter Kutzer, shortstop Ernst Nagel, catcher Felix Meyer, and right fielder Kmoch—contributed two hits each. Through five games, three Comfort players were hitting over .400—Kutzer (.500), Nagel (.500), and Bergmann (.437).[45]

Pankratz pitched well the following Sunday, but the Broncos were stymied by Boerne's Edgar Bergmann, who shut them out, 4–0, allowing only three hits. After a week off, Comfort edged Kerrville, 3–2, on May 28 when Joe Pankratz held the Braves to six hits and ignited the Broncos' game-winning run rally with a single in the eighth inning.[46]

At the end of May, Comfort was the sole club besides Alamo Heights playing over .500 ball, holding second place with a 4–3 record, two games behind Alamo Heights (6–1).[47] With Pankratz gaining momentum on the mound, the Broncos hosted Alamo Heights on June 4 in a critical game. With a win, Comfort would move within a game of first place, but a loss would leave them three games behind the Firemen—a wide margin in an 18-game season.

Joe Pankratz struggled early—the Firemen scored a run in each of the first three innings—but the Broncos exploded in the bottom of the third for seven runs against Alamo Heights starter Menger, then added three more in the fourth to end Menger's day on the mound. Alamo Heights scored in the fourth and the sixth, but Pankratz shut the Firemen down in the final three innings to preserve a 10–6 Comfort victory,[48] drawing the Broncos (5–3) within one game of the Firemen (6–2). Pankratz yielded 11 hits and seven walks but stopped the Firemen batters when it counted, and he also contributed two hits. Ernst Nagel continued to swing a potent bat for Comfort, knocking out two hits.

On the same day, Bandera defeated Kerrville, 6–3, behind a strong outing by former Kerrville pitcher Wood Thornberry and three hits by second baseman F. Hamilton. Boerne had the day off.[49] Bandera, Kerrville, and Boerne were now all tied for third place—or last place, depending on how one looked at it—each

Figure 28. Bandera Cowboys uniform of Fabian Anderwald. (Courtesy of Audra L. Rose-Kight.)

struggling with a record of 3–5. Alamo Heights had the day off on June 11, so when Comfort traveled to Bandera that day, the Broncos could climb within one-half game of the first place Firemen by defeating the Cowboys. However, Comfort stumbled, losing 2–1 in a game called after six innings due to rain.[50] Comfort protested the decision of the umpires—hired by Bandera, the home team—to stop the game:

> Either Bandera's Umpire [*sic*] didn't know the rules or didn't think, when he pulled a disappearing act in the seventh inning when rain interrupted play. He didn't even think to call the game. In fact, he was one of the first to leave the diamond. The ruling on games of this nature is that the umpire must wait 30 minutes before he can make his decision, and that both teams have to be on hand. All the Comfort boys stayed on the field, and even had the diamond in good shape a half hour after the rain was over. While Bandera left the park as soon as it started.
>
> Their claim to the game is that they were leading after the sixth, and as the seventh was not finished, the score falls back to the last completed inning. Which is true enough only they didn't follow out all of the rule.[51]

Though there is no newspaper report of the league's subsequent decision on the protest, it was presumably denied since Bandera's fourth win—the Cowboys' third in a row—stood for the remainder of the season. This victory moved the Cowboys into sole possession of third place with a 4–5 record. As it turned out, Bandera's truncated win marked the apex of the Cowboys' 1933 season.

As in Comfort, rain wreaked havoc in Boerne that afternoon, but in that case, umpires washed out a likely victory for Kerrville. The Braves were leading the White Sox, 7–0, in the bottom of the fourth inning when it began to rain. The Braves needed to play just one more inning for the game to be considered an official game even if rain ended the contest later. The *Kerrville Mountain Sun* reported that the "raindrops were very gentle," but the umpire (hired by the home team, Boerne) "called it a day," apparently refusing to wait for the rain to dissipate.[52] The rainout meant that instead of a win for Kerrville, the game would be made up between the two clubs at the end of the season. (The Mountain League standings as of June 11 are shown in Table 11.)[53]

Table 11. Mountain League Standings, June 11, 1933

	W	L	GB	Pct.
Alamo Heights	6	2	---	.750
Comfort	5	4	1½	.556
Bandera	4	5	2½	.444
Kerrville	3	5	3	.375
Boerne	3	5	3	.375

Between June 11 and June 18, Kerrville made a major change in its roster after starting pitcher Haskell Archer abruptly left the team to pitch for Comfort. Based on the games for which box scores exist, Archer fashioned a 3–3 record in his time with Kerrville, giving up 68 hits and 34 runs in 60 1/3 innings for a TRA of 5.07.[54] Kerrville added pitcher Harvey Hardy[55] to replace Archer. Hardy pitched well for Mason in 1932, then started the 1933 season with Junction in the Hill Country League. In fact, pitching for Junction early in 1933, Hardy fired a no-hitter against Mason on April 23[56] before leaving the Mountaineers to join the Braves.

It is unknown if Archer jumped to Comfort voluntarily—the Broncos were looking for pitching help and they appeared to be the better team at that point—or whether the Braves acted first by adding Hardy as their primary starter, forcing Archer to look elsewhere to pitch. Whatever the reason for Archer's move to Comfort, he impressed fans in his June 18 debut when the Broncos trounced Boerne, 9–3,[57] improving Comfort's season mark to 6–4. Although Archer yielded 10 hits, he kept the ball on the ground, resulting in two Comfort double plays thanks to some slick fielding by shortstop Ernst Nagel, who also pounded out two hits.[58]

At the same time, Kerrville, looking like an also-ran at that point with a 3–5 record, was anxious to shore up its roster. In addition to Harvey Hardy replacing Archer on the mound, the Braves recruited a new shortstop with a powerful bat, Travis McNair. After the controversial June 11 rainout in Boerne, the Braves had a day off on June 18,[59] so they would have to cool their heels with their two new players until they hosted first-place Alamo Heights on June 25 and second-place Comfort the following Sunday before playing the Firemen again on July 4. Facing the top two teams in the league in the next three games, Kerrville's season was on the brink.

Hardy rose to the challenge when he made his first start against Alamo Heights on June 25, pitching a 4–0 shutout, giving up just four hits, walking none and striking out eight.[60] McNair, hitting in the leadoff spot, also made a favorable impression on Braves fans, contributing two hits in his Kerrville debut.

The next Sunday, the Braves faced Haskell Archer, their erstwhile teammate, when they hosted Comfort. The Braves could manage only eight hits off Archer while Hardy struggled after his brilliant effort against Alamo Heights, giving up 15 hits in a 5–1 Comfort win.[61] Kerrville now stood 4–6 for the season, well behind Alamo Heights (8–3) and Comfort (7–4).

Two days later, the Braves faced Alamo Heights again as part of a July 4 doubleheader played at the Boerne Independence Day celebration at the Kendall

County Fairgrounds.[62] Despite just two days of rest since his loss to Comfort, Hardy pitched even better against the Firemen this time, holding them to just one hit. However, the Firemen managed a run without benefit of a hit in the second inning when they scored on a fielder's choice after Hardy hit two batters with a pitch. It looked like the 1–0 lead might hold up because Firemen lefty Charley Suche stymied the Braves through seven innings. In the top of the eighth inning, the Braves rallied as Jake Goss and Travis McNair rapped singles with one out. First baseman Clergy Hollimon then smashed a two-run double for a 2–1 Kerrville lead. The Braves added a run in the ninth on an error by Firemen third baseman Weston, a sacrifice bunt, and a fielder's choice. Hardy held the Firemen scoreless in the ninth, securing the 3–1 win for the Braves.[63]

Hardy continued to dominate the opposition, defeating Bandera, 8–3, on July 9 to lift the Braves to .500 with a 6–6 mark. Through four games, Travis McNair was hitting .471 (eight hits in 17 at-bats). Thanks to Hardy and McNair, Kerrville was turning its season around.

After Comfort's 5–1 win over Kerrville on July 2, the Broncos braced for another dogfight at Alamo Heights on July 9. Comfort (7–4) was just one-half game behind the first-place Firemen (8–4) who lost to Kerrville in Hardy's pitching gem on July 4. A win would vault the Broncos into first place.

Haskell Archer came into the game having won his first two starts for Comfort, including the 5–1 win over his former teammates at Kerrville. Alamo Heights countered with Menger—an odd choice since Nealon and Suche were both solid pitchers and the Broncos had shellacked Menger in the Firemen's 10–6 loss to the Broncos on June 4.

Archer pitched well until the third when Alamo Heights scored three runs. Menger coughed up two runs in the seventh to cut the Firemen lead to 3–2. After Alamo Heights added a run in the bottom of the seventh, the Firemen brought in Charley Suche to relieve Menger. Suche held them scoreless, then Alamo Heights batters added two runs in the bottom of the eighth for a 6–2 lead. Comfort scored twice in the top of the ninth, but Suche fanned Skeeter Pankratz to end the rally, giving the Firemen a 6–4 win and cementing their position in first place with a one-and-one-half game lead. (Table 12 shows the Mountain League standings as of July 9.)[64]

Table 12. Mountain League Standings, July 9, 1933

	W	L	GB	Pct.
Alamo Heights	9	4	---	.692
Comfort	7	5	1½	.583
Kerrville	6	6	2½	.500
Boerne	4	7	4	.364
Bandera	4	8	4½	.333

On July 16, Kerrville hosted Boerne in a face-off between Hardy and Boerne's Edgar Bergmann, one of the best pitchers in the league despite his team's disappointing record. Boerne scored first after player-manager Clarence Holekamp singled and advanced to second on a wild pitch and then to third on a passed ball. Clarence Bourgeois singled him in for a 1–0 White Sox lead. The Braves knotted the score on an unearned run in the third when leadoff hitter Staudt walked and advanced to second on a sacrifice bunt, then scored on an error by White Sox third baseman Cheese Bremer.

The big blow of the game came in the fifth when newcomer Travis McNair stroked a two-run homer after Hardy singled for a 3–1 Kerrville advantage. The Sox rallied in the sixth. After two outs, Cheese Bremer singled then stole second and trotted home when Hardy fired two wild pitches. Hardy then stiffened, holding the Sox scoreless in the last three innings and earning the 3–2 victory for the Braves. Hardy whiffed nine, limiting the White Sox to just four hits. On the same afternoon, Comfort (8–5) handed Bandera its fourth straight loss, 11–3, to remain one game ahead of the Braves (7–6).

Kerrville enjoyed a day off in the league schedule on July 23[65] while Comfort traveled to Boerne. The Broncos jumped on Edgar Bergmann for four runs in the first inning. But despite their disappointing season, the White Sox (5–7) did not flinch, getting a run back in the bottom of the first and scoring another in the sixth. The White Sox then erupted for four runs on five hits off Haskell Archer in the seventh inning, and they added an insurance run in the eighth. The Braves rallied, scoring a run in the ninth, but Bergmann shut the door for a 7–5 come-from-behind win for Boerne.[66] White Sox left fielder Albert Uecker stroked three hits, including a double. Archer allowed 14 hits to Boerne and issued two bases on balls. The loss dropped Archer's record to 3–2 since joining the Broncos.

On July 30, Kerrville's game at Alamo Heights was rained out. To fill a league off day, Comfort scheduled an exhibition game against the Fredericksburg Giants, still playing in the HCL, but their game was also rained out.

Kerrville (7–6) was one-half game behind Comfort (8–6), but tied in the loss column, as the Braves and the Broncos prepared to meet on August 6 in Comfort.[67] Fans looked forward to another pitching tug-of-war between Harvey Hardy, the new sensation for Kerrville, and Haskell Archer, the former Kerrville hurler. The *Comfort News* proclaimed:

> A very important game of ball will be played on the local diamond Sunday when the Comfort Broncos battle with the Kerrville Braves for second place in the Mountain League. The Home Orchestra will be on hand to urge the local boys on to victory.
>
> This game should be a thriller and deserves the support of the local fans.
>
> Let's be there![68]

Instead of a thriller, the game turned out to be a laugher for Kerrville. Hardy continued his effective hurling, holding Comfort to eight hits and striking out four while the Braves solved Archer's offerings for 13 hits, including three by leadoff hitter Staudt. The Braves were leading, 4–1, after eight innings when they added three insurance runs in notable fashion. After Staudt and Goss singled to open the ninth, they advanced to second and third on a wild pitch. Travis McNair hit a sharp grounder through Bronco third baseman Skeeter Pankratz, scoring Staudt and Goss on the misplay as McNair dashed all the way to third, making it a three-base error. McNair then stole home to cap a decisive 7–1 victory for Kerrville, moving the Braves (8–6) into second place, one-half game ahead of Comfort (8–7). The Braves were now riding a four-game winning streak.

In the meantime, Alamo Heights lost to Boerne, 4–1, as the White Sox continued to play the role of spoiler, improving to a 7–8 record after winning three in a row. Edgar Bergmann shut down the Firemen, holding them to seven hits while Boerne roughed up Firemen hurler Clark Nealon for 10 hits. Sox first baseman Gus Wendler banged out three hits while second baseman Rudy Leidl and shortstop Gus Pfeiffer added two hits each.[69]

Alamo Heights was now 10–5, ahead of Kerrville (8–6) and Comfort (8–7) with three games left in the season. The Firemen traveled to Comfort on August 13. A win by the Firemen would eliminate the Broncos from the pennant race (although they could still tie Kerrville for second place).

This time Charley Suche toed the rubber for Alamo Heights while Joe Pankratz returned to the mound for Comfort, replacing Archer as the starter after the latter had allowed 14 combined runs in his last two starts. Pankratz pitched effectively while Suche had an off day. The Broncos stroked 13 hits, as five hitters contributed two hits, including center fielder Felix Meyer, who hit a double and a triple, scoring three runs. Comfort knocked Suche out of the game in the fourth inning after he gave up six runs, but reliever Nealon did not fare much better, allowing three more runs as the Broncos romped to a 9–4 win over the Firemen.[70]

Kerrville shut out Bandera, 7–0, behind Hardy's nifty two-hitter for the team's fifth straight win. Clergy Hollimon knocked out three hits for the Braves, including a home run.[71] (Table 13 shows the Mountain League standings as of August 13.)[72]

Table 13. Mountain League Standings, August 13, 1933

	W	L	GB	Pct.
Alamo Heights	10	6	---	.625
Kerrville	9	6	½	.600
Comfort	9	7	1	.563
Boerne	7	8	2½	.467
Bandera	4	12	6	.250

Alamo Heights was scheduled for a day off on August 20 while Kerrville and Comfort both played at home, the Braves meeting the White Sox and the Broncos facing the Bandera Cowboys, who had lost seven in a row. If Kerrville and Comfort both won, the Braves would tie Alamo Heights for first and Comfort would stand just one-half game behind.

Archer returned to the mound for Comfort, holding Bandera to seven hits as the Broncos handled the Cowboys, 5–1.[73] Second baseman West, right fielder Paul Weiss, and shortstop Ernst Nagel each contributed two hits to the Broncos' cause.

On the same day, Kerrville faced a more arduous task, facing the White Sox, who were enjoying a late-season resurgence:

> A recent winning streak has placed the White Sox back in the running for championship honors, and the Braves are expecting the stiffest kind of competition in Sunday's joust. By way of assisting to make the league race an extremely tight affair, the Boerne club in its last three tussles defeated Comfort, Bandera, and Alamo Heights. This endeavor scrambled the dope all over the hills and once more made the White Sox a feared foe of all the contending teams.[74]

True to form, fellow hurlers Harvey Hardy and Edgar Bergmann were both sharp in the contest, Hardy yielding eight hits while Bergmann allowed only six. The sole run came in the third inning when Hardy singled and was sacrificed to second before McNair, "the classiest shortstop ever seen hereabouts,"[75] drove him in with his second hit, "a sizzling liner between right and center."[76] Boerne's first baseman Gus Wendler knocked out four of the eight White Sox hits, but Hardy kept the Sox off the scoreboard for a 1–0 victory.[77] With his second shutout in a row, Hardy had now pitched 24 consecutive scoreless innings, raising his league record to 7–1.[78] Boerne center fielder Clarence Bourgeois kept the game close with his impressive defensive play: "A dumpy gent by the name of Bourgeois burglarized the Braves out of at least two safe hits. During the afternoon, he roamed all around the outfield and snared four long drives, two of which ordinarily would have been extra base blows."[79]

Hardy's shutout of the White Sox tied Kerrville with Alamo Heights for first place, both clubs holding 10–6 records. Nearly moribund on July 2 when they were 4–6, the Braves won six in a row, thanks in large part to Hardy's dominance on the mound and McNair's powerful bat. Comfort was only one-half game behind at 10–7. As a result, the Mountain League standings were now closer than ever on August 20, as shown in Table 14.[80]

Table 14. Mountain League Standings, August 20, 1933

	W	L	GB	Pct.
Alamo Heights	10	6	---	.625
Kerrville	10	6	---	.625
Comfort	10	7	½	.588
Boerne	7	9	3	.438
Bandera	4	13	6½	.235

Baseball fans in Alamo Heights, Kerrville, and Comfort were dizzy with pennant fever. Alamo Heights and Kerrville had two games left. The Firemen traveled to Bandera on August 27, then visited Kerrville on September 10 for a makeup of the game rained out on July 30. Both of Kerrville's games were makeup games—at Boerne on September 3 (a makeup game for the rainout on June 11 when Kerrville was leading, 7–0, despite just "very gentle" raindrops) and at home against Alamo Heights on September 10 (the makeup for the rainout on July 30). Comfort had one game left at Boerne on August 27.

The *Comfort News* gleefully reported the possible outcomes in the race for the Mountain League pennant, albeit not entirely accurately:

> If Comfort beats Boerne, the Broncos are sure of a tie, for second place. If Kerrville wins both of its games, the Braves will be on top with Comfort and Alamo Heights for second. If Kerrville loses both games, Alamo Heights will remain on top with Comfort in undisputed possession of second place [assuming Comfort defeated Boerne]. If Boerne beats Kerrville, and Kerrville wins one [against Alamo Heights], the three leading teams will be in a tie for first place [again, assuming Comfort prevailed over Boerne].[81]

As expected, Alamo Heights defeated Bandera, 3–0, as Clark Nealon hurled a four-hit shutout on August 27, although the Cowboys put up a valiant effort despite having lost eight in a row.[82] Bandera pitcher F. Hamilton allowed seven hits, including two each by Firemen shortstop Gus Haycock and catcher Jelly Harris.

On the same day, Boerne hosted Comfort in a must-win game for the Broncos. For some reason, Christie Lindemann started for Comfort rather than Haskell Archer or Joe Pankratz, but it was not Lindemann's day. The White Sox exploded for five runs in the fifth inning, knocking Lindemann out of the game in favor of Archer, but the Broncos could not recover. The White Sox prevailed, 7–4, leaving the Broncos with a final record of 10–8, behind Alamo Heights (now 11–6 after their win over Bandera) and Kerrville (10–6).[83] The *Comfort News* lamented that after this loss, Comfort had only "a very slim chance" for the playoffs since the Braves would have to lose both of their remaining games. This seemed unlikely since "the Braves have been playing exceptionally good ball."[84]

Yet, Kerrville's task was not easy, facing a veteran Boerne club and first-place Alamo Heights in successive makeup games. On September 3, Kerrville traveled to the Kendall County Fairgrounds to meet the White Sox in a matchup of two hot pitchers—Harvey Hardy and Edgar Bergmann. Boerne ace Edgar Bergmann had given up only two runs in his past 18 innings, downing Alamo Heights, 4–1, but losing to Kerrville, 1–0. Boerne was now eliminated from the pennant race, but the Sox were improving after winning three of their last four games—the only blemish in that span was their 1–0 loss to the Braves.

Before the Boerne game, Kerrville's ace pitcher Harvey Hardy and slugging shortstop Travis McNair signed professional contracts with the Beaumont Exporters of the Texas League for 1934:

> Two members of the Kerrville Braves, now engaged in a warm finish fight for the Mountain League champions, will be given spring tryouts with the Beaumont, Texas League club, next March.

> Harvey Hardy, star hurler of the independent league, and Travis McNair, shortstop and balance wheel of the Kerrville infield, have signed contracts with Beaumont and will report to the Exporters next season. Manager Bob Coleman of the Beaumont club has invited McNair to come to San Antonio next Monday and appear in his line-up against the San Antonio Missions in the Labor Day double-header, which will close the Texas League season. A large number of Kerrville fans probably will accompany McNair and watch his debut in class A baseball.
>
> Hardy has won nine out of 10 times hurled for the Braves this season[85] and his consistent mound work came to the attention of the Beaumont club officials, who lost no time in signing both him and McNair. The fast little infielder has a batting record of .447 for the season.[86]

With a professional tryout in his back pocket, Hardy must have been on an emotional high when he took the mound against Boerne, but the White Sox scored in the second inning on a base hit by first baseman Gus Wendler, stopping his scoreless string at 25 innings. The Braves responded in the top of the third when catcher Beaver singled in two runs. The White Sox tied the score at 2–2 in the seventh after Wendler scored on an error by Braves second baseman Morris but Hardy and Bergmann kept the game tied through nine, sending the game to extra innings.

In the bottom of the 12th, Hardy retired the first batter but walked Boerne's Clarence Bourgeois, who advanced to second on a passed ball. After leadoff batter Rudy Leidl was intentionally walked to set up a double play, right fielder Harry Schweppe singled to right, scoring Bourgeois for a 3–2 White Sox win.[87] Hardy suffered just his second loss of the season despite striking out 12 batters. Bergmann earned the win, allowing 10 hits while striking out six.

In spite of the tough loss, the mood of the Braves lightened when Alamo Heights stunned the Hill Country by announcing it was withdrawing from the league to play in the Winter League in San Antonio.[88] Despite Kerrville's loss to Boerne, the exit of Alamo Heights meant that the Braves and Comfort would play for the league title as the top two remaining teams, Kerrville with a record of 10–7 and Comfort at 10–8.

However, Alamo Heights quickly reversed its decision to withdraw. This about-face had two immediate consequences. First, three teams—Alamo Heights, Kerrville, and Comfort—were again competing for two playoff spots (first place and second place). Second, the Braves would now be required to play the Firemen in their makeup game scheduled for September 10.[89] If Kerrville defeated the Firemen, the Braves would tie for the pennant, assuring them of a slot in the league championship series with Alamo Heights. If they lost, Alamo Heights would take first place alone while Kerrville would fall into a tie with Comfort for second place at 10–8, forcing a playoff game between those two clubs for the right to play Alamo Heights for the league title. After a coin flip, Kerrville hosted the game with Alamo Heights.[90] The league supplied umpires from the Southwestern Officials Association, apparently to avoid any bias by the men in blue.[91] The league and the teams agreed to raise the admission price for the game from 25 cents to 35 cents, with both teams splitting the gate evenly.[92]

Harvey Hardy again took the mound for the Braves, while the Firemen tabbed Clark Nealon. The game was tied, 1–1, in the fifth inning when Alamo Heights erupted for four runs on five hits against Hardy. The Braves rallied to plate a run in the fifth inning on Louie Wootton's double then scored three more to tie the game at 5–5 in the sixth, thanks to three Firemen errors combined with a single by Jess Hollimon and a double by Staudt.[93]

Hardy promptly gave up the go-ahead run in the top of the seventh. After walking leadoff batter Crawford, he allowed singles to Jim Riley and Sheridan to score a run. A squeeze bunt by outfielder Turner secured an insurance run. Nealon held the Braves scoreless over the final three innings for a 7–5 victory, grabbing the Mountain League pennant for the Firemen.[94] (The final standings for the 1933 Mountain League are shown in Table 15).[95]

Table 15. Mountain League Final Standings, 1933

	W	L	GB	Pct.
Alamo Heights	12	6	---	.667
Kerrville	10	8	2	.556
Comfort	10	8	2	.556
Boerne	9	9	3	.500
Bandera	4	14	8	.222

With the regular season complete, Kerrville's loss to Alamo Heights dropped it into a tie with Comfort for second place. The "slim chance" of Comfort tying for second place—according to the *Comfort News* two weeks earlier—had in fact come to pass, thanks to Kerrville's two losses in makeup games with Boerne

Figure 29. Comfort Broncos jacket. (Courtesy of Shirley Pankratz Solis.)

and Alamo Heights. The Braves and the Broncos would now meet in a playoff game to determine the opponent for Alamo Heights in the Mountain League championship series. Kerrville again won a coin flip to host the playoff game on September 17.[96]

While the Braves continued to rely on their ace, Harvey Hardy, Comfort made a change. Instead of starting Haskell Archer, who had lost to the Braves, 7–1, on August 6, the Broncos returned Joe Pankratz to the mound. Fans flocked to the game, drawing Kerrville's largest crowd of the season.[97]

Despite the frenzy of the home fans, the game did not start well for the Braves. A muddy diamond from recent rains did not help. Comfort scored first, plating two runs without benefit of a hit in the third inning. After Joe Pankratz reached base when Hardy plunked him with a pitch, he advanced to second on a wild pitch. On a groundball hit by West, Pankratz was caught in a rundown between second and third but eluded his pursuers and scored on an errant throw to third base, while West advanced all the way to third on the play. West then scored when Hardy fielded a groundball but threw wildly to first. After Kerrville scored a run on a double by Morris, Comfort added two runs in the fifth inning on a double by Felix Meyer and a single by Morris Goforth for a 4–1 Comfort lead through seven innings.

For his part, Joe Pankratz dominated Braves hitters, holding Kerrville to just two hits through seven innings, but the pitcher tired in the eighth. He walked leadoff hitter Staudt before allowing a run on singles by Jake Goss, Travis McNair, and Clergy Hollimon. Pankratz then walked in another run to cut Comfort's lead to 4–3 before he escaped the jam.

After the Broncos failed to score in the top of the ninth, the Braves rallied in the bottom half. After one out, Staudt beat out an infield hit. Jake Goss hit a groundball to shortstop Ernst Nagel "with an easy double play in sight,"[98] but the infielder booted the ball for an error, putting the tying and winning runs on base. Pankratz then induced Travis McNair, one of the best hitters in the league, to pop out to short. With two outs, Comfort was one out from advancing to the championship series, but Kerrville first baseman Clergy Hollimon dropped a blooper into the outfield to score Staudt with the tying run. The next batter, Kerrville third baseman Louie Wootton, smashed a sizzling line drive down the third base line to score Goss with the winning run for a thrilling 5–4 victory, sending Kerrville into the championship series against Alamo Heights.[99] The *Kerrville Mountain Sun* boasted that the Braves "slipped into the championship playoff by the margin of a frog's eyebrow."[100]

Fans expected a close championship series between Alamo Heights and Kerrville. While the Firemen had a better regular season record (12–6), the Braves (10–8) derailed the Firemen in three out of the five games between the two clubs.[101] Admission was set at 25 cents for adults and 10 cents for children. The gate from the series would be shared among the two series participants and the other three Mountain League teams. Seventy-five percent of the gate was set aside for the two series teams. The series winner would receive 60 percent of that sum while the losing team would receive 40 percent. The remaining 25 percent of the gate would be shared equally among the other three clubs—Comfort, Boerne, and Bandera.[102]

The first game of the series was scheduled to start on September 24 at Tech Field, the home of the Texas League's San Antonio Missions,[103] but the game was rained out and rescheduled for Wednesday, September 27.[104] The makeup game featured two strikeout artists with professional contracts: Harvey Hardy of Kerrville, whose Mountain League exploits had already been rewarded with a professional tryout for the next season, and Charley Suche of Alamo Heights, the young southpaw who had signed a contract with the Cleveland Indians but deferred his professional career to pursue a college education.[105]

Kerrville struck in the first inning when Staudt, the Braves' speedy leadoff hitter, singled, advanced to second on a walk, stole third base, and scored on an infield out. The Firemen tied the game in the fourth inning on a play that can be described as a "Little League home run." Braves shortstop Travis McNair dropped Gus Haycock's pop fly in short left field for an error, then compounded the misplay by throwing wildly when trying to nab Haycock at second base. Haycock sped all the way home to score on McNair's two errors on the play.

After that, Hardy and Suche traded zeros on the scoreboard as the game remained deadlocked at 1–1 through nine innings. In the bottom of the 10th, Firemen player-manager Jim Riley beat out an infield hit, then Sheridan sacrificed him to second. Hardy walked Jelly Harris before Nealon bunted safely. With the bases loaded, Suche gave himself the victory by hitting a deep sacrifice fly, scoring Riley for a 2–1 win and a 1–0 series lead for Alamo Heights.[106] Hardy struck out 14 in a losing effort, while Suche struck out nine.[107]

The series returned to Kerrville on October 1 where the clubs fought to a 6–6 tie through 12 innings. Pitcher Clark Nealon went the distance for Alamo Heights, but the normally reliable Hardy was not effective on the mound for Kerrville, giving up six runs in the first two-and-one-third innings. Third baseman Louie Wootton relieved Hardy, pitching nine-and-two-thirds innings of scoreless ball which allowed the Braves to rally, tying the score in the seventh on hits by Travis McNair, Louie Wootton, and Hardy.[108]

Neither team scored after the seventh inning, but Kerrville missed some golden opportunities to snatch the victory in the 12th inning. Jess Hollimon started the frame by slugging a double, but on appeal he was called out for missing first base. After Wootton doubled on a deep drive to the outfield, Hardy singled, but Wootton "was held at third and there he was nipped on a throw by [pitcher] Nealon."[109] After Morris lined out to end the threat, the umpire promptly called the game on account of darkness. Baserunning miscues likely cost Kerrville a win.

The tie game would be made up on October 8 as if it were a rainout. That is, a completely new game would be played rather than starting in the 13th inning of the previous game. However, there was some question of where it would be played. Under the original schedule, the third game was to be played on Comfort's diamond, a neutral site. After review, league president H. O. Adler decided the next game would be played at Comfort as the "third game" and that if Kerrville evened the series at 1–1, the pivotal game would be played at Kerrville.[110]

Fireballer Charley Suche returned to the mound for the Firemen while Kerrville countered with Louie Wootton who pitched so effectively in long relief in the tie game.[111] After Kerrville scored a run in the first inning, Alamo Heights scored a run in the fourth and four runs in the fifth for a 5–1 lead. Suche's control faltered in the eighth inning when the Braves scored three runs to close within one run, but the Firemen added two insurance runs in the top of the ninth. Suche, who struck out nine, held the Braves scoreless in the ninth, preserving a 7–4 victory, to win the first Mountain League championship series, two games to none.[112]

Kerrville outhit the Firemen, 11–9, as four Braves slapped two hits apiece (Goss, Hollimon, Wootton, and Beaver). But Suche pitched out of trouble, stranding 14 men on base. The Braves' defense failed them as they committed six infield errors while allowing Alamo Heights six stolen bases.[113] Firemen catcher Jelly Harris banged out three hits, including a triple, while stealing two bases and scoring twice. For Kerrville, Jake Goss, Clergy Hollimon, Louie Wootton, and Beaver each rapped two hits.[114] Firemen shortstop Gus Haycock displayed "some fancy fielding that cut off several runs."[115]

Overall, the first season of the Mountain League was a triumph. Despite the early lead of Alamo Heights, the league enjoyed a riveting pennant race that was not decided until the final game of the season. Kerrville's walk-off win in the second-place playoff game against Comfort could not have been more dramatic. Topping off the season, the championship series gripped Hill Country baseball fans like never before. The rainout of the first game created even more suspense before the thrilling 2–1 win by the Firemen in the makeup game. In the next game, the "what ifs" that baseball fans love to ponder were as prevalent as ever when the two teams fought to a 6–6 tie called for darkness, but not before Kerrville lost several opportunities to win the game due to poor baserunning. After all that, the victory of Alamo Heights in the decisive game was almost anticlimactic.

The success of Alamo Heights can be attributed to a good balance of hitting, speed, and pitching. In the 14 of 18 league games for which statistics were available, Feille hit .362, slamming nine extra-base hits for a .638 slugging percentage, while player-manager Jim Riley hit .370 with five doubles. In just nine games, shortstop Gus Haycock hit .382 with a slugging percentage of .559. Since the Firemen won all four of the league games for which box scores were not found, it is likely that the actual hitting stats of Feille, Riley, and Haycock (and all Firemen hitters for that matter) were even more impressive. The Firemen enhanced their offense with speed, leading the league in stolen bases with 27 (again, in just 14 games). On the mound, Charley Suche and Clark Nealon provided a strong one-two punch. (See Appendix D for team and individual statistics for all Mountain League teams in 1933.)

Kerrville saved its season by adding pitcher Harvey Hardy and shortstop Travis McNair in June. Hardy compiled a 7–3 record in the second half of the season, giving up only 21 runs and striking out 76 batters in 90 innings for an excellent TRA of 2.10. Playing in the last 10 games of the season, McNair hit .341 with a .477 slugging percentage. Several Kerrville regulars contributed as well. First baseman Clergy Hollimon led the team in hits with 22 for a .301 average while right fielder Staudt maintained a torrid pace as leadoff batter, hitting .345.

Comfort struggled on the mound as Haskell Archer disappointed Bronco fans with a 4–3 record after arriving from Kerrville. Comfort's offense was the best in the league. In the 15 league games for which box scores exist, the Broncos scored 108 runs—an average of more than seven runs per game. Left fielder Walter Kutzer fueled the offense from the leadoff spot, hitting .339, while center fielder Felix Meyer hit .345 and new shortstop Ernst Nagel hit .339. Joe Pankratz hit .313 while manning second base and stabilizing the pitching department late in the season, producing an outstanding 4–1 record.

While champion Alamo Heights, along with contenders Comfort and Kerrville, could be proud of their seasons, it was a different story for Boerne. The White Sox, managed by Clarence Holekamp, were surely disappointed with a fourth-place finish. Led by ace pitcher Edgar Bergmann (he crafted a 7–4 record in games for which box scores exist) and four players with batting averages higher than .350 (shortstop Gus Pfeiffer, second baseman Rudy Leidl, left fielder Albert Uecker, and center fielder Clarence Bourgeois), the White Sox should have challenged for the flag. To the chagrin of Boerne fans, however, the White Sox were never in contention. After a 2–1 record early in the season, the White Sox swooned, losing five of six games before rebounding to reach .500 in the last game of the season.

Bandera finished last but briefly gave fans hope in the middle of the season. Starting 1–5, Bandera defeated Boerne, Kerrville, and Comfort in successive games to move into third place, but they lost their last nine games to finish with a 4–14 record. The Cowboys averaged only 3.2 runs per game,[116] lowest in the league, while giving up nearly nine runs a game, in part due to a lack of fielding prowess.[117] Pitcher Wood Thornberry pitched well early in the season, winning three of his first five games, including a 3–1 victory over Boerne in which he struck out 11, and a win over Kerrville, 6–3, when he struck out 14.

However, Thornberry may have hurt his arm at that point in the season because after that, he allowed more than two hits per inning and more than 12 runs per nine innings.[118] Thornberry's ineffectiveness in the last half of the season, combined with a weak offense and spotty fielding, doomed the Cowboys to a last-place finish.

By all accounts, the teams were enthusiastically supported by their fans, especially in Kerrville and Comfort. Certainly, the natural rivalries among Kerrville, Boerne, Comfort, and Bandera boosted fan interest and attendance. In addition, the proximity of league teams, the primary reason the league was formed, benefited the clubs and the players alike with shorter travel times and lower travel expenses. The only disappointment from the 1933 season was that the series between the winners of the Mountain League and the HCL never came to fruition.

In the meantime, all was not well in the HCL in 1933. Fredericksburg withdrew from the league at the end of the first half of the season. The controversy began early in the year when Llano initially withdrew from the league "as a result of the [league] directors' allowance of a forfeit to Mason of the game played between the two clubs . . . on the grounds that Llano used ineligible players."[119] Two weeks later, however, the league reinstated Llano, allowing the Cowboys to retain all players except a pitcher named Goodman.[120] The league then had to decide how to address the two league games (versus San Saba and Fredericksburg) that were missed by the Cowboys due to their temporary withdrawal. In their two-week hiatus from the league, Llano played San Saba and Fredericksburg as originally scheduled but they played them as "exhibition" games.[121] In these "exhibition" games, Llano defeated San Saba, 5–2, on April 16 then lost to Fredericksburg, 13–3, on April 23.[122]

League standings at the end of the first half show Fredericksburg and Llano tied with 9–3 records[123] while the other four teams played 13 games. Llano's 9–3 record included a later "makeup" victory over San Saba in the second game of a doubleheader on June 11 but not the Giants' 13–3 "exhibition" thrashing of the Cowboys on April 23. The *Fredericksburg Standard* claimed that the club managers had agreed before the April 23 "exhibition" game that it would count in the standings if Llano returned to the league.[124] If the "exhibition" game were counted in the league standings, the Giants would win the first-half title, earning a berth in the championship series at the end of the season.

However, the league required Llano to make up both games the Cowboys missed in the regular schedule. Since the Cowboys had already won their makeup game with San Saba, the only makeup game to be played was against

Fredericksburg, thus disregarding the Giants' "exhibition" win on April 23 and giving the Cowboys a second opportunity against the Giants. The league's decision caused league president R. E. Jordan, the sportswriter for the *Fredericksburg Standard*, to resign due to a "[l]ack of harmony and a dilly-dally policy on behalf of the league directorate."[125] At the same time, the Giants protested the decision by withdrawing from the Hill Country League:

> The one act that had quite a bearing on the club's decision to withdraw was the ruling of the league directors to give Llano a chance to make up the two games their club missed while temporarily out of the league on their own motion. This ruling the Fredericksburg directors regarded as a penalty against their own team forced by Llano's failure to carry out its regular schedule.[126]

For the remainder of 1933, Fredericksburg "freelanced" games with other teams, including games against Boerne and Comfort.[127] On September 24, the Giants closed the 1933 season by crushing Boerne, 16–1.[128] Elias Klaerner and Ernst Kott each had three hits for the Giants.[129]

Eden, a small town 30 miles west of Brady, replaced the Giants in the HCL for the remainder of the 1933 season.[130] Despite the withdrawal of the Giants, stalwarts of the league, the HCL completed the 1933 season, albeit with some disruption. One week after Fredericksburg withdrew, Junction, sporting an abysmal 1–14 record (and an overall HCL record of 8–55 since 1931), dropped out of the league, reducing the league to five teams.[131] Although Junction had managed to win only one game before disbanding, their lone victory was memorable—Harvey Hardy's no-hit shutout of Mason, 2–0,[132] before Hardy joined Kerrville in the Mountain League in June.

After Fredericksburg's withdrawal, Llano became the first-half champion with a 9–3 record.[133] Mason (8–3) later edged Llano (8–4) by one-half game to grab the second-half crown, earning the right to challenge the Cowboys for the HCL title.[134] (For the 1933 HCL standings, see Appendix G.)

In the first game at Robinson State Park, pitcher Earl Van Huss settled down after giving up four runs in the third inning to secure a 7–5 win and a 1–0 series lead for Llano.[135] In the second game at Mason, Llano enlisted Fredericksburg star pitcher Hugo Klaerner, who signed a professional contract in July 1933 about the same time the Giants withdrew from the HCL. Klaerner pitched for the Waco Cubs/Pine Bluff Judges of the Dixie League for the remainder of the 1933 season, but after his minor league season ended, Klaerner returned home, playing for the Giants in their last game (their 16–1 whipping of Boerne), then offering his services to Llano. Surprisingly, the HCL did not object to Llano's use of Klaerner for the 1933 championship series despite his professional status. In the second game, Klaerner relieved Llano ace Van Huss in the first inning after the starter issued two walks and allowed a double. Klaerner limited Mason's scoring to one run in the inning, then kept the Mavericks scoreless until the ninth inning when they rallied to score four runs, but Klaerner held on to secure Llano's third consecutive HCL title with a 7–5 win.[136]

The *Llano News* reported that the gate receipts for the championship series were $126 for each game. If admission prices were 25 cents for adults, more than 500 fans attended each game. Although the anticipated series between Llano, the HCL champion, and Alamo Heights, the Mountain League winner, did not happen, Llano did plan to play a series against the Texon Oilers, the West Texas champions for the previous five seasons.[137]

In four seasons, the HCL lost its four most southern teams: Boerne after 1930, Comfort after 1931, Kerrville after 1932, and then Fredericksburg midway through the 1933 season. In the meantime, Boerne, Comfort, and Kerrville formed the Mountain League with Bandera and Alamo Heights, enjoying a dynamic 1933 season. Fredericksburg, a natural rival to Kerrville, Comfort, and Boerne, would soon see fit to join the Mountain League, adding a powerful ballclub, and generating even more fervor among Hill Country baseball fans who eagerly anticipated the 1934 season.

Before proceeding to 1934, however, we first consider a Mountain Leaguer's "day in the sun" in chapter 11 and then survey the rustic ballparks of the Hill Country in chapter 12.

CHAPTER 11

CHARLEY SUCHE

From the Mountain League to the Major Leagues

The Mountain League featured a future major leaguer in its inaugural season. Alamo Heights pitcher Charley Suche was barely 18 years old when he pitched the Firemen to the 1933 league championship. Standing 6′2″ and weighing 190 pounds, the lanky southpaw would pitch for several minor league teams before appearing for the proverbial "cup of coffee" in the major leagues.

The ninth of ten children, Charley was born on August 5, 1915, in Cranes Mill, a small burg in Comal County, Texas.[1] Shortly after he graduated from high school in May 1933, scout Joe Slapnicka signed Suche to a professional contract with the Cleveland Indians with the stipulation that he finish his college education at Baylor University before his pro career began.[2] Since he was still available to play ball during the summer of 1933, Alamo Heights added him to the roster where he played a key role in the championship run of the Firemen.

Suche apparently waived the education contingency in his contract because in 1934, he began pitching in Cleveland's minor league system, winning 19 games for Fargo-Moorhead in the Northern League. He returned to Fargo-Moorhead in 1935, winning 22 games. He met his future wife, Grayce, while pitching for Fargo-Moorhead. Charley and Grayce married in Cass County, North Dakota, on November 8, 1935.

Suche had less success the next two seasons but in 1938,[3] he led Wilkes-Barre of the Eastern League with a 3.10 ERA (despite a 6–13 record), resulting in a late-season call-up by the Cleveland Indians.[4] The Indians were in third place but were out of contention with the first-place Yankees on September 18 when Suche pitched in his sole major-league game.

On that day, future Hall of Famer Bob Feller, just 19 years old, started the second game of a Sunday doubleheader in Cleveland against the Philadelphia Athletics.[5] Feller fashioned a 17–11 record in 1938, but he did not shine this day. The Athletics sent Feller to the showers in the fifth inning after he issued

Figure 30. Charley Suche. (Published under license of Texas Bay Mare.)

five walks and allowed five hits, giving up six runs.[6] Southpaw veteran Al Milnar relieved Feller, but he failed to retire a batter, yielding two walks, two hits, and a wild pitch (although one Philadelphia runner was thrown out at the plate). The Athletics now led, 7–0.[7] With two outs, Cleveland manager Ossie Vitt summoned 23-year-old Suche to the mound for his major-league debut. Suche retired Indians catcher Hal Wagner on a ground out to second base to end the inning.[8]

It so happened that Suche led off the bottom of the fifth inning. Suche smashed a double against Athletics pitcher Bud Thomas. However, Suche's joy over his extra-base hit quickly turned to embarrassment. He was doubled off second base after Lyn Lary hit a line drive to Athletics second baseman Dario Lodigiani.[9]

In the top of the sixth, Suche struck out the first batter, pitcher Bud Thomas, but Athletics slugger Wally Moses doubled, and Billy Werber drove him in with a single before stealing second. Giving up the run must have rattled Suche because he walked the next two batters, Sam Chapman and Nick Etten, to load the bases with one out. Philadelphia's Bob Johnson then stepped to the plate and singled in two more runs. After Suche issued another walk, Irv Bartling singled in the fourth run of the inning. Hal Wagner, up for the second time in the game against Suche, hit a sacrifice fly to center to score Johnson. Suche retired Thomas for the final out after allowing five runs, giving the Athletics a 12–0 lead.[10]

Clay Smith relieved Suche to start the seventh inning but gave up two more runs. After seven innings, the game was mercifully called on account of darkness, resulting in an abbreviated 14–3 Philadelphia victory.[11]

In one-and-one-third innings, Suche walked three and gave up four hits, allowing four runs.[12] Suche remained on the Cleveland bench for the remaining two weeks of the 1938 season. He never appeared again in the majors, leaving him with a lifetime ERA of 27.00. On the positive side, he doubled in his only major-league at-bat for a batting average of 1.000 and a slugging percentage of 2.000.

For the 1939 season, Suche returned to Wilkes-Barre but was traded to Hartford, a Boston Braves affiliate in the Eastern League. He managed a combined record of 8–11 for the season.[13] In 1940, Suche remained in Hartford, dropping to a 4–10 record with a 4.34 ERA.[14] After his disappointing season, he was demoted in 1941 to Boston's Class B affiliate at Bridgeport, a member of the Interstate League. Suche ended his professional career there, posting a 7–11 record with a 3.77 ERA.[15]

Suche played service ball in World War II, where he combined with two other pitchers, Marius Russo and major leaguer Tommy Bridges, to hurl a no-hitter on September 17, 1944.[16] After the war, Suche returned to Texas. According to the 1950 census, Suche lived with Grayce and five-year-old daughter, Janet, in Bandera County. Charley listed his occupation as a "combination man" in the telephone industry.[17]

Suche died on February 11, 1984, in San Antonio, where he is buried in Sunset Memorial Park.[18]

CHAPTER 12

GREEN CATHEDRALS

Hill Country Ballparks

Baseball fans love not just the game of baseball—they also cherish the ballparks where it is played. Indeed, we often imagine baseball as tied to a specific place, usually the ballpark where we first experienced the thrill of a game as youngsters. In our minds, these diamonds become sacred spaces, frozen in time. So, it is not surprising that one of the best baseball books ever published dubbed ballparks as "green cathedrals."[1]

Hill Country town teams played in a variety of "green cathedrals" over the years. Typically, the ballparks were marked by wooden grandstands holding from 200 to 1,000 fans. Many were prominent features of their town such as Fair Park in Fredericksburg and Robinson State Park (now a city park) in Llano. Others no longer feature a baseball diamond, but the grandstands remain for other uses, such as the Kendall County Fairgrounds in Boerne. Still others have disappeared, such as Kerrville's former ballpark, where the space is now occupied by an industrial building. Only hints of Comfort's Faltin Field remain—its location is now a vacant field where one can see faint impressions of the former infield.

Before we turn to the 1934 season, we pause to review the hallowed grounds where the crack of a bat, the smack of a ball in a leather glove, and the chatter of infielders were heard on Sunday afternoons nearly 100 years ago.

BOERNE

In 1910, the Boerne White Sox signed a four-year lease of the property at the northeast corner of what is now North School Street and Johns Road where Boerne Middle School North now stands. The White Sox played their games at this location for several years.[2] In 1913, the Kendall County Fair Association acquired the title to what is now the fairgrounds on River Road. Not long after that, the White Sox moved their games to the fairgrounds, where they played during the Hill Country League and Mountain League eras. The ball field was

Figure 31. Boerne White Sox catcher Harry Phillip outside the Kendall County Fairgrounds. (Courtesy of Tom Phillip.)

located inside a horse racing track. The grandstands overlooked both the horse track and the diamond, as shown in the photograph on p. 141.

Unlike other league ball fields, the fairgrounds diamond did not have a grass infield, resulting in "hot" groundballs for infielders. According to reports by the

Figure 32. White Sox catcher Harry Phillip on the diamond at the Kendall County Fairgrounds. Note the fence for the horse track between the grandstands and the diamond. (Courtesy of Tom Phillip.)

Fredericksburg Standard, the diamond had a "sun field" and a "tricky uphill outfield."[3] The fairgrounds remain in use for the annual Kendall County Fair, but it no longer has a baseball field. Later, starting sometime in the 1940s, the White

Figure 33. Boerne White Sox practice at the Kendall County Fairgrounds. (Courtesy of Tom Phillip.)

Figure 34. A pickoff attempt at the Kendall County Fairgrounds circa 1950. (Courtesy of Patrick Heath Public Library, Boerne, Texas.)

Sox began to play at Bower Field—a baseball diamond located on Johns Road that remains in use today. However, after their move to Bower Field, the White Sox occasionally played at the fairgrounds during the annual Kendall County Fair, as shown in the photograph on p. 142.

COMFORT

In the 1920s and 1930s, the Comfort Broncos played at Faltin Field at the corner of Eighth Street and Main Street. In newspaper advertisements for Comfort ball games in that era, the Broncos' home diamond is referred to as "League Park," but it is believed that League Park and Faltin Field are one and the same. The Broncos played at Faltin Field until the 1940s when they moved to Market Platz (now known as Altgelt Field) on Seventh Street where junior high school football games are now played. In 1950, the Broncos moved again to Comfort Community Park, a new diamond on US Highway 87 North owned by veteran Comfort ballplayer Joe Pankratz. It was the first ballpark in the Hill Country with lights, which attracted teams from San Antonio and other towns. In the 1960s, however, the Kerrville club, now known as the Indians, purchased the ballpark from the Broncos and moved it, piece by piece, to Kerrville.[4]

During the years Comfort played in the Hill Country League (1930–31) and the Mountain League (1933–35), Faltin Field may not have had the same seating capacity and other amenities enjoyed by other diamonds in the Mountain League. Regarding the Mountain League championship series between Fredericksburg and Comfort in 1935, the *Fredericksburg Standard* reported that the Broncos' home field "does not have the proper seating and other facilities necessary for a championship game."[5] After the Broncos left Faltin Field, the land was given to the Comfort school district by Albert Faltin and used as a high school baseball diamond for many years. Today, Faltin Field is flat, open land bordered by a community garden, but one can still see an area of brown dirt that may have served as the infield for Faltin Field.

FREDERICKSBURG

The Giants played their home games at Fair Park in the heart of the city. Like Boerne's diamond at the Kendall County Fairgrounds, the diamond at Fair Park was surrounded by a horse racing track. Occasionally, horse races and baseball games would be held on the same day. Today the site is occupied by an H-E-B grocery store and the remnant of Fair Park, known now as Old Fair Park, located near the intersection of East Ufer Street and South Lincoln Street. Old Fair Park contains lighted baseball and softball diamonds.

Figure 35. Comfort's Faltin Field. (Courtesy of Comfort Heritage Foundation, Inc., Comfort, Texas.)

Figure 36. Comfort Broncos, 1924. Top row (L–R): manager Ernst Doebbler, Chester Faltin, Bill Pape, Walter Stahmann, Edgar Steves, Udo Schellhause, Arthur Bergmann, scorekeeper Jim Saylor. Bottom row (L–R): Buck Nowlin, F. M. "Pat" Faust, Guy Reese, Morris Goforth, Joe Pankratz, Felix Meyer, Bill Haufler. This photograph was likely taken at Faltin Field. (Courtesy of Comfort Heritage Foundation, Inc., Comfort, Texas.)

KERRVILLE

In 1922, the Kerrville Black Athletics played a game at the "Fair Grounds," which may have been the grounds of the West Texas Fair held in Kerrville for several decades starting in 1899.[6] The site was on the river side of the intersection of Water Street and Junction Highway, called Five Points.[7]

Before 1925, the Kerrville Athletics played at a ballpark located in the 1600 block of Broadway and Water Street.[8] The main entrance was at the corner of Broadway and G Avenue.[9] However, in 1923, the Kerrville Athletics played Junction at the Fair Grounds while their ballpark was occupied by a Presbyterian Encampment.[10] This became a recurring problem so the next year, the Athletics moved their games to a temporary site at the northeast corner of McFarland and Paschal. The team removed the stands from the old diamond on Broadway but there was no money to reconstruct them at the new location. The Athletics did, however, construct temporary stands there to allow the team to finish the 1924 season.[11]

In January 1925, Kerrville businessman Ben Smith came to the rescue by forming a plan to construct permanent stands, dugouts, and fences after procuring a ten-year lease on the property. Smith secured a pledge of $3,000 from Kerrville banker and businessman Louis A. Schreiner conditioned upon other businessmen raising an additional $1,000 to cover the $4,000 cost of construction.[12] Smith's plan succeeded, enabling him to supervise the completion of the new ballpark in time for the Athletics' 1925 season. The ballpark, containing two grandstands (one holding 500 fans and the other holding 200 fans),[13] was christened with a doubleheader before a sellout crowd on April 5. In the first game, the Athletics lost to a US Army base team, Kelly Field, 2–1, while in the nightcap, the Black Athletics and another Black team, U.S. Tire Chain Company, were tied, 3–3, when the game was called in the fifth inning due to darkness.[14] The *Kerrville Mountain Sun* was effusive in its praise of the new park, commenting that "[n]o city in Southwest Texas has a better ball park."[15]

The ballpark at McFarland and Paschal hosted Kerrville's first major-league game in 1930 when, as discussed in chapter 4, the New York Giants and Chicago White Sox traveled from San Antonio to play an exhibition game won by the White Sox, 9–6.[16] The site was no longer used as a ballpark when the Schreiner Wool and Mohair Commission Company completed a large warehouse at that location in 1937.[17] It is not known where the Kerrville Braves played after that. Today the site is occupied by a plumbing business. After 1941, the Kerrville All-Stars, as the Black team was later known, played at Carver Park at 820 Webster.[18]

The Legion Cubs, who played independently before joining the Mountain League in 1935, played their home games on the Veterans Administration Hospital grounds in Kerrville.[19] Federal regulations prohibited the Cubs from charging admission fees to their games, so the club could generate funds to cover expenses only by asking fans for voluntary donations.

LLANO

In 1924, Isaiah and Naomie Robinson conveyed title to 42.5 acres on the south side of the Llano River to the state of Texas for a new state park to be named after the Robinsons.[20] The property featured live oak and pecan trees as well as pens that had once held herds of cattle before ranchers drove them north to market.[21] Before giving title to the state, the Robinsons used the property for public recreation purposes such as picnics, barbecues, and Independence Day celebrations.[22] As a result, this property was known to Llano residents as the "picnic grounds." Due to its prior recreational use and its natural beauty, the property was well suited for a state park.

During the 1930s, the Llano Cowboys played baseball at Robinson State Park on the former "picnic grounds."[23] Since there was no fence on the diamond, automobiles parked beyond the outfielders. A batted ball that rolled into the parked automobiles was a ground rule double, limiting runners to two bases. As noted in chapter 4, this ground rule affected the outcome of at least one game when a runner on first base was required to return to third base, instead of scoring, on a hit into the parked automobiles.

After the Hill Country League disbanded following the 1936 season, the ball field was occasionally used as a landing strip for airplanes.[24] In 1953, the park was acquired by the city of Llano.[25] The city still operates the park today as Robinson City Park.

BANDERA

The location of the ballpark in Bandera is not definitively known, but the most likely site for the diamond in Bandera is the southeast corner of 14th Street and Cypress where Hevenor Feed & Supply is located today. An aerial photograph circa 1920 seems to confirm this, showing an open field with the faint outline of a diamond.

CHAPTER 13

A BUNCH OF SANDLOTTERS

Mountain League, 1934

As the calendar turned to 1934, economic prospects brightened a bit in the Hill Country. The projected mohair market was strong.[1] With robust prices, Texas was expected to produce five-and-one-half million pounds of mohair, with Kerrville's Schreiner Wool and Mohair Commission Company alone generating one million of those pounds.[2]

However, bank robberies remained a concern, perhaps because the infamous Texas outlaws, Bonnie Parker and Clyde Barrow, known usually just as Bonnie and Clyde, inspired a rash of criminality.[3] On February 2, three heavily armed men robbed the Coleman National Bank in Coleman, Texas, 50 miles north of Brady.[4] The robbers briefly kidnapped six bank employees but released them after the criminals escaped south into the Hill Country with $24,000.[5] The Texas Rangers engaged in a fierce gunfight with one of the robbers on the road between Johnson City and Blanco. The Rangers fired a machine gun, but the bandit escaped "in a hail of bullets."[6] Several days later, all three robbers were apprehended and arrested.[7] A bank robbery in Marble Falls[8] and the assault and robbery of a truck driver by Comfort youths[9] reminded Hill Country residents that times remained desperate for some.

In early 1934, baseball in the Hill Country was in a state of flux. Both the HCL and the Mountain League faced the departure of top-notch teams before the 1934 season. In the HCL, Fredericksburg withdrew in the middle of the 1933 season, but the league dearly wanted the Giants—one of the best teams in the league—to return to the fold. In the Mountain League, the 1933 champion, Alamo Heights, decided to join the Class A Bexar County (San Antonio) League for the 1934 season.[10] The Mountain League clubs viewed Fredericksburg as the natural choice to replace Alamo Heights because Kerrville, Comfort, and Boerne were all established rivals of the Giants—ball games with those clubs drew large crowds. Where the Giants would land was critical to the fortunes of both leagues.

As part of its effort to woo Fredericksburg, the HCL invited the Giants to attend the annual league meeting scheduled for late January 1934 in Llano.[11] By then, however, Fredericksburg had already decided to join the Mountain League. The Giants, undoubtedly impressed by the league's engrossing pennant race in 1933, could not pass up the chance to renew its internecine battles with Kerrville, Comfort, and Boerne. On January 23, 1934, the Mountain League formally approved Fredericksburg's addition to replace Alamo Heights.[12]

The Mountain League hoped to add a sixth team in 1934 to eliminate the off Sundays that result from a five-team schedule. At a meeting on March 6, 1934, the league invited the Hondo Bronchos to join the league.[13] Hondo was piloted by Al Hollmig, the popular former Giants player.[14] However, nothing came of this attempt to add the team.

Despite the Mountain League's failure to attract a sixth team, the prospects for a successful season were good. The incoming Giants were a formidable team. They won the 1930 HCL championship and played in the HCL championship series in 1931. Although Fredericksburg slumped in 1932, the Giants were in first place when they withdrew from the HCL in 1933. Adding the Giants was indeed a feather in the cap for the Mountain League.

Fredericksburg's roster from the tumultuous 1933 season was mostly intact for the upcoming campaign, but the Giants lost their star pitcher, Hugo Klaerner, when he signed a professional contract with the Chicago White Sox in July 1933.[15] Since Hugo was now a professional, his brother, Chester "Smokey" Klaerner, was expected to step into Hugo's role as the Giants' ace pitcher. Chester was a top-flight pitcher and older brother of right fielder Alfons Klaerner. As insurance, the Giants returned veteran pitcher Rod Sanders to their roster. Third baseman Elias Klaerner and pitcher-outfielder Phillip Klaerner, cousins to Hugo, Chester, and Alfons,[16] also returned for 1934 along with hard-hitting outfielder Edgar Klett. To prepare for the season, the Giants played an exhibition game against the Deike Brothers all-brother team on March 25.[17]

The Boerne White Sox were looking for redemption in 1934. Although they fielded a seasoned team, the Sox finished the 1933 season at 9–9 in fourth place—not good enough for Clarence Holekamp's talented squad. Like Fredericksburg, the White Sox boasted two sets of siblings. Edgar Bergmann toed the rubber for the White Sox as their ace pitcher, while his younger brother Walter waited in the wings. Although Edwin Uecker and his twin brother, Albert, were now over

30 years old and would play backup roles in 1934, their younger brother Johnny Uecker was ready to step in at third base. Another brother, August "Tuddy" Uecker,[18] took over as catcher. The White Sox also counted on second baseman Rudy Leidl, shortstop Gus Pfeiffer, center fielder Clarence Bourgeois, and left fielder Harry Schweppe as key players in their pursuit of the 1934 flag.

Kerrville lost to Alamo Heights in the 1933 championship series, but the Braves' hopes for 1934 suffered a catastrophe—a nearly complete turnover of their roster. It is not clear why this occurred except that both Harvey Hardy, the pitcher who carried the Braves to the 1933 championship series, and Travis McNair, their powerful shortstop, had signed professional contracts with the Beaumont Exporters of the Texas League for the 1934 season. Star third baseman-pitcher Louie Wootton, along with catcher Jess Hollimon and his brother, first baseman Clergy Hollimon, left the club to play for the Legion Cubs, an independent team.[19] Only four players (and only two regulars, outfielder Monk Warren and Jake Goss, who would serve as player-manager) returned from the 1933 season, requiring a move to enlist younger players including Warren Toler, a hard-throwing young southpaw.[20] It remained to be seen whether the youth movement would bear fruit for Kerrville. However, the Braves did add a solid player in Jim Riley, former player-manager of Alamo Heights. Catcher Ben Grantham also returned to the team,[21] but he ended up playing only two games for the Braves in 1934.

After tying for second place in 1933, the Comfort Broncos hoped to reach the next level. Unlike the Kerrville Braves, who defeated the Broncos in the 1933 second-place playoff game, Comfort returned most of its roster in 1934. The team again featured the Pankratz brothers—pitcher-shortstop Joe Pankratz and third baseman Skeeter Pankratz. Another set of Bergmann brothers—catcher Arthur Bergmann and center fielder Harry Bergmann[22]—together with left fielder Walter Kutzer, second baseman West, and center fielder Felix Meyer, constituted a well-balanced offense that led the league in runs the previous season. The Broncos tapped Christie Lindemann as their top pitcher for 1934 since Haskell Archer did not return to the club, although Joe Pankratz would also see some action on the mound.

The good news for the Bandera Cowboys heading into 1934 was that many of the players returned from the 1933 team, but after finishing in last place with a 4–14 mark, the Cowboys hoped for significant improvement from their nucleus of players led by pitcher-second baseman F. Hamilton, shortstop Bob Mansfield, catcher Thallman, and second baseman Billings. After a difficult 1933 season, pitcher Wood Thornberry did not return.

For the 1934 season, the schedule consisted of 16 games—two games fewer than 1933—starting on April Fools' Day and running through August 12. Unlike the "unbalanced" schedule in 1933, each team would play an equal number of games (four) against every other team.

The season opened with high hopes in all five towns. Fredericksburg won its first league game with a thrilling victory over Comfort at Fair Park. The Giants had to rally to grab the victory. Comfort pitcher Joe Pankratz was holding a 3–1 lead in the seventh when the Giants tied the game after Chester Klaerner tripled and scored before Elias Klaerner also crossed home plate on a throwing error by left fielder Walter Kutzer. The Giants won the game when Edgar Klett led off the 10th with a base hit that he stretched into a double. After Klett advanced to third on a fly ball, Chester Klaerner tapped a single into right field to give the Giants a 4–3 victory in their first Mountain League contest.[23] Rod Sanders earned the complete game victory.

In the other Opening Day game, Edgar Bergmann pitched a four-hit shutout, leading Boerne over Kerrville, 9–0. Five White Sox hitters—second baseman Rudy Leidl, shortstop Gus Pfeiffer, first baseman Gus Wendler, third baseman Johnny Uecker, and left fielder Albert Uecker—stroked two hits each. Bandera had the first Sunday off—the consequence of a five-team circuit.

It did not take long for the cream to rise to the top of the league. Fredericksburg won its first five games, including a 28–1 drubbing of Bandera on April 15 and a 23–1 victory over Kerrville on May 6. In the latter game, catcher-outfielder Alfons Klaerner knocked out five hits including two doubles and a home run.[24] The following Sunday, the Giants crushed Kerrville, 19–10. Right fielder Red Schnerr drove in five runs on three hits, including a double and a triple, while center fielder Edgar Klett and pitcher Elias Klaerner slammed home runs.[25]

Boerne won its first six games. Like the Giants, the White Sox achieved two lopsided victories early in the season, 17–1, over Bandera on May 6, and 15–1 against Comfort on May 13, when the White Sox bombed Bronco pitcher Joe Pankratz for 14 hits and 15 runs in the first three innings.[26] Shortstop Gus Pfeiffer rapped three hits, including a double and triple, to lead the Sox.[27]

The first showdown between the undefeated Giants (5–0) and White Sox (6–0) took place on May 20 at Boerne's home diamond at the Kendall County Fairgrounds. The Giants took a 3–1 lead against Boerne pitcher Arthur Schulze before Edgar Bergmann relieved him in the fourth with one out and the bases loaded. Bergmann retired the side without further damage then stifled the Giants' hitters with his curveball, allowing only three singles over five-and-two-thirds innings of relief. The White Sox added a run in the fourth on a single by Gus Pfeiffer after Rudy Leidl doubled. Down 3–2 in the bottom of the seventh, Tuddy Uecker (brother of Albert, Edwin, and Johnny) slammed a two-run triple off Chester Klaerner for a 4–3 lead.[28] Bergmann stopped the Giants over the final two innings, preserving the win and giving the Sox sole possession of first place with a 7–0 record.[29]

While Boerne and Fredericksburg started the season with winning streaks, Kerrville and Bandera struggled mightily. After the Braves lost to Fredericksburg, 19–10, on May 13, they were 0–6 as their young players struggled. The Cowboys stood 0–4 after they lost to Boerne on May 6, 17–1. One of the clubs would earn its first win when Kerrville traveled to Bandera on May 20.

Davenport, Bandera's best pitcher, started against Kerrville's Gowen who was making his first appearance on the mound. After Kerrville plated a run in the first, Bandera pounced on Gowen. Catcher Thallman started the Cowboys' rally with a single. Knibbe tripled before Davenport slapped a two-run single. An error by Braves second baseman Jim Riley (the former player-manager of Alamo Heights), a triple by F. Hamilton, and a single by third sacker Cravey completed the Cowboys' five-run inning, knocking out Gowen. With that cushion, Davenport cruised to an 8–1 win, dropping the Braves to 0–7 and setting up the rematch between the clubs the following Sunday in Kerrville.[30]

Unlike the first game between the two clubs, the second game on May 27 was close, necessitating extra innings. This time, the Braves started lefty Warren Toler against right-hander Clay Wright for the Cowboys. The clubs traded unearned runs in the first inning before the Cowboys snagged another in the third when third baseman D. Gray scored on an error after smashing a double.

Wright held onto the 2–1 Bandera lead until the ninth inning. Kerrville first baseman Zeke Myers started the inning by beating out an infield hit. Second baseman Larrimore sent Myers to third with a double, which brought F. Hamilton from second base to the mound in relief of Wright. Kerrville catcher George Brown greeted Hamilton with a game-tying single, but Hamilton settled down to squelch any further scoring, sending the game to the 10th inning.

Toler shut down the Cowboys in the top of the 10th, giving up a harmless single by Hamilton. Braves center fielder Louis Fisher[31] led off the bottom of the 10th with a single and moved to second on a wild throw by F. Hamilton on a grounder. After Fisher was bunted to third, Myers laid down a squeeze bunt to score Fisher with the winning run, rewarding the Braves with a nail-biting 3–2 victory.[32] The *Kerrville Mountain Sun* reported that the win aroused the generosity of local businessmen, who offered players "drinks on the house" in more than one establishment after the game.[33] Bandera remained in fourth place with a 1–5 mark, but Kerrville (1–7) had at least broken into the win column.

Bandera's loss left the Cowboys one game behind Comfort. The Broncos stood at 2–4 after losing two games each to Fredericksburg and Boerne, including the humiliating 15–1 loss to the White Sox on May 13. After Joe Pankratz faltered as the team's pitcher early in the season, giving up 15 runs in three innings to the White Sox, the Broncos returned to Christie Lindemann who steadied the mound corps. Comfort proceeded to win three of its next four games, including two victories over Kerrville. Third baseman Skeeter Pankratz, catcher Arthur Bergmann, and center fielder Felix Meyer led the offense as the Broncos scored a season-high 12 runs in a shutout shellacking of Kerrville on June 10[34] after bouncing Bandera, 8–5, the previous week.[35] After 10 games, the Broncos posted a 5–5 mark, but they remained well behind the pace set by the front-running Giants and the White Sox.

After Boerne dropped Fredericksburg to second place with the 4–3 win on May 20, the Giants edged Comfort, 3–2, in 10 innings on May 27, rallying to tie the score in the ninth before right fielder Stahl singled home the winning run in the 10th.[36] Comfort's Joe Pankratz, now playing shortstop after losing his role as starting pitcher, stroked three hits in the losing effort.[37] Fredericksburg's narrow victory improved their record to 6–1, setting up a rematch with undefeated Boerne on June 3.

With aces Chester "Smokey" Klaerner and Edgar Bergmann on the mound, fans expected another close contest, but the Giants blew the game open in the second inning. After the Giants scored a run on an error, Bergmann hit Giants second sacker Henry Langerhans with a pitch and gave up a run-scoring single to Giants catcher Felix Hahn. Chester Klaerner then contributed to the cause by slugging a three-run home run to right field, making the score 5–0.[38]

After the Giants added a run in the third, Elias Klaerner launched a two-run homer in the following inning, increasing the lead to 8–0. Klaerner's blast was "the longest home run to left center that was ever driven out on the local lot."[39] Chester Klaerner shut out the White Sox, scattering seven hits while cruising to an easy 11–0 win. The Giants were now tied with the White Sox for first place, both clubs sporting identical 7–1 records. (Table 16 shows the Mountain League standings at the midpoint of the season.)[40]

Table 16. Mountain League Standings, 1934 (midpoint)

	W	L	GB	Pct.
Fredericksburg	7	1	---	.875
Boerne	7	1	---	.875
Comfort	3	4	3½	.429
Bandera	1	6	5½	.143
Kerrville	1	7	6	.125

Over the next four Sundays, both the Giants and the White Sox went undefeated. Fredericksburg's wins included a 14–1 laugher over Kerrville on July 4, a game in which the Giants stole nine bases (four by Phillip Klaerner) and drew nine walks,[41] and a 20–3 decimation of Comfort on July 8, when eight players had two or more hits.[42] Boerne's four wins included a 16–0 crushing of Kerrville on July 8,[43] but three weeks earlier, Comfort had managed to throw a scare into the White Sox. Boerne eked out a 3–2 win over the Broncos, thanks to Johnny Uecker's four hits, including a triple and a home run.[44]

By mid-July, the Giants and White Sox were headed for another first-place face-off, with both clubs carrying 11–1 records. Tensions were high as the clubs took the field in Boerne on July 15. The *Fredericksburg Standard* reported that the Kendall County sheriff had added special deputies for the game but this "did not seem to bother Manager Saenger's charges."[45]

For the third time this season, Chester "Smokey" Klaerner matched up with Edgar Bergmann in a contest of the two best pitchers in the league. The White Sox threatened to score when Johnny Uecker opened the second inning with a long triple. However, when Harry Phillip hit a pop fly into shallow center, Giants second baseman Henry Langerhans made the catch, then whirled and fired a strike to catcher Felix Hahn, nabbing Uecker at the plate for a double play.

The Giants got on the scoreboard in the third inning when Chester Klaerner scored on a groundout after advancing to third on a tailor-made double play grounder that White Sox shortstop Gus Pfeiffer misplayed. The Giants added to their lead in the sixth. After one out, third baseman Lawrence Peter doubled before Elias Klaerner singled, sending Peter to third. When Elias Klaerner stole second, the catcher's throw bounced into center field, allowing Peter to score. Edgar Klett tripled, scoring Elias Klaerner, before Alfons Klaerner drove in Klett to give the Giants a 4–0 lead. Langerhans singled but Bergmann got out of the inning when Hahn hit a line drive to third baseman Johnny Uecker, who doubled Alfons Klaerner off third base.[46]

Fredericksburg added two insurance runs in the seventh. With the bases loaded, Pfeiffer misplayed another groundball,[47] allowing a run to score, then Edgar Klett hit a sacrifice fly to increase the lead to 6–0. The White Sox scored on a groundout in the seventh but could manage no further damage against Chester Klaerner who allowed seven hits, walking none and striking out six en route to a 6–1 victory, dropping Boerne to second place with a 11–2 record with just three Sundays left in the season.[48]

After a week off, the White Sox would meet the Giants for the last time on July 29. Since early in the season, it had been a foregone conclusion that the Giants and the White Sox would meet in the championship series as the top two teams in the league, but both teams sought home-field advantage as well as bragging rights that the pennant would confer.

While the Giants and the White Sox competed for first place, the struggle to avoid the cellar remained as tight as ever. After games on July 8, Bandera held a 1–10 record while Kerrville stood at 1–11. Their only wins were against each other; the teams split their first two games on May 20 and May 27. The Braves and the Cowboys were scheduled to play again on July 15 in Bandera and July 22 in Kerrville. There is no box score for the July 15 game, but Bandera won in front of its home crowd, 8–4,[49] giving the Cowboys a 2–10 record, one-and-one-half games ahead of the Braves. The *Kerrville Mountain Sun* reported that Crooks pitched well for the Braves, but Kerrville errors and timely Bandera hits led to the defeat.[50] Bandera's D. Gray went the distance on the mound to earn the win.

Kerrville was eager to avenge its loss the following Sunday on the Braves' home field. Warren Toler, the young portsider, started for the Braves, while the Cowboys countered with Davenport, their most consistent pitcher. Eight errors by the Cowboys would be their undoing.

The Braves pounced on Davenport in the first inning. Leadoff hitter McBryde singled. After advancing on an infield out, McBryde scored on a single by player-manager Jake Goss. With two outs, Brown singled, sending Goss to third who then scored on an error for a 2–0 lead. In the second, Toler aided his own cause by singling, advancing on an error, and scoring on a double by right fielder Monk Warren for a 3–0 lead, knocking Davenport out of the box. The Braves added a run in the fourth when Larrimore reached first on an error, advanced to second on another error, and scored on Warren's single.

The Cowboys managed only five hits off Toler, who struck out eight. Bandera's only run came in the sixth on a sacrifice fly with the bases loaded and none out, but Toler fanned Thallman and induced Billings to ground out, ending the threat. Toler shut down the Cowboys in the last three innings to earn the 4–1 win for the

Braves.[51] Bandera dropped to a 2–11 record but was still one-half game ahead of Kerrville (2–12) with one game left in the season. Bandera had an easier task in their final game, playing Comfort on July 29 while Kerrville faced the juggernaut Giants on August 5 after a week off.

In late July, all that remained of the season was the pennant race between Fredericksburg and Boerne. After the White Sox lost to the Giants on July 15, they enjoyed an off day on July 22 while Fredericksburg shortstop Louis Schneider smacked four hits to lead the Giants to a 13–6 win over Comfort.[52] The victory over the Broncos gave the Giants a 13–1 record, one-and-one-half games ahead of Boerne, holding an 11–2 mark. On July 29, Boerne traveled to Fredericksburg for a crucial game. Since only two games remained in the season, a Giants victory would clinch the pennant.

For the fourth time this season, Edgar Bergmann faced Chester "Smokey" Klaerner on the mound. Like in the July 15 contest, the Giants broke the game open early against Bergmann. Chester Klaerner opened the bottom of the third inning with a single. After an error by shortstop Gus Pfeiffer, Smokey scored when center fielder Clarence Bourgeois muffed a fly ball hit by Phillip Klaerner, but Bourgeois recovered to throw out Klaerner at second base. Lawrence Peter and Elias Klaerner both singled, scoring another run. Edgar Klett doubled, scoring Peter, but Elias Klaerner was thrown out at the plate. Alfons Klaerner then slammed a two-run home run for a 5–0 lead by the Giants.

The Giants added a run in the fourth on three errors and a single by Phillip Klaerner. Down 6–0, Sox pitcher Arthur Schulze relieved Bergmann in the fifth, but the Giants struck for three more runs on a run-scoring single by Felix Hahn and a two-run double by Smokey Klaerner for a 9–0 advantage. Boerne managed two runs in the eighth inning. With runners on second and third, Rudy Leidl hit a foul pop fly into right field, which second baseman Henry Langerhans caught but he threw the ball into the Giants' dugout, allowing both runners to score. Smokey Klaerner then shut the door, holding the Sox to six hits, striking out three in the 9–2 victory.[53] Fredericksburg took its third consecutive game from Boerne, improving to a 14–1 record and clinching the pennant as Boerne dropped to 11–3.

Fredericksburg and Boerne both finished the regular season with shutouts on August 5. The Giants crushed Kerrville, 22–0, when Phillip Klaerner gave up just one hit.[54] Giants left fielder Edgar Klett smashed two home runs and a double against the outmatched Braves, and second baseman Henry Langerhans hit a home run and a double while stealing four bases. The *Fredericksburg Standard* lamented Kerrville's decline on the diamond in 1934:

> A bunch of "sand lotters" that started clowning before the game started, and got worse as the game progressed put on a poor exhibition of baseball at Fair Park last Sunday. Just why Kerrville should be represented by such a club we can't understand. Formerly all athletic contests, and especially baseball, between Fredericksburg and Kerrville were a sight to see. There is no doubt but what they were "a sight" last Sunday, but not to see. Shades of the "old spirit" were evident when Kerrville's grandstand first baseman [Myers] left the field after an umpire's decision. Men of his caliber, that refuse to take the umpires ruling, are better off in the dugout.[55]

Not to be outdone, Boerne finished the regular season by downing Comfort, 11–0.[56] Edgar Bergmann returned to form, shutting out the Broncos on seven hits while Sox third baseman Johnny Uecker drove in four runs and right fielder Paul Weiss (a former Comfort player) and center fielder Clarence Bourgeois each contributed three hits.

The Giants finished with a 15–1 record, ahead of Boerne at 12–3.[57] Kerrville's loss to the Giants left them in last place with a 2–13 record, one-half game behind Bandera who had finished the season on July 29 with a loss to Comfort, 7–5, ending with a 2–12 record. After reaching the .500 mark at 5–5, Comfort lost three of its last four games—two to the Giants and one to the White Sox—to finish third with a 6–8 mark, a disappointing season for the Broncos after tying for second place in 1933 with a winning record (10–8). (The final 1934 Mountain League standings are shown in Table 17.)[58]

Table 17. Mountain League Final Standings, 1934

	W	L	GB	Pct.
Fredericksburg	15	1	---	.938
Boerne	12	3	2½	.800
Comfort	6	8	8	.429
Bandera	2	12	12	.143
Kerrville	2	13	12½	.133

At the conclusion of the regular season, a coin flip decided that the first game of the championship series between Fredericksburg and Boerne would be played at Fredericksburg's Fair Park on August 12.[59]

Hill Country fans could not have hoped for a better game to start the series—yet another showdown between Fredericksburg's Chester Klaerner and Boerne's Edgar

Bergmann. The Giants scored in the bottom of the first, when Edgar Klett smashed a double after Phillip Klaerner singled. The Sox countered with a run in the fourth. After Rudy Leidl hit a two-bagger off the glove of center fielder Elias Klaerner, Harry Schweppe walked and Gus Wendler singled to left, scoring Leidl to tie the game.

The Sox grabbed a 3–1 lead in the fifth when they scored two runs on singles by Gus Pfeiffer, Paul Weiss, Edgar Bergmann, and Rudy Leidl. The Giants cut the lead in half in the bottom of the fifth. After Elias Klaerner stole second base with two outs, he scored when Klett beat out an infield hit and third baseman Johnny Uecker threw wildly to first base for an error.

With the White Sox leading 3–2 in the top of the eighth, Leidl singled and advanced to second on a passed ball, scoring when Wendler's fly ball fell safely for a double. The Giants responded in the bottom of the inning. Henry Langerhans doubled and Deike[60] singled him to third. Felix Hahn hit a deep sacrifice fly to score Langerhans, cutting the lead to 4–3, heading into the ninth.

The White Sox failed to score in the top of the ninth, but they were just three outs away from taking the first game of the series. To the consternation of White Sox fans, Bergmann could not hold the lead as doubles by brothers Phillip Klaerner and Elias Klaerner tied the score, sending the game to extra innings.

With Fredericksburg fans sitting anxiously on the edge of their seats, Chester Klaerner walked Schweppe to start the 10th inning. After advancing to second on another passed ball—Giants catcher Felix Hahn had four passed balls in the game—Johnny Uecker singled and when right fielder Deike "was slow in returning the ball, Schweppe scored."[61] A force out and a double play ended the inning but for the second time in two innings, the White Sox held a one-run lead with just three outs needed for a victory.

In the bottom of the 10th, Bergmann struck out Deike while Hahn grounded out to Bergmann. With two outs and the bases empty, Chester Klaerner worked a walk. Bergmann got two strikes on leadoff hitter Louis Schneider, but Schneider smashed a line drive to right. Boerne right fielder Paul Weiss "came in fast but the ball hopped badly and rolled nearly to the racetrack fence with Weiss in hot pursuit as C[hester] Klaerner romped home with the tying run,"[62] and Schneider followed him across the plate for a game-winning, inside-the-park home run.[63]

It was a devastating 6–5 loss for Boerne manager Clarence Holekamp and the White Sox. Chester Klaerner did not have his best stuff and twice they were on the verge of winning in the final inning, but they failed to nail down the victory. The second game of the series was scheduled for the following Sunday, August 19, in Boerne.

The clubs took the field at the Kendall County Fairgrounds before "one of the largest crowd [*sic*] ever assembled to witness a championship contest in the Hill

Country."[64] Unlike in the first game, Chester Klaerner and Edgar Bergmann both pitched effectively, but five errors by the Boerne infield (three by shortstop Gus Pfeiffer and two by third baseman Johnny Uecker) proved fatal for the White Sox. In the top of the first, the Giants scored the only earned run of the game when Edgar Klett hit a scorching single after Deike and Phil Klaerner both hit safely. The Giants added three unearned runs on two infield errors in the inning for a 4–0 lead.

Boerne broke through with an unearned run in the fourth, when Harry Schweppe reached first on shortstop Louis Schneider's error, advanced to second on a ground out, and scored on a line drive single by Gus Wendler, the first hit of the game by the White Sox. The Giants added a run in the fifth on an error by Johnny Uecker after singles by Chester Klaerner and Felix Hahn. With a four-run lead, Klaerner held Boerne hitless the rest of the way, twirling a nifty one-hitter for a 5–1 victory that earned the Mountain League championship for Fredericksburg.[65]

The Giants celebrated their title by playing three exhibition games the following weekend at the Gillespie County Fair, winning all three.[66] The opening game on Friday saw the Giants shut out the Farmer Boys League All-Stars, 5–0, as Phillip Klaerner threw a two-hitter.[67] On Saturday, Red Schnerr slammed a home run, leading the Giants to an 11–8 victory over the Comfort Broncos. Fredericksburg closed out the fair on Sunday with a 10–7 win over a team of combined players from Comfort and Boerne. Louis Schneider, normally the Fredericksburg shortstop, went the distance on the mound while Edgar Bergmann suffered yet another loss to the Giants.[68]

Table 18. Mountain League All-Star Team, 1934

Position	Player	Team
Catcher	Felix Hahn	Fredericksburg
First Base	Gus Wendler	Boerne
Second Base	Joe Pankratz	Comfort
Shortstop	Louis Schneider	Fredericksburg
Third Base	Phillip Klaerner	Fredericksburg
Left Field	Edgar Klett	Fredericksburg
Center Field	Elias Klaerner	Fredericksburg
Right Field	Skeeter Pankratz	Comfort
Pitchers	Chester Klaerner	Fredericksburg
	Edgar Bergmann	Boerne

After the season, the *Fredericksburg Standard* selected a Mountain League all-star team for 1934 (Table 18).[69] Boerne fans might be excused if they objected to the *Standard*'s failure to name third baseman Johnny Uecker and second baseman Rudy Leidl to its all-star squad. Of course, this was not an official all-star team, but merely the opinion of the *Standard*, undoubtedly from a hometown standpoint. The *Standard* also praised the efforts of Giants manager Felix Saenger who for 12 years had been "managing the Giants and getting practically nothing out of it," selflessly devoting his time to advance the Giants' cause.[70]

The Giants (15–1) recorded some eye-popping statistics on their way to the Mountain League championship. (See Appendix E for statistics for all Mountain League teams in 1934.) In the 15 regular season games for which box scores are available, they scored 185 runs—more than 12 runs per game—while allowing fewer than three runs per game. Left fielder Edgar Klett hit .448 with 16 extra-base hits—an average of more than one per game—for a whopping slugging percentage of .925. He also stole nine bases. If the Mountain League had named the most valuable player for 1934, Klett would have certainly been so recognized. Center fielder Elias Klaerner (.435) and right fielder-third baseman Red Schnerr (.413) hit over .400, while pitcher Chester Klaerner (.392) was close. On the mound, Chester Klaerner was 10–1, striking out 80 and allowing only 25 runs in 95 innings for an exceptional TRA of 2.37.[71]

While the White Sox (12–3) were disappointed at falling short of the championship, Boerne did enjoy a resurgence in 1934. The Sox offense was led by third baseman Johnny Uecker, who batted .370 with three triples (tied with his brother, Tuddy Uecker) and a .555 slugging percentage, and second baseman Rudy Leidl who hit .352 and led the team in runs (11). Shortstop Gus Pfeiffer hit .311. Ever reliable Edgar Bergmann starred on the mound, engineering an 8–3 record in the 13 games for which box scores exist, allowing just 33 runs in 85 innings for a TRA of 3.49.

After challenging for the pennant in 1933, the Comfort Broncos (6–8) took a step backward, especially late in the season, when the team gave up 44 runs in their last four games, including a 20–3 debacle at Fredericksburg. One bright spot was catcher Arthur Bergmann, who improved his batting average from .229 to .364 in 1934. The Pankratz brothers continued to shine as well. Third baseman Skeeter Pankratz hit .265 while pitcher-shortstop Joe Pankratz hit .295. However, Joe Pankratz's effectiveness on the mound dropped off significantly in 1934, as he gave up 30 runs in 28 1/3 innings early in the season for a 1–3 record with a TRA of 9.52. After the fifth game of the season, he was moved from the mound to shortstop in favor of Christie Lindemann who fared only slightly better, fashioning a 2–4 record with a TRA of 5.87.

Bandera (2–12) floundered through another season, but the Cowboys did escape the cellar in 1934, edging Kerrville by one-half game for fourth place. Shortstop Bob Mansfield hit an astounding .579 with a .947 slugging percentage, but for unknown reasons, he played in only half of the games. Pitcher-right fielder Davenport hit .272 while second baseman-pitcher F. Hamilton hit .241. Other regulars struggled at the plate as reflected by their anemic batting averages: First baseman Blackwell (.091), second baseman Billings (.154), catcher Thallman (.217), third baseman D. Gray (.179), and right fielder Knibbe (.179). Davenport led the mound corps with a 1–3 record, striking out 27 hitters in 30 2/3 innings, but he also walked 18 batters and gave up 38 hits, resulting in a TRA of 7.63. Sharing the pitching duties, F. Hamilton went 0–3, giving up 17 runs in 20 innings for a TRA of 7.65. However, D. Gray was effective as a reliever, allowing only three runs in 11 1/3 innings for a TRA of 2.38.

Kerrville (2–13) sank like a rock in 1934. The league runner-up in 1933, the Braves dropped to the cellar after losing key performers from the prior season. In the 13 games for which box scores exist, the Braves were outscored by their opponents, 146–33. However, a few bright spots can be found—second baseman C. Gray hit .316 with a .474 slugging percentage and player-manager Jake Goss hit .282. Young strikeout artist Warren Toler showed some promise, nabbing both Braves' victories by defeating Bandera, 3–2, in ten innings on May 27 and stopping the Cowboys again, 4–1, on July 22 when he struck out eight, allowing just five hits. Yet he could not duplicate this success against other clubs, ending with a 2–6 record and a TRA of 10.75.

In retrospect, the 1934 season was a mixed bag for the Mountain League. The addition of Fredericksburg was a brilliant stroke, bringing a highly talented squad to the league. The thrilling pennant race and the championship series between Boerne and Fredericksburg captivated fans, reinforcing the notion that in its finest form, Hill Country baseball was superb.

On the other hand, the season revealed a large gap between the top two teams and the bottom dwellers—Kerrville and Bandera—with both squads losing multiple games by embarrassing scores. In addition, neither the Braves nor the Cowboys won a game except against the other. The challenge for 1935 would be to make the Mountain League more competitive from top to bottom.

In the meantime, Mason dropped out of the Hill Country League, leaving Llano as the only original league member remaining from the inaugural 1930 season just four years earlier.[72] Of the eight teams that began the 1934 season in the HCL, none were south of Llano, thus completing its evolution into a northern Hill Country league.[73] The Richland Springs Lions,[74] who joined the HCL in the second half of 1933, won the first half of the 1934 season with a 9–1 record, while the San Saba Rangers took the second-half flag at 8–2 (after a 2–9 record in the first half).[75] (For the 1934 HCL standings, see Appendix G.) The Llano Cowboys, who finished 11–9, failed to make the championship series, ending their three-year reign as HCL champions.[76]

San Saba won the HCL title by pounding Richland Springs, 11–4, in the decisive third game of the championship series.[77] Although the HCL began the season with eight clubs,[78] Brady and Menard were "dropped from the schedule on June 10,"[79] revealing the instability of the league amid tough economic conditions. Despite the Depression, the HCL hoped to continue in 1935 with its six remaining teams.

As the Hill Country began to feel the brumal chill of the offseason, baseball fans, still blessed with two leagues—the HCL in the northern tier and the Mountain League in the southern tier—could not wait for the sure signs of spring: bluebonnets and baseball. Fredericksburg and Boerne expected to challenge for the Mountain League title, but a pressing question during the offseason would be whether Comfort, Kerrville, or Bandera could join the fray at the top in 1935.

Two months after the Fredericksburg Giants celebrated their Mountain League title, shocking news reverberated throughout the Hill Country. On October 21, pitcher Rod Sanders was killed in an altercation at a dance hall in Mason. Sanders died from the loss of blood after his brother-in-law, Wes Ritter, and another Mason man, Roy Taylor, slashed him with a knife.[80] Sanders's death certificate concluded that he was stabbed in the back. The newspaper accounts do not disclose the nature of the dispute leading to the stabbing, but Ritter was reported to be in serious condition with a head wound.[81] Ritter and Taylor were arrested and placed on bonds of $3,000 and $2,000, respectively.

Sanders, only 26 when he was killed, pitched for Mason, Kerrville, Fredericksburg, and Pontotoc in his Hill Country career. He enjoyed his finest season with Fredericksburg in 1931 when he won 13 of 16 starts for the Giants. His stellar season with the Giants earned him a professional contract with the St. Louis Cardinals, who assigned him to Springfield of the Western Association for 1932.[82] Apparently, he did not make the club[83] because he returned to the Mountain League in 1932, splitting his season between Fredericksburg and Kerrville, but he slumped to a combined 2–5 record. After playing sporadically in 1933, Sanders started the first game of the 1934 season for Fredericksburg, defeating Comfort 4–3 in 10 innings,[84] but he did not appear again for Fredericksburg. (See Appendices A–E for Sanders's complete statistics.)

After his single start for Fredericksburg in the Mountain League, Sanders jumped to Pontotoc in the HCL for the remainder of the 1934 season, although the reasons for his move are unknown. After withdrawing from the HCL just six games into the 1931 season, Pontotoc returned to the HCL in 1934. With Sanders as the Pirates' primary starter, Pontotoc managed to last the entire season, putting up a .500 record—6–6 in the first half and 5–5 in the second half.[85]

On May 6, Sanders matched up against Vernon Taylor, the former University of Texas star who was pitching once again for Brady. Despite giving up four triples, Sanders bested Taylor in an 8–5 victory.[86] The following Sunday, Sanders limited Brady to four hits, but the Turks edged the Pirates, 3–2.[87]

On July 8, Sanders ran into a buzz saw against Llano, losing at home, 8–3. Sanders struck out 10 but allowed 10 hits and three walks.[88] Five weeks later, Sanders avenged this loss when the visiting Pirates trounced Llano, 11–2, on August 12 in the penultimate game of the HCL season.[89] Sanders cruised to the win, limiting the Cowboys to five hits. When he walked off the mound at Robinson State Park that Sunday afternoon, little did he know that this game would be his final victory.[90]

CHAPTER 14

HUGO KLAERNER

Major Leaguer, Musician, and County Sheriff

A familiar Hill Country veteran enjoyed a meteoric rise to the major leagues in 1934 after starring for Fredericksburg and Kerrville in the Hill Country League. Known to his teammates and friends as "Dutch" or "Hoog," Hugo Klaerner was regarded as the best pitcher in the Hill Country League from 1930 to 1933. Hugo (pronounced "HOO-go") was the older brother of Chester "Smokey" Klaerner and Alfons Klaerner and a cousin to Phillip Klaerner and Elias Klaerner—all outstanding players for the Giants.

Hugo was born on October 15, 1908, in Fredericksburg. He started pitching in sandlot ball at age 15. Six years later in 1929, Hugo tried out for the San Antonio Indians. They sent him to Laredo for spring training, where he broke the ring finger of his right (pitching) hand. When he tried to start pitching again, he kept rebreaking the finger. He gave up the game for a while to allow his finger to heal, but when it did so, it was crooked and stiff. However, this turned out to be an advantage, because his stiff finger allowed him to put a different kind of spin on the ball. Some sportswriters called his new pitch a "sailer" but later it was simply known as Klaerner's slider.[1]

After returning home, Hugo became the star pitcher for the Fredericksburg Giants when they began play in the Hill Country League, leading them to the inaugural championship in 1930.[2] In 1931, however, Hugo left the team "on account of differences with the Giants management."[3] As recounted in chapter 6, he pitched for Kerrville for much of 1931 before returning to the Giants late in the season, pitching in the HCL championship series that the Giants lost to Llano.[4] Hugo remained with the Giants through early July in the 1933 season.

Shortly after Fredericksburg withdrew from the HCL midway through the 1933 season (see chapter 10), Hugo signed a professional contract with the Chicago White Sox, leaving the Giants to pitch for the Waco Cubs/Pine Bluff Judges of the Dixie League. For the Judges, Hugo fashioned a 5–2 record with a 2.66 ERA in the second half of 1933.[5] After his minor league season ended,

Klaerner pitched Llano to the 1933 HCL championship, defeating Mason, 7–5, in the decisive game.[6]

Hugo never pitched in the Mountain League, but in March 1934, he did work out with the Giants[7] before Fredericksburg began its first Mountain League season. After "spring training" with the Giants, Hugo rejoined the Judges for the 1934 season—now playing solely in Pine Bluff, Arkansas—where he went 24–7 with a 2.61 ERA in the East Dixie League.[8]

His performance at Pine Bluff attracted the attention of the Chicago White Sox, who were in the throes of a youth movement. The White Sox called Klaerner up in September 1934 as a 25-year-old rookie. He joined a last-place club, although the Sox roster included future Hall of Famers outfielder Al Simmons and shortstop Luke Appling.

After his rapid ascent to the majors, Klaerner started three games, all during a long Comiskey Park homestand.

START ONE: WASHINGTON 7, CHICAGO 4

Klaerner's first start came against the Washington Senators on Monday, September 10. Although they were the defending American League champions, the Senators stood at 61–73 as Hugo took the mound, well out of the 1934 pennant race. Klaerner was likely nervous in his first look at the majors because he did not have his best control, walking two batters in the first inning, but he was able to work out of the jam. In the bottom of the first, Simmons homered, giving the White Sox and Klaerner a 1–0 lead. In the second, though, the Senators tied the game when Ossie Bluege singled after a double by Luke Sewell.

Klaerner held the Senators in check while the Sox regained the lead in the fifth. Klaerner helped his cause by leading off the inning with a double. After a walk, another rookie, Charlie Uhlir, singled Klaerner home and Simmons singled in another run for a two-run Sox margin. Once again, Klaerner could not hold the lead in the ensuing inning. After walking two batters, Klaerner gave up a two-run double to Senators right fielder John Stone, tying the score again at 3–3 in the sixth inning.

After the Sox failed to score in their half of the sixth, disaster struck for Klaerner in the seventh. Senators Heinie Manush and Fred Schulte opened the inning with singles and were sacrificed to third. Sox player-manager Jimmy Dykes ordered Klaerner to intentionally walk Luke Sewell to load the bases and set up a double play. Pinch hitter Cliff Bolton foiled the strategy by slugging a grand slam into Comiskey Park's right field lower deck for a 7–3 Senators lead. Klaerner finished the seventh inning without further damage but was relieved

Figure 37. Hugo Klaerner, Chicago White Sox. (Courtesy of the Gillespie County Historical Society, Fredericksburg, Texas.)

in the eighth. The White Sox scored a run in the eighth inning but could score no more in a 7–4 loss.[9]

Klaerner allowed nine hits and seven walks in his seven innings, striking out three in the losing effort. Hugo was undoubtedly disappointed, but he must have also thought that if he could just sharpen his control, he could be a winning major league pitcher.

START TWO: PHILADELPHIA 9, CHICAGO 4

One week later, Klaerner made his second start against the Philadelphia Athletics—formerly a powerhouse team that won the World Series in 1929 and 1930 and the American League pennant in 1931, but in 1934 the Athletics finished below .500 for the first time in 10 years. First baseman Jimmie Foxx was the only star remaining from the Athletics' dominant teams.

Unlike his first start when he avoided trouble in the first inning, Klaerner floundered this time. After a leadoff single and wild pitch, Bob Johnson singled in a run. Klaerner struck out Jimmie Foxx but then walked Pinky Higgins. With two outs, Eric McNair launched a home run into the left field stands for a 4–0 Philadelphia lead. Klaerner continued to struggle in the second. After he retired the first two batters, Doc Kramer singled then Klaerner walked the next two batters to load the bases for the dangerous Foxx who promptly singled in two runs. Klaerner struck out Higgins to end the threat.

Down 6–0, the Sox rallied. As in his first game, Klaerner doubled in the third. After a walk to Jocko Conlan, Simmons doubled, scoring Klaerner and Conlan. In the fourth, the Sox cut the lead to 6–4 on two run-scoring singles. They might have scored more but Klaerner, on first base after a fielder's choice groundout, was thrown out at third base on the second run-scoring single. The score remained 6–4, until Klaerner tired in the ninth. After two walks, McNair struck again, hitting his second home run of the game, securing the A's 9–4 victory.[10]

Klaerner pitched a complete game in the losing effort, giving up nine runs on 10 hits and seven walks while striking out six. Hugo's lack of control again sealed his fate. White Sox Manager Jimmy Dykes would give Klaerner one more start in the 1934 season.

START THREE: CLEVELAND 9, CHICAGO 8

The trouble started right away for Klaerner in his third start on Saturday, September 22 against the Cleveland Indians. He allowed a leadoff single before walking Earl Averill. Hal Trosky then stroked his 34th home run of the season against the upper-deck façade in right field for a three-run blast, giving the

Figure 38. Hugo Klaerner. (Courtesy of Kevin Klaerner.)

Indians a 3–0 lead before Klaerner retired a batter. Klaerner allowed no further damage in the first, but in the next inning, the Indians' Milt Galatzer doubled and Averill walked with one out. After Trosky singled in Galatzer to put the Sox behind, 4–0, Dykes had seen enough, relieving Klaerner in the second inning. Joe Vosmik, the next batter, singled in Averill to make the score 5–0. However, the

White Sox rallied, scoring single runs in the second, fourth, and sixth innings, then plating four runs in the seventh to grab a 7–5 lead, taking Klaerner off the hook for a loss. The Indians answered with four runs of their own in the eighth and eventually won the game, 9–8.[11] Klaerner pitched only one-and-one-third innings, giving up five runs on five hits and two walks, striking out none.

Regrettably, Klaerner would never pitch in the major leagues again. He finished his brief career with a 0–2 record and a 10.90 ERA. In 17 1/3 innings, he walked 16 and struck out nine, giving up four home runs.[12] Klaerner's lack of control and his proclivity for giving up the long ball proved to be his downfall in his brief tenure with the Chicago White Sox.

Although he never saw major league action again, Hugo enjoyed a long career in the minors. He won 20 games for Longview in the West Dixie League in 1935, including a perfect game.[13] Hugo pitched 24 complete games, compiling a 1.80 ERA in 248 innings.[14] He then went 15–12 for Oklahoma City in the Texas League the following year. He pitched for the St. Paul Saints in the American Association and Shreveport in the Texas League before hanging up his professional spikes at the age of 33 in 1942.[15] After his playing career ended, he returned to Fredericksburg where he pitched for the Giants through the 1940s.

Hugo married Esther Petermann on June 17, 1935, during his 20-win season for Longview. Hugo and Esther had six children: Travis, Evelyn, Gladys, Carlos, Tommy, and Patrick.[16] After Hugo returned to Fredericksburg, he continued a family tradition in law enforcement.

Hugo's father, Alfred Klaerner,[17] served as the sheriff of Gillespie County (Fredericksburg is the county seat) from 1918 to 1920 and then was elected again in 1924, serving until 1942.[18] Hugo's uncle, John Klaerner, also served as county sheriff, holding the office from 1900 to 1910. Given his family history, it was natural for Hugo to run for election as county sheriff, which he did at the age of 42. Elected in 1950, Hugo served for 30 years, retiring in 1980.[19] As a result, a member of the Klaerner family held the position of Gillespie County sheriff for 60 years between 1900 and 1980.[20]

Hugo's courage as sheriff was on full display in 1971 when he captured a murder suspect without incident. On September 28, 1971, Kendall County Sheriff Douglas Kuebel was shot and killed in the early morning hours when he responded to a domestic disturbance six miles north of Boerne. Hugo and two other officers sped toward Kendall County to assist in the apprehension of the suspect. As they entered Interstate 10 near Comfort, they spotted the suspect's vehicle. Eyeing the police car, the suspect left the interstate highway, leading the officers on a high-speed chase. Hugo and officers finally stopped the

Figure 39. Fredericksburg Giants. Hugo Klaerner is standing, far left. (Courtesy of Kevin Klaerner.)

suspect's vehicle 18 miles west of Comfort. When Hugo and the officers forced the suspect out of his car, he complied without a struggle. The murder weapon, a shotgun, was found inside the vehicle.[21]

Apart from baseball and law enforcement, music was predominant in Klaerner's life, as it was for many Germans in the Hill Country. Both a singer and a musician, Klaerner's favorite hobby was playing the tuba, bass horn, and baritone brass wind instruments.[22] For many years, he was a member of Pehl's Old-Time German Oompah Band which "put Fredericksburg on the map" by playing engagements in all corners of Texas.[23] Klaerner "could blow that big bass horn, or his baritone and tuba to the great enjoyment and delight of the audiences."[24] Klaerner also sang with the local Mannerchor, participating in the annual Saengerfest in Fredericksburg.[25] He also sang in the choir at Zion Lutheran Church where he was a lifelong member.[26]

Two years after he retired as sheriff, Klaerner passed away at the age of 73 in 1982. Fredericksburg grieved his loss:

> Our community has lost a good man, a respected citizen, a beloved family man, former Sheriff, Hugo Klaerner. There are not many towns in Texas, in the U.S., that can boast of having had, or still have, a sheriff who not only enforced the law rigidly, fearlessly, with tact, who combined his time by rendering enjoyment to friends, his countrymen, with music and song.[27]

Hugo Klaerner starred in baseball, reaching the major leagues as a pitcher; mastered multiple musical instruments, playing in German bands in his hometown; and steadfastly served his community as sheriff. He embodied much of the well-rounded German life in the Hill Country—excelling in sports and music while later plying a distinguished career in law enforcement.

CHAPTER 15

LIFE GETS SERIOUS

Mountain League, 1935

In 1935, the market for mohair enjoyed heavy sales, improving the outlook of ranchers raising goats.[1] Still in the throes of the Depression, however, some Hill Country residents sought illegal means to share in the wool and mohair markets. In early January, after an investigation assisted by the Texas Sheep and Goat Raisers Association (TSGRA), two men from the Camp Verde area between Kerrville and Bandera were charged with stealing goats.[2] A week later, two Kerrville men were charged with stealing 60 sheep.[3] The TSGRA promised more prosecutions if necessary to protect the livelihood of their member ranchers.

At about the same time, world affairs came to Fredericksburg. Two years after Adolf Hitler ascended to power in Germany, Dr. Hans Luther, the German ambassador to the United States and former chancellor of Germany, chose to visit Fredericksburg, which was well known as a bastion of German settlers. Fredericksburg held a banquet attended by 80 persons in his honor at the Nimitz Hotel.[4] After being presented with a ten-gallon Texas cowboy hat, Dr. Luther spoke on "the political and social changes in Germany during the past 2 years and expressed confidence in the people's ability to work out satisfactorily their problems."[5] It was not reported if any of the German Texans in attendance were alarmed by the Nazi government's policies, including the Nazis' harsh consolidation of power after they gained control in the 1933 election. However, nonagenarian August Hoffman, the oldest resident of Gillespie County and reportedly the sole survivor of the "Massacre on the Nueces" in 1862,[6] was introduced to the audience to much acclaim.[7]

Perhaps reflecting a recovering economy, the Mountain League added a sixth team in 1935. By doing so, the league eliminated the off days that resulted from a five-team schedule. For a while, it looked like Center Point would be the new team, but those efforts failed when the town could not field a representative squad.[8] Instead, the Mountain League invited the Legion Cubs to join as the sixth club.[9]

Legion was not a town in the traditional sense. An area near Kerrville became known as Legion in the early 1920s when the Texas Department of the American Legion owned the land and unfinished buildings that later became the United States Veterans Administration Hospital.[10] Both the hospital and the community itself were known as Legion.[11] By 1970, Legion was incorporated into the city of Kerrville, but in 1935, Legion was a separate community that fielded its own team.[12] The Cubs played their home games on the hospital grounds, putting the team at a financial disadvantage because federal government regulations prohibited the Cubs from charging an admission fee on federal property.[13] Hence, the only recourse of the Cubs for recouping club expenses was to ask fans for voluntary donations when attending games.[14]

Since the Mountain League now had six teams, the league changed the playoff rules to provide that the second- and third-place teams would play a one-game playoff to determine who would meet the first-place team in a best-of-three championship series.[15] As a result, three of the six teams would play in the Mountain League postseason. With an even number of teams, the league schedule consisted of 20 games (four games against each team) with no off days, beginning April 14 and ending August 25.[16]

Spirits were high, especially in Boerne and Fredericksburg, as the 1935 season approached. Columnist Perry Winkle[17] of the *San Antonio Evening News* sang the praises of the White Sox: "Boerne White Sox, sporting one of the classiest uniformed teams in the Mountain League this year, are out to cop a championship under the leadership of Clarence Holekamp, who has piloted the team since 1923, being in harness 12 years and one of the best known skippers in this section of the state."[18]

Winkle pointed out that Edgar Bergmann was returning as the ace pitcher of the White Sox along with slugger Johnny Uecker, while Fredericksburg lost their top pitcher, Chester "Smokey" Klaerner, who signed a professional contract with the New York Giants:[19] "The big reason for the preseason thrill at Boerne rests in the fact their ancient rival, the Fredericksburg Giants, are without the services of Smokey Klaerner. It was Smokey who jinxed the Sox last year and he's out of the way now, having been given a trial in major league ball."[20]

Winkle predicted the White Sox would take the 1935 title, disenchanting many Giants fans:

> Boerne is a good town. The boys are always welcome as opponents in other burgs, and so far the writer hasn't been offered any alibis as to

> why Boerne lost to Fredericksburg last year, which is about the best advertising the town could get—that of giving the other fellow credit for winning the game whenever he is lucky enough to do so.
>
> And this year the writer picks Boerne to cop the flag, passing up the Giants this season, to the big surprise of the Fredericksburg fans. Boerne is overdue and this time the line is clear, so "Engineer" Holekamp should be able to bring the "Boerne Flyer" into Pennantville on time.[21]

The following week, Winkle reported the hostile response of Fredericksburg fans to his prediction of a Boerne championship:

> Having selected Boerne as our choice for the title victory this year, the writer has been requested to avoid Fredericksburg until after Sept. 1. The fans are quite het up [*sic*] over that prediction of a Boerne victory, due chiefly to the fact our prediction clicked last year when we went down the line for Boss Saenger and "crowned" the Giants champs—and they won.
>
> The prediction of doom is not what gets the Fredericksburg fans "on us," it's the desertion. In their opinion, we should have stuck by the Giants, now that Chester is gone, and the team is in need of moral support. Red-hot letters have trickled in upon us from Fredericksburg. These letters point out that Fredericksburg is still on the map.[22]

To mollify the Fredericksburg fans, Winkle extolled the many virtues of the Giants:

> There is no denying it, these Giants are tough, despite the loss of "Lil Chester,' the smoke-ball whiz-bang. Our friend Felix Saenger has work ahead of him to win the flag, but a good start is half the battle, so the Giants figure to whip the field often enough to make the playoffs, and then put on steam and take the playoff games.
>
> The batting power of the Giants is apparent. Six of them hit better than .328 last year. Elias Klaerner and Edgar Klett batted .402 with Klaerner hitting 7 homers, 10 triples, and 13 doubles for the season.[23]
>
> Other sluggers returning to Saenger's roster include Alford [*sic*] Klaerner,[24] .345; Phil Klaerner, .338; Felix Hahn, .349; and Red Schnerr, .328.[25]

Phillip Klaerner would take over the role of starting pitcher from his cousin, Chester "Smokey" Klaerner. Much of the Giants' success in 1934 stemmed from Chester's sparkling work on the mound, especially in big games against Boerne. Phillip Klaerner had big shoes to fill if the Giants were to continue their winning ways.

After praising both the White Sox and the Giants in previous columns, Perry Winkle paused before Opening Day on April 14 to pay tribute to the Mountain League:

> Baseball leagues are, generally speaking, hotbeds of strife and dissension. Clubs get mad at each other, quit, cracking up loops. New members come in, more grief, and while all this may be well from the added interest among fans, its nice to go to a meeting and expect to meet some one who is glad to see you.
>
> However, on the field, the Mountain League is the reverse. Umpires demand big fees, scorekeepers don't like their jobs, and it's rumored that Adler and Faust [league president and secretary-treasurer, respectively] don false whiskers, so they can see the game, but not be drawn into any rows of the contending nines.
>
> The Mountain League is a serious setup of teams. Losing managers feel all broken up over the loss of game, for the fans in "them thar mountains" are hard to suit. "Give us a winner" is not a plaint, it's a threat.
>
> Tomorrow, three managers will be saddened by losses. Three others will be on speaking terms with the angels, at least, their spirits will be soaring up into ethereal heights.
>
> Life is serious—life is real, in the Mountain League.[26]

Life would indeed get serious and real in the Mountain League this season but not in the way Winkle, or anyone else, could have foreseen on Opening Day.

Boerne and Fredericksburg would clearly vie for the championship. Other than losing Chester Klaerner to a professional contract, the Giants roster changed little. For its part, Boerne returned the same veteran club, but the White Sox did add a powerful bat at a key position—former Fredericksburg and Comfort shortstop Ernst Nagel.[27]

Of course, the question remained whether any of the other four teams would be strong enough to mount a challenge to the White Sox and Giants. As a new club, the Legion Cubs were an unknown quantity, but the team's roster did include at least one veteran player who played for Kerrville in the Braves' 10–8 season in 1933—the versatile Louie Wootton, who hit .295 in 1933 and would play five positions in 1935. Apart from Wootton, most of the Cubs were untested. They were led by player-manager Bob Barry, a former Kerrville player, who would occasionally pitch in 1935.

Of the other three clubs, Comfort seemed most likely to take a step forward due to the Broncos' nucleus of veteran ballplayers—slugging shortstop Joe Pankratz and his brother, third baseman Skeeter Pankratz, as well as catcher Arthur Bergmann, center fielder Felix Meyer, and first baseman Morris Goforth. Joe Pankratz would pitch only sparingly in 1935, perhaps due to a sore arm lingering from 1934. Rookie Harold Krauter would assume the role of starting pitcher. His success on the mound, or lack of it, would go far in determining Comfort's fortunes in 1935.

Kerrville and Bandera were simply hoping for improvement after dismal seasons the year before. In Kerrville, the entire board of directors resigned, necessitating an all-new set of directors to step in for 1935.[28] Key players returning to Kerrville, helmed by player-manager Ben Grantham, included middle infielder C. Gray, catcher-first baseman Clergy Hollimon, and outfielders Jake Goss, Monk Warren, and Louis Fisher. Kerrville also added promising first baseman Maybeaux to its roster. Warren Toler was slotted to toe the rubber again for the Braves, but he would rotate starting duties with six-foot-six Slim Esbeck[29] in Kerrville's effort to escape the cellar. To break from the past, the Braves sported new uniforms—gray with royal blue and cardinal red trimmings. Their socks were white, banded with red and blue stripes.[30]

Outfielders Tommy Dugosh, a former Boerne and Comfort player, and Knibbe returned to Bandera, along with second baseman-pitcher F. Hamilton, shortstop R. Click, and pitcher-outfielder Davenport. The Cowboys added catcher Adamietz, shortstop Rugh, and pitcher Charlie Gray,[31] among others, in hopes of much-needed improvement.

As in 1934, Boerne and Fredericksburg shot out of the gate to start the 1935 season. The White Sox spoiled the home debut of the Legion Cubs on April 14 with a 12–1 thrashing.[32] Newcomer Ernst Nagel smashed four hits, including a double, to lead the Boerne onslaught. The next week in Boerne, left fielder Harry Schweppe hit safely in all four of his at-bats, leading the White Sox over the Cubs, 12–2.[33] Edgar Bergmann went seven innings then turned the mound duties over to his younger brother Walter for the final two frames. In a closer contest the next Sunday, the White Sox handed Comfort its first loss, 7–5, when center fielder Clarence Bourgeois produced a three-run homer in the eighth inning.[34]

Similarly, Fredericksburg started off with Phillip Klaerner shutting out Bandera twice in a row, winning 5–0 at Bandera on April 14,[35] then dominating the Cowboys, 13–0, a week later at Fair Park when Klaerner contributed four hits to the offense.[36] In their third game of the season, catcher Andy Andrews, a former Kerrville player, blasted a home run among three hits as the Giants tamed the Legion Cubs, 6–4.[37]

Legion had the misfortune to begin the season with two games each against powerful Boerne and Fredericksburg, losing their first three games, but they were spared further damage on May 5 when their second game against Fredericksburg was rained out. Since Boerne's May 5 game against Comfort was also rained out, the White Sox and the Giants would meet in Boerne on May 12 with identical 3–0 records.

Columnist Perry Winkle noted the excitement that was building for the first clash of the season between Fredericksburg and Boerne:

> The White Sox, led by [manager Clarence] Holekamp and [business manager Udo] Harz, are stepping along as advertised, and the critical Boerne fans are insisting on the genuine article this year, meaning the championship, not the runners-up consolation.
>
> The "Jolly Jints" are out to bust up a lot of bubbles like the White Sox make when they're in the "wash," but the Sox are used to being "cleaned" ever so often, and they can take it. However, in the game Sunday a new angle crops up, and they must deliver for [pitcher Edgar] Bergmann.
>
> Bergmann might have won last year, had it not been for [Chester] Klaerner's great pitching. This year that alibi is out. The Sox have to deliver the groceries, and this humble scribe sees a dark future for the Hose, if they can't click against Phil Klaerner.
>
> Knowing this, the towns, both Fredericksburg and Boerne, will trek to White Sox diamond [*sic*] to watch Dame Fortune and the Fates decide the future of two good ballclubs. The issue involves more than a ball game; it involves the future of Boerne as a team of big-timers, and the future of Phil Klaerner as the "man of the hour" for Fredericksburg.[38]

When game day arrived, the White Sox struck first in the second inning against Phillip Klaerner. After Gus Wendler and Clarence Bourgeois singled, catcher Harry Phillip bunted to advance Bourgeois to second, but Klaerner threw wildly to first, allowing Wendler to score. Edgar Bergmann hit a sacrifice fly to left field, scoring Bourgeois for a 2–0 lead.

The Giants tied the game in the fourth. After Alfons Klaerner singled and Elias Klaerner doubled, Edgar Klett stroked a two-out, two-run single. The White Sox responded with a run in their half of the fourth inning on a single by Harry Schweppe after singles by Harry Phillip and Edgar Bergmann. The Giants took their first lead in the sixth. Klett's double scored Henry Langerhans who had reached first on an error by third baseman Johnny Uecker before Red Schnerr singled in Klett with the go-ahead run for a 4–3 Giants lead.

The wheels came off for Fredericksburg in the eighth inning. With one out, Bergmann and Rudy Leidl singled before Schweppe doubled, scoring Bergmann. Pfeiffer hit a sacrifice fly, scoring Leidl. With two outs, Uecker made up for his earlier error by smashing a triple, driving in Schweppe. Giants third baseman Alfons Klaerner booted Ernst Nagel's groundball, allowing Uecker to score the fourth run of the inning, giving the Sox a 7–4 lead.

Edgar Bergmann gave up two hits in the ninth but with one out and two runners on base, he retired Phillip Klaerner and Alfons Klaerner on popouts to grab the 7–4 win, putting Boerne in first place at 4–0.[39] The Giants fell into a second-place tie with the surprising Comfort Broncos who were also 3–1, their only loss coming at the hands of the White Sox.

The White Sox would not have long to rest on their laurels since they traveled to Fredericksburg the next Sunday. Unlike the first contest, this game turned out to be a classic dogfight between Edgar Bergmann and Phillip Klaerner. The Giants scored a run in the second on a single by Phil Klaerner after Klett advanced to second on an error by third baseman Johnny Uecker. The White Sox responded with a run in the sixth inning. Leidl singled to center and advanced to second when center fielder Elias Klaerner bobbled the ball. Schweppe singled, scoring Leidl to tie the game, but Schweppe was thrown out at second base trying to advance on the throw to the plate.

Fredericksburg threatened in the eighth inning but could not score. Elias Klaerner opened the inning with a single, his third hit of the game, before catcher Andrews walked. Klett cracked what appeared to be a base hit, but Andrews slipped in the mud from heavy rain the day before and was forced out at second base. Phil Klaerner walked to load the bases with one out. First baseman Stahl attempted a squeeze bunt but popped out to Sox catcher Harry Phillip, who fired the ball to third to catch Elias Klaerner off the bag for a nifty inning-ending double play.

After Phillip Klaerner retired the Sox in order in the top of the ninth, Red Schnerr led off with a single in the Giants' half of the inning. Shortstop Vincent Ransleben, new to the Giants in 1935, laid down a perfect sacrifice bunt. Sox catcher Harry Phillip fielded it, but his throw sailed wild, enabling Schnerr to advance to third with no outs. Leadoff hitter Alfons Klaerner then singled in Schnerr with the winning run for a heart-stopping 2–1 victory.[40]

Bergmann and Klaerner both pitched effectively although Bergmann gave up 11 hits while Klaerner allowed only eight. They each struck out just three hitters, relying more on guile than blazing speed to stifle their opponents. With the win, the Giants were now tied for first place with Boerne at 4–1. After a rainout at home against Bandera on the same day, Comfort stood one-half game behind the leaders with a 3–1 mark.

The White Sox may have had a sense of déjà vu after the game since the outcome was reminiscent of agonizing losses to the Giants in 1934. But with Boerne and Fredericksburg tied at the top of the standings and Comfort close behind, Mountain League fans were anticipating another robust pennant race.

Boosted by their win against Boerne, the Giants traveled to Comfort on May 26. The Broncos were hoping to catch Fredericksburg napping and stake their claim as a true contender this season. Comfort's new pitcher, Harold Krauter, was splendid in his early starts. Coming into the game against the Giants, Krauter had thrown three shutouts in four starts—two against Kerrville and one against Bandera. The sole blemish on Krauter's record was the 7–5 loss to Boerne on April 28.[41] Shortstop Joe Pankratz, catcher Arthur Bergmann, and second baseman Robert Lindner led the offense, which was averaging over seven runs per game—impressive even though most of their early season games were against Kerrville and Bandera.

Wasting no time in front of their home fans, the Broncos scored three runs in the first inning off Phillip Klaerner. With one out, Joe Pankratz singled and Dick Spenrath was safe on an error by Giants second baseman Henry Langerhans. After Klaerner hit Arthur Bergmann with a pitch to load the bases, Robert Lindner laid down a squeeze bunt, scoring Pankratz. When Phil Klaerner's throw to first went astray, Spenrath also scored. Bergmann then scored the third run on an infield hit by center fielder Felix Meyer.

Fredericksburg pushed its first run across the plate in the sixth. After Langerhans singled and advanced to second on a fielder's choice, he scored on an error by shortstop Joe Pankratz. The Broncos responded in the bottom of the sixth. After Skeeter Pankratz reached base on shortstop Ransleben's error, first baseman Goforth singled him home, giving the Broncos a 4–1 lead.

After hurling eight strong innings against the vaunted Giants, Krauter tired in the ninth. Edgar Klett singled for Fredericksburg and Phillip Klaerner hit a long triple to right, scoring Klett. Klaerner scored on a groundout to draw the

Giants within a run, but Krauter struck out pinch hitter Felix Hahn to end the game. Krauter allowed just five hits while walking one batter and striking out three for a well-deserved 4–3 win.[42] Krauter was now 4–1, allowing just 10 runs in his five starts.

While the Broncos improved to 4–1, and Boerne easily handled Kerrville, 8–0, to claim first place with a 5–1 record,[43] the Giants were stunned to find themselves in third place with a 4–2 record. This disappointing turn of events caused Giants manager, Felix Saenger, to tender his resignation.[44] It is unknown if his resignation was purely voluntary. The Giants replaced Saenger with catcher Andy Andrews, who would serve as a player-manager.[45] Andrews had taken over the catching duties from veteran Felix Hahn. His first test as a skipper would be the rematch with Comfort at Fair Park on June 2, the following Sunday.

This time against the Broncos, Phillip Klaerner was sharper, striking out seven batters in the first three innings. The Giants gave him a two-run lead in the second inning, but Comfort got a run back in the third when Joe Pankratz doubled, scoring Krauter, who had walked. However, on the play, Pankratz was thrown out at third trying to stretch his hit into a triple. The Broncos tied the game in the sixth when Dick Spenrath singled, Arthur Bergmann sacrificed him to second, and Robert Lindner singled, scoring Spenrath.

The Giants broke Krauter's spell against them in the sixth inning when six consecutive Giants reached base safely—Phillip Klaerner doubled, Red Schnerr doubled, Stahl singled, Weise walked, Vincent Ransleben singled, and Edgar Klett singled. After Krauter retired Elias Klaerner and Alfons Klaerner, Andrews singled—his third hit of the day in his debut as player-manager. Mercifully, Krauter retired Phil Klaerner for the final out, but not before the Giants scored five runs for a 7–2 lead. The Broncos could not score again until the ninth when they pushed two runs home on two hits and an error, but they fell short, 7–4.[46] By avenging their prior loss to Comfort, the Giants returned to second place at 5–2 while Comfort fell to third with a 4–2 record. Boerne kept winning, trouncing Kerrville, 10–2, to retain the top spot with a 6–1 mark.[47]

At the same time, the rest of the league struggled. By June 2, Bandera had lost its first seven games. It was little consolation that after Fredericksburg thrashed the Cowboys, 13–0, on April 21, Bandera's other losses were by less embarrassing margins. Bandera suffered two one-run losses during that span. Kerrville edged the Cowboys, 8–7, on May 5 when Braves player-manager Ben Grantham slugged a home run and two singles.[48] On June 2, the Cowboys could not take advantage of eight Legion errors, losing, 4–3, when Cubs left fielder

Baker smacked a home run off Bandera right-hander Charlie Gray with two outs in the bottom of the ninth.[49] Gray struck out 10 in a strong effort.

Kerrville showed some promise early in the season with three consecutive wins—two against Bandera and one against Legion. With a 3–2 record, Braves fans dared to dream that they could return to the top of the league. However, Kerrville stumbled, first losing to Legion, 9–6, when former Brave Louie Wootton smashed three hits including a double,[50] then falling to Boerne as Edgar Bergmann pitched a two-hit shutout, 8–0.[51] The White Sox bounced the Braves again, 10–2, on June 2 at the Kendall County Fairgrounds when Ernst Nagel continued his hot hitting with four hits while Rudy Leidl added a home run.[52] The three-game losing streak dropped the Braves to fifth place with a 3–5 record, ahead of only winless Bandera.

Legion lost its first four games, including an 8–3 loss at Kerrville,[53] reflecting the struggles of their starting pitcher, Walter Albrecht, who allowed 22 runs in 25 innings for a TRA of 7.92. Legion then replaced Albrecht with former Kerrville and Comfort hurler Haskell Archer, who also carried a potent bat. The addition of Archer paid immediate dividends for the Cubs because the next week, Legion defeated Kerrville, 9–6, when the Cubs rallied to score five runs in the eighth inning, highlighted by a grand slam by Archer, who earned the win in relief.[54] A solo home run by center fielder Clergy Hollimon accounted for the other run in the rally.

The Cubs then edged Bandera twice, first rallying to win in 10 innings, 5–3, on May 26,[55] when Archer notched another win in relief. On June 2, with two outs and the bases empty in the ninth, left fielder Baker slammed a walk-off home run to gain the win, 4–3, giving Archer his third straight come-from-behind win as a reliever.[56] These comeback victories improved Legion's record to 3–4, elevating the Cubs to fourth place, ahead of Kerrville (3–5) and Bandera (0–7).[57] After a poor start in their first season in the league, Legion was finding a groove.

As the summer heated up in June, Boerne and Fredericksburg continued to roll. The White Sox and the Giants were not scheduled to meet again until July 21 and July 28. In the meantime, the leaders feasted on the other clubs.

After sweeping two games with the Braves in late May, Boerne proceeded to stomp feeble Bandera, 13–2, on June 9.[58] Right fielder Gus Pfeiffer led Boerne's 15-hit attack with three hits, including a double and triple, while center fielder Clarence Bourgeois slammed a home run. Pitchers Arthur Schulze and Edgar Bergmann allowed the Cowboys just five hits. The following Sunday, Edgar Bergmann and Schulze combined to shut out the Cowboys, 8–0.[59] First baseman Gus Wendler drove in four runs while left fielder Harry Schweppe banged out three hits. In four games with Kerrville and Bandera, Boerne outscored them, 39–4.

On June 23, Edgar Bergmann whitewashed Legion, 8–0,[60] holding the Cubs to four hits. White Sox leadoff hitter Rudy Leidl stroked three hits while shortstop Ernst Nagel drove in three runs. One week later, the White Sox traveled to Legion where they prevailed, 8–5.[61] In this game, Legion protested an umpire's call at a critical juncture. Little did the teams, or anyone else, realize at the time that the league's decision on this protest would soon have cataclysmic consequences for Boerne and the Mountain League.

Meanwhile, Fredericksburg plowed a similar path to the White Sox, holding off host Kerrville, 7–4, on June 9 when Phillip Klaerner struck out the final two Braves in the ninth with the tying run at the plate.[62] The next Sunday, Elias Klaerner took the mound as the Giants crushed the Braves, 12–1, at Fair Park.[63] The Giants took advantage of 12 walks issued by three Braves pitchers (Toler, Redmond, and Esbeck) while third baseman Alfons Klaerner drove in four runs.

On the same day, left fielder Edgar Klett smashed two doubles and a triple to lead the Giants past Bandera, 13–1.[64] When the Giants traveled to Bandera one week later, Alfons Klaerner took the mound for the first time this season, shutting out the Cowboys, 16–0, while scattering seven hits. Elias Klaerner drove in five runs on four hits.[65] Like Boerne, Fredericksburg dominated Kerrville and Bandera, outscoring them 48–6 in their four June games.

While the Giants and White Sox surged, Comfort faltered, losing two games to improving Legion. On June 9, newcomer Haskell Archer pitched Legion past the Broncos, 3–2, when the Cubs rallied for two runs in the ninth to defeat Comfort's stalwart pitcher, Harold Krauter.[66] The next week, the Cubs whitewashed the Broncos, 13–0. Archer and Bill Dickey combined for a four-hit shutout while the Cubs bombed two Bronco pitchers, twin brothers Hilmar Stieler and Arthur Stieler, for 14 hits, including seven for extra bases.[67]

After their dual spankings by Legion, the Broncos recovered to take two games from Kerrville—the first by a score of 6–1 on June 23 when Harold Krauter returned to the mound, allowing just six hits to gain the win.[68] Comfort also won the return match, 12–6, on June 30 despite a first inning, three-run homer by Braves catcher Jess Hollimon.[69] After the Braves' early lead, the Broncos stormed back by knocking around Braves pitchers Warren Toler and Slim Esbeck for 18 base hits, including three hits each by Comfort third baseman Skeeter Pankratz, left fielder Thomas, and Krauter.

At the end of June, Boerne held first place with a 10–1 record while the Giants stood one game behind at 9–2. Comfort remained within striking distance at 6–4, while improving Legion had won five of its last seven games to enter the playoff picture. (Table 19 shows the Mountain League standings on June 30.)[70]

Table 19. Mountain League Standings, June 30, 1935

	W	L	GB	Pct.
Boerne	10	1	---	.909
Fredericksburg	9	2	1	.818
Comfort	6	4	3½	.600
Legion	5	6	5	.455
Kerrville	3	9	7½	.250
Bandera	0	10	9½	.000

On July 7, Edgar Klett smashed a home run and a double to pave the way for the Giants' win over Legion, 6–2, aided by five errors by the Cubs.[71] Giants' pitcher Phillip Klaerner started the game but was relieved in the fifth inning by his brother, Elias Klaerner, with the bases loaded and none out. Elias limited the damage to one run, preserving a 3–1 lead, which the Giants never relinquished. The two Klaerners allowed Legion 11 hits but just two runs.

While the Giants were defeating the Cubs, Comfort traveled to Boerne hoping to keep their title dreams alive while the White Sox sought to extend their six-game winning streak. Comfort scored in the top of the first. Skeeter Pankratz singled for the Broncos and Christie Lindemann reached base on an error by White Sox shortstop Gus Pfeiffer. Edgar Bergmann walked the dangerous Joe Pankratz to load the bases with one out. Catcher Arthur Bergmann laid down a bunt and beat it out for an infield single, scoring Skeeter Pankratz. The Broncos tallied another run on a groundout for an early 2–0 lead.

In the second, Boerne rallied to tie the score. Gus Wendler and Clarence Bourgeois hit consecutive singles, both scoring on Harry Phillip's smashing liner. The game remained tied until the sixth, when the White Sox pushed another run across on a double by Clarence Bourgeois and a single by Edgar Bergmann. Bergmann made it stand up, holding the Broncos scoreless over the last three innings for a come-from-behind victory, 3–2, improving Boerne's record to 11–1.[72] Bergmann gave up just four hits, walked two and struck out five. Hilmar Stieler pitched effectively in a losing effort.[73]

Boerne's elation from the narrow victory over the Broncos was short-lived. Later the following week, the league formally considered Legion's protest of its loss to the White Sox 10 days before. When Boerne defeated Legion, 8–5, on June 30, the White Sox scored four of their eight runs in the fourth inning. In that inning, Legion disputed a call by the umpires. After appeals to the umpires fell on deaf ears, Legion protested the game. However, the protest would not be decided until the week *after* Boerne's 3–2 squeaker over Comfort on July 7.

The accounts of Legion's protest and the disputed call vary. What appears to be the most likely scenario was described by the *Kerrville Mountain Sun*.[74] With no one out and a runner on first base in the fourth inning, Boerne's batter hit a groundball that struck the runner advancing to second base. The umpires, hired by Legion as the home team, ruled the runner safe at second and the batter out.[75] The next batter struck out but Boerne went on to score four runs in the inning before the side was retired.

According to baseball rules, when a batted ball strikes a runner before passing an infielder, the umpires call the runner out for interference and the ball is dead. Other runners, if any, would be required to return to their last occupied base although the batter-runner would be awarded first base on the interference call. If the runner struck by the batted ball was not called out but instead was permitted to remain on second base, the umpires ruled incorrectly. Legion presumably claimed in its protest that the four runs would not have scored in the inning but for the erroneous ruling by the umpire. Since Boerne won, 8–5, those four runs decided the outcome of the game.

Contrary to the account in the *Kerrville Mountain Sun*, the *Fredericksburg Standard* described the disputed play differently:

> In the course of the game with no man out (Boerne at bat), and a man on first base, a ball was hit to the second baseman who scooped up the ball, touched the runner that was forced at second, and threw out the man on first. The umpire declared the man on second safe and the man at first out, the next man up struck out. Had both of the men been out as they should have this would have retired the side. Instead with two outs, several more runs were scored which proved to be the margin of victory.[76]

This account mentions nothing about a batted ball striking the runner. Instead, it suggests that the umpire called the runner safe at second despite the infielder tagging the runner out. In such a case, Legion would have been protesting a judgment call of the umpires—a protest much less likely to succeed than one objecting to the improper application of baseball rules.

League directors met in Comfort on Wednesday, July 10,[77] 10 days after the disputed game. Mountain League president H. O. Adler had a conflict of interest in Legion's protest due to his role as president of the White Sox. As a result, the directors stepped into the fray, deciding to uphold Legion's protest and ordering

Legion and Boerne to replay the June 30 game in its entirety,[78] although the *Fredericksburg Standard* indicated that the game would be replayed only if it had a bearing on the final standings.[79]

The White Sox reacted immediately and harshly. On Friday, July 12, the White Sox announced their withdrawal from the Mountain League.[80] To make their decision abundantly clear, the White Sox failed to appear in Comfort on Sunday, July 14 to play the scheduled game with the Broncos, resulting in a 9–0 forfeit.[81] The White Sox announced that they would continue to play baseball for the remainder of the season by scheduling games with independent teams.[82] Boerne's withdrawal ended the capable tenure of H. O. Adler as Mountain League president.

The *Fredericksburg Standard* reproached the White Sox for their withdrawal:

> To say the least, Boerne's action as the leading team of the league with admittedly the best roster in the league and best support was unsportsmanlike. Their action after finding that the decision had not been rendered in their favor smacks of the attitude of the small child who "takes its dolls home to play" when things are not in its favor . . .
>
> We're sorry Boerne quit, not because we think the league will fold up with them out, nor because it will cheat the fans out of the best games of the season, but because by doing so they defeated the very purpose of the league—"[t]o promote and promulgate good sportsmanship."[83]

While the White Sox were surely disappointed that the league would require them to replay the Legion game, it is hard to understand their decision to withdraw. After all, the White Sox were in first place and seemingly had a good chance to unseat Fredericksburg as league champion in 1935 even if they were forced to replay the Legion game. The perspective of the White Sox might have been conveyed in Boerne's weekly newspaper, but the *Boerne Star* suffered a fire in 1940, destroying its archives and eliminating it as a contemporary source of information for this dispute.

Moreover, it is difficult to assess Legion's protest, and the league's decision upholding it, because the newspaper reports are incomplete and contradictory. Assuming that the runner was struck by the groundball, the runner should have been called out, the ball declared dead, and the batter-runner should have been awarded first base. Thus, a proper ruling by the umpires would have resulted in one out on the play—the same number of outs which resulted from the umpires' erroneous on-field decision. The only difference is that there would have been a runner on first base (the batter awarded first on the interference) rather than a runner on second. The next batter struck out, but the White Sox proceeded to plate four runs before the third out was recorded. In this scenario, Boerne would still have scored four runs even if the umpires had made the correct call on the diamond.

Legion may have argued that the disputed play should have resulted in a double play, contending that if the umpires had ruled properly, the inning would have ended without Boerne scoring any runs because the next batter struck out.[84] If Boerne had not scored four runs in the inning, the White Sox would have lost the game 5–4 instead of winning 8–5 However, if this were Legion's contention, it was fatally flawed because the disputed play could *not* have resulted in a double play. Since the ball was dead as soon as it struck the runner, the batter-runner could not have been thrown out at first. If Legion's protest were upheld on the grounds that the umpires should have awarded Legion a double play, Boerne's objection to the league's decision was well taken.

If the runner had not been not struck by the groundball but instead the second baseman fielded the groundball, tagged the runner, and threw to first, beating the batter-runner, then Legion protested an umpire's judgment call. Since baseball rules consider all judgment calls (such as safe or out calls) to be final, the call would not normally be overturned by protest, absent egregious circumstances. As a result, if the league upheld Legion's protest of a judgment call, it is not surprising that Boerne would take exception.

Even apart from these permutations, comments by our old friend Perry Winkle, columnist of the *San Antonio Evening News*, suggest another possible basis for Boerne's objection to the protest. A week after Boerne's withdrawal, Winkle commented:

> Mountain League "bosses" have red faces today, Boerne White Sox quit, advertised their reasons and we are sorry to have to admit that [business manager] Udo Harz and [manager] Clarence Holekamp did the right thing by throwing their franchise back at the "bosses" and quitting.
>
> Articles of a constitution were agreed upon, and like that of the good old U.S.A., the league "bosses" have no business fooling with a "live wire." And they were "shocked" when Boerne refused to be taken for a "ride."[85]

These remarks imply that in addition to any substantive concerns, Boerne objected to the procedure by which the protest was upheld, possibly claiming that it failed to comply with the league constitution. On this point, the original report of the protest in the *Fredericksburg Standard* sheds some light, noting that even though Legion had immediately protested the game after the umpire's disputed call, "the umpire did not publicly announce to the fans that the balance of the game was being played under protest" in violation of the league constitution, which required the public announcement of a protested game.[86]

Thus, Boerne may have argued that the protest was procedurally defective and should not have been considered by the league because the umpires failed to announce the protest at the game as required by the league constitution. Mr. Winkle, a presumably disinterested journalist, concluded that Boerne's withdrawal was justified, lending credence to the actions of the White Sox, though it is unfortunate that no newspaper accounts give us the full story.

In any event, the White Sox announced they were quitting the Mountain League after the league upheld Legion's protest and required the teams to replay the game. It is unknown if other teams made overtures to dissuade the White Sox from proceeding with its withdrawal. If such entreaties were made, the White Sox were implacable—they withdrew from the league rather than replay the protested game. The truncated league continued the season without Boerne while the White Sox played independent teams for the remainder of the year.

The primary impact of Boerne's withdrawal was reflected in the league standings. Without Boerne, Fredericksburg now found itself in first place by a comfortable margin while Comfort sat in second place. But the biggest impact was on Legion and Kerrville, two teams that were nearly out of playoff contention before Boerne's withdrawal. Now they were competing for third place, the final playoff spot under the league's new playoff rules for 1935, which remained in effect despite the reduction of the league to five teams after Boerne's exit. (Table 20 shows the Mountain League's initial standings after Boerne's withdrawal and games played on July 14.)[87]

Table 20. Mountain League Standings, July 14, 1935 (initial)

	W	L	GB	Pct.
Fredericksburg	11	2	---	.846
Comfort	7	5	3½	.583
Legion	5	8	6	.385
Kerrville	4	10	7½	.286
Bandera	1	11	9½	.083

However, it can be inferred from standings published later that the league decided not to count the Cubs' losses to Boerne on June 23 and June 30 (leaving them with a 5–6 record as of July 14), nor would it count Comfort's 3–2 loss to Boerne on July 7 or Boerne's 9–0 forfeit to Comfort on July 14 (giving the Broncos a 6–4 record as of July 14). These games had begun the second half of the season and were the third and fourth games of the season played by both Legion and Comfort against the White Sox while the other teams had played just two against Boerne at the time of Boerne's withdrawal. By not counting these additional games played by Legion and Comfort against Boerne, all the teams remaining after the withdrawal were on equal footing in the standings because they had each played two games against the White Sox.[88] (The revised league standings as of July 14 are shown on Table 21.)

Table 21. Mountain League Standings, July 14, 1935 (after adjustment)

	W	L	GB	Pct.
Fredericksburg	11	2	---	.846
Comfort	6	4	3½	.600
Legion	5	6	5	.455
Kerrville	4	10	7½	.286
Bandera	1	11	9½	.083

Legion sought to take advantage of its new opportunity to make the playoffs by adjusting the Cubs' mound corps. Going forward, the Cubs would occasionally use shortstop Louie Wootton as a starting pitcher, perhaps because Haskell Archer, their best pitcher, showed signs of fatigue after the latest thrashing by the Giants. On July 21, Wootton pitched well enough to beat Kerrville, 9–6, in 10 innings on July 21[89] and contributed at the plate as well, singling in the go-ahead runs in the three-run 10th inning for the Cubs.

The following week Legion returned Archer to the mound. He allowed nine hits but only two runs as Legion again defeated Kerrville, 7–2.[90] The Cubs managed only six hits, but Kerrville pitcher Warren Toler issued four walks while Braves fielders made five costly errors behind him. Rather than contending merely for third place, Legion, now above .500 at 7–6, set its sights on second-place Comfort.

At first, the Broncos kept pace with Legion, thanks to a doubleheader sweep of Bandera on July 21 by scores of 8–6 and 15–3.[91] Skeeter Pankratz led the

Broncos, stroking seven hits in the twin bill. After that, however, Comfort took a nosedive, losing three in a row. Perhaps overconfident after their sweep the week before, the Broncos dropped a 2–1 decision to Bandera on July 28[92]—only the second win of the season for the Cowboys. Bandera pitcher Charlie Gray held the Broncos to two hits just one week after they jumped on Cowboys pitching for 23 runs in two games.

Fredericksburg piled on Comfort, sweeping the Broncos in successive weeks, dropping Comfort into third place. On August 4, Comfort pitcher Harold Krauter lost, 5–4, when the host Giants scored the deciding run in the bottom of the eighth without benefit of a base hit—after an error and a walk, the runners advanced on a sacrifice bunt before the lead runner scored on Phil Klaerner's sacrifice fly.[93] In the rematch a week later in Fredericksburg, Giants right fielder Red Schnerr slapped four hits, scoring three times, to lead the Giants to a 9–4 win.[94] For unknown reasons, Krauter did not pitch this game. Instead, Hilmar Stieler started on the mound, allowing 13 hits while failing to strike out a batter in suffering the loss, leaving Comfort with an 8–7 mark for the season.[95] The Giants' sweep of the two games clinched the pennant for Fredericksburg with a 13–2 record.

Elsewhere, Legion had an easier task than Comfort, playing Bandera in successive weeks. On August 4, Legion scored seven runs in the third inning then held off a Cowboys rally to nab the victory, 10–7.[96] The following Sunday, young southpaw Bill Dickey pitched the Cubs to a 7–5 win over Bandera, for the team's fourth win in a row.[97] The winning streak moved the Cubs, now 9–6, into second place, one game ahead of Comfort after the Broncos three-game losing streak dropped them to 8–7.

Legion and Comfort were scheduled to play each other the last two weeks of the regular season, first at Legion on August 18, then at Comfort on August 25. Since Kerrville dropped out of playoff contention by losing three consecutive games, falling to a 4–13 record, Legion and Comfort would both make the playoffs, but the final two games would decide home-field advantage for the playoff game between the second- and third-place teams.

Based on his win against Bandera the week before, Legion started Bill Dickey in the first game between the clubs on August 18 instead of either their best pitcher, Haskell Archer, or part-time hurler Louie Wootton. Comfort countered with its best pitcher, Harold Krauter.

After the teams traded runs in the first inning, the Broncos pounded Dickey in the second. Archer relieved Dickey but not before the Broncos scored five runs when catcher Arthur Bergmann and outfielder Walter Kutzer each bashed home runs. Left fielder Christie Lindemann contributed three hits while Krauter kept the Cubs in check, holding them to eight hits and striking out five, in a 10–6 Comfort win.[98]

Since both clubs were now tied with 9–7 records,[99] the last game of the regular season would determine second place. This time it was Comfort that made a puzzling decision on a starting pitcher. Instead of starting Krauter, who defeated the Cubs the week before, the Broncos started Hilmar Stieler, who pitched effectively in only one of his four previous starts. Legion started Louie Wootton, who found his rhythm as a pitcher late in the season after starring at shortstop most of the year.

The Cubs and the Broncos were tied 3–3 in the fifth inning when Legion jumped on Stieler, scoring six runs, and knocking him out of the game in favor of Krauter. Haskell Archer, playing second base this game, stroked six hits while right fielder Joe Woods[100] slugged a home run as Legion sailed to an 18–4 victory at Comfort. Wootton gave up seven hits, striking out 12, to earn the win, nabbing second place for the Cubs.[101]

After the Giants clinched the pennant, they crushed visiting Kerrville, 19–5, on August 18,[102] scoring their 19 runs on 14 hits, including home runs by Phillip Klaerner and first baseman Henry Langerhans. Elias Klaerner pitched the complete game victory. The next Sunday, the Giants visited Kerrville where the Braves played tougher.[103] Behind Red Schnerr's two doubles and a single, the Giants prevailed, 6–3, despite a home run by Braves player-manager Ben Grantham. Phillip Klaerner returned to the mound, allowing six hits, to win the season finale. The first-place Giants finished the regular season with a 15–2 record, five games ahead of second-place Legion.

As in 1934, Kerrville and Bandera finished at the bottom of the standings. After winning three games in a row in late April and May, the Braves lost 12 of their next 13 games, defeating only Bandera, 8–2, on July 7 when Ben Grantham rapped three hits.[104] Kerrville finished in fourth place at 4–14.

Bandera did not earn its first win of the season until the Cowboys defeated Kerrville on July 14, winning, 9–6.[105] The Cowboys' only other win came against Comfort on July 28, when Charlie Gray's two-hitter gave them a 2–1 victory.[106] Bandera finished in last place with a 2–16 record, their season mercifully ending on August 11 because Boerne's withdrawal canceled the Cowboys' last two games of the season originally scheduled against the departed White Sox. (The final 1935 Mountain League standings[107] are shown on Table 22.)

Table 22. Mountain League Final Standings, 1935

	W	L	GB	Pct.
Fredericksburg	15	2	---	.882
Legion	10	7	5	.588
Comfort	9	8	6	.529
Kerrville	4	14	11½	.222
Bandera	2	16	13½	.111

With the regular season now completed, the Mountain League turned to the postseason beginning with the playoff game on September 1 between the second- and third-place teams. As the second-place club, Legion chose to play its playoff game against Comfort at Kerrville's ballpark.[108] Since those clubs had played each other the last two weeks of the regular season, it would be the third consecutive game between the Cubs and Broncos. The winner would face Fredericksburg in the best-of-three championship series.

For the playoff game, both teams called on starting pitchers who had managed wins against their opponent. Comfort started Harold Krauter who defeated Legion on August 18 while Legion tabbed Louie Wootton, who handled Comfort in the Cubs' lopsided win on August 25.

Either the playing field in Kerrville was in poor condition or both teams suffered from nerves because they committed 13 errors—six by Comfort and seven by Legion.[109] Comfort scored twice in the first inning. After Christie Lindemann and Joe Pankratz singled, Arthur Bergmann laid down a squeeze bunt, scoring Lindemann, but Pankratz also scored when pitcher Wootton threw wildly to second base. Legion fought back in the bottom of the first, scoring a run on a single by Baker after Kaiser singled and stole second base—his first of three stolen bases. Haskell Archer then singled but Baker was thrown out at the plate on a perfect throw by center fielder Walter Kutzer.

The Broncos added a run in the third when Joe Pankratz reached third on a rundown play and then scored on a passed ball. The Cubs responded with a run in the bottom of the third, when the Broncos infield committed four errors. After Legion tied the game at 3–3 in the fourth, Comfort grabbed the lead for good in the fifth inning. Christie Lindemann doubled home a run before Harold Krauter scored on an infield out. The Broncos added three more runs in the sixth inning. With runners at first and third, Dick Spenrath rapped a hot grounder to shortstop Powell, but second baseman Archer failed to cover second, allowing the runner on third to score. Lindemann's third hit of the game plated two more runs for an 8–3 Comfort lead.

Legion rallied in the seventh. After Kaiser beat out an infield hit and stole second, Baker singled him home and Clergy Hollimon doubled to score Baker, cutting the deficit to 8–5. But Comfort responded in the top of the ninth with four runs—one on an error and three more on two-out singles by Robert Lindner, Morris Goforth, and Spenrath.

Krauter held Legion scoreless in the bottom of the ninth to preserve a 12–5 victory, sending Comfort into the championship series against Fredericksburg.[110] Krauter gave up nine hits, striking out just two, but he was good enough to dash the hopes of the Cubs. Wootton took the loss, allowing 12 hits.

The first game of the championship series was originally scheduled for September 8 in Fredericksburg, but the league decided to postpone the game for a week to avoid a conflict with the Golden Jubilee Fair in Fredericksburg.[111] The opening game was now scheduled for September 15 at Fair Park. It was reported that Comfort chose to play its home game on September 22 at the Kerrville ballpark because the Broncos' Faltin Field did "not have the proper seating and other facilities necessary for a championship game."[112] Perhaps this account was not accurate because, as it turned out, the second game of the series was in fact played at Faltin Field, not in Kerrville.

To stay sharp until September 15, the Giants hosted the Brady Turks of the Hill Country League on September 8. Edgar Klett, Alfons Klaerner, and Phillip Klaerner each stroked three hits—both Klaerners hit two doubles—leading the Giants to a 9–1 win.[113]

In the first game of the championship series, the clubs started their top pitchers, Phillip Klaerner, the Giants' "Black Ace,"[114] and Comfort's Harold Krauter. The Giants opened the scoring in the second inning. After a walk and an error put two men on, singles by Vincent Ransleben, Henry Langerhans, Phil Klaerner, and player-manager Andy Andrews produced four runs.

Down 5–0 after the Giants added another run in the fourth, the Broncos scored a run in the fifth inning on singles by Joe Pankratz and Walter Kutzer followed by an error. The Giants piled on in the bottom of the fifth, producing five runs on three singles and two doubles for a 10–1 lead. It was all over but the shouting. The teams traded runs late in the game, but the Giants breezed to a 13–3 victory.[115] Phillip Klaerner starred both at the plate and on the mound, rapping four hits (a single, two doubles, and a triple), scoring four runs and driving in three, while scattering eight hits and striking out seven Broncos without issuing a walk.

In addition to Phillip Klaerner's four-hit game, right fielder Red Schnerr smashed three hits, including a double, while second baseman Weise drove in three runs on two hits. Krauter suffered through the Giants' attack, going the distance for Comfort, giving up 17 hits and 13 runs. The Broncos would now have to win two games in a row as the teams prepared to play the second game of the series in Comfort.

The Broncos returned Krauter to the mound, hoping for a much-improved performance against the Giants' vaunted offense. Unlike the first game, this game would be a tightly pitched clash between Krauter and Phillip Klaerner. The Giants scored first in the third inning. After Red Schnerr was safe on an error by Bronco third baseman Skeeter Pankratz, player-manager Andy Andrews tripled him home. Krauter stranded Andrews on third, inducing Elias Klaerner to ground out to third. Comfort tied the score in the bottom of the third. Dick Spenrath singled and was sacrificed to second. After Phillip Klaerner struck out Christie Lindemann, Skeeter Pankratz blasted a triple to center, scoring Spenrath.

The Giants came right back in the fourth. Edgar Klett singled, and Felix Hahn sacrificed him to second. Light-hitting shortstop Vincent Ransleben doubled, scoring Klett for a 2–1 Giants lead. Both pitchers held their opponents in check until the seventh when Fredericksburg added a run after Phillip Klaerner singled, advanced to second on a groundout to first, and scored on a single by Andrews—his second run batted in of the game.

With the Giants leading, 3–1, heavy rainfall began in the eighth inning while the Giants were batting. The umpires called the game on account of rain.[116] Since the teams had played at least five full innings, it was an official game, resulting in a shortened 3–1 victory,[117] earning the 1935 Mountain League championship for the Giants—their second league title in a row.[118] Although Krauter pitched much more effectively in this game, the Broncos could muster just four hits off Phillip Klaerner, who kept the Comfort batters off balance all day.

The champions did not stay idle for long. The following Sunday, the Giants traveled to Richland Springs to meet the Hill Country League All-Stars,[119] consisting of players mostly from Llano, Richland Springs, and Brownwood.[120] The Giants lost, 7–4, after the All-Stars scored four runs in the eighth inning on four hits and three errors.[121] On October 6, Fredericksburg hosted the All-Stars at Fair Park, where the Giants avenged their prior loss by sweeping a doubleheader by scores of 10–3 and 5–2.[122] Phillip Klaerner pitched a complete game victory in the first game, then saved the nightcap after Red Schnerr smashed a grand slam.[123]

After Boerne's departure in July, Fredericksburg dominated the Mountain League, cruising to a 15–2 record and winning the championship series against a solid Comfort club. (See Appendix F for team and individual statistics for all Mountain League teams in 1935, including Boerne.) The Giants averaged more than eight runs per game, outscoring their opponents by a phenomenal 99-run margin, 140–41. Left fielder Edgar Klett hit .435 with power, slugging 10 extra-base hits (six doubles, three triples, and one home run) for a .652 slugging percentage. Klett led the team in hits (30) and runs scored (21) and was second in stolen bases with six. New player-manager Andy Andrews hit .370 with a .543 slugging percentage while right fielder Red Schnerr hit .354, leading the team in doubles (eight) and stolen bases (seven). On the mound, Phillip Klaerner admirably filled the gap when his cousin, Chester "Smokey" Klaerner, left the Giants to pursue professional baseball. Phillip crafted an outstanding 10–2 mark, giving up just 34 runs in 97 innings for a nifty TRA of 3.15. Phillip's brother, Elias Klaerner, and his cousin, Alfons Klaerner, also pitched effectively when Phillip needed a rest.[124]

Comfort returned to a winning record in 1935, making its first championship series appearance. Second baseman Robert Lindner led the Broncos offense, hitting .351, while third baseman Skeeter Pankratz hit .299. A perennial star, shortstop Joe Pankratz hit just .263 but made the most of his hits, leading the team in runs with 14. Harold Krauter led the pitching staff with a 7–4 record, giving up 48 runs in 102 innings for a respectable TRA of 4.23. However, Hilmar Stieler lost four games without a victory, allowing more than 10 runs per nine innings. The Broncos put up a spirited effort in the postseason, defeating Legion to advance to the championship series, but they were outclassed by the Giants.

The Legion Cubs made an impressive debut in the Mountain League. Led by two versatile players, Louie Wootton (shortstop, center fielder, and pitcher) and Haskell Archer (pitcher, second baseman, and outfielder), the Cubs came on strong after losing their first four games to finish second with a 10–7 record, but they fell short in the second-place playoff game against Comfort. Wootton hit .308, leading the team in runs scored (19). Archer hit .317, tying Wootton for the team lead in hits with 20. On the mound, Archer won six games without a loss,[125] a vast improvement over his 1933 season with Kerrville and Comfort when he was a combined 7–6.[126] Others did not pitch nearly as well, including Albrecht, who lost three games early in the season without a win, permitting 22 runs in 25 innings. Wootton engineered a 2–1 mark when called on to pitch. The torrid finish of the Cubs gave their fans reason to be optimistic for 1936.

Kerrville managed to avoid the cellar in 1935, but with a 4–14 record, the Braves did not see much improvement over their last-place finish the season before. Player-manager Ben Grantham hit .308, leading the team in hits with 18 while playing catcher and second baseman. First baseman Maybeaux and outfielder Louis Fisher contributed to the offense, hitting .294 and .318, respectively, but they played part-time roles. Pitcher Warren Toler struggled to a 1–8 record, allowing 62 runs in 64 2/3 innings for a TRA of 8.62. His counterpart, Slim Esbeck, did not fare much better, finishing 1–4, giving up 35 runs in 43 innings (TRA 7.33). Clearly, the Braves needed an infusion of talent, especially on the mound, to improve in 1936.

For the third season in a row, Bandera labored near the bottom of the standings, ending in the cellar with a 2–16 record. Their first victory came at the expense of Kerrville, 9–6, on July 14 after the Cowboys lost their first 12 games.[127] Bandera's only other win was Charlie Gray's surprising 2–1 win over Comfort on July 28.[128] As in 1934, Bandera had difficulty scoring runs. Second baseman F. Hamilton led the team in hitting with a .281 average—the only regular to hit over .250. Several other starters did not climb above the .200 mark: center fielder Tommy Dugosh (.128), right fielder Knibbe (.146), catcher Adamietz (.122), and third baseman Click (.103). Charlie Gray notched both of Bandera's victories but otherwise struggled on the mound, allowing 47 runs in 61 innings for a TRA of 6.93.

While the Mountain League completed its season, crowning the Fredericksburg Giants as repeating champions, the Boerne White Sox continued their winning ways against non-league opponents after their withdrawal from the league. On July 21, the Sunday after their withdrawal from the league, the White Sox met the Converse Cubs in Boerne. Converse must have had a strong team because they played the White Sox tough. Edgar Bergmann yielded 10 hits but allowed only a single run to outpitch the Cubs' Lefty Mayer in a 2–1 White Sox win.[129] Shortstop Ernst Nagel led the Sox with two hits. The *San Antonio Express* account of the game reported that "[n]ow playing independent ball, the White Sox would like games with some of the stronger amateur Southwest Texas teams" and urged interested teams to contact Udo Harz, business manager of the White Sox.[130]

In August, the White Sox played a home-and-home series with the Pleasanton All-Stars. On August 11, the White Sox traveled to Pleasanton (30 miles south of San Antonio) for the first game. The White Sox teed off on All-Stars pitcher S. Ward, scoring 10 runs in the first six innings. Catcher Harry Phillip led the Sox attack with three hits, including a double and triple, while Gus Pfeiffer added two hits including a double. The *San Antonio News* blamed the loss on All-Stars manager Mose Dixon: "The big reason the All-Stars got the short end was that [Dixon] didn't start the game as pitcher, but finished it nicely, holding the Sox scoreless in the last three frames. However, Mose was given the blame by Pleasanton fans for the loss, as he under-rated the invaders a bit and it was a costly mistake."[131]

The following Sunday, Dixon did not make the same error in Boerne. Starting the game this time, Dixon, "the ancient speed king," limited the White Sox to six hits as the All-Stars prevailed, 5–2.[132] Walter Bergmann, Edgar's younger brother, pitched well as the starting pitcher but allowed the All-Stars to score all five of their runs in the fourth inning. Johnny Uecker rapped three hits for the White Sox.

On September 1, the White Sox met the Converse Cubs again in Boerne, but this time, the Sox humiliated the Cubs, scoring 15 runs in the eighth inning![133] Johnny Uecker hit two triples in that inning and was on deck when the third out was recorded. The game account in the *San Antonio Light* did not report the final score or other details of the game, perhaps to avoid further embarrassment of Converse.

Three weeks later, the White Sox traveled to New Braunfels to play the Dittlinger Millers on the final day of the Comal County Fair.[134] This was the same team that defeated Fredericksburg, 6–5, on July 28 on one of the Giants off days created by Boerne's departure from the Mountain League, so the Millers were a tough opponent. Even though Edgar Bergmann allowed 11 hits and walked five, the White Sox held on to win, 3–2. Harry Schweppe and Gus Pfeiffer notched two hits each, Pfeiffer driving in two runs and Schweppe knocking in the other Sox run.

In compiling an 11–1 record for their partial season in the Mountain League, the White Sox commanded respect, featuring veteran ballplayers at every position. In league play, shortstop Ernst Nagel, new to the White Sox in 1935, led the team in both batting average (.423) and slugging percentage (.558).[135] Gus Pfeiffer, who moved from shortstop to right field to make room for Nagel, hit .396/.542 (batting average/slugging percentage) while second baseman Rudy Leidl (.415/.528) and left fielder Schweppe (.353/.412) also excelled.

Although some box scores are skimpy on pitching statistics, resulting in incomplete season records, Edgar Bergmann generated a record of at least 9–1, giving up just 23 runs in 82 innings for an outstanding TRA of 2.52. Boerne players and fans surely pondered what might have transpired if the White Sox had not withdrawn from the league after 12 games. Would they have vanquished the rival Giants and won the 1935 Mountain League title? They would never know.

Amid the tempestuous Mountain League season, the Hill Country League plodded along with six teams in the northern tier of the Hill Country, including the Brownwood Bears (Brownwood is located 46 miles northeast of Brady).[136] After winning three consecutive Hill Country League titles in 1931–33 and serving as one of the strongest teams in the HCL since its inception in 1930, Llano stumbled to a 2–17 overall mark for the 1935 season.[137] Newcomer Brownwood took advantage of the Cowboys' steep decline, grabbing the first-half crown with an 8–2 record while Richland Springs and San Saba, the 1934 HCL champions, tied for the second-half flag with 8–2 records.[138]

In the playoff game to decide the second-half winner, Richland Springs disposed of San Saba, 2–0, to advance to the best-of-five championship series against Brownwood.[139] The series went the distance, but the Bears defeated Richland Springs in the decisive fifth game, 6–1, to win the 1935 HCL crown.[140] (For the 1935 HCL standings, see Appendix G).

As the 1935 baseball season wound down in October, baseball fans in the Hill Country could only ponder what 1936 would bring. Would Boerne return to the Mountain League, renewing its bitter feud with Fredericksburg? If not, would the Mountain League continue to operate in 1936? If the Mountain League disbanded, would Boerne, Fredericksburg, Comfort, Kerrville, Legion, and Bandera move to the Hill Country League, creating the southern circuit that the HCL directors had rejected in 1933? A pall of uncertainty hung over both players and fans in the benumbing winter months as they patiently counted the days until the crack of the bat rang out again on Hill Country diamonds in the 1936 season.

CHAPTER 16

EDGAR BERGMANN

A Pillar of Boerne

Many of the ballplayers who played in the Mountain League during the Depression were the great-grandsons of the earliest German settlers in the Hill Country and became stalwarts of their communities for many years after they hung up their spikes. Edgar Bergmann—ace pitcher for the Boerne White Sox—is a prime example.

Edgar's great-grandfather, Christian Bergmann, married Johanna Christiane Luise (or Louise) Dressler in 1842 in Germany. The couple and their three sons, including Edgar's grandfather, Karl (or Carl or Charles) Heinrich Bergmann, immigrated to Texas in 1854, moving to the Boerne area one year later to farm on their new land.[1] Karl Bergmann grew up in Boerne and married Pauline Vogt in 1881. Edgar's father, Louis Adolph Bergmann, was born to Karl and Pauline in Comfort in 1889. Louis married Ida Mary Minnich on May 9, 1911, in Boerne. Louis and Ida had four sons and a daughter. Three of the sons played for the White Sox: Edgar, born August 12, 1912; Walter, born December 21, 1913; and Elmer, born May 17, 1922.

Edgar Bergmann graduated from Boerne High School and attended night classes at Trinity University. Edgar turned 21 in 1933, the first year of the Mountain League. He was a fierce competitor, using his pinpoint control to thwart opposing hitters. In the three years in the Mountain League (1933–35), Bergmann was consistently effective, compiling a 23–8 record.[2] Bergmann and Chester Klaerner of Fredericksburg stood out as the top pitchers in the league during these years.

After the Mountain League folded before the 1936 season, Bergmann continued to pitch for the White Sox for many years. However, in 1940, Bergmann pitched for the Owl Café in the Spanish-American League in San Antonio.[3] Bergmann played for a semiprofessional team in San Antonio for several years, but it is not known which team (it may have been the Owl Café team).[4] He also played in the San Antonio City League, where he was selected as the most outstanding player four times.[5]

Figure 40. Edgar Bergmann, Boerne White Sox pitcher. (Courtesy of Betsy Bergmann Sueltenfuss.)

Bergmann returned to the White Sox after his tenure in San Antonio. As late as 1951, when he was 39 years old, Bergmann straddled the rubber for the White Sox as his brother, Walter, served as his catcher.[6] (It should be noted that third baseman Johnny Uecker and outfielder Clarence Bourgeois were also still playing for the White Sox in 1951.) The Bergmann brothers played in the same lineup on many occasions.[7] All the Bergmann brothers, but especially Edgar, were anchors of the Boerne White Sox for many years, although Walter did sign a professional contract and played for a time in the Rio Grande Valley League.[8]

While pitching for the White Sox, Edgar worked in the lumber business. In 1931, Bergmann began working for the Ebensberger and Son Lumber Yard at 231 South Main Street in Boerne—a company that started in the 1880s. After leaving Ebensberger in 1937, Bergmann worked for George C. Vaughn Lumber and Wilson Lumber Company in San Antonio. In 1957, Bergmann and his wife, Ruby, purchased the former Ebensberger Lumber Yard where Bergmann had worked in his younger days, starting the Bergmann Lumber Company at the same location. Bergmann's White Sox teammate, shortstop Ernst Nagel, was one of the first employees of Bergmann Lumber Company.

In 1969, the Bergmanns purchased the property directly across the street at 236 South Main.[9] This property included the building operated as a general store for many years by H. O. Adler, president of the Boerne White Sox and the Mountain League.[10] The property also included the old Theis House built in 1858. After restoring these buildings, the Bergmann Lumber Company reopened at this location on March 1, 1969. Edgar owned the Bergmann Lumber Company for 40 years, from 1957 until his death in 1997.

While operating Bergmann Lumber Company, Edgar was an active leader in the Boerne community, serving as president of the Kendall County Fair Association, a director of Boerne State Bank, a life member of Boerne Turn Verein (a German bowling club), a director of the Boerne Berges Fest, a board member of the Boerne Public Library,[11] and a member of the Kendall County Historical Commission. He was also active in the Boerne *Gesangverein* (a German singing club), the Grange, the South Texas Racing Association, and the Texas Lumbermen's Association.

Ruby served the community in many ways as well. In addition to her participation in the Boerne *Gesangverein*, the Grange, and the Kendall County Fair Ladies' Auxiliary, Ruby was a founding member of the Boerne Area Historical Preservation Society. Edgar and Ruby were both active members of First Baptist Church in Boerne.

Edgar passed away on January 6, 1997. One month later, Ruby died. They left four children: Barbara, Donald, Betsy, and Randy. Donald worked at Bergmann Lumber Company for a time starting in 1975 after serving in the military, and later managed Alamo Lumber Company locations in both Freer and Alice, Texas.

Figure 41. Edgar Bergmann, Boerne businessman. (Courtesy of Betsy Bergmann Sueltenfuss.)

After college, Randy Bergmann returned to Boerne in 1971 and managed the Bergmann Lumber Company, assuming ownership upon his father's death in 1997 and operating it until the business closed in 2017. The Bergmann family still owns the property today, which is now leased to the Tusculum Brewing Company, a local brewpub that has retained the historical nature of the building constructed by H. O. Adler in 1911.

Edgar Bergmann was a pillar of the Boerne community. A star of the Boerne White Sox for several decades, Bergmann later ascended to the role of prominent businessman and civic leader. Bergmann's life demonstrates how deeply Hill Country ballplayers were interwoven into the fabric of their communities. A number were baseball heroes who became renowned leaders in business or government as well as many local organizations and institutions. But none were more prominent than Edgar Bergmann, who left a dual legacy of baseball stardom and devotion to the Boerne community.

CHAPTER 17

DEAD AS A DODO BIRD

League Vicissitudes, 1936 and Beyond

The economic outlook of the Hill Country was improving in 1936. Kerrville banker and businessman Louis A. Schreiner returned from his wedding in New York City to report that the industrial centers in the East were optimistic.[1] More importantly for the Hill Country, Schreiner projected a strong wool and mohair market with higher prices in 1936, aided by new uses found for mohair fabric and a cold winter, which increased demand for wool.[2]

Despite the reviving economy, the outlook for baseball in the Hill Country was less than sanguine in early 1936. Boerne's withdrawal in 1935 exposed some cracks in the foundation of the Mountain League. The first rumblings of trouble came when Fredericksburg decided in early 1936 to return to the Hill Country League, joining five northern Hill Country towns—Brady, Mason, Llano, Richland Springs, and Lampasas.[3] Perhaps Fredericksburg was so incensed by Boerne's withdrawal in 1935 that the Giants would not have stayed in the Mountain League even if Boerne did return. Or perhaps the White Sox failed to announce their intentions soon enough; they did not decide to rejoin the Mountain League until early March 1936. By that time, the Giants had already chosen to return to the HCL. Boerne, Bandera, Kerrville, Legion, and Comfort did make a last-ditch effort, formally inviting Fredericksburg to remain in the Mountain League, but the Giants declined.[4]

The belated invitation to Fredericksburg amounted to the last gasp of the Mountain League. After the Giants reaffirmed their decision to move to the HCL, Kerrville announced that it would also join the HCL, increasing the league's number of teams to seven.[5] Three weeks later, however, the Braves suddenly disbanded, deciding not to field a team at all for the 1936 season.[6]

Not long after Kerrville's exit, Comfort also chose not to play baseball in 1936, sealing the fate of the Mountain League. Only three clubs remained—Boerne,

Legion, and Bandera—not enough to sustain the league.[7] After the Mountain League dissolved, each of these three teams initially chose to play independently, although two would end up playing in leagues before the season ended.

Regarding the demise of the Mountain League, columnist Perry Winkle offered the following commentary, alluding to the controversy that led to Boerne's withdrawal in 1935:

> The Mountain League crashed due to the fact it had more managers, directors, secretaries, business managers and team directors than anything else. The towns built up impressive front offices, Directors by the carload were lined up.
>
> The manager had to have a business manager, assistant managers, and self-styled coaches also dogged his footsteps.
>
> The president of the league had a flock of directors to advise him. He was not supposed to be either fair or intelligent, so the towns protected him by sending a flock of directors down to a meeting to shout down the president, the managers, and the umpires.
>
> The Mountain League had too much management and too little anything else.[8]

In the absence of the Mountain League, Bandera, along with two other small Hill Country towns, Center Point and Medina, tried to form a new league, but their efforts failed when Boerne decided not to join the endeavor.[9]

Beginning its independent play on March 8, Boerne defeated the Meggs Servicemen—a team sponsored by a filling station—in 10 innings, 8–7.[10] Starting pitcher Walter Bergmann, Edgar's younger brother, kept Meggs scoreless but when Edgar relieved Walter, he gave up a 4–0 lead, allowing seven unanswered runs. The White Sox rallied to tie the score in the ninth before pushing across the winning run in the bottom of the 10th. The following week, *San Antonio Evening News* columnist Perry Winkle praised Boerne, managed this season by first baseman Gus Wendler, and its redoubtable ballplayers:

> The Boerne White Sox are not just a ball team. They're more of an institution . . .
>
> Boerne citizens know that the White Sox are a good investment as an ad for their community, so they ante up without argument every year. Boerne has no oil fields, gold mines, mineral waters, or army posts to help it get ahold of ballplayers.

> The roster is composed of hometown boys who can be counted on for a game, whether there's a dime in the cash drawer or not.[11]

Playing independent ball must not have suited Boerne for long, because the White Sox joined the South Central League (SCL) before the opening of the SCL season on May 3. Ironically, the SCL included three teams located east of San Antonio—Luling, Seguin, and Gonzales—all much farther away than Boerne's Mountain League opponents had been. On the other hand, New Braunfels—a natural Hill Country rival to Boerne—also played in the SCL.

The White Sox defeated the Gonzales Indians, 5–1, in their first SCL game. Walter Bergmann scattered eight hits for the win.[12] Even though the White Sox managed only four hits, they took advantage of nine walks issued by Indians pitcher Forshagen to claim their inaugural SCL victory. On May 10, Boerne traveled to Luling where they defeated the Redwings, 9–6, behind Johnny Uecker's two doubles and a home run.[13] Walter Bergmann earned the win despite allowing 14 hits. Boerne won its third consecutive game the following Sunday when the White Sox hosted the Seguin Pale Hose.[14] The White Sox pushed across the only run of the game in the 14th inning, when second baseman Rudy Leidl walked, stole second, and then scored on an error by the Seguin shortstop for a 1–0 victory.[15] Walter Bergmann went the distance, shutting out the Pale Hose for 14 innings.

Later in the season, on July 19, Boerne traveled to Luling, where the Redwings held them scoreless for a 7–0 victory—the third consecutive shutout by Luling pitchers.[16] After giving up five runs, Boerne's Walter Bergmann was relieved in the seventh by his brother, Edgar. White Sox second baseman Rudy Leidl accounted for two of the team's hits.

Other than these four games, we found no accounts of games played by Boerne in the SCL in 1936. However, the White Sox did not ignore their rivalry with Fredericksburg even though the clubs were now in different leagues. The White Sox hosted Fredericksburg on July 4 as the featured game for Boerne's Independence Day celebration at the Kendall County Fairgrounds. The Giants pulled out a thrilling win, 3–1, in 12 innings,[17] scoring the decisive runs on a throwing error by Sox catcher Harry Phillip and a single by Giants second baseman Paul Weise. On Friday, August 28, the two teams opened the Gillespie County Fair, the Giants defeating the White Sox, 6–3.[18] Fredericksburg pitcher Pete Petermann, new to the club in 1936, held the White Sox to six hits, while Edgar Bergmann took the loss.

Legion initially decided to disband in 1936, encouraging its players to join the Kerrville Braves. When the Braves abruptly dissolved their team, however, the Legion club was resurrected. Kerrville returned the favor by encouraging Braves players to join the Cubs.[19] Legion club secretary Clay Neal commented, however, that the Cubs would not join a league until "the team is better organized."[20]

Legion ultimately joined the HCL, replacing Lampasas, which folded. By early August, Legion compiled a dreadful 1–9 record. Legion's final regular season game with the Llano Cowboys on August 16 was not played, Legion apparently forfeiting the game. In fact, forfeits were a recurring problem for the HCL in 1936.[21] As a result, the *Fredericksburg Standard* dubbed the 1936 season the "Forfeit Year."[22]

Unlike Boerne and Legion, which joined leagues in 1936, Bandera remained independent. Although records are scanty, the *Bandera New Era* did report a seesaw game on April 12 between Bandera and Legion before the Cubs joined the HCL. Legion scored early but Bandera rallied to take the lead, 7–6, in the bottom of the eighth. The Cubs overcame Bandera by scoring five runs in the top of the ninth to win, 11–7.[23] The newspaper noted that the Cowboys would play Harper on the following two Sundays, but no record was found of any Bandera games for the remainder of 1936.

Despite the HCL's troubles, Fredericksburg continued its dominance of Hill Country baseball, winning the HCL pennant by a five-game margin with a 16–3 record. Fredericksburg's player-manager Andy Andrews led his team by example, topping the Giants with an astounding .566 batting average (30 hits in 53 at-bats). He also led the team in RBIs with 23. Five other regulars hit at least .333: Paul Weise (.355), Elias Klaerner (.353), Felix Hahn (.350), Pfeil[24] (.344), and Phillip Klaerner (.333). Edgar Klett, the putative Mountain League MVP in 1935, slumped a bit in 1936 but still batted .309 and drove in 21 runs.[25] One of the Pankratz brothers—probably Skeeter[26]—hit .315 and was second on the team in runs scored. He played for the Giants after Comfort failed to field a team in 1936.[27] (Table 23 shows the final 1936 HCL standings.)[28]

Table 23. HCL Final Standings, 1936

	W	L	GB	Pct.
Fredericksburg	16	3	---	.842
Richland Springs	11	8	5	.579
Llano	11	9	5½	.550
Brady	10	10	6½	.500

Junction	4	4	6½	.500
Mason	4	8	8½	.333
Lampasas	2	7	9	.222
Legion	1	9	10½	.100

The top four teams made the playoffs under the HCL playoff format in 1936. The generous playoff system and league instability resulted in some intrigue. On July 3, the HCL invited former member Junction to join the league, replacing the Mason franchise, which ceased operations.[29] The HCL advised Junction that if they finished in the top four spots, they would make the playoffs. On August 9, the last Sunday of the regular season, Junction romped over Llano, one of the league's best teams, 24–8, giving them a final record of 4–4 in their abbreviated league play. Junction finished tied for fourth place with the Brady Turks, who also ended the season at .500 but played a full season slate for a 10–10 mark.[30] Shortly after the end of the regular season, the HCL directors held a meeting without Junction representatives in attendance. Ten days later, the HCL notified Junction that the league directors had broken the fourth-place tie by a coin toss, which eliminated Junction in favor of Brady.[31]

When the playoffs began, the first-place Giants met third-place Llano while second-place Richland Springs faced the fourth-place Brady Turks. The Giants and the Cowboys split their first two games, Fredericksburg winning the first game, 6–4, while Llano shut out the potent Giants, 1–0, in the second game.[32] In the decisive game at Fair Park, the Giants stopped Llano, 7–0, advancing to the championship series against Richland Springs, who had defeated Brady by winning a doubleheader, 6–2 and 9–3, after losing the first game of the series, 7–0.[33]

The Giants rallied to win the first game of the series against Richland Springs in walk-off fashion, 10–9. Down by a run with two outs and nobody on base in the bottom of the ninth, Elias Klaerner doubled and Pfeil[34] walked. Red Schnerr then stepped to the plate and smacked a double—his second of the game—to drive in the winning runs.[35] Elias Klaerner earned the win in relief.

In the second game at Richland Springs, the Giants grabbed the HCL title by scoring five runs in the seventh inning for an 8–3 win. Red Schnerr and Elias Klaerner both smacked triples, while Klaerner also started a triple play with a running catch in deep right field. The Giants earned their third consecutive league title after winning Mountain League championships in 1934 and 1935.[36] In seven years of league play—five in the HCL and two in the Mountain League—the Giants now owned four league titles.

Figure 42. Boerne White Sox, 1938. Back row (L–R): Walter Bergmann, Gus Wendler, Leroy Katzer, Johnny Uecker, Johnny Leidl, William Behr, unknown player. Front row (L–R): Harry Phillip, David Epperson, Clif Patton, Ray Minor Sr., Clarence Bourgeois. (Courtesy of Tom Phillip.)

Figure 43. Fredericksburg Giants, 1940. Bat boys, front (L–R): Roy Stroeher, Wilfred Seipp. Front row (L–R): George Zenner, Henry Henke, Alfred Grobe, Arno Icke, Stanley "Red" Schnerr, Ben Mogford, Vincent Ransleben, Alois Jenschke, Max Moellering, and Otto "Britton" Schneider Jr. Back row (L–R): Edgar Marschall, business manager, Elias "Red" Klaerner, Edgar Klett, George Zimmerman, Hugo Klaerner, Alfred Enderlin, Louis "Schramm" Schneider, Eugene Jung, and scorekeeper Elton Jordan. (Courtesy of Schneider Collection, Gillespie County Historical Society, Fredericksburg, Texas)

Figure 44. Comfort Broncos. Standing (L–R): Bernard Stieler, Hilmar Stieler, Morris Goforth, Joe Pankratz, Arthur Bergmann, Ernst "Skeeter" Pankratz, manager F. M. "Pat" Faust. Kneeling (L–R): Christie Lindemann, Robert Lindner, Harold Krauter, Chester Spenrath, Walter Kutzer. (Courtesy of Comfort Heritage Foundation, Inc., Comfort, Texas.)

Despite the spirited ending of the 1936 season, the HCL was pronounced "dead as a dodo bird"[37] in March 1937 when only two teams—Fredericksburg and Richland Springs—showed up for the league meeting in Llano.[38] Later that month, a new league, the South Texas League, was formed at the instigation of Perry Winkle, the intrepid sports columnist of the *San Antonio Evening News*.[39] Fredericksburg and Boerne joined the league's Northern Division[40] with the Pearsall Rangers[41] and a combined team, Hondo-D'Hanis.[42] The *Fredericksburg Standard* predicted that the 1937 schedule would be "the toughest [Fredericksburg] has yet faced in any league competition."[43]

Perhaps considering the stiffer opposition, the Giants added three former Comfort stars to their roster—shortstop Joe Pankratz, third baseman Skeeter Pankratz, and catcher Arthur Bergmann.[44] However, the *Fredericksburg Standard*'s prediction proved to be prophetic when the Giants finished with a 5–7 record, tied for third with Boerne.[45] Although the Giants carried a .304 team batting average (led again by Edgar Klett at .461),[46] the Giants suffered from poor pitching and spotty fielding.[47] The *Standard* lamented that this was "their worst [finish] in their history as members of an organized league."[48] After Hondo-D'Hanis and Pearsall ended the season tied for first place with records of 7–5, Hondo-D'Hanis won the championship series between the two clubs to claim the Northern Division title.[49]

Starting in 1938, Fredericksburg, Boerne, and Comfort played independently for three years until the HCL was reformed in 1941 with six teams (Fredericksburg, Boerne, Kerrville, Comfort, Stonewall, and Harper)[50] but the league lasted just one year, likely affected by the outbreak of World War II.

After that, the Giants, White Sox, and Broncos resumed their independent play through the war years. A new iteration of the HCL formed again in 1947, but Fredericksburg, Boerne, and Comfort continued to play independent ball until 1949, when the three clubs joined the HCL where they competed through at least 1953.[51]

The Boerne White Sox continued to play through at least 1967, competing in yet another version of the HCL in 1962 and 1963 (when the league added the Kerrville All-Stars, a Black team),[52] the Cosmopolitan League in 1966,[53] and the Metropolitan League in 1967.[54] The Fredericksburg Giants continued to play through 1963—the final season of the Hill Country League.[55]

After the demise of the Mountain League following the 1935 season, Fredericksburg, Boerne, Comfort, Kerrville, and Bandera—five of the earliest and most prominent settlements in the Hill Country—would never compete again in the same league. For years afterward, fans would reflect fondly on the halcyon days when Hill Country baseball boasted two strong leagues, the original Hill Country League (1930–36) and its counterpart, the Mountain League (1933–35.)

CHAPTER 18

BASEBALL WAS KING

Kerrville Black Baseball, 1922–1970

Sadly, like major league baseball before 1947, when Jackie Robinson broke the color barrier, Hill Country baseball was divided by race in the Depression years. Teams in the Hill Country League and the Mountain League were all-White. Yet like professional Negro League teams, Black town teams played in the Hill Country with the same passion and ability as their White counterparts despite the walls of segregation.

For at least 100 years after the Civil War ended slavery, Black residents of Texas faced "a combination of class disadvantage, differentiation, and imposed caste"[1] resulting from segregation:

> [Black Texans] had always lived in a separate country, with separate laws, from the dominant white. The change from slavery to elaborate caste was probably as inevitable as a similar situation inevitably created caste in India, Ethiopia, and Hispanic America generations earlier. The tragedy, and error, was that the new caste system provided no means for eventual social elevation and change; it did nothing to provide [Black Texans] the means for eventual entrance into American life on an equal, if separate, basis with white society. But then few caste systems ever do. The faceless slave became the faceless sharecropper and handyman, whose name history continued to ignore.[2]

Black residents often lived in fear of racial violence that maintained White control. In fact, Texas ranked third in the nation in lynchings between 1900 and 1910 with more than 100.[3] One of the most barbarous lynchings occurred in Waco in 1916 when a mob beat, stabbed, mutilated, hanged, and burned Jesse Washington[4]—a lynching that later became known as the "Waco Horror."

Despite the brutality of the Jim Crow era, Texas was home to many talented Black baseball players, including Hall of Famer Rube Foster, who was born in

Calvert. Foster started his professional career in 1898 with the Waco Yellow Jackets, an independent Black team, before starring as a pitcher for the Chicago American Giants, among other prominent teams, in the early twentieth century.[5] After his playing career ended, Foster was instrumental in forming the Negro National League (NNL) in 1920.[6]

Smokey Joe Williams, born in Seguin, Texas, began his professional career with the San Antonio Black Bronchos in 1905. Another Hall of Famer and one of the finest Negro League hurlers, Williams enjoyed a long career, pitching for the Chicago Giants, the New York Lincoln Giants, and the Homestead Grays, among others, before retiring in 1932.[7]

The son of Texas sharecroppers,[8] Hall of Fame catcher Biz Mackey played for the San Antonio Black Aces. After signing with the Indianapolis ABCs, Mackey played on some of the best Negro League teams, including the Hilldale Daisies, Philadelphia Stars, and Newark Eagles. Wielding a powerful bat and known as a superior defensive catcher, Mackey is regarded as second only to Josh Gibson among Negro League catchers. His career spanned from the first season of the NNL in 1920 to 1947, the year Jackie Robinson integrated the major leagues.[9] Mackey is credited with mentoring another Hall of Fame catcher, Roy Campanella, before "Campy" began his marvelous career with the Brooklyn Dodgers in 1948.[10]

Hall of Fame shortstop Willie Wells also hailed from Texas—Austin was his hometown. Playing for the San Antonio Black Aces when he caught Rube Foster's eye, Wells soon developed into an NNL standout for the St. Louis Stars and later the Chicago American Giants. Playing from 1924 to 1948, Wells is considered one of the greatest shortstops of all time.[11]

Other prominent Negro League players from Texas included catcher Louis Santop (Tyler), pitcher Bill Foster (Rube's younger half brother, also born in Calvert), pitcher Hilton Smith (Giddings), and pitcher Andy Cooper (Waco)—all members of the National Baseball Hall of Fame in Cooperstown.

With plentiful talent in Texas, the first Black semiprofessional league in the Lone Star State began play in 1920.[12] The Texas Colored League (TCL) was "part of a larger movement by African Americans throughout the state and country to establish their own cultural and community institutions during a period of intense racial segregation."[13] The TCL included the San Antonio Black Aces and Austin Black Senators, along with teams in Dallas, Fort Worth, Houston, Waco, Beaumont, Shreveport (Louisiana), and Galveston. Players worked at full-time jobs while playing baseball on the weekends, receiving little in the way of additional income.[14]

In the 1920s, thanks to the TCL, Black semiprofessional baseball "established itself with fans as a dominant sport."[15] Negro League teams, recognizing the semiprofessional talent in Texas, did not hesitate to recruit Black Texans. For example, in 1920, the Indianapolis ABCs, a charter member of the NNL, signed six players from the San Antonio Black Aces, including Biz Mackey.[16] Nevertheless, fluctuating attendance hurt team finances, causing the TCL to dissolve after the 1923 season.[17] Although the TCL ultimately failed, many Black semiprofessional teams survived and even thrived, including the San Antonio Black Aces and the Austin Black Senators, due in part to the greater freedom to schedule games attractive to fans without the constraints of a league schedule.[18]

As semiprofessional Black baseball grew in popularity in the 1920s, it became important to Black Texans "as a force of identity and cultural pride [that] grew with the number of teams playing baseball."[19] With the growing demand for baseball and a plethora of talent, the first fully professional Black league in Texas, the Texas-Oklahoma-Louisiana League (TOL), formed in 1929. The TOL included the Dallas Black Giants, the Fort Worth Black Panthers, the Houston Black Buffaloes, and the San Antonio Black Indians.[20]

The TOL was "a watershed for black baseball in Texas."[21] Patterned after Rube Foster's NNL, the TOL soon gained notoriety in the Black baseball world. TOL President Quincy J. Gilmore was a former president of the Kansas City Monarchs, the most prestigious NNL team. At the end of the inaugural TOL season in 1929, Gilmore used his connections to arrange a postseason series between the Monarchs, who had won the NNL pennant, and the TOL champions, the Houston Black Buffaloes.[22] The Texas Black press deemed the series the "colored world's championship."[23] Although Kansas City swept the series in four games, playing for the "colored world's championship" was a notch in the TOL's belt.

When teams played during the day, it was often difficult for working fans to attend games, but the TOL and NNL pioneered new approaches to make games more accessible. To combat dwindling attendance late in the 1930 season, the Black Buffaloes began playing their home games under floodlights at night—an innovation that the Kansas City Monarchs instituted earlier that year.[24] The use of lights for night games by the Buffaloes and the Monarchs preceded the first use of lights by American or National League teams by five years.[25]

Houston repeated its TOL championship in 1930, meeting the NNL champion Chicago American Giants in a best-of-five-game postseason series. This time, the press touted the series as the "Negro National Baseball Championship."[26] Chicago won the series but required all five games to prevail over the Black Buffaloes.

Despite these promising beginnings, the Depression ultimately took its toll on the TOL as attendance declined amid rising economic pressures. The TOL folded after the 1931 season but not before leaving an indelible mark on Black baseball in Texas and indeed the nation:

> During its three-year existence, the Texas-Oklahoma-Louisiana League reached near equality with the other black leagues in the country. It was a source of racial pride and community identity for black Texans. Its end . . . also showed the significant economic impact of the Great Depression on Texas and the country. However, the TOL bestowed a lasting reputation for African American baseball in Texas and left a permanent imprint on the Negro leagues and the game of baseball.[27]

Rube Foster's willingness to match the champions of the NNL against the TOL champion in 1929 and 1930 affirmed the high level of talent in the TOL. But during the first third of the twentieth century, there was more to Black baseball in Texas than either the TOL, the first professional league, or even the TCL, the first semiprofessional league. The landscape of Black baseball in Texas also included town teams playing outside large cities.

The Hill Country did not enjoy a large enough Black population to field a professional team in the TOL or a semiprofessional team in the TCL, but in Kerrville, the largest city in the Hill Country, a Black town team flourished for many years. Black people first came to Kerr County as slaves around 1856. The 1860 census showed 49 slaves in the county, about half of whom were owned by one planter.[28] Following emancipation after the Civil War, 90 Black people resided in Kerr County in 1870—nearly 9 percent of the county's total population at that time.[29] Many Black families chose to stay in Kerr County, including several families whose descendants later played baseball, such as the Blanks, Fifer, Hardy (or Hardee), and Butler families.[30] Around 1900, Kerrville received an influx of Black families, who moved from Bandera County due to a rabies scare posed by mountain lions roaming the area.[31]

Kerrville had the highest concentration of Black residents in the Hill Country.[32] By 1930, the Black community counted nearly 500 residents, about 4.7 percent of the county's growing population.[33] As a result, Kerrville's Black community was large enough to support a town team, unlike other Hill Country cities, although Black teams also played from time to time in Llano, Mason, Harper, Hondo, and Fredericksburg.

In contrast to large cities such as Houston or Dallas, where Black newspapers covered the local African American community, Kerrville had only two

White-owned newspapers. Their coverage of the Kerrville Black community was sparse and often reflected racial stereotypes. Newspaper articles about Black people were rare—except for stories of those arrested for committing crimes. The Kerrville newspapers did carry a few stories on the Black baseball team, but even when stories were published, they were brief. As a result, it is difficult to document fully the history of Kerrville's Black team, but we can piece together a cogent narrative from the limited newspaper reports that were published.

As early as 1922, Kerrville fielded a team known as the Black Athletics.[34] In July 1922, the Black Athletics traveled to Llano to play the Llano Black Aces. Behind the pitching of Jim Butler, the Black Athletics bombed the Black Aces, 23–6.[35] The next month, Butler hit a grand slam to lead the Black Athletics to victory over the visiting San Antonio Black Wonders, 11–6,[36] at the "Fair Grounds." As noted in chapter 12, the "Fair Grounds" may have been the grounds of the West Texas Fair, held in Kerrville for several decades starting in 1899.[37]

The Black Athletics played the San Antonio Black Wonders often. In 1924, the two clubs had a thrilling 15-inning affair in Kerrville. Jim Butler pitched all 15 innings, striking out 32 while the Black Wonders pitcher named Washington struck out 30 batters! Butler also knocked out four hits while Lester Fifer[38] smashed a home run along with three other hits. However, the Black Athletics lost the game, 6–5. The *Kerrville Mountain Sun* noted that "[q]uite the crowd witnessed the game and all report that it was one of the best played contests seen this season and a number have asked for another game in the near future."[39]

It was not uncommon for Black teams to play each other following games between White teams, making a doubleheader played on the same field. In 1925, one of those doubleheaders christened the new Kerrville ballpark built by Ben Smith at the northeast corner of Paschal and McFarland.[40] In that twin bill, two White teams, the Kerrville Athletics and Kelly Field, an army team, played the first game. The Athletics prevailed, 2–1, in 10 innings. In the nightcap, the Black Athletics played a Black team from San Antonio representing the U.S. Tire Chain Company, known as the Tire Changers. Playing the second game of a doubleheader had its disadvantages for the Black teams, because the game had to be called on account of darkness after the top of the fifth inning, resulting in a 3–3 tie.[41] The *Kerrville Mountain Sun* reported that the tie game with the Tire Changers:

> . . . . rankled in the breasts of a bunch of colored athletes in the Alamo City the belief that they were a superior lot of ball tossers and fence busters and that no bunch with calluses on their feet could beat them.

> Likewise in the colored section of this city [Kerrville] rumor was rife that the local colored team was far superior to the chicken connoisseurs from any city, San Antonio or otherwise.
>
> In fact, both bunches got real chesty with their prediction of what might have happened on that eventful day had it not got dark so soon, with the result that challenges and counter challenges were hurled back and forth between the two camps to such an extent that sporting blood was up to a fever pitch.
>
> The San Antonio boys said they could and the Kerrville bunch said they doubted it, so a return game was arranged for last Sunday.
>
> Kerrville's sporting blood had reached such a high point the fateful morning that the local team could not wait for the San Antonio bunch to get here, so they fared forth to meet them.[42]

To settle the tie between the two teams, the Black Athletics and the Tire Changers agreed to play several weeks later in Comfort—a shorter trip from San Antonio for the Tire Changers. In that rematch, the Black Athletics edged the Tire Changers, 7–6, but that was not the end of baseball in Comfort that day:

> At the completion of the game more words passed and the boastful spirit of the Alamo City Athletes caused them to make the prediction that the score was an accident, so the limousines were cranked and the warring factions came on toward the originally appointed ground [in Kerrville], where after the close of the White game that afternoon a second contest was staged.[43]

After all the braggadocio, Doyle, the Black Athletics' pitcher, shut out the Tire Changers, 6–0, on the Kerrville diamond although the newspaper report did not state whether the teams played a full nine innings.[44] In any event, the victory of the Black Athletics quelled any further remonstrances from the visiting Tire Changers.[45] Upon recounting these events, the *Kerrville Mountain Sun* commented that "[b]aseball fans of this city are missing a good lot of interesting sport when they fail to remain after the regular White game to see the colored boys play."[46]

Baseball was an integral part of everyday life in the Black community, especially on significant holidays such as Juneteenth, which commemorates June 19, 1865—the day that Union Major General Gordon Granger issued an order in Galveston proclaiming freedom for all slaves in Texas, thus fully ending slavery after the Civil War. Since the order specifically ended slavery in Texas, Black Texans were keen to celebrate Juneteenth and remain so today.

A two-day Juneteenth celebration occurred in 1927. Kerrville's Black team, now known as the Black Bear Cats, observed Juneteenth—the *Kerrville Mountain Sun* referred to the holiday as "Emancipation Day"—by playing both a Sunday game on June 19 and a rare Monday game. A Black team from Beeville served as the opponent in both games. Behind pitcher Doyle, Kerrville won on Sunday, 8–3. With Butler on the mound for Monday's game, the Black Bear Cats trimmed the Beeville squad, 6–3.[47]

Strangely, in 1928, the team was referred to in newspaper accounts as both the Black Athletics and the Black Bear Cats.[48] Perhaps the newspaper had not caught up with the change to Black Bear Cats in the preceding season. In any event, on May 20, 1928, the Black Athletics fell to the San Antonio Black Sox, 4–3, in San Antonio.[49] Wren pitched well, allowing just four hits, but the Black Athletics "lost on errors."[50] Soil Brown and Taylor were the hitting stars for the Black Athletics.[51]

Later that season, a game with the Uvalde Black Sox ended in controversy. According to the *Kerrville Mountain Sun*:

> The Black Bear Cats, Kerrville's colored ball team, came out with the small end of all-7 score in their Sunday fracas with the Uvalde Black Sox, when the winning team became disgruntled and left the field at the end of the eighth inning.
>
> Up to the time of ceasing hostilities it was a dandy ball game, with just enough argument on the side to make the large crowd of spectators think that they were going to see a real bang-up free-for-all within a few minutes.[52]

The newspaper account did not provide any details on the imbroglio that led to one of the teams leaving the field. It is not even clear from the report which team left the field, but it appears to have been the Bear Cats—presumably resulting in a forfeit.

On August 19, 1928, the Bear Cats took on the San Antonio Black Sox again, but this time, the game ended in a 13–13 tie after 10 innings in San Antonio.[53] Following the game, Kerrville manager Charles Nesby announced that the clubs would resolve the tie the following Sunday in Kerrville. The rematch turned out to be a doubleheader. The Bear Cats took both games by identical scores of 7–6.[54]

In 1929, the team became known first as the Kerrville Black Boosters, then the Black All-Stars. The Kerrville Athletics, the White team, were reorganized in 1929 as the Tourists following a brief hiatus.[55] Because the Tourists were given preference for using the local diamond, the Black Boosters were forced to play most of their games on the road in 1929. Nevertheless, Black Boosters manager Hezekiah Lott was quick to thank local businesses for securing new uniforms for the team.[56]

Kerrville could hold its own against ballclubs from large cities even apart from San Antonio. In July 1929, the Black Athletics, as they were called again briefly, defeated the Fort Worth Black Cats, 10–7, in Kerrville.[57] First baseman Ed Nesby was the star of the game for the Black Athletics. According to the *Kerrville Mountain Sun*, the Fort Worth Black Cats played in the "Texas Colored Baseball League." Notably, the "Texas Colored Baseball League" may have been the professional Texas-Oklahoma-Louisiana League. The Fort Worth Black Panthers played in the TOL so the newspaper may have mistakenly referred to the team as the "Black Cats." Indeed, in 1931, the Fort Worth club in the TOL became known as the Black Cats. If the Fort Worth Black Cats were actually the Fort Worth Black Panthers of the TOL, the Black Athletics' victory in 1929 was quite an accomplishment, the defeat of a professional ballclub.

At the same time, the Black Athletics were equally willing to play clubs from any small towns in the region that boasted a Black team. For example, the Black Athletics opened the 1930 season against a team from Hondo, south of Bandera. The two clubs fought to a 1–1 tie which was called due to darkness after 13 innings.[58] Taylor pitched the first 10 innings for Kerrville, striking out 21 batters. Ed Nesby then took the mound, holding the Black Giants scoreless until darkness ended the game as a tie.

Although Kerrville was by far the most prominent Black team in the Hill Country, it was not the only one. In 1932, the *Junction Eagle* announced that on Sunday, May 29, the Mason Black Mavericks would meet the Fredericksburg Black Giants on Fireman Field in Junction.[59] Admission prices of 25 cents for adults and 15 cents for children would be charged. The Black Giants enlisted an unnamed "bowlegged negro from Kerrville" who "will furnish comedy as well as a demonstration of real baseball ability."[60] For their part, the Mason Black Mavericks offered another unnamed player who was "the best negro twirler in West Texas."[61] The virulent racism of the day is illustrated by the last sentence of the *Junction Eagle* article, which quoted local baseball fan Ches Goodwin as saying that "this will be the first "[N-word] baseball game ever played in Junction, and should draw a record attendance."[62] No report of the game itself was found.

As a result, the identities of the "bowlegged negro from Kerrville" and the "best negro twirler in West Texas" remain unknown.

By 1932, the Depression was now in full swing, but the Kerrville Black team flourished in this era, drawing many fans to the ball games. The Black All-Stars became a focal point of the community. Even more so than the fans of White teams in the Mountain League, the Black community passionately supported their heroes on the diamond. In the face of both racism and economic hardships during the Depression, baseball served to foster local pride, but it also reinforced the need for those in the Black community in Kerrville to support one another. A sense of unity was essential to survival in a segregated environment, especially when jobs were scarce.

Under Jim Crow segregation, Black residents in Kerrville were permitted to reside only within a segregated area, which consisted of approximately 20 square blocks north of downtown, generally bounded by Schreiner Street on the south, Wallace Street on the west, what is now Carver Park on the north, and Hays Street on the east.[63] Black people were prohibited from going to movie theaters, hotels, and public swimming pools.[64] Black children attended the segregated Colored School,[65] later renamed Doyle School, on Barnett Street. There were two all-Black churches—the Barnett Chapel Methodist Church on Paschal, the oldest Black church in Kerr County, and the Mount Olive Baptist Church on West McFarland Drive.[66] The Colored School and the two churches served as foundational institutions in the close-knit Black community.

Black people operated several businesses in Kerrville, including a laundromat, gas station, taxi service, and others.[67] In addition, seven "juke joints" were located within a two-block area. Not only did the juke joints ply customers with Texas barbecue, but they also provided a community gathering place to dance under the stars, play dominoes, and shoot pool.[68] The Pleasure Garden, located on Webster Avenue behind the Doyle School, brought well-known blues artists to Kerrville, including Big Joe Turner, Big Mama Thornton, and B. B. King.[69]

But for the Black community of Kerrville in those days, "baseball was king."[70] Attending the games of the All-Stars was "a family reunion," where residents could catch up with relatives, friends, and neighbors.[71] Youngsters worshipped their heroes on the diamond but also boisterously competed for foul balls landing outside the diamond—they were paid for each foul ball returned to the team as well as empty beer and soft drink bottles found under the stands.[72]

Young men aspired to play for the All-Stars. When a ballplayer graduated from high school, it was considered a high honor to be invited to play for the club.[73] At the same time, their parents expected the club not only to oversee their development as players but to protect them from vices as well. For example, when the All-Stars manager invited Joe Lewis to join the club upon his high school graduation, his mother would allow him to play only if the manager assured her that he would not be permitted to drink alcohol.[74] The older players on the All-Stars often viewed themselves as role models for the younger players, both on and off the diamond, exhorting them to respect their parents and elders.[75]

Like players on the White town teams, the All-Stars mostly played for the love of the game, although players did occasionally receive a small cash payment if the gate proceeds allowed surplus revenues to be distributed to the players.[76]

Doubleheaders were the highlight of both Juneteenth and Independence Day. The festivities often included a parade as well as a ladies softball game and a "Fat and Over 40" baseball game before the All-Stars' twin bill.[77] Home games of the All-Stars were always well attended, but many fans also supported the team by traveling to road games. In later years, this included a Black-owned taxi service that provided transportation to the games.[78]

While the Black All-Stars often played on the same diamond as White teams by playing the second game of a doubleheader against another Black team, they did occasionally play White teams. After the Kerrville Braves concluded their season in the Hill Country League, they played the Black All-Stars on September 18, 1932, as the first game of a three-game series. Part of the motivation for the game was that the proceeds would "go into the badly depleted treasury of the Braves, who closed the season on the red ink side of the ledger."[79] According to the *Kerrville Mountain Sun*, the All-Stars boasted a phenomenal season record of 38–4.[80] The Braves prevailed over the Black All-Stars but barely:

> The Braves were victorious . . . but they were pressed to the limit to win the decision by an eyebrow. The final score was 7 to 6 and the dusky pastimers outslugged the Hill Leaguers, 11 to nine.
>
> A rousing eighth-inning rally by the All-Stars shelled Hugo Klaerner off the pitching mound and a succession of extra-base hits gave the colored boys four runs. Maxwell relieved Klaerner and chunked the last frame. The All-Stars added another run at his expense.
>
> Colander[81] started on the hillock for the All-Stars and the Braves routed him in the third after three singles, an error and a wild pitch had netted them four runs. The Tribe kept pecking away at Overton, the relief pitched [*sic*] and managed to win the verdict in the ninth after one man had been retired. Joe Pankratz, "Red" Klaerner, and Beaver led the Braves at bat.

> Blanks of the All-Stars slammed out a homer in the second inning with nobody on the runway. Four of the All-Star safeties were two-baggers.[82]

Although the All-Stars fell short by one run, they hit four doubles and a home run, knocking Hugo Klaerner out of the game—an accomplishment since Klaerner was the premier pitcher in the Hill Country and a future major leaguer. Moreover, the Braves enlisted two exceptional Fredericksburg players (Hugo Klaerner and his cousin, center fielder Elias Klaerner) after the Giants failed to make the 1932 playoffs. The All-Stars thus stood toe-to-toe with a club sporting a roster that was markedly stronger than the Braves' regular season club. In addition to the two Klaerners, the Braves included Joe and Skeeter Pankratz, two outstanding Comfort players who starred for Kerrville in 1932 when Comfort dropped out of the Hill Country League. The Pankratz brothers returned to the Broncos in 1933.

The *Kerrville Mountain Sun* published a box score for the clash between the Braves and the All-Stars. It was rare for newspapers in those days to publish box scores for Black teams even when they played a White team. Since this is the only known box score for a game involving Kerrville's Black team during the Depression years, it is replicated in full in Table 24.[83]

Table 24. Box Score: Braves vs. All-Stars

BRAVES	**POS**	**AB**	**R**	**H**	**O**	**A**	**E**
Staudt	ss	5	1	1	2	3	1
J. Pankratz	2b	2	4	2	1	2	1
Grantham	c	5	0	0	8	0	1
E. Klaerner	cf	3	0	2	1	0	0
Beaver	1b	4	0	2	13	0	1
King	2b	4	0	0	0	2	0
Saenger	rf	2	0	0	2	0	0
E. Pankratz	lf	4	1	1	0	0	0
H. Klaerner	p-2b	4	1	1	0	5	0
Maxwell	p	0	0	0	0	0	0
Totals		**34**	**7**	**9**	**27**	**12**	**5**
ALL-STARS	**POS**	**AB**	**R**	**H**	**O**	**A**	**E**
Dillworth	2b	4	0	0	4	3	1
Nesby	1b	5	0	0	10	0	0

Dimry	lf	5	2	2	0	1	1
Brown	ss	5	1	2	0	3	1
Walker	cf	5	1	1	8	0	0
Blanks	c	5	2	2	5	0	0
Edwards	3b	4	0	2	2	2	2
Colander	p-rf	4	0	2	1	1	0
Overton	rf-p	4	0	0	0	3	0
Totals		**41**	**6**	**11**	**25***	**13**	**5**

* One out when winning run scored.

Score by Innings										R	H	E
Braves	0	0	4	0	1	0	1	0	1-	7	9	5
All-Stars	0	1	0	0	0	0	0	4	1-	6	11	5

Home run: Blanks; two-base hits: J. Pankratz, Brown, Walker, Edwards, Colander; sacrifice hit, E. Klaerner; stolen bases: J. Pankratz, Dimry 2, Blanks; innings pitched by H. Klaerner 8, with 10 hits and 6 runs, by Colander with 3 hits and 4 runs; base on balls off Overton 3; struck out by H. Klaerner 8, by Colander 1, by Overton 4; hit batsmen, by H. Klaerner (Dillworth), by Colander (J. Pankratz), by Overton (J. Pankratz); wild pitch, Colander; double play, Brown to Dillworth to Nesby. Time: 2:20. Umpires: J. Frost and Hughes.

It is worth noting that Jack Frost, a Black umpire, officiated the game. Although it would be expected for a Black umpire to work a game involving Black teams, this was a game between White and Black teams. Even more significant is the fact that Jack Frost was occasionally hired by the Comfort Broncos to umpire their games against White opponents.[84] According to Comfort pitcher Clemens Heinen, Frost was well respected as an umpire. Heinens commented that "I was the pitcher at that time, and I always found Frost fair and square."[85]

While the Braves and the All-Stars originally planned to play a three-game series, the second game scheduled for September 25 was rained out. Since no record of another game between the Braves and the All-Stars could be found on the following Sundays, the third game may have been canceled after the rainout. As a result, the box score for the September 18 game is even more precious to the historical record of the All-Stars.

The All-Stars opened the 1933 season on a chilly Sunday afternoon on March

26 by hosting the Mason Black Wonders—another Black team from a town in the Hill Country. The Black All-Stars edged Mason, 7–6, in 10 innings.[86] Charley Callander pitched until the ninth, when he was relieved by Nesby, who earned the win. Jim Pollard was now the Kerrville manager.

Another round of ball games on Sunday and Monday highlighted the Juneteenth celebration in 1933. On Sunday, there was another White-Black doubleheader at which "bargain double-header prices" of 35 cents for adults and 10 cents for children were charged.[87] As in previous years, the first game featured two White teams—the Kerrville Braves trounced the Mountain Home "Hot Timers," 11–1, filling an off day in the Braves' Mountain League schedule. In the second game, the San Antonio Black Missions defeated the Black All-Stars, 7–2.[88] On Monday, however, the Black All-Stars rebounded, winning 6–4 thanks to a long home run by Charley Callander. The *Kerrville Mountain Sun* commented:

> Large crowds were reported to have been in attendance both days, entertainments aside from baseball games attracting many. A 12-piece negro orchestra furnished music each day, while several colored boys did a "buck-and-wing" to the great delight of the crowd.
>
> Kerrville's annual "June-teenth" celebration came to a close Monday night, or rather, the wee small hours of Tuesday morn, the occasion being a platform dance.[89]

As in 1932, the All-Stars played a White team at the end of the 1933 season. This time, the Black All-Stars played the club from nearby Legion on October 8, 1933. Although the newspaper report does not explicitly state that the Legion team was White, it refers to three players—Beaver, Wood, and McDonald—who later played for Legion in the 1935 Mountain League season. As a result, it is reasonable to conclude that this was a game between White and Black teams.[90] The *Kerrville Mountain Sun* reported on Legion's 10–8 victory:

> Before one of the largest crowds to witness a game played on the local diamond, the Legion baseball club defeated the reinforced Kerrville Black All-Stars by the score of 10–8, in one of the most thrilling and exciting games played this season.
>
> Both teams played good ball, although both starting pitchers, Beaver for Legion, and Wilson for the All-Stars, were hit rather freely. Wood, left-hander for Legion, displayed a brand of relief pitching that was really amazing, striking out the first two men to face him and registering

> a total of five strikeouts for the four innings he pitched. He was credited with the win.
>
> Brown of the All-Stars hit a home run in the second with the bases empty,.and Kaiser of Legion duplicated this feat with one man on second base. McDonald, Henry and George of Legion each garnered three hits apiece, one of the hits of McDonald and George was a triple, while Henry hit a double. Kaiser, in addition to his home run, also got a single. George made a sensational catch in left field that was the high-light of the game. Nesby, Calander,[91] Blanks, Brown and Joe each got two hits for the All-Stars.
>
> In addition to this thrilling game, the crowd was treated to yells from the Kerrville All-Stars booster girls club. They surely did liven things up and the crowd greatly appreciated their cheers.[92]

Starting in 1934, Kerrville's Black team changed its nickname again—this time to the Black Braves, presumably in reference to the Kerrville Braves, the local White team now playing in the Mountain League.[93] Kerrville's Black team remained the Black Braves until at least 1942, after which the team nickname reverted to the Black All-Stars, or just the All-Stars.[94] The officers of the Black Braves elected in 1934 were President Thomas Blanks, Secretary Ben Nelson, and managers Charles Nesby and Jim Pollard.[95]

The Black Braves attracted White fans as well as Black. The Black Braves opened the 1934 season with an 11–10 victory over the Missouri Pacific Black team from San Antonio, rallying for four runs in the ninth inning.[96] The *Kerrville Mountain Sun* highlighted that "[m]anagers Jim Pollard and Chas. Nesby expressed their appreciation for the good turn-out of white fans."[97] Even so, the reigning segregation required separate sections for White and Black fans.

There is some indication that in 1934, rather than playing their entire schedule independently, Kerrville played in the West Texas Negro League, although little is known about this venture.[98] On July 4, 1934, the Black Braves split a July 4 doubleheader with the Smithville Black Bears, losing the first game, 3–2, thanks to five Kerrville errors, but winning the second, 7–2, behind pitcher Charley Callander[99] who was aided by four double plays.[100] The newspaper account noted that after the doubleheader, the Black Braves stood 11–4 on the season.[101]

The Black Braves played an odd game in 1935 when they met the Waelder Black Sox at the Kerrville ballpark. After seven innings of scoreless ball, the Black Braves exploded for eight runs in the eighth inning to win, 8–0.[102] Alexander and Maxwell shared pitching duties in the shutout.[103] A week before that, the

Black Braves defeated a team from Center Point, 11–0.[104]

The Black Braves enjoyed a successful season in 1936 despite losing their first contest to the Austin Black Senators, 19–1.[105] Since the Black Senators had played five years earlier in the TOL, a professional league, this lopsided score was not necessarily surprising. But after the loss, Manager Jim Pollard recruited several new ballplayers for the club.[106] His efforts paid off because two weeks later, the Black Braves responded by edging the San Antonio Black Missions, 9–8.[107]

Another unusual game occurred on April 12, 1936, when the Black Braves met the Smithville Black Bears, who featured a catcher called "The Lazy Man." This unconventional catcher sat behind home plate in a rocking chair during part of the game as an added attraction for fans.[108] The "Lazy Man" may have drawn curious fans to the game, but Kerrville defeated the Black Bears, 11–4.[109] The following week, the Black Braves sported flashy new uniforms donated by local businessmen when they faced the Hondo Black Tigers.[110]

Starting on April 26, 1936, the Black Braves played a three-game series with the San Antonio Black Giants. The first two would be played in Kerrville while the third game would be played at Tech Field in San Antonio. The clubs split the first two games. Kerrville prevailed in the first game, 5–4, but lost the second game, 4–3.[111] In the final game in San Antonio, the Black Braves pounded out the win, 11–7.[112] Clarence Clark stroked three hits (a triple, double, and single), while Dimery contributed three hits for the Black Braves.[113]

As noted earlier, newspaper coverage of Black baseball was spotty at best. Unlike front-page coverage afforded to White teams, the meager accounts of Black games were often buried deep in the back of the newspaper. Although the scarce accounts in Kerrville newspapers were generally respectful, overt racism did occur. While the most offensive racial epithet was not used as in the *Junction Eagle* in 1932, the *Kerrville Times* unashamedly employed racial stereotypes in an article in 1937:

> According to Charles Callander, empressario [*sic*] for the Kerrville Black Braves Baseball team, the ball park has been cleared and all is in readiness for a big game Sunday afternoon. The trouble with Charlie's team right now is that they do not know who the opposing team will be. As he "shines 'em up" for his customers, his gold teeth gleam when he smiles and assures us, "It sho' will be a good game, whoever we play, suh."[114]

The Kerrville All-Stars continued to play for many years after surviving the Depression. While many other Black teams faded away in Texas, the popularity

Figure 45. Kerrville All-Stars, 1940s Standing, top row (L–R): Clifford Fifer, Roy Neal, Jake Miller, Merrill Neal, Junior Nesby, Preston Nesby, Felton Brown, and team manager Jack Frost. Bottom row, seated (L–R): Bill Haynes, Clifton Fifer Sr., Coach William Sims, Phillip Sorrell, Joe Beasley, and Lawrence Norris. The photo was taken at the baseball field in Carver Park. (Courtesy of Clifton Fifer Jr.)

Figure 46. Kerrville All-Stars, 1947. The names of the players in this photograph have not survived. (Reprinted courtesy of *The Kerrville Daily Times*, Kerrville, Texas.)

Figure 47. Earnest Fifer, 1969 All-Stars at Carver Park. (Courtesy of Clifton Fifer Jr.)

Figure 48. Lionel Jefferson, 1969 All-Stars at Carver Park. (Courtesy of Clifton Fifer Jr.)

of the All-Stars persisted in Kerrville more than three decades later. Although Jim Crow segregation remained in effect for nearly 20 years after Jackie Robinson broke the color barrier in 1947, the walls of segregation began to crumble a bit in 1960 when a later iteration of the Hill Country League added the All-Stars as the seventh team, joining six White teams—the Kerrville Kats, the Fredericksburg Giants, Pat's Cubs (another Fredericksburg team), the Boerne White Sox, Helotes, and Camp Stanley. The *Kerrville Times* noted that the All-Stars,

Figure 49. Kerrville All-Stars jacket, 1962. (Jacket courtesy of Clifton Fifer Jr.)

managed by Clifton Fifer Sr., had played exhibition games with the teams in the Hill Country League for several seasons, always attracting large crowds.[115]

In the opening game of the 1960 season, Pat's Cubs trounced the Black All-Stars, 24–8, scoring 11 runs in the first inning.[116] Clifton Fifer Sr. was the most effective of the many Kerrville pitchers, but the All-Stars suffered from shaky fielding. Catcher Charlie Nesbitt led the All-Stars with three hits.

The following Sunday, the Black All-Stars defeated Helotes, 7–3, for their first victory in the formerly all-White league.[117] Vernon Shields and Bubba Warrants smashed home runs to lead the attack. After their first six games, the Black All-Stars held a 3–3 record in the league.[118]

In 1962, the All-Stars finished in sixth place (out of eight teams) with a 5–9 record but ahead of the last-place Kerrville Kats who were 2–12.[119] The All-Stars remained in the Hill Country League through the 1963 season but returned to playing independent ball for the 1964 season.[120] The Black All-Stars played through the 1970 season[121] before suffering their demise like other town teams in the Hill Country.

Kerrville's Black baseball team, best known in its later years as the All-Stars, was a bellwether for the Black community. Indeed, celebrations of Juneteenth—that most cherished holiday—always featured baseball. Holiday or not, ball games were a means for expressing pride and cohesion in the face of segregation. Sitting shoulder-to-shoulder to cheer on their diamond heroes evoked a sense of unity in the Black community that could not be fully expressed in other ways during the Jim Crow era.

In addition, while Jim Crow did not end until 30 years after the Depression, it is not difficult to envision that Kerrville's Black team played an early role in dispelling racial stereotypes by playing in front of White fans and, more importantly, by playing occasionally against White teams. When White ballplayers shared the diamond with Kerrville's Black players who competed with the same prowess and mettle, it became harder to deny the common bonds of humanity.

EPILOGUE

Baseball as Balm

Despite the depredations of the Depression, town baseball thrived in the Hill Country. Baseball became an outlet to relieve the economic stress suffered by many. Enjoying a game in the stands on an effulgent Sunday afternoon with family, friends, and neighbors and relaxing at a postgame picnic provided a numinous respite from temporal concerns.

More than that, though, baseball united people. By cheering on their local stars, fans not only lived vicariously through their diamond exploits, but many also found that the bonds of German propinquity served as a shield against the most devastating effects of economic hardship. Taking home bragging rights when their local nine defeated a nearby town team was simply a bonus.

That is not to say that the Depression did not affect Hill Country baseball. The Hill Country League formed in 1930 just as the Depression gained a foothold. Led by Chink Taylor, a former major leaguer, the Llano Cowboys were a magnificent team, winning three consecutive HCL titles in 1931–33 after losing the inaugural championship series to Fredericksburg in 1930. Fredericksburg fielded a potent club featuring as many as five members of the Klaerner family including Hugo, a future major leaguer.

In addition to Fredericksburg and Llano, the HCL included Boerne, Comfort, and Kerrville, but these southern towns soon withdrew from the league due to the expense of traveling to northern towns such as Llano and Mason, and later, Brady and Junction. Kerrville, Comfort, Boerne, and previously independent Bandera formed the Mountain League in 1933 to minimize expenses by playing closer to home. Fredericksburg joined the Mountain League in 1934 to reunite the Giants with Boerne, Comfort, and Kerrville.

In retrospect, the Mountain League, beginning play in 1933, represented the apotheosis of Hill Country baseball. Towns in the league embodied the earliest settlements[1] from the mid-nineteenth century—Fredericksburg was the second German settlement in the Hill Country, while settlements in Boerne, Comfort, Kerrville, and Bandera soon followed.[2] In 1934 and 1935, the Mountain League teams reflected the core of German culture in the Hill Country, naturally intensifying the competition on the diamond.[3]

While the Fredericksburg–Llano rivalry in the HCL was strong, the Mountain League fomented the most ferocious rivalries. Fredericksburg and Boerne were the best teams in the Mountain League, resulting in bare-knuckle battles that left the loser longing for revenge. Boerne and Comfort were ardent intra-county rivals located only 15 miles apart. Fredericksburg and Kerrville, always competitors as the two largest cities in the Hill Country, sought to achieve symbolic dominance by prevailing on the diamond. Despite the fervid nature of all these matchups, some newspaper accounts suggest that Fredericksburg and Comfort may have enjoyed the most heated rivalry of all.

In that light, the dissolution of the Mountain League after Boerne's withdrawal in 1935 was disheartening. Although baseball continued to thrive in the Hill Country for many years after the Mountain League faded into history, resulting in later iterations of the Hill Country League as well as other leagues, the five "core" teams of the Mountain League—Fredericksburg, Boerne, Comfort, Kerrville, and Bandera—would never play in the same league again.

The quality of play in the Hill Country was high. Several ballplayers signed professional contracts and a few even made brief appearances in the major leagues. Fredericksburg pitcher Hugo Klaerner started three games for the 1934 Chicago White Sox. Alamo Heights hurler Charley Suche pitched one game for the Cleveland Indians in 1938. Boerne shortstop Charlie English (who moonlighted while playing at Fort Sam Houston) played parts of four seasons in the major leagues with the Chicago White Sox, the New York Giants, and the Cincinnati Reds. Klaerner, Suche, and English all enjoyed relatively long careers in the minor leagues.

Many other Hill Country ballplayers signed professional contracts or obtained tryouts after playing in the Hill Country League or the Mountain League, such as pitcher Chester "Smokey" Klaerner (Fredericksburg), pitcher Walter Bergmann (Boerne), pitcher Harvey Hardy (Mason and Kerrville), shortstop Travis McNair (Kerrville), first baseman Archie Peel (Llano), pitcher Roswell "Rod" Sanders (Mason, Fredericksburg, Kerrville, and Pontotoc), catcher Ben Grantham (Kerrville), pitcher Anton Leidl (Boerne and Kerrville), infielder Karl Kott (Fredericksburg), and pitcher Vernon Taylor (Kerrville, Brady, and Llano). As a result, there is no question that there was an abundance of baseball talent in the Hill Country.

Off the diamond, many of the ballplayers grew into community leaders, such as Hugo Klaerner who served as Gillespie County sheriff for 30 years, and Boerne pitcher Edgar Bergmann, who thrived as a successful businessman and civic leader in Boerne. Klaerner and Bergmann were quintessential Hill Country Germans both on the diamond and in their work lives—superbly skilled but not flashy, stolid yet staunchly competitive.

As we have seen, however, the Mountain League and the Hill Country League are far from the entire story of Hill Country baseball. The Kerrville Black team, variously known as the Black Athletics, Black Braves, Black Bear Cats, and the Black All-Stars (but best known later as the All-Stars), played tremendous baseball. The team was even more significant to the Kerrville Black community than Hill Country or Mountain League teams were to their fans. Baseball united the Black community in its struggle for survival against the twin evils of the Depression and the grievous racism of the Jim Crow era.

While it is proper to condemn the segregation and searing racial injustice that repressed Black ballplayers and their fans alike, there were signs—small but noteworthy—that the foundations of racism were beginning to show some cracks. For example, Kerrville's Black team sporadically met White teams such as in 1932 and 1933, when the Black Braves played the Kerrville Braves and Legion Cubs, respectively. Several newspaper accounts also reveal that a significant number of White fans attended the Black team's games (albeit in a separate section of the stands). While these occasional interactions between races do not in any way mitigate the atrocity of Jim Crow segregation, they can be viewed as small harbingers—tentative "baby steps"—on a long, painful journey which eventually culminated in the elimination of de jure segregation and Jim Crow laws 30 years later.

Baseball at the town level no longer plays a dominant role in the Hill Country,[4] or anywhere else for that matter. Through television and social media, professional sports now command our society's attention. Moreover, both high school and college sports have replaced local baseball and amateur sports in general as the basis for rivalries among communities.

Yet one must wonder whether we have lost something quite valuable. Baseball during the Depression brought a critical sense of belonging to people in the Hill Country at a time when life had become more challenging. Sunday afternoon town baseball not only strengthened local identities through the crucible of competition but also reinforced common bonds with nearby communities. Whether it was the residents of the German-dominated towns of Fredericksburg, Llano, Boerne, Kerrville, or Comfort, or whether it was the residents of the Kerrville Black community, baseball engendered a much-needed sense of connection.

Indeed, baseball enabled Hill Country residents to stand together in the face of a withering economic storm. In the case of Kerrville's Black residents, baseball also provided what may have been the only public outlet for the expression of pride and unity in the face of segregation and crushing racism. For both the descendants of early German settlers and the descendants of slaves, town baseball served as an analgesic balm in the Depression years, soothing the privations of the times while adumbrating a brighter future to come.

ACKNOWLEDGMENTS

I have many people to thank for their assistance in the creation and development of this book.

As noted in the preface, Paul Barwick started me on this journey at the Old Jail Museum in Boerne, then was kind enough to review the initial draft.

Early on, Robin Stauber of the Patrick Heath Public Library (PHPL) in Boerne directed me to the library's file on the Boerne White Sox and encouraged my curiosity. Caren Creech of the PHPL helped me to connect with Texas Tech University Press at the Boerne Book Festival.

Diane Miller, director of the Butt-Holdsworth Memorial Library in Kerrville, provided some helpful articles on baseball in the Hill Country and gave me wonderful connections to others. One of those connections was Clifton Fifer Jr., the son of Kerrville All-Stars player Clifton Fifer Sr. Mr. Fifer generously opened his scrapbook on the All-Stars and shared his time. He also reviewed an early draft of the chapter on the Kerrville Black team. Shirley Lewis, widow of former All-Stars player Joe Lewis, shared her wonderful memories of the team and the times in which they played.

Anne Stewart and Margaret Kutzer Morries of the Comfort Heritage Foundation opened their Comfort baseball file to me and generously gave of their time in responding to my research inquiries. Shirley Pankratz Solis and JoAnn Stiles, daughters of Comfort ballplayer Joe Pankratz, and Joyce Pankratz, daughter of Comfort player Skeeter Pankratz, shared their memories of their fathers and other Broncos of long ago. Shirley also made available her excellent book, *Comfort Broncos, 1922–1958*, which chronicles the history of the Broncos in newspaper articles and wonderful photographs. The Comfort Heritage Foundation keeps a copy of her book on hand. In addition, Joyce's research discovered a key article about Dizzy Dean in the *Comfort News*.

Evelyn Weinheimer of the Pioneer Museum in Fredericksburg directed me to articles on the Fredericksburg Giants compiled by the museum and shared her recollections of Hugo Klaerner as county sheriff. She also assisted with the museum's photographs of the Fredericksburg team that grace this book.

Rebecca Norton, Executive Director of the Frontier Times Museum in Bandera, connected me to Roy Dugosh and Cecil LeStourgeon, who graciously assisted me in tracking down the possible locations of the ballparks in Bandera.

The San Antonio African American Community Archive and Museum (SAAACAM) provided extensive research on Negro League baseball in San Antonio and Texas. Many thanks to SAAACAM's Caira Spenrath, Cristal Mendez, and Gwyn Hartung.

Several descendants of ballplayers generously provided me with assistance. Betsy Bergmann Sueltenfuss, daughter of Boerne White Sox pitcher Edgar Bergmann, was generous with her time, providing much information as well as photographs of her father. Tom Phillip, son of Boerne White Sox player Harry Phillip, graciously provided many team photos of the White Sox as well as individual photos. A number of these photos are included in this book. Audra Rose-Kight and Jim Anderwald provided a wonderful photograph of Fabian Anderwald's Bandera Cowboys uniform and shared information about Bandera's ballclub. Hugo Klaerner's grandson, Lieutenant Kevin Klaerner of the Kendall County Sheriff's Office, took off an entire afternoon to drive me to Fredericksburg for an interview with his uncle, Travis Klaerner, who shared memories of his father, Hugo Klaerner, and his uncle, Chester Klaerner. I was saddened to learn that Travis passed away before completion of this book.

Colleagues at the Genealogical Society of Kendall County (GSKC) were also generous with their time. Hal Harwell reviewed the legal description of the 1910 lease of the Boerne White Sox. Based on his extensive Boerne subdivision records, Hal was able to determine the location of the property. Hal also assisted with other helpful bits of Boerne history. GSKC President Jan Carr encouraged and supported my efforts in ways she will never know.

I was also blessed by the assistance of several historians and archivists. Boerne historian Bryden Moon provided insight on the German settlement of Boerne and the Hill Country. Llano historian Patty Schneider Pfister generously provided invaluable information about Robinson State Park and the history of baseball in Llano. She also discovered a wonderful photograph of the Llano Cowboys. Cristele Richins, a museum representative of the Llano County Historical Museum, also provided research assistance. Andrew Crews, Archivist-Librarian of the San Antonio Public Library, kindly tracked down some obscure articles in the San Antonio newspapers. Jackie Davis of the Fort Sam Houston Museum assisted my research on Dizzy Dean while he pitched for Fort Sam Houston in the late 1920s.

Travis Snyder, editor in chief of the Texas Tech University Press, provided a sure and steady hand during the publication process.

Christopher J. Wickham, professor emeritus of German at the University of Texas at San Antonio, kindly provided guidance on several German words and terms. However, any errors regarding the German language are solely mine.

World Series champion and Boerne resident Jeremy Affeldt generously authored the foreword, which sets the tone for this book so well.

A huge thank-you to all of you. I can never repay the kindness you have shown to a newcomer to Boerne and the Hill Country.

In addition to my gratitude for the many blessings above, I am thankful beyond measure for the unending love, support, and encouragement of my beautiful wife, Nancy.

Above all, I give all glory to Jesus Christ, my Lord and Savior, my Rock and Redeemer.

NOTES ON TEAM STATISTICS COMPILED FROM BOX SCORES

Since there was little newspaper coverage of Kerrville's Black team, we found only one box score for games played by the Kerrville Black Athletics or Black Braves (the nicknames the team sported in the early 1930s). This box score is shown in chapter 18. Even if box scores had been published, Kerrville newspapers did not report on more than a few Black games each year. As a result, we were not able to compile team or individual statistics in any year for that team.

We were able to compile statistics for three Hill Country League seasons (1930–32) and the only three Mountain League seasons (1933–35) but it was not an easy task. Only the *Fredericksburg Standard* and *Comfort News* published team statistics for the local team at season's end, but it was done haphazardly.

To generate standard statistics for all teams, we compiled statistics from box scores to the extent they were available from local newspapers. Box scores were usually, but not always, published for the local team in the *Fredericksburg Standard*, *Comfort News*, *Kerrville Mountain Sun,* and *Llano News.* The *Boerne Star* suffered a fire in 1940, destroying all copies of past editions, so box scores from that publication are not available for any pre-1940 season. In addition, we found only two Mountain League box scores in the *Bandera New Era.* As a result, Mountain League box scores for the games of the Boerne White Sox and the Bandera Cowboys are available *only* when they played Kerrville (*Kerrville Mountain Sun*), Comfort (*Comfort News*) or Fredericksburg (*Fredericksburg Standard*),[5] but even then, a box score would occasionally be absent from those newspapers. Box scores for Alamo Heights games in 1933 were only sporadically published in either the *San Antonio Express* or the *San Antonio Light.* Apart from the few box scores in the San Antonio newspapers, box scores for Alamo Heights games are available only if they appeared in the Kerrville or Comfort newspapers. Some box scores were found in the Mason, Brady, and Junction newspapers, but many were not. Hill Country League games involving Mason, Brady, and Junction in 1930–32 were most available when they played

Fredericksburg, Llano, and Kerrville where box scores were often published in the local newspaper.

Based on available box scores, we have compiled statistics for three seasons of the Hill Country League (1930–32) and the three seasons of the Mountain League (1933–35). These are found in Appendices A–F. Since box scores were typically not available for all games played by a team, the statistics in the appendices are usually based on fewer than the full schedule of games for a season. Of course, this distorts the actual statistics, at least to some extent. For example, Alamo Heights was just 8–6 in the 14 games for which box scores exist from the 1933 season, but they finished 12–6, having won all four of the other games. As a result, the statistics shown in Appendix A likely understate the performance of Alamo Heights players, perhaps significantly. Nevertheless, we believe it is still useful to compile the statistics for the games that we do have because they illustrate the relative performance of the players and teams in the Hill Country League and the Mountain League.

Several comments are in order on two aspects of the statistics in the appendices. First, most of the available box scores did not list runs batted in at all or did so only occasionally, making compilation of RBIs for a season impossible in most cases. As a result, the statistics do not include RBIs.

Second, with few exceptions, the available box scores did not identify the number of *earned* runs given up by pitchers. Instead, only the *total* runs (earned and unearned) given up by a pitcher were listed in box scores. As a result, the earned run average (ERA) of pitchers cannot be calculated. In place of ERA, the statistics below use total run average (TRA), calculated in the same way as ERA but using *total* runs (earned and unearned) rather than *earned* runs. While not as accurate in measuring a pitcher's performance as ERA, TRA helps us to compare the relative performance of pitchers while recognizing that one must consider the fielding prowess, or lack thereof, of the team behind them on the diamond.

Third, most box scores did not list walks for individual batters. Without this data, it is impossible to compile on-base percentages (OBP) for hitters. As a result, we compiled batting average and slugging percentage for each hitter, but we were not able to calculate OBP or OPS (on-base percentage plus slugging percentage).

Finally, due to deficient information from some box scores, there are some statistics that could not be compiled without much guesswork and speculation. For example, a box score with multiple pitchers might not show how many innings were pitched by each pitcher, thus making it impossible to determine the innings pitched and the number of runs allowed by each pitcher. Where season statistics could not be compiled at all on account of these deficiencies, they are indicated by a question mark. When we found statistics for most games but not all, the season totals reflect only the known statistics. In those cases, we have placed a question mark next to the applicable statistics, denoting their incomplete nature.

With these caveats, the yearly statistics for each team in the Hill Country League (1930–32) and the Mountain League (1933–35) are found in Appendices A–F. In addition, Appendix G contains the Hill Country League standings for 1933–36.

ABBREVIATIONS FOR APPENDICES

PLAYER POSITION (POS)

1b: first baseman
2b: second baseman
3b: third baseman
c: catcher
cf: center fielder
if: infielder
lf: left fielder
of: outfielder
p: pitcher
ph: pinch hitter
rf: right fielder
ss: shortstop

STATS

2B: doubles
3B: triples
AB: at bats
BA: batting average
BB: walks
G: games played
GB: games behind
GS: games started (pitchers)
H: hits
HBP: hit by pitch
HR: home runs
IP: innings pitched
L: losses
Pct.: (winning) percentage
R: runs
SB: stolen bases

SO: strikeouts
SP: slugging percentage
TRA: total run average
W: wins
WP: wild pitches

APPENDIX A: HILL COUNTRY LEAGUE STANDINGS AND TEAM STATISTICS, 1930

1930 Hill Country League Standings

Team	W	L	GB	Pct.
Fredericksburg	19	7	---	.731
Llano	18	7	½	.720
Boerne	17	9	2	.654
Kerrville	10	15	8½	.400
Comfort	8	18	11	.308
Mason	5	21	14	.192

Championship Series: Fredericksburg defeated Llano, two games to one.

Boerne White Sox (17–9)*									**Manager Ed Kaiser**		
Player	**POS**	**G**	**AB**	**R**	**H**	**2B**	**3B**	**HR**	**BA**	**SP**	**SB**
Bremer	3b	25	98	14	35	6	2	0	.357	.459	8
A. Uecker	rf-p	25	97	22	21	3	0	0	.216	.247	5
R. Leidl	2b	25	109	29	39	3	2	0	.358	.431	3
Holekamp	1b	24	105	12	22	2	0	0	.210	.229	1
Myler	p-rf	22	77	20	31	4	2	0	.403	.506	3
E. Harz	cf	20	69	8	17	2	1	0	.246	.304	2
Dunsmore	c	16	60	7	15	2	0	0	.250	.283	3
English	ss	16	67	20	22	2	2	1	.328	.463	2
W. Kalisky	c-rf	14	54	6	15	1	1	0	.278	.333	3
Schweppe	lf	13	38	5	5	0	1	0	.132	.184	1
Pfeiffer	cf-rf	11	31	3	5	0	0	0	.161	.161	1
Dugosh	p	8	15	0	0	0	0	0	.000	.000	0
Johnston	rf-1b	4	18	2	5	1	1	0	.278	.444	0
Hudson	ss	3	6	1	1	0	0	0	.167	.167	0
A. Leidl**	ss	4	16	3	4	1	0	0	.250	.313	0

Player	POS	G	AB	R	H	2B	3B	HR	BA	SP	SB
Schrader	rf-cf	4	4	1	1	0	0	0	.250	.250	0
Collins	ph	3	1	1	0	0	0	0	.000	.000	0
Wendler	1b	3	11	3	2	0	0	0	.182	.182	1
A. Bergmann***	rf-lf	2	6	0	0	0	0	0	.000	.000	0
Bourgeois	rf	2	0	0	0	0	0	0	.000	.000	0
Phillip	ph	1	0	0	0	0	0	0	.000	.000	0
Hargrove	p	1	0	1	0	0	0	0	.000	.000	0
R. Uecker****	ph	1	1	0	1	0	0	0	1.000	1.000	1
Total		**25**	**883**	**158**	**241**	**27**	**12**	**1**	**.273**	**.334**	**34**

Pitcher	G	GS	W/L	IP	H	R	TRA	BB	SO	HBP	WP
Myler	21	17	13–5	146⅔	143	66	4.05	18?	139	9	0
Dugosh	8	7	4–2	47	45	22	4.21	8?	35	4	0
A. Uecker	1	1	0–1	9	11	11	11.00	?	?	0	0
Hargrove	1	0	0–0	5⅔	9	2	3.18	2	5	0	0
Total	**25**	**25**	**17–8**	**208⅓**	**208**	**101**	**4.36**	**28?**	**179?**	**13**	**0**

* These statistics include only 25 (of 26) Hill Country League regular season games—statistics for 15 games were taken from available box scores, while statistics for the other 10 games were compiled from the 1930 Boerne White Sox scorebook in the Dietert Historical Archives at Boerne's Patrick Heath Public Library. The statistics do not include exhibition games.

** Anton Leidl played 16 games for Kerrville.

*** "A. Bergmann" is Anton Bergmann.

**** "R. Uecker" may be Johnny Uecker, whose first name was "Reinwald" ("Johnny" was a nickname).

1930 Comfort Broncos (8–18)*						**Manager Ernst Doebbler**					
Player	**POS**	**G**	**AB**	**R**	**H**	**2B**	**3B**	**HR**	**BA**	**SP**	**SB**
Goforth	1b	18	72	5	17	1	0	1	.236	.333	1
Meyer	cf-c	18	68	12	12	4	1	1	.250	.382	1
J. Pankratz	ss-2b	17	60	11	18	2	2	1	.300	.450	3
S. Pankratz	3b	16	58	5	12	0	1	1	.207	.293	0
Lindner	lf-rf	15	61	1	12	1	0	0	.197	.213	0
Wendler	ss-2b	15	57	3	17	1	2	0	.298	.386	0

Maddox	p-2b	13	35	4	3	1	0	0	.086	.114	0
Nowlin	c	12	47	3	7	1	0	0	.149	.170	0
Bergmann**	rf-lf	9	35	3	7	2	0	0	.200	.257	0
Weiss	cf-rf	7	20	2	6	1	1	0	.300	.550	1
Marberger	p-lf	6	17	3	3	0	0	1	.176	.353	0
Allerkamp	2b-rf	5	13	2	0	0	0	0	.000	.000	0
Kutzer	rf-2b	5	12	2	3	0	0	0	.250	.250	0
Wright	2b-rf	3	6	2	1	0	0	0	.167	.167	0
King	2b	3	9	1	1	0	0	0	.111	.111	0
Haufler	p	2	3	0	0	0	0	0	.000	.000	0
West	3b	2	6	0	0	0	0	0	.000	.000	0
A. Bergmann**	rf-ss	2	7	0	0	0	0	0	.000	.000	0
H. Bergmann	cf-rf	2	6	0	0	0	0	0	.000	.000	0
Cheatham	p	2	0	0	0	0	0	0	.000	.000	0
Stieler	cf	1	3	0	1	0	0	0	.333	.333	0
Watt	p	1	3	0	1	0	0	0	.333	.333	0
Benecker	rf	1	2	0	0	0	0	0	.000	.000	0
Krauter	p	1	0	0	0	0	0	0	.000	.000	0
Lindemann	p	1	0	0	0	0	0	0	.000	.000	0
Total		**18**	**600**	**59**	**121**	**14**	**7**	**5**	**.202**	**.273**	**6**

Pitcher	**G**	**GS**	**W/L**	**IP**	**H**	**R**	**TRA**	**BB**	**SO**	**HBP**	**WP**
Maddox	13	8	4–7	86	93	61	6.38	?	79	10	4
Marberger	5	5	0–3	32	42	20	5.63	3	23	1	0
J. Pankratz	3	0	0–0	11⅔	4	3	2.31	?	15	1	1
Haufler	2	2	0–2	10	9	5	4.50	?	10	0	2
Watt	1	1	1–0	9	4	0	0.00	1	10	1	0
Cheatham	1	1	0–1	6	8	4	6.00	2	2	0	0
Krauter	1	1	0–0	1⅓	4	3	18.00	?	?	0	0
Lindemann	1	0	0–0	1	4	4	36.00	2	0	0	0
Total	**18**	**18**	**5–13**	**157**	**168**	**100**	**5.73**	**?**	**139?**	**13**	**7**

* These statistics include only 18 (of 26) Hill Country League regular season games. Statistics were taken from the published box scores available from newspaper accounts. Some box scores were either not published or not available.

** "A. Bergmann" is Arthur Bergmann. "Bergmann" is probably Arthur Bergmann as well. If so, the statistics of "Bergmann" and "A. Bergmann" should be combined.

1930 Fredericksburg Giants (19–7)*									Manager Al Hollmig		
Player	**POS**	**G**	**AB**	**R**	**H**	**2B**	**3B**	**HR**	**BA**	**SP**	**SB**
Hollmig	1b	26	90	18	32	4	2	1	.356	.478	1
Knopp	2b	24	102	17	24	4	0	1	.235	.304	2
U. Henke	c	23	90	6	20	4	1	0	.222	.289	3
Fuller	ss-3b	23	88	13	25	2	1	0	.284	.330	0
Durst	cf	23	90	15	24	3	2	0	.267	.344	5
Klett	rf-lf	22	82	14	22	3	1	2	.268	.402	7
Peter	ss	21	77	12	22	2	2	0	.286	.364	1
E. Henke	lf-rf	20	68	8	13	1	0	0	.191	.206	4
H. Klaerner	p-of	20	62	9	22	1	1	0	.355	.403	3
Hahn	3b-c	17	52	4	9	2	0	0	.173	.212	0
E. Klaerner	rf-lf	16	49	6	11	1	0	1	.224	.306	1
Probst	p-cf	10	30	4	8	0	0	0	.267	.267	2
Deike**	ss-2b	8	22	1	5	0	0	0	.227	.227	1
C. Klaerner	p	7	17	1	5	0	0	1	.294	471	0
Total		**26**	**919**	**128**	**242**	**27**	**10**	**6**	**.263**	**.334**	**30**

Pitcher	G	GS	W/L	IP	H	R	TRA	BB	SO	HBP	WP
H. Klaerner	18	12	10–4	110⅔	101	57	4.64	?	135	3	1
Probst	9	9	6–2	64⅔	53	24	3.34	?	41	2	1
C. Klaerner	6	4	3–1	38	35	14	3.32	2	33	0	1
E. Henke	2	1	0–0	9	15	14	14.00	3	12	0	1
Total	**26**	**26**	**19–7**	**222⅓**	**204**	**109**	**4.41**	**?**	**221**	**5**	**4**

* These statistics include all 26 Hill Country League regular season games. Statistics were taken from the published box scores available from newspaper accounts. The statistics do not include: 1) two exhibition games played at the Gillespie County Fair against Llano and Comfort on August 22 and August 23, respectively, and 2) the championship series against Llano.

** "Deike" is Levi Deike, one of the famous Deike brothers. See chapter 2.

1930 Kerrville Tourists/Athletics (10–15)* Manager H. C. Holchak											
Player	**POS**	**G**	**AB**	**R**	**H**	**2B**	**3B**	**HR**	**BA**	**SP**	**SB**
Baker	lf-cf	23	86	5	20	1	0	0	.233	.244	3
C. Hollimon	rf-1b	22	73	6	24	4	0	1	.329	.425	1
A. Saenger	2b-rf	20	84	7	18	2	0	0	.214	.238	0
Warren	cf-rf	17	39	1	6	0	0	0	.154	.154	1

A. Leidl**	ss-p	16	65	11	19	3	2	1	.292	.446	0
Andrews	c-1b	14	56	8	15	5	1	0	.268	.393	3
Wootton	3b-cf	14	40	1	6	3	0	0	.150	.225	0
Hall	ss-3b	13	37	4	9	1	0	0	.243	.270	1
Coleman	ss-p	10	46	4	10	3	1	0	.217	.326	2
Trapp	c-1b	9	30	6	9	1	0	0	.300	.333	1
Swayze	p-of	9	26	5	7	1	0	0	.269	.308	4
Scarborough	rf-lf	9	28	0	1	0	0	0	.036	.036	1
J. Hollimon	2b-lf	8	18	2	4	1	1	0	.222	.389	0
Thornberry	p	8	27	4	5	0	0	0	.185	.185	2
Lawrence	1b-c	8	33	2	6	2	0	0	.182	.242	0
Vaughan	cf	7	16	1	1	0	0	0	.063	.063	1
Morris	3b	7	15	0	1	0	0	0	.066	.066	0
Michon	rf	5	21	2	3	0	0	0	.143	.143	1
Grantham	3b-rf	5	12	1	3	0	0	0	.250	.250	0
Anderson	lf-rf	5	13	1	2	0	0	0	.154	.154	0
Rice	3b	5	20	2	2	0	0	0	.100	.100	2
Garrett	lf-rf	4	6	0	0	0	0	0	.000	.000	0
Lochte	3b-lf	3	2	0	1	0	0	0	.500	.500	0
Hamilton	ss-of	2	6	0	0	0	0	0	.000	.000	0
McDonald	rf	2	1	0	0	0	0	0	.000	.000	0
C. Klaerner	p	1	4	0	0	0	0	0	.000	.000	0
Taylor	3b	1	4	1	0	0	0	0	.000	.000	0
Perez	p	1	4	0	1	0	0	0	.250	.250	0
Murdock	p	1	4	0	0	0	0	0	.000	.000	0
Bryant	cf	1	4	0	1	0	0	0	.250	.250	0
Stewart	3b	1	2	1	1	0	0	0	.500	.500	0
Wheeler	rf	1	1	0	0	0	0	0	.000	.000	0
Holchak	ph	1	1	0	0	0	0	0	.000	.000	0
Benedict	ph	1	0	0	0	0	0	0	.000	.000	0
Total		**24**	**824**	**75**	**175**	**27**	**5**	**2**	**.212**	**.264**	**23**

Pitcher	**G**	**GS**	**W/L**	**IP**	**H**	**R**	**TRA**	**BB**	**SO**	**HBP**	**WP**
Thornberry	8	8	3–4	78	59	23	2.65	?	83	2	1
A. Leidl**	8	6	3–3	48⅓	38	26	4.84	?	53	4	3
Swayze	8	7	2–5	60	51	33	4.95	?	66	4	7
C. Klaerner	1	1	0–1	11	3	3	2.45	3	10	0	0

Pitcher	G	GS	W/L	IP	H	R	TRA	BB	SO	HBP	WP
Perez	1	1	0–1	8	14	9	10.13	0	3	0	0
Murdock	1	1	1–0	9	4	0	0.00	3	12	1	0
Wootton	1	0	0–0	2	4	4	18.00	0	1	0	0
Saenger	1	0	0–0	1	1	1	9.00	2	2	0	0
Coleman	1	0	0–0	0	0	0	---	1	0	1	0
Total	**24**	**24**	**9–14***	**217⅓**	**174**	**99**	**4.10**	**?**	**231**	**12**	**11**

* These statistics include only 24 (of 26) Hill Country League regular season games, including a 15-inning 2–2 tie with Llano on April 27 which did not count in the standings, but the statistics for that game *are* included in the above statistics *except* for pitchers' win-loss records, resulting in a 9–14 combined pitching record. Statistics were taken from the published box scores available from newspaper accounts. Some box scores were either not published or not available.

** Anton Leidl played four games for Boerne.

1930 Llano Cowboys (18–7)*									**Manager Jack Holloway/ Chink Taylor****		
Player	**POS**	**G**	**AB**	**R**	**H**	**2B**	**3B**	**HR**	**BA**	**SP**	**SB**
Hutto	p-of	23	93	17	32	3	2	0	.344	.419	2
Colllings	3b	23	103	16	24	2	1	0	.233	.272	4
Reed	ss	22	95	28	29	3	2	0	.305	.379	8
Taylor	2b-cf	20	81	35	37	12	4	2	.457	.777	13
P. McLeod	c-cf	18	71	10	19	1	0	1	.268	.324	1
Holloway	1b	17	69	11	26	6	4	0	.377	.570	2
Draper	p-cf	17	64	5	11	2	0	0	.172	.203	1
Mather	cf-rf	16	70	13	29	1	5	0	.414	.571	3
Duncan	lf-rf	12	48	6	14	1	0	0	.292	.313	2
Lewis	c-1b	11	39	9	12	2	2	0	.308	.462	4
Pinckney	2b	9	41	11	13	3	0	0	.317	.390	5
D. McLeod	lf-1b	5	19	4	3	0	0	0	.158	.158	2
White	p	3	10	1	1	0	0	0	.100	.100	0
Randolph	rf	2	11	1	3	0	0	0	.273	.273	0
Brydson	c	2	10	0	3	0	0	0	.300	.300	0
Nixon	of	2	3	0	1	0	0	0	.333	.333	0
Chapman	lf	2	5	0	0	0	0	0	.000	.000	0
Simpson	cf-rf	2	4	0	0	0	0	0	.000	.000	0
Speagle	1b	1	6	1	1	0	0	0	.167	.167	0

Cross	p	1	1	0	0	0	0	0	.000	.000	0
Decker	2b	1	3	0	0	0	0	0	.000	.000	0
Roberts	cf	1	2	0	0	0	0	0	.000	.000	0
Barrett	2b	1	3	0	0	0	0	0	.000	.000	0
Brewer	c	1	3	1	1	0	0	0	.333	.333	0
Shankel	c	1	2	0	1	0	0	0	.500	.500	0
Leverett	rf	1	1	0	0	0	0	0	.000	.000	0
Nichols	ph	1	1	0	0	0	0	0	.000	.000	0
McDougal	3b	1	4	0	0	0	0	0	.000	.000	0
Hammontree	rf	1	1	0	0	0	0	0	.000	.000	0
Cross	p	1	1	0	0	0	0	0	.000	.000	0
Brown	ss	1	4	1	0	0	0	0	.000	.000	0
Total		**24**	**868**	**170**	**260**	**36**	**20**	**3**	**.300**	**.397**	**47**

Pitcher	**G**	**GS**	**W/L**	**IP**	**H**	**R**	**TRA**	**BB**	**SO**	**HBP**	**WP**
Draper	16	15	12–3	137⅓	110	57	3.74	36	124	11	3
Hutto	6	6	3–2	50⅓	48	25	4.47	?	35	1	0
White	3	3	2–1	25	24	9	3.24	5	32	1	0
Cross	1	0	0–0	1⅓	1	0	0.00	1	1	0	0
Total	**24**	**24**	**17–6***	**214**	**183**	**91**	**3.83**	**42?**	**192**	**13**	**3**

* These statistics include only 24 (of 26) Hill Country League regular season games, including a 15-inning 2–2 tie with Kerrville on April 27 which did not count in the standings, but the statistics for that game *are* included in the above statistics *except* for pitchers' win-loss records, resulting in a 17–6 combined pitching record. Statistics were taken from the published box scores available from newspaper accounts. Some box scores were either not published or not available. The statistics do not include the championship series against Fredericksburg.

** Jack Holloway started the season as manager, but after Taylor joined the club in May 1930, he must have taken over as a player-manager because E. E. Martin selected Taylor as the top manager in the Hill Country League when he named the All-Star team. See chapter 4.

1930 Mason Mavericks (5–21)*									**Manager unknown**		
Player	**POS**	**G**	**AB**	**R**	**H**	**2B**	**3B**	**HR**	**BA**	**SP**	**SB**
Loeffler	3b-cf	16	59	1	11	0	1	1	.186	.271	0
Hoffman	1b-2b	15	53	3	8	1	0	0	.151	.170	1
Kygar	c	13	48	4	3	0	0	0	.063	.063	1
Nobles	lf-2b	13	38	2	6	0	0	0	.158	.158	0

Player	POS	G	AB	R	H	2B	3B	HR	BA	SP	SB
Sanders	p	13	35	1	4	0	0	0	.114	.114	2
J. Brown	ss-p	13	52	9	12	4	0	0	.231	.308	1
Evans	rf-cf	12	39	3	5	2	0	0	.128	.179	1
Vogel	c-cf	10	39	3	8	0	0	0	.205	.205	1
Hatch	p-1b	10	31	6	7	1	0	0	.226	.258	0
Keller	2b-ss	10	40	8	12	1	0	0	.300	.325	1
Lang(e)	cf-lf	7	20	1	4	0	0	0	.200	.200	0
R. Brown	3b-p	5	20	5	6	1	1	0	.300	.450	4
Latham	rf-2b	5	20	1	3	0	0	0	.150	.150	0
Tate	rf-lf	5	13	1	1	0	0	0	.077	.077	2
Shearer	lf-rf	4	8	1	1	1	0	0	.125	.250	0
H. Schmidt	lf	2	5	1	1	0	0	0	.200	.200	0
C. Schmidt	1b	1	0	1	0	0	0	0	.000	.000	1
Garner	rf	1	1	0	0	0	0	0	.000	.000	0
Total		**16**	**521**	**51**	**92**	**11**	**2**	**1**	**.177**	**.211**	**15**

Pitcher	G	GS	W/L	IP	H	R	TRA	BB	SO	HBP	WP
Sanders	13	11	3–9	97⅓	107	59	5.46	?	101	3	1
Hatch	5	3	0–3	22⅓	46	37	14.90	?	10	3	2
Loeffler	3	2	0–1	12	9	5	3.75	0	9	1	0
Vogel	1	0	0–0	2⅓	5	5	19.29	2	1	0	0
R. Brown	1	0	0–0	0	2	2	Inf	0	0	0	0
Total	**16**	**16**	**3–13**	**134**	**169**	**108**	**7.25**	**?**	**121**	**7**	**3**

* These statistics include only 16 (of 26) Hill Country League regular season games. Statistics were taken from the published box scores available from newspaper accounts. Some box scores were either not published or not available.

APPENDIX B: HILL COUNTRY LEAGUE STANDINGS AND TEAM STATISTICS, 1931

1931 Hill Country League Standings

Team	W	L	GB	Pct.
Fredericksburg	20	6	---	.769
Llano	16	7	2½	.696
Kerrville	13	12	6½	.520
Mason	10	14	9	.417
Comfort	8	15	10½	.348
Junction	6	19	13½	.240

Championship Series: Llano defeated Fredericksburg, two games to none.

1931 Comfort Broncos (8-15)*									Manager unknown		
Player	**POS**	**G**	**AB**	**R**	**H**	**2B**	**3B**	**HR**	**BA**	**SP**	**SB**
R. Leidl	2b	14	60	12	17	2	2	0	.283	.383	0
Wendler	ss-3b	14	56	6	16	0	2	1	.286	.411	3
Goforth	1b	14	54	6	13	2	1	0	.241	.315	3
J. Pankratz	3b-ss	13	48	7	15	3	1	0	.313	.417	4
S. Pankratz	cf	12	45	6	14	1	2	0	.311	.422	0
Meyer	c-of	12	46	6	10	1	0	0	.217	.239	0
Bergmann**	lf	9	30	0	6	0	1	0	.200	.267	0
Myler	p	8	31	3	8	1	1	0	.258	.354	1
West	rf-lf	8	30	2	3	0	0	0	.100	.100	0
Bremer	rf-3b	7	24	5	9	3	3	0	.375	.750	1
Tomlinson	c	7	15	1	2	0	0	0	.133	.133	0
Kutzer	rf	4	11	0	2	0	0	0	.182	.182	1
Dugosh	p	4	4	0	0	0	0	0	.000	.000	0
Haufler	p	3	6	1	1	0	0	0	.167	.167	0
Gaffney	p	1	3	0	0	0	0	0	.000	.000	0

Player	POS	G	AB	R	H	2B	3B	HR	BA	SP	SB
Stewart	p	1	3	0	0	0	0	0	.000	.000	0
Loessberg	p	1	4	0	0	0	0	0	.000	.000	0
Total		**14**	**470**	**55**	**116**	**13**	**13**	**1**	**.247**	**.336**	**13**

Pitcher	G	GS	W/L	IP	H	R	TRA	BB	SO	HBP	WP
Myler	8	7	3–4	67⅔	48	24	3.19	18	31	3	1
Dugosh	4	2	0–2	10⅓	18	14	12.19	4	11	0	1
Haufler	3	2	0–2	15⅓	22	17	9.98	6	4	2	1
Loessberg	1	1	0–1	9	15	10	10.00	2	2	1	1
Stewart	1	1	0–1	8	8	8	9.00	1	3	2	0
Gaffney	1	1	1–0	9	4	0	0.00	2	6	2	0
Total	**14**	**14**	**4–10**	**119⅓**	**115**	**73**	**5.50**	**33**	**57**	**10**	**4**

* These statistics include only 14 (of 23) Hill Country League regular season games. Statistics were taken from the published box scores available from newspaper accounts. Some box scores were either not published or not available.

** "Bergmann" is likely Arthur Bergmann.

1931 Fredericksburg Giants (20–6)*								**Manager Felix Saenger**			
Player	**POS**	**G**	**AB**	**R**	**H**	**2B**	**3B**	**HR**	**BA**	**SP**	**SB**
Hollmig	1b	23	81	19	28	5	2	1	.346	.494	3
Peter	3b	22	76	17	18	1	1	0	.237	.276	2
Knopp	ss-2b	21	76	14	16	5	1	2	.211	.382	2
Klett	lf-rf	20	80	22	20	3	7	1	.250	.500	2
Nagel	ss-2b	19	69	6	12	0	1	0	.174	.203	1
Hahn	c-ss	19	68	13	18	5	0	0	.265	.338	1
Durst	cf	19	74	14	13	4	1	0	.176	.257	0
Sanders	p	16	54	4	20	0	0	0	.370	.370	2
E. Klaerner	rf-lf	16	59	8	13	0	2	0	.220	.288	1
U. Henke	c-1b	14	44	9	9	0	0	0	.205	.205	0
E. Henke	lf	13	49	8	12	2	1	1	.245	.388	4
Fuller	2b-ss	8	33	6	14	3	2	0	.424	.636	0
C. Klaerner	p-2b	7	23	3	2	0	1	0	.087	.174	0
H. Klaerner	3b-rf	3	2	1	0	0	0	0	.000	000	0
P. Klaerner	p-rf	3	6	2	2	0	0	1	.333	.833	0
Kott	ss	1	3	1	0	0	0	0	.000	.000	1
Total		**23**	**797**	**147**	**197**	**28**	**19**	**6**	**.247**	**.353**	**19**

Pitcher	G	GS	W/L	IP	H	R	TRA	BB	SO	HBP	WP
Sanders	16	16	13–3	131	95	56	3.85	30	118	9	9
C. Klaerner	6	6	5–1	53	39	18	3.06	11	32	3	2
P. Klaerner	2	1	0–1	9⅔	20	12	11.17	7	7	0	0
Hollmig	1	0	0–0	7	8	4	5.14	0	2	0	0
Total	**23**	**23**	**18–5**	**200⅔**	**162**	**90**	**4.04**	**48**	**159**	**12**	**11**

* These statistics include only 23 (of 26) Hill Country League regular season games. Statistics were taken from the published box scores available from newspaper accounts. Some box scores were either not published or not available. The statistics do not include the championship series against Llano.

1931 Junction Firemen (6–19)*					**Manager Ches (Pratt) Goodwin**						
Player	**POS**	**G**	**AB**	**R**	**H**	**2B**	**3B**	**HR**	**BA**	**SP**	**SB**
Motley	c-2b	15	53	4	6	1	0	0	.113	.132	1
McWright	cf-1b	15	54	5	14	1	2	0	.259	.352	1
Gardner	p-2b	15	45	6	12	0	4	0	.267	.444	1
Blackburn	ss-c	14	51	5	13	2	0	2	.255	.412	4
Camp	3b-rf	14	49	7	15	3	0	0	.306	.367	1
Kindrick	2b-lf	12	41	3	4	1	0	0	.098	.122	0
Hord	lf-rf	9	29	1	4	0	0	0	.138	.138	2
Dechert	1b-lf	8	24	2	5	0	0	0	.208	.208	0
Dunbar	lf-rf	7	22	1	3	0	0	0	.136	.136	0
Ratliff	ss-p	7	26	3	9	3	1	0	.346	.538	2
Buster	p-1b	6	15	0	3	0	0	0	.200	.200	1
Holland	3b-p	3	3	0	1	1	0	0	.333	.667	0
Hendricks	rf-lf	3	10	1	1	0	0	0	.100	.100	0
Moore	3b-rf	3	10	0	0	0	0	0	.000	.000	0
Hickerson	lf-rf	2	4	0	0	0	0	0	.000	.000	0
Ragland	p	2	1	0	0	0	0	0	.000	.000	0
Huddleston	rf-ss	2	3	0	0	0	0	0	.000	.000	0
Webber	1b	2	6	1	0	0	0	0	.000	.000	0
Robertson	p	2	2	0	0	0	0	0	.000	.000	0
Babb	p	1	2	0	0	0	0	0	.000	.000	0
Richardson	p	1	1	0	1	0	0	0	1.000	1.000	0
Goodwin	rf	1	3	0	0	0	0	0	.000	.000	0
White	p	1	2	0	0	0	0	0	.000	.000	0
Total		**15**	**456**	**39**	**91**	**12**	**7**	**2**	**.200**	**.270**	**13**

Pitcher	G	GS	W/L	IP	H	R	TRA	BB	SO	HBP	WP
Gardner	9	8	2–6	67	61	50	6.72	14	48	3	5
Buster	3	1	0–1	17⅓	31	16	8.31	6	5	0	2
Ratliff	2	1	0–1	9	14	14	14.00	1	3	0	0
Ragland	2	0	0–0	2⅔	0	0	0.00	1	2	0	0
Robertson	2	1	0–1	11⅓	15	10	7.94	5	7	1	1
Babb	1	1	0–1	5⅓	14	12	20.25	2	4	1	0
Richardson	1	1	0–1	2⅔	10	11	37.13	2	1	0	0
White	1	1	0–1	6	8	6	9.00	1	6	1	0
Holland	1	1	0–1	1	2	5	45.00	3	2	1	0
Total	**15**	**15**	**2–13**	**122⅓**	**155**	**124**	**9.12**	**35**	**78**	**7**	**8**

* These statistics include only 15 (of 25) Hill Country League regular season games. Statistics were taken from the published box scores available from newspaper accounts. Some box scores were either not published or not available.

1931 Kerrville Braves (13–12)*						**Manager Dick Bischofhausen/ Nelson Davis**					
Player	**POS**	**G**	**AB**	**R**	**H**	**2B**	**3B**	**HR**	**BA**	**SP**	**SB**
Grantham	c-2b	22	75	10	23	2	3	0	.307	.413	5
A. Leidl	p-cf	22	79	20	24	6	0	3	.304	.494	3
C. Hollimon	1b	21	82	2	19	4	1	0	.232	.305	1
Baker	lf-3b	19	70	6	12	3	0	0	.171	.214	7
Wootton	3b/of	19	67	6	10	2	1	0	.149	.209	1
H. Klaerner	p-3b	15	52	5	14	2	0	0	.269	.308	4
Saenger	cf-rf	14	48	7	10	0	0	0	.208	.208	4
Beaver	2b-rf	13	38	3	7	2	0	0	.184	.237	1
Hall	ss-3b	12	43	4	11	2	1	0	.256	.349	1
Staudt	ss-2b	11	31	4	7	0	1	0	.226	.290	1
Warren	of	10	17	3	3	1	0	0	.176	.235	1
Cannon	ss-p	7	29	4	8	0	0	0	.276	.276	5
Bischofhausen	of	6	15	0	4	0	0	0	.267	.267	0
Owens	rf	6	19	5	4	0	1	0	.210	.316	0
Kelley (Kelly)	ss-rf	5	11	0	1	0	0	0	.091	.091	0
Markt	rf-2b	5	10	0	1	0	0	0	.100	.100	0
Myler	p-cf	4	13	2	3	1	0	0	.231	.308	0
Michaels	c-ss	4	14	5	6	0	0	2	.429	.857	1

J. Hollimon	2b-rf	3	7	1	1	0	0	0	.143	.143	0
Johnston	c	3	10	0	1	0	0	0	.100	.100	0
Archer	rf-lf	2	5	1	3	1	0	0	.600	.800	0
Taylor	3b-cf	2	8	1	2	0	0	0	.250	.250	0
Crooks	cf-lf	2	3	0	0	0	0	0	.000	.000	0
Riley	rf	2	6	2	2	0	0	0	.333	.333	0
Gotthardt	2b	1	3	0	0	0	0	0	.000	.000	0
Mueller	p	1	5	0	3	0	0	0	.600	.600	0
Wilson	rf	1	4	1	1	0	0	0	.250	.250	0
Holchak	ss	1	2	0	0	0	0	0	.000	.000	0
Goodwin	p	1	0	0	0	0	0	0	.000	.000	0
Total		**23**	**766**	**92**	**180**	**26**	**8**	**5**	**.235**	**.309**	**35**

Pitcher	**G**	**GS**	**W/L**	**IP**	**H**	**R**	**TRA**	**BB**	**SO**	**HBP**	**WP**
H. Klaerner	13	11	6–5	114	108	47	3.71	23	106	0	5
A. Leidl	8	8	4–4	65	53	32	4.43	20	67	4	4
Myler	2	2	1–1	15	14	10	6.00	2	10	4	0
Mueller	1	1	0–1	10⅓	11	7	6.10	5	7	0	0
Goodwin	1	1	0–1	1⅓	6	3	20.25	0	2	0	0
Total	**23**	**23**	**11–12**	**205⅔**	**192**	**99**	**4.40**	**50**	**192**	**8**	**9**

* These statistics include only 23 (of 25) Hill Country League regular season games. Statistics were taken from the published box scores available from newspaper accounts. Some box scores were either not published or not available.

1931 Llano Cowboys (16–7)*						**Manager C. L. "Chink" Taylor**					
Player	**POS**	**G**	**AB**	**R**	**H**	**2B**	**3B**	**HR**	**BA**	**SP**	**SB**
Mather	rf	17	76	16	27	0	5	0	.355	.487	8
P. McLeod	c-3b	17	66	3	15	1	1	0	.227	.273	1
Reed	ss-3b	17	70	16	21	3	0	1	.300	.386	4
J. Pinckney	2b-3b	16	71	13	15	1	0	0	.211	.225	2
C. Taylor	cf-3b	15	55	18	20	3	3	3	.364	.691	8
C. Brewer	lf-1b	15	57	11	21	3	2	1	.368	.544	8
Van Huss	p	13	47	4	9	2	0	0	.191	.234	0
Peel	1b-p	13	46	12	22	3	3	2	.478	.804	3
H. Collings	3b	12	42	4	10	0	0	0	.238	.238	1
D. McLeod	1b-lf	4	11	0	0	0	0	0	.000	.000	0
Decker	ss-2b	3	6	0	0	0	0	0	.000	.000	0

Player	POS	G	AB	R	H	2B	3B	HR	BA	SP	SB
Davis	1b	3	12	5	5	0	0	0	.417	.417	1
Young	p-lf	3	6	0	1	0	0	0	.167	.167	0
Riddle	cf	3	12	4	3	1	0	0	.250	.333	0
Draper	p	3	8	0	3	0	0	0	.375	.375	0
E. Brewer	c	2	2	1	1	0	0	0	.500	.500	0
T. Pinckney	ss-2b	2	8	1	1	0	0	0	.125	.125	0
R. Barrett	rf	1	2	0	1	0	0	0	.500	.500	0
D. Barrett	2b	1	4	0	0	0	0	0	.000	.000	0
Holloway	c	1	5	0	0	0	0	0	.000	.000	0
Simpson	lf	1	5	2	3	0	0	0	.600	.600	0
McDonald	p	1	2	1	1	0	0	0	.500	.500	0
Pankey	rf	1	0	0	0	0	0	0	.000	.000	0
Total		**17**	**613**	**111**	**179**	**17**	**14**	**7**	**.292**	**.400**	**36**

Pitcher	G	GS	W/L	IP	H	R	TRA	BB	SO	HBP	WP
Van Huss	13	11	10–2	99⅔	75	32	2.89	30	60	5	1
Draper	3	3	2–1	24	22	5	1.88	4	21	2	0
Young**	3	2	1–0	21⅓	19	12	5.06	9	20	4	3
Peel	2	0	1–0	2⅔	4	3	10.13	1	2	1	1
McDonald	1	1	0–0	2⅓	6	9	34.70	1	3	0	0
Total	**17**	**17**	**14–3**	**150**	**126**	**61**	**3.66**	**45**	**106**	**12**	**5**

* These statistics include only 17 (of 23) Hill Country League regular season games. Statistics were taken from the published box scores available from newspaper accounts. Some box scores were either not published or not available. The statistics do not include the championship series against Fredericksburg.

** Young also recorded one balk.

1931 Mason Mavericks (10–14)*										**Manager unknown**	
Player	**POS**	**G**	**AB**	**R**	**H**	**2B**	**3B**	**HR**	**BA**	**SP**	**SB**
Brown	ss	12	52	10	11	2	2	0	.212	.327	1
Hatch	p-of	12	47	9	17	1	2	2	.361	.596	1
Schmidt	1b	11	43	5	11	0	0	1	.256	.326	1
Barrett	2b	10	36	4	8	1	0	0	.222	.250	0
Loeffler	of-p	9	24	2	3	0	0	0	.125	.125	0
Simpson	3b	9	32	2	1	0	0	0	.031	.031	0
Hoffman	lf-p	9	34	3	8	3	1	0	.235	.382	0

Holloway	c-of	7	21	3	5	0	0	0	.238	.238	1
Evans	rf	7	30	5	11	1	0	0	.367	.400	1
Vogel	c	6	24	4	5	0	0	1	.208	.333	1
Dannheim	of-3b	6	20	3	4	0	1	0	.200	.300	1
Kygar	c	5	13	0	4	0	0	0	.308	.308	0
Draper	p	5	16	2	3	0	1	0	.188	.313	0
Lange	lf-cf	5	17	2	2	0	1	0	.118	.235	0
Wagner	rf-2b	2	2	0	1	0	0	0	.500	.500	1
Keller	2b	1	4	0	1	0	0	0	.250	.250	0
Humphrey	3b	1	5	3	1	0	0	0	.200	.200	1
Total		**12**	**420**	**57**	**96**	**8**	**8**	**4**	**.229**	**.314**	**9**

Pitcher	**G**	**GS**	**W/L**	**IP**	**H**	**R**	**TRA**	**BB**	**SO**	**HBP**	**WP**
Hatch	8	7	3–4	55⅔	57	36	5.82	25	20	1	2
Draper	5	5	0–5	40⅔	42	20	4.42	7	31	0	0
Hoffman	2	0	0–0	9⅓	12	8	7.71	5	4	2	1
Loeffler	1	0	0–0	1⅓	1	0	0.00	1	2	1	0
Total	**12**	**12**	**3–9**	**107**	**112**	**64**	**5.38**	**38**	**57**	**4**	**3**

* These statistics include only 12 (of 24) Hill Country League regular season games. Statistics were taken from the published box scores available from newspaper accounts. Some box scores were either not published or not available.

APPENDIX C: HILL COUNTRY LEAGUE STANDINGS AND TEAM STATISTICS, 1932

1932 Hill Country League Standings – First Half

Team	W	L	GB	Pct.
Mason	10	3	---	.769
Llano	9	4	1	.692
Fredericksburg	8	5	2	.615
Kerrville	6	7	4	.462
Brady	5	8	5	.385
Junction	1	12	9	.077

1932 Hill Country League Standings – Second Half

Team	W	L	GB	Pct.
Llano	11	1	---	.917
Brady	6	4	4	.600
Fredericksburg	6	5	4½	.545
Mason	5	6	5½	.455
Kerrville	5	7	6	.417
Junction	0	10	10	.000

Championship Series: Llano defeated Mason, two games to one.

1932 Brady Turks (11–12)*								Manager Luke Vogel			
Player	**POS**	**G**	**AB**	**R**	**H**	**2B**	**3B**	**HR**	**BA**	**SP**	**SB**
L. Vogel	c-cf	15	62	14	20	4	2	0	.323	.452	1
Samuelson	cf-2b	14	61	11	16	1	0	1	.262	.328	0
Pearson	1b	13	49	8	14	1	0	0	.286	.306	0
Prewitt (Pruitt)	lf-rf	13	53	5	13	3	1	0	.245	.340	1
H. Jones	3b	12	45	8	12	2	0	0	.267	.311	2
V. Taylor	p	9	26	4	9	0	0	0	.346	.346	1

Player	POS	G	AB	R	H	2B	3B	HR	BA	SP	SB
W. Jones	ss	8	23	1	6	0	0	0	.261	.261	2
G. Reed	rf-lf	6	17	1	2	0	0	0	.118	.118	0
Gardner	lf	6	25	4	10	2	2	0	.400	.640	0
Holt	of-c	6	14	1	4	2	0	0	.286	.429	0
Hill	ss-2b	6	19	6	4	0	0	0	.211	.211	0
Tongate	2b	5	16	4	5	2	0	0	.313	.438	0
Hunter	3b-1b	5	17	6	9	0	2	0	.529	.647	1
Gleaton	ss	4	13	0	4	1	0	0	.308	.385	0
S. Smith	of-3b	3	12	1	1	0	0	0	.083	.083	0
Harris	p	3	6	1	2	0	1	0	.333	.667	0
Archer	p-cf	3	11	2	5	1	1	0	.455	.727	1
Faught	2b	3	11	2	3	0	1	0	.273	.455	0
Campbell	p	2	4	0	0	0	0	0	.000	.000	0
F. Vogel	rf-p	2	7	1	1	0	0	0	.143	.143	0
Webb	p	1	3	0	2	0	0	0	.667	.667	0
Petty	p	1	0	0	0	0	0	0	.000	.000	0
Linkenboger	cf	1	4	0	1	0	0	0	.250	.250	0
Page	rf	1	1	0	0	0	0	0	.000	.000	0
Total		**15**	**499**	**80**	**143**	**19**	**10**	**1**	**.287**	**.371**	**9**

Pitcher	G	GS	W/L	IP	H	R	TRA	BB	SO	HBP	WP
V. Taylor**	9	8	4–4	72⅓	67	31	3.86	20	69	2	3
Harris	3	0	0–1	11⅔	10	5	3.86	2	13	0	0
Archer	2	2	1–0	15⅔	12	10	5.74	10	11	2	0
Campbell	2	2	0–2	14	19	9	5.79	5	8	0	0
F. Vogel	1	1	0–1	5⅔	11	6	10.13	0	0	1	0
Webb	1	1	1–0	7	10	6	7.71	1	6	0	0
Petty	1	1	0–1	2	6	5	22.50	2	3	0	0
Total	**15**	**15**	**6–9**	**128⅓**	**135**	**72**	**5.05**	**40**	**110**	**5**	**3**

* These statistics include only 15 (of 23) Hill Country League regular season games. Statistics were taken from the published box scores available from newspaper accounts. Some box scores were either not published or not available.

** According to one report, Taylor's complete season record was 8–5. *Fredericksburg Standard*, September 9, 1932, 3.

1932 Fredericksburg Giants (14–10)*									Manager Felix Saenger		
Player	**POS**	**G**	**AB**	**R**	**H**	**2B**	**3B**	**HR**	**BA**	**SP**	**SB**
E. Klett	lf	24	99	21	45	7	10	2	.455	.788	6
E. Klaerner	rf-lf	24	103	14	36	1	1	1	.350	.408	5
Hahn	c	23	69	14	20	1	1	1	.290	.377	0
Peter	2b-ss	23	80	6	21	3	1	0	.263	.325	0
R. Klett	3b-2b	20	57	12	14	2	0	0	.246	.281	5
Deike	ss	20	85	17	19	0	0	0	.224	.224	0
Knopp	if-of	20	56	12	16	3	1	0	.286	.375	1
H. Klaerner	p-cf	19	78	21	29	3	1	0	.372	.436	3
Schneider	3b	18	64	7	15	2	1	0	.234	.297	1
P. Klaerner	of-p	18	60	7	9	3	1	1	.150	.300	0
Probst	1b-p	14	40	3	7	1	1	0	.175	.250	0
C. Klaerner	p-rf	9	27	8	10	0	2	1	.370	.630	0
Hollmig	1b	7	31	5	9	1	0	0	.290	.325	0
Wendler	ss	3	13	6	5	0	0	0	.385	.385	1
A. Klaerner	p	3	2	1	0	0	0	0	.000	.000	0
Sanders	p	2	4	3	0	0	0	0	.000	.000	0
Lee	ph	1	0	0	0	0	0	0	.000	.000	0
Pfeil	2b	1	0	0	0	0	0	0	.000	.000	0
Total		**24**	**868**	**157**	**255**	**27**	**20**	**6**	**.294**	**.392**	**22**

Pitcher	G	GS	W/L	IP	H	R	TRA	BB	SO	HBP	WP
H. Klaerner	12	9	6–4	87⅓	67	46	4.74	28	72	5	2
C. Klaerner	8	8	5–3	62⅔	47	20	2.87	20	49	4	0
P. Klaerner	4	2	2–1	18⅓	21	7	3.44	1	13	2	0
Probst	3	2	0–1	16	20	21	11.81	6	5	2	0
A. Klaerner	3	1	0–0	6⅓	?	?	?	0	3	0	1
Sanders	2	2	1–1	18?	14	10	5.00?	1	11	0	1
Knopp	1	0	0–0	0 ⅓	0	0	0.00	1	0	0	0
Total	**24**	**24**	**14–10**	**209?**	**169?**	**104?**	**4.48?**	**57**	**153**	**13**	**4**

* These statistics include all 24 Hill Country League regular season games. Statistics were taken from the published box scores available from newspaper accounts.

1932 Junction Mountaineers (1–22)*									Manager [?] Blackburn		
Player	**POS**	**G**	**AB**	**R**	**H**	**2B**	**3B**	**HR**	**BA**	**SP**	**SB**
Buster	1b-p	15	62	4	21	2	0	0	.339	.371	3
S. Goodwin	2b-of	15	51	8	6	0	1	0	.118	.157	2
Blackburn	ss-2b	14	56	7	19	0	4	0	.352	.482	1
W. C. Smith	c-rf	10	22	2	4	0	0	0	.182	.182	0
Gardner	1b-p	9	36	2	13	2	1	1	.361	.583	0
Goodman	p-of	9	30	6	8	1	2	0	.267	.433	0
Motley	c-ss	8	26	2	8	1	0	0	.308	.346	2
King	lf-2b	8	33	2	7	0	0	0	.212	.212	3
W. A. Smith	3b-ss	7	27	6	2	0	0	0	.074	.074	2
L. Ragland	p-of	7	21	4	5	0	0	0	.238	.238	0
Tomberlin	rf-cf	7	24	0	3	0	0	0	.125	.125	0
James	cf-ss	5	18	2	3	0	0	0	.167	.167	0
D. Taylor	3b-2b	4	12	0	3	0	0	0	.250	.250	0
Cummings	c-1b	3	10	3	2	0	0	0	.200	.200	2
Ard	lf-rf	3	6	1	2	0	0	0	.333	.333	0
Carl Taylor	2b-lf	3	9	0	0	0	0	0	.000	.000	0
Ratliff	ss	3	10	0	1	0	0	0	.100	.100	0
Barber	3b	3	10	0	2	0	0	0	.200	.200	0
Ramsey	2b-3b	3	7	2	1	0	0	0	.143	.143	1
McWright	cf	3	11	3	6	2	0	0	.545	.727	0
Moore	rf	2	8	1	4	0	0	0	.500	.500	0
Hannah	lf-p	2	7	0	1	0	0	0	.143	.143	0
J. Ragland	lf-1b	2	4	0	0	0	0	0	.000	.000	0
Ragland**	lf	2	6	0	0	0	0	0	.000	.000	0
McKinney	ph	1	1	0	0	0	0	0	.000	.000	0
R. Smith	c	1	2	2	1	0	0	0	.500	.500	0
Craven	rf	1	3	0	1	0	0	0	.333	.333	0
P. Ragland	rf	1	3	1	0	0	0	0	.000	.000	0
Standifer	p	1	1	0	0	0	0	0	.000	.000	0
Brady	ss	1	2	0	0	0	0	0	.000	.000	0
McLendon	cf	1	0	0	0	0	0	0	.000	.000	0
Tomlinson	lf	1	2	0	0	0	0	0	.000	.000	0
Northcutt	p	1	1	0	0	0	0	0	.000	.000	0
Total		**15**	**521**	**58**	**123**	**8**	**8**	**1**	**.236**	**.288**	**16**

Pitcher	G	GS	W/L	IP	H	R	TRA	BB	SO	HBP	WP
Goodman	8	7	1–6	57⅔	77	75	11.71	17?	52?	4	1
L. Ragland	6	3	0–3	23⅔?	35?	35?	?	12?	10?	0	0
Buster	4	3	0–3	22	?	34	13.90	13	9	1	0
Hannah	1	1	0–1	8	9	6	6.75	2	8	0	0
Northcutt	1	1	0–1	2	?	9	40.50	3	0	0	1
Standifer	1	0	0–0	?	?	?	?	?	?	?	?
Gardner	1	0	0–0	3	5	3	9.00	0	9	0	0
??	1	0	0–0	1⅔	3	3	16.20	0	0	0	0
Total	**15**	**15**	**1–14**	**118?**	**129?**	**165?**	**12.58?**	**47?**	**88?**	**5**	**2**

* These statistics include only 15 (of 23) Hill Country League regular season games. Statistics were taken from the published box scores available from newspaper accounts. Some box scores were either not published or not available.

** It is not clear whether "Ragland" is L. Ragland, J. Ragland, or P. Ragland.

1932 Kerrville Braves (11–14)*								Manager Nelson Davis			
Player	**POS**	**G**	**AB**	**R**	**H**	**2B**	**3B**	**HR**	**BA**	**SP**	**SB**
Grantham	c-2b	25	103	16	28	4	2	0	.272	.350	6
Staudt	rf-cf	23	92	11	20	3	1	0	.217	.272	2
J. Pankratz	3b-p	21	74	22	19	2	1	2	.257	.392	8
S. Pankratz	ss-3b	20	77	13	17	4	0	0	.221	.273	3
Wootton	cf-p	14	46	4	14	2	0	0	.304	.348	4
Baker	lf-3b	14	51	3	12	1	0	0	.235	.255	5
Beaver	2b-1b	14	44	9	14	1	0	0	.318	.341	3
Morris	2b-rf	10	35	3	11	1	0	0	.314	.343	2
Myler	p-of	8	30	3	5	1	0	0	.167	.200	1
Carr	ss	7	27	5	5	0	0	0	.185	.185	1
Currie (Curry)	1b-of	8	29	7	12	1	0	0	.414	.448	0
Rowe	of-ss	6	24	1	5	1	0	0	.208	.250	0
Sanders	p	6	15	0	4	0	0	0	.267	.267	0
Crooks	lf-3b	6	13	4	1	1	0	0	.077	.154	0
Weiss	1b	6	26	6	8	1	0	1	.308	.462	0
King	2b-ss	5	20	5	7	0	0	0	.350	.350	2
Haufler	p-rf	5	21	1	5	1	0	0	.238	.286	0
Wendler	1b-2b	4	13	3	2	0	1	0	.154	.308	0
Johnson	cf	2	7	0	3	0	0	0	.429	.429	1

Player	POS	G	AB	R	H	2B	3B	HR	BA	SP	SB
Reno	2b-ss	3	12	2	1	0	0	0	.083	.083	0
Gray	3b	2	6	2	1	0	0	0	.167	.167	0
Saenger	lf-rf	2	6	1	3	0	0	0	.500	.500	0
J. Hollimon	c	2	7	1	2	0	0	0	.286	.429	0
Michaels	c-1b	2	8	1	1	1	0	0	.125	.250	0
Warren	cf	2	6	1	2	0	0	0	.333	.333	0
Marberger	1b	2	6	1	1	0	0	0	.167	.167	0
C. Hollimon	1b	2	7	1	2	0	0	0	.286	.286	0
Anderson	rf	2	9	1	2	0	0	0	.222	.222	0
Alexander	cf-2b	2	1	0	1	0	0	0	1.000	1.000	0
Wartenbach	?	1	6	1	0	0	0	0	.000	.000	0
Foster	cf	1	5	0	0	0	0	0	.000	.000	0
Noble	ss	1	4	0	0	0	0	0	.000	.000	0
Goforth	1b	1	4	0	1	0	0	0	.250	.250	0
Taylor	p	1	4	1	3	0	0	0	.750	.750	0
White	p	1	4	0	0	0	0	0	.000	.000	1
Ratliff	2b	1	4	1	3	0	0	0	.750	.750	0
Perry	p	1	3	0	0	0	0	0	.000	.000	0
McNair	p	1	4	1	0	0	0	0	.000	.000	0
R. Leidl	rf	1	1	0	0	0	0	0	.000	.000	0
Myer	rf	1	3	2	0	0	0	0	.000	.000	0
C. Fletcher	lf	1	3	1	2	0	0	0	.667	.667	0
McDonald	1b	1	5	0	1	0	0	0	.200	.200	0
Maxwell	p	1	2	0	0	0	0	0	.000	.000	0
Stahl	3b	1	4	0	0	0	0	0	.000	.000	0
Total		**25**	**871**	**134**	**218**	**25**	**5**	**3**	**.250**	**.301**	**39**

Pitcher	G	GS	W/L	IP	H	R	TRA	BB	SO	HBP	WP
Myler	8	7	4–3	59⅔	70	30	4.53	11	33	3	0
Sanders	6	5	1–4	40⅓	38	27	6.02	7	29	3	2
Haufler	4	2	1–4	30	?	?	?	?	?	?	?
Grantham	2	2	1–1	17	23	11	5.82	4	13	0	0
Wootton	2	1	1–0	9?	?	?	?	?	?	?	?
J. Pankratz	2	2	1–1	15	19	11	6.60	2	4	0	0
McNair	1	1	0–1	9	17	11	11.00	6	6	1	0
Maxwell	1	1	0–1	0	2	4	Inf	2	0	1	1

Perry	1	1	0–1	8	16	10	11.25	1	3	0	0
White**	1	1	0–1	9	16	8	8.00	0	8	0	0
Taylor	1	1	1–0	9	6	6	6.00	3	8	1	0
??	1	1	1–0	9	11	7	7.00	?	?	?	?
Total	**25**	**25**	**11–14**	**214?**	**218?**	**125?**	**5.26?**	**36?**	**104?**	**9?**	**3?**

* These statistics include all 25 Hill Country League regular season games. Statistics were taken from the published box scores available from newspaper accounts.

** White also recorded one balk.

1932 Llano Cowboys (20–5)*					**Manager C. L. "Chink" Taylor**						
Player	**POS**	**G**	**AB**	**R**	**H**	**2B**	**3B**	**HR**	**BA**	**SP**	**SB**
P. McLeod	c-3b	23	90	20	30	3	3	1	.333	.433	13
Taylor	cf	23	93	38	40	9	4	0	.430	.613	29
M.A. Reed	ss-1b	23	97	25	26	2	1	0	.268	.309	6
R. Bounds	3b-2b	22	92	12	27	2	0	0	.293	.315	3
Van Huss	p-lf	20	69	3	11	1	1	0	.159	.203	1
Mather	rf	20	91	23	35	5	1	2	.385	.527	7
C. Brewer	lf-p	19	71	12	18	1	0	0	.254	.268	9
Pinckney	2b	11	51	8	12	2	1	0	.235	.314	3
R. Brown	ss	10	41	14	16	3	4	0	.390	.659	2
B. Moore	of-1b	10	37	6	10	1	0	1	.270	.378	1
F. Bounds	ss-3b	9	39	9	12	1	0	0	.308	.333	3
Collings	1b-3b	8	25	2	1	0	0	0	.040	.040	0
Peel	1b	7	33	4	9	2	1	0	.273	.394	0
Falk	lf	4	17	2	6	2	0	0	.353	.471	0
Draper	p	4	14	2	4	0	0	0	.286	.286	0
E. Brewer	c	3	5	1	1	0	0	0	.200	.200	0
Holt	ph	1	1	0	0	0	0	0	.000	.000	0
Petty	p	1	1	0	0	0	0	0	.000	.000	0
C. McLeod	rf	1	0	0	0	0	0	0	.000	.000	0
Total		**23**	**867**	**181**	**258**	**34**	**16**	**4**	**.298**	**.388**	**77**

Pitcher	**G**	**GS**	**W/L**	**IP**	**H**	**R**	**TRA**	**BB**	**SO**	**HBP**	**WP**
Van Huss	19	17	13–4	158	138	68	3.87	27	96	13	2
Draper	4	3	3–1	25⅓	22	15	5.33	7	23	2	1

Pitcher	G	GS	W/L	IP	H	R	TRA	BB	SO	HBP	WP
C. Brewer	3	2	2–0	20	24	5	2.25	2	3	1	0
Petty	1	1	0–0	3	3	1	3.00	1	2	0	0
Total	**23**	**23**	**18–5**	**206⅓**	**187**	**89**	**3.88**	**37**	**124**	**16**	**3**

* These statistics include only 23 (of 25) Hill Country League regular season games. Statistics were taken from the published box scores available from newspaper accounts. Some box scores were either not published or not available. The statistics do not include the championship series against Mason.

1932 Mason Mavericks (15–9)* Manager Johnny "Old Man" Fuller											
Player	**POS**	**G**	**AB**	**R**	**H**	**2B**	**3B**	**HR**	**BA**	**SP**	**SB**
Kygar	c	16	63	7	8	3	0	0	.127	.175	1
Hatch	cf-p	15	40	14	11	1	1	0	.275	.350	4
Hoffman	3b-p	15	58	3	16	0	2	0	.276	.345	2
Hardy	p-lf	15	54	6	12	2	0	0	.222	.259	0
Schmidt	1b	14	67	10	16	1	2	0	.239	.313	1
L. Brown	ss	13	53	12	15	3	0	0	.283	.340	5
J. Fuller	2b-cf	12	35	4	7	2	0	0	.200	.257	3
J. Brown	3b-ss	11	37	5	6	0	0	0	.162	.162	1
Evans	rf	10	32	5	11	2	1	0	.344	.469	3
Donheim (Dannheim)	of-2b	9	21	8	5	1	0	0	.238	.286	0
Nobles	2b-3b	9	27	3	8	0	0	0	.296	.296	0
Latham	3b-2b	8	28	1	4	1	0	0	.143	.179	1
Josefson	rf-cf	7	28	10	9	2	0	0	.321	.393	0
Loeffler	3b-rf	2	5	0	0	0	0	0	.000	.000	0
Wagner	3b	1	5	0	0	0	0	0	.000	.000	0
Heinrichs	lf	1	2	2	0	0	0	0	.000	.000	0
Rhode	p	1	1	0	0	0	0	0	.000	.000	0
Total		**16**	**556**	**90**	**128**	**18**	**6**	**0**	**.230**	**.284**	**21**

Pitcher	G	GS	W/L	IP	H	R	TRA	BB	SO	HBP	WP
Hardy**	14	14	8–5	117	125	64	4.92	12	67	7	2
Hatch	3	1	0–3	14	25	15	9.64	4	9	3	0
Hoffman	1	1	0–0	2	4	3	13.50	2	0	0	0
Rhode	1	0	0–0	3	0	0	0.00	3	5	1	0
Total	**16**	**16**	**8–8**	**136**	**154**	**82**	**5.43**	**21**	**81**	**11**	**2**

* These statistics include only 16 (of 24) Hill Country League regular season games. Statistics were taken from the published box scores available from newspaper accounts. Some box scores were either not published or not available. The statistics do not include the championship series against Llano.

** According to one report, Hardy's complete season record was 11–6. *Fredericksburg Standard*, September 9, 1932, 3.

APPENDIX D: MOUNTAIN LEAGUE STANDINGS AND TEAM STATISTICS, 1933

1933 Mountain League Standings

Team	W	L	GB	Pct.
Alamo Heights	12	6	---	.667
Kerrville	10	8	2	.556
Comfort	10	8	2	.556
Boerne	9	9	3	.500
Bandera	4	14	8	.222

Second-Place Playoff Game: Kerrville defeated Comfort, 5–4.

Championship Series: Alamo Heights defeated Kerrville, two games to none.

1933 Alamo Heights Firemen (12–6)*									Manager Jim Riley		
Player	**POS**	**G**	**AB**	**R**	**H**	**2B**	**3B**	**HR**	**BA**	**SP**	**SB**
Riley	1b-c	14	54	9	20	5	0	1	.370	.519	2
Feille	rf-cf	14	47	13	17	6	2	1	.362	.638	3
Villaret	2b	14	54	4	11	1	1	0	.204	.259	1
Turner	lf-cf	13	52	6	13	0	0	2	.250	.365	5
Sheridan	3b-rf	13	45	6	10	3	1	0	.222	.333	5
Harris	c	12	41	4	11	2	2	0	.268	.415	6
Nealon	p	9	25	0	2	0	0	0	.080	.080	0
Haycock	ss	9	34	13	13	2	2	0	.382	.559	0
Suche	p-cf	8	24	2	1	0	0	0	.042	.042	0
Weston	3b-rf	4	13	4	4	1	0	0	.308	.385	2
Crawford	rf	4	10	3	3	0	0	0	.300	.300	0
Whitney	cf-rf	5	14	2	2	0	0	0	.143	.143	1
Menger	p-rf	5	12	2	1	0	0	0	.083	.083	0
Niemic	ss-3b	4	16	3	4	1	1	0	.250	.438	0

Player	POS	G	AB	R	H	2B	3B	HR	BA	SP	SB
Shuhardt	rf-lf	3	7	0	1	0	0	0	.143	.143	0
Harrell	ss	2	9	1	4	0	1	0	.444	.667	2
Funk	rf	1	1	0	0	0	0	0	.000	.000	0
Paden	c	1	4	0	0	0	0	0	.000	.000	0
Thompson	ss	1	5	1	0	0	0	0	.000	.000	0
Total		**14**	**467**	**73**	**117**	**21**	**10**	**13**	**.251**	**.364**	**27**

Pitcher	G	GS	W/L	IP	H	R	TRA	BB	SO	HBP	WP
Nealon	8	6	4–2	61	54	23	3.39	5	27	1	2
Suche	7	6	3–3	49	49	20	3.67	13	36	0	3
Menger	2	2	1–1	10⅓	18	13	11.32	1	2	0	0
Total	**14**	**14**	**8–6**	**120⅓**	**121**	**56**	**4.19**	**19**	**65**	**1**	**5**

* These statistics include only 14 (of 18) Mountain League regular season games. Statistics for 12 games were taken from newspaper box scores. The statistics for the other two games were gleaned from the 1933 Boerne White Sox scorebook. Some box scores were either not published or not available. The statistics do not include exhibition games or the games in the championship series against Kerrville.

1933 Bandera Cowboys (4–14)*									**Manager unknown**		
Player	**POS**	**G**	**AB**	**R**	**H**	**2B**	**3B**	**HR**	**BA**	**SP**	**SB**
F. Hamilton	2b-p	13	47	3	15	0	1	0	.319	.362	0
Thornberry	p-c	13	52	7	15	1	3	0	.288	.423	0
B. Mansfield	ss	12	48	8	15	1	1	1	.313	.438	1
Billings	rf-2b	11	34	3	10	0	0	0	.294	.294	1
Dugosh	rf-lf	11	29	4	7	1	0	0	.241	.276	0
Hayes	if	11	46	4	12	3	0	0	.261	.336	1
Brady	lf-p	10	28	3	9	3	0	0	.321	.429	0
E. Mansfield	1b	9	29	2	7	2	0	0	.241	.310	0
Thallman**	c-3b	8	19	2	3	0	0	0	.158	.158	0
Zumwalt	c	8	30	1	7	2	0	0	.233	.300	0
L. Hamilton	lf-c	7	23	3	3	0	0	0	.130	.130	0
Short	cf-p	5	15	3	2	0	0	0	.133	.133	1
E. Jenschke	3b	4	15	1	3	2	0	0	.200	.333	0
L. Jenschke	cf	4	15	0	0	0	0	0	.000	.000	0
Bants	of	3	11	1	2	0	0	0	.182	.182	0

S. King	3b-1b	3	12	1	2	0	0	0	.167	.167	0
Risinger	2b	2	6	1	1	0	0	0	.167	.167	0
Kalka	1b	2	6	0	0	0	0	0	.000	.000	0
Bray	rf	1	1	0	1	0	0	0	1.000	1.000	0
Gray	p	1	1	0	1	0	0	0	1.000	1.000	0
Flaherty	c	1	2	0	0	0	0	0	.000	.000	0
T. Thalmann	1b	1	1	0	0	0	0	0	.000	.000	0
Davenport	lf	1	1	0	0	0	0	0	.000	.000	0
Jureski	p	1	1	1	0	0	0	0	.000	.000	0
I. Jenschke***	rf	1	1	2	0	0	0	0	.000	.000	0
Total		**14**	**473**	**50**	**115**	**15**	**5**	**1**	**.243**	**.302**	**4**

Pitcher	**G**	**GS**	**W/L**	**IP**	**H**	**R**	**TRA**	**BB**	**SO**	**HBP**	**WP**
Thornberry	11	9	3–7	65	85	62	8.58	22	66	1	6
F. Hamilton	7	3	0–2?	23⅔	21	16	6.08	4	8	1	0
Brady	1	0	0–0	2⅔	4	0	0.00	0	1	0	0
Gray	1	1	0–1	?	?	?	?	4	1	1	0
Short	1	0	0–0	?	?	?	?	5	2	1	0
Jureski	1	1	0–1	?	?	?	?	?	?	?	?
Billings	1	0	0–0?	?	?	?	?	?	?	?	?
Total	**14**	**14**	**3–11**	**?**	**?**	**?**	**?**	**?**	**?**	**?**	**?**

* These statistics include only 14 (of 18) Mountain League regular season games. Statistics for 12 games were taken from newspaper box scores. The statistics for the other two games were taken from the 1933 Boerne White Sox scorebook. Some box scores were either not published or not available. The statistics do not include exhibition games.

** "Thallman" was sometimes spelled "Thalman" or "Thalmann."

*** "I. Jenschke" is listed in the Boerne White Sox scorebook for the game on July 30. It is possible that this was E. Jenschke or L. Jenschke.

1933 Boerne White Sox (9–9)*					**Manager Clarence Holekamp**						
Player	**POS**	**G**	**AB**	**R**	**H**	**2B**	**3B**	**HR**	**BA**	**SP**	**SB**
R. Leidl	2b-3b	18	78	17	29	7	0	0	.372	.462	1
A. Uecker	lf-p	18	76	7	28	7	2	0	.368	.513	3
Bourgeois	cf	18	68	9	24	2	1	0	.359	.412	3
Wendler	1b-ss	18	70	9	19	4	1	0	.271	.357	4
Phillip	c-3b	17	65	4	17	1	0	0	.262	.277	4

Player	POS	G	AB	R	H	2B	3B	HR	BA	SP	SB
Schweppe	rf-lf	16	53	4	13	1	0	0	.245	.264	1
E. Bergmann	p	16	41	4	9	1	0	0	.220	.244	0
Pfeiffer	ss	14	59	13	25	5	0	0	.424	.508	2
Bremer	3b	13	50	9	9	0	0	0	.180	.180	3
T. Uecker	c	8	27	3	3	1	1	0	.111	.222	0
Holekamp	2b-1b	6	16	3	5	1	0	0	.313	.375	0
Harz	lf-rf	5	9	0	0	0	0	0	.000	.000	0
E. Uecker	p	3	8	1	1	0	0	0	.125	.125	0
J. Bergmann	?	3	8	2	0	0	0	0	.000	.000	2
Dugosh	p	3	1	0	0	0	0	0	.000	.000	0
Schultz	p	2	1	0	0	0	0	0	.000	.000	0
A. Bergmann	c	1	4	2	2	0	0	0	.500	.500	0
Collins	c	1	1	0	0	0	0	0	.000	.000	0
Newton	p	1	1	0	0	0	0	0	.000	.000	0
J. Uecker	rf-1b	1	5	0	0	0	0	0	.000	.000	0
Total		**18**	**641**	**87**	**184**	**30**	**5**	**0**	**.287**	**.349**	**23**

Pitcher	G	GS	W/L	IP	H	R	TRA	BB	SO	HBP	WP
E. Bergmann**	16	13	7–4?	10⅔	101	35	3.10	18	51	5	0
A. Uecker	4	1	1–0?	11⅔	13	8	6.17	6	2	0	0
E. Uecker**	3	3	0–2?	10	13	12	10.80	2	0	0	0
Schultz	2	0	0–0	3⅓	7	2	5.40	1	0	0	0
Dugosh**	2	1	0–0?	2	1	4	18.00	0	1	0	0
Schweppe	1	0	0–0	3⅔	5	2	4.91	3	0	0	0
Newton	1	0	0–1	2⅔	5	3	10.13	1	2	1	0
Total	**18**	**18**	**8–7****	**135**	**145**	**66**	**4.40**	**31**	**56**	**6**	**0**

*These statistics include all 18 Mountain League regular season games (except for pitching statistics as noted in ** below). Statistics for 14 games were taken from available box scores, while statistics for the other four games were taken from a Boerne White Sox scorebook for 1933. The statistics do not include exhibition games.

**The Boerne White Sox scorebook for 1933 did not record when pitchers relieved the starting pitcher. As a result, for three of these games in which the starting pitcher was relieved, it is impossible to determine the winning or losing pitcher or compile statistics for innings pitched, hits, runs, walks, strikeouts, etc. Statistics for pitchers with a question mark next to their win-loss record reflect only those 15 games in which complete statistics could be compiled.

1933 Comfort Broncos (10–8)[*]										Manager unknown	
Player	**POS**	**G**	**AB**	**R**	**H**	**2B**	**3B**	**HR**	**BA**	**SP**	**SB**
S. Pankratz	3b-lf	15	62	12	17	0	1	0	.274	.306	0
Meyer	cf-c	14	55	12	19	3	3	0	.345	.509	1
Nagel	ss	14	62	11	21	4	0	0	.339	.403	4
J. Pankratz	2b-p	14	48	12	15	1	1	0	.313	.375	1
Goforth	1b	14	58	9	18	2	1	0	.310	.379	0
Kutzer	lf	13	56	13	19	0	1	0	.339	.375	1
West	2b-rf	13	50	9	15	1	0	0	.300	.320	1
Weiss	rf-cf	13	47	8	13	2	2	0	.277	.404	0
Lindemann	p-rf	10	23	3	7	1	0	0	.304	.348	0
A.Bergmann	c-lf	10	35	4	8	2	0	0	.229	.286	0
Archer	p	7	27	3	5	0	0	0	.185	.185	0
H. Bergmann	cf-3b	6	14	7	6	1	0	0	.429	.500	0
Kmoch	cf-rf	4	12	4	6	0	0	1	.500	.750	0
Marquardt	rf	1	0	0	0	0	0	0	.000	.000	0
???	2b	1	0	1	0	0	0	0	.000	.000	0
Total		**15**	**549**	**108**	**169**	**17**	**9**	**1**	**.307**	**.376**	**8**

Pitcher	G	GS	W/L	IP	H	R	TRA	BB	SO	HBP	WP
Archer	7	7	4–3	61	67	28	4.13	13	22	1	0
J. Pankratz[**]	6	5	4–1	50⅔	57	29	5.15	16	14	7	1
Lindemann[**]	3	3	2–1	19⅓	27	14	6.52	4	15	4	0
Total	**15**	**15**	**10–5**	**131**	**151**	**71**	**4.88**	**33**	**51**	**12**	**1**

[*] These statistics include only 15 (of 18) Mountain League regular season games. Statistics were taken from the published box scores available from newspaper accounts. Some box scores were either not published or not available. The statistics do not include exhibition games or the second-place playoff game with Kerrville.

[**] The April 23 box score vs. Kerrville does not clearly assign hits, runs, or HBP between pitchers Lindemann and J. Pankratz; the author assigned these stats on a "best guess" basis.

The following 1933 hitting statistics for *all 18 regular season games* of the Comfort Broncos were published in the *Comfort News.*[*]

Player	AB	R	H	BA
Nagel	69	11	25	.362
Kutzer	59	13	21	.356
Weiss	58	11	18	.310
J. Pankratz	55	13	17	.309
Goforth	69	12	21	.305
A. Bergmann	61	13	18	.295
Meyer	72	13	20	.278
West	62	9	17	.273
Lindemann	27	3	7	.257
S. Pankratz	73	12	18	.245
Archer	29	3	6	.207
H. Bergmann	3	0	0	.000
Totals	**637**	**113**	**187**	**.294**

[*] *Comfort News,* August 31, 1933, 8.

1933 Kerrville Braves (10–8)[*]								**Manager E. M. Hughes**			
Player	**POS**	**G**	**AB**	**R**	**H**	**2B**	**3B**	**HR**	**BA**	**SP**	**SB**
Warren	cf-rf	18	60	10	13	1	0	0	.217	.233	2
Goss	lf-rf	17	58	8	18	0	0	0	.310	.310	0
Staudt	rf-ss	16	55	13	19	1	0	0	.345	.364	1
C. Hollimon	1b-c	16	73	12	22	3	0	1	.301	.384	0
Wootton	3b-p	16	61	10	18	3	2	1	.295	.459	3
Beaver	c-2b	16	59	7	14	1	0	1	.237	.305	0
Morris	2b-ss	14	48	5	11	1	0	0	.229	.250	3
McNair	ss	10	44	7	15	3	0	1	.341	.477	1
Hardy	p	10	38	3	9	0	0	0	.237	.237	0
Archer	p-rf	7	26	6	12	1	0	0	.462	.500	1
Myers	lf-rf	7	19	0	2	1	0	0	.105	.157	0
Grantham	c-lf	6	23	5	10	2	0	0	.435	.522	2
Coleman	lf-rf	4	18	3	4	1	0	0	.222	.278	0
Maxwell	1b-p	4	9	1	0	0	0	0	.000	.000	0
Baker	lf	2	5	0	1	0	0	0	.200	.200	0
McElroy	cf-2b	2	3	0	0	0	0	0	.000	.000	0
J. Hollimon	c	1	4	1	2	0	0	0	.500	.500	0

Gray	ss	1	4	0	1	0	0	0	.250	.250	0
Saenger	rf	1	3	0	0	0	0	0	.000	.000	0
Tarver	cf	1	3	0	1	0	0	0	.333	.333	0
Foster	ph	1	1	0	1	0	0	0	1.000	1.000	0
Total		**18**	**614**	**91**	**173**	**18**	**2**	**4**	**.282**	**.337**	**13**

Pitcher	**G**	**GS**	**W/L**	**IP**	**H**	**R**	**TRA**	**BB**	**SO**	**HBP**	**WP**
Hardy	10	10	7–3	90	70	21	2.10	14	76	6	5
Archer	7	6	3–3	60⅓	68	34	5.07	13	28	2	2
Maxwell	2	2	0–2	6⅔	16	15	20.25	2	3	2	0
Wootton	1	0	0–0	4	2	3	6.75	0	5	2	0
Total	**18**	**18**	**10–8**	**161**	**156**	**73**	**4.08**	**29**	**112**	**12**	**7**

*These statistics include all 18 Mountain League regular season games. Statistics were taken from the published box scores available from newspaper accounts. Statistics do not include exhibition games, the second-place playoff game with Comfort, or the championship series games against Alamo Heights.

APPENDIX E: MOUNTAIN LEAGUE STANDINGS AND TEAM STATISTICS, 1934

1934 Mountain League Standings

Team	W	L	GB	Pct.
Fredericksburg	15	1	---	.938
Boerne	12	3	2½	.800
Comfort	6	8	8	.429
Bandera	2	12	12	.143
Kerrville	2	13	12½	.133

Championship Series: Fredericksburg defeated Boerne, two games to none.

1934 Bandera Cowboys (2–12)*									Manager unknown		
Player	**POS**	**G**	**AB**	**R**	**H**	**2B**	**3B**	**HR**	**BA**	**SP**	**SB**
Blackwell	1b	8	33	1	3	1	1	0	.091	.182	1
Davenport	p-rf	7	11	3	3	0	1	0	.273	.454	0
F. Hamilton	2b-p	7	29	2	7	1	0	0	.241	.276	0
Thallman**	c	7	23	1	5	0	0	0	.217	.217	1
D. Gray	3b-of	7	28	2	5	1	1	0	.179	.286	1
Knibbe	rf	7	28	1	5	0	1	0	.179	.250	0
Billings	2b-3b	7	13	2	2	1	0	0	.154	.231	0
I. Jenschke***	of-if	6	13	1	2	1	0	0	.154	.231	1
Dugosh	lf-cf	6	17	4	1	0	0	0	.059	.059	0
Mansfield	ss	5	19	6	11	0	2	1	.579	.947	2
R. Click****	3b-of	5	19	0	4	1	0	0	.211	.263	0
L. Hamilton	c-ss	5	17	1	5	0	1	0	.294	.411	0
Wright	p-rf	4	5	1	1	0	0	1	.200	.800	1
Brady	lf	4	10	0	1	0	0	0	.100	.100	0
L. Jenschke	cf-3b	4	16	1	1	0	0	0	.063	.063	1
Cravey	3b	1	5	0	1	0	0	0	.200	.200	0
Total		**8**	**286**	**26**	**57**	**6**	**7**	**2**	**.199**	**.290**	**8**

Pitcher	G	GS	W/L	IP	H	R	TRA	BB	SO	HBP	WP
Davenport	6	3	1–3	30⅔	38	26	7.63	18	27	0	1
F. Hamilton	4	2	0–3	20	25	17	7.65	6	11	0	1
D. Gray	3	0	0–0	11⅓	13	3	2.38	1	8	0	0
Wright	3	3	0–1	9	17	14	14.00	6	7	1	2
Total	**8**	**8**	**1–7**	**71**	**93**	**60**	**7.61**	**31**	**53**	**1**	**4**

* These statistics include only 8 (of 14) Mountain League regular season games. Statistics were taken from the published box scores available from newspaper accounts. Some box scores were either not published or not available.

** "Thallman" was sometimes spelled "Thalman" or "Thalmann."

*** Two box scores listing only "Jenschke" were attributed to I. Jenshcke based on position.

**** A box score listing "Cook" at third base was attributed to Click based on later box scores.

1934 Boerne White Sox (12–3)*								Manager Clarence Holekamp			
Player	**POS**	**G**	**AB**	**R**	**H**	**2B**	**3B**	**HR**	**BA**	**SP**	**SB**
J. Uecker	3b	13	54	9	20	1	3	1	.370	.555	0
R. Leidl	2b	13	54	11	19	3	0	0	.352	.407	3
Pfeiffer	ss	13	61	9	19	3	2	0	.311	.426	2
Bourgeois	cf	13	50	9	12	3	1	1	.240	.400	1
E. Bergmann	p-rf	13	35	0	8	2	0	0	.229	286	1
Wendler	1b	13	48	8	8	2	1	0	.167	.250	0
T. Uecker	c	12	37	2	11	2	3	0	.297	.514	0
Schweppe	lf-rf	12	47	5	14	5	0	0	.298	.404	0
Phillip	rf-c	10	36	4	6	0	0	0	.167	.167	0
Schulze	p	6	6	1	0	0	0	0	.000	.000	0
A. Uecker	lf	4	19	2	6	3	1	0	.316	.579	2
Weiss	lf-rf	2	7	2	4	0	0	0	.571	.571	0
W. Bergmann	p	2	2	0	1	0	0	0	.500	.500	0
E. Uecker	p-rf	2	2	1	0	0	0	0	.000	.000	0
W. Uecker**	ph	2	2	0	0	0	0	0	.000	.000	0
Bremer	rf	1	2	1	2	0	0	0	1.000	1.000	1
A. Bergmann	c	1	3	2	1	1	0	0	.333	.667	1
Total		**13**	**465**	**66**	**131**	**25**	**11**	**2**	**.282**	**.396**	**11**

Pitcher	G	GS	W/L	IP	H	R	TRA	BB	SO	HBP	WP
E. Bergmann	12	11	8–3	85	82	33	3.49	9	58	0	2
Schulze	6	2	2–0	26	30	10	3.46	7	3	0	0
E. Uecker	1	0	0–0	4	2	0	0.00	1	2	0	0
W. Bergmann	1	0	0–0	1	1	0	0.00	0	0	0	0
Total	**13**	**13**	**10–3**	**116**	**115**	**43**	**3.34**	**17**	**63**	**0**	**2**

*These statistics include only 13 (of 15) Mountain League regular season games. Statistics were taken from the published box scores available from newspaper accounts. Some box scores were either not published or not available. These statistics do not include the championship series against Fredericksburg.

** "W. Uecker" may have been Tuddy (middle name Wilhelm) Uecker, brother of Albert, Edwin, and Johnny. If so, the statistics of "W. Uecker" should be combined with "T. Uecker."

1934 Comfort Broncos (6–8)*									**Manager unknown**		
Player	**POS**	**G**	**AB**	**R**	**H**	**2B**	**3B**	**HR**	**BA**	**SP**	**SB**
A. Bergmann**	c-cf	11	44	6	16	2	0	0	.364	.409	0
J. Pankratz	ss-p	11	44	6	13	1	0	0	.295	.318	0
H. Bergmann	lf-ss	11	44	4	13	0	1	1	.295	.409	2
S. Pankratz	3b	11	49	6	13	1	0	0	.265	.286	0
Kutzer	2b	11	46	3	11	0	0	0	.239	.239	1
Goforth	1b	11	49	3	10	0	2	0	.204	.286	0
Meyer	cf	10	45	9	13	3	1	0	.289	.400	0
Lindemann	p-rf	8	29	3	3	0	0	0	.103	.103	1
Spenrath	rf-c	8	24	0	2	0	0	0	.083	.083	0
Weiss	rf	4	15	1	3	0	0	0	.200	.200	0
Treiber	2b-p	3	9	0	0	0	0	0	.000	.000	0
Lindner	ss-rf	2	5	0	2	0	0	0	.400	.400	0
Mertz	p-rf	2	4	0	0	0	0	0	.000	.000	0
Nagel	ss	1	4	1	1	0	0	0	.250	.250	0
Kmoch	cf	1	4	0	1	0	0	0	.250	.250	0
Total		**11**	**415**	**42**	**101**	**7**	**4**	**1**	**.243**	**.287**	**4**

Pitcher	G	GS	W/L	IP	H	R	TRA	BB	SO	HBP	WP
Lindemann	6	6	2–4	46	58	30	5.87	17?	15?	0	2
J. Pankratz	4	4	1–3	28⅓	45	30	9.53	9?	10?	2	1
Mertz	2	0	0–0	8	7	4	4.50	0	0	0	0

Pitcher	G	GS	W/L	IP	H	R	TRA	BB	SO	HBP	WP
Treiber	1	1	0–1	8	17	11	12.38	2	2	1	0
A. Bergmann**	1	0	0–0	4	6	10	22.50	5	2	0	1
S. Pankratz	1	0	0–0	2⅔	4	4	13.50	?	?	0	0
Total	**11**	**11**	**3–8**	**97**	**137**	**89**	**8.26**	**33?**	**29?**	**3**	**4**

* These statistics include only 11 (of 14) Mountain League regular season games. Statistics were taken from the published box scores available from newspaper accounts. Some box scores were either not published or not available.

** "A. Bergmann" is Arthur Bergmann.

1934 Fredericksburg Giants (15–1)*								**Manager Felix Saenger**				
Player	**POS**	**G**	**AB**	**R**	**H**	**2B**	**3B**	**HR**	**BA**	**SP**	**SB**
Klett	lf	15	67	25	30	6	4	6	.448	.925	9
E. Klaerner	cf-p	15	69	24	30	3	3	3	.435	.696	12
Schneider	ss-2b	15	79	27	29	7	1	1	.367	.494	6
P. Klaerner	3b-p	15	71	20	24	4	1	0	.338	.423	9
Langerhans	2b-ss	14	60	16	19	4	0	2	.317	.483	8
Schnerr	rf-3b	13	46	17	19	2	3	2	.413	.674	5
C. Klaerner	p-1b	13	51	14	20	1	3	1	.392	.588	1
A. Klaerner	rf-c	12	47	18	15	2	0	2	.319	.553	3
Peter	1b	11	46	6	17	2	0	0	.370	.413	0
Stahl	1b	10	14	4	6	2	0	0	.429	.571	0
Hahn	c	9	41	10	10	1	0	0	.244	.268	0
Jenschke	2b-3b	7	19	1	1	0	0	0	.053	.053	0
Itz	1b	3	7	3	2	0	0	0	.286	.286	0
Deike	2b	1	0	0	0	0	0	0	.000	.000	0
Sanders	p	1	3	0	0	0	0	0	.000	.000	0
Total		**15**	**620**	**185**	**222**	**34**	**15**	**17**	**.358**	**.576**	**53**

Pitcher	G	GS	W/L	IP	H	R	TRA	BB	SO	HBP	WP
C. Klaerner	11	10	10–1	95	67	25	2.37	24	80	2	2
P. Klaerner	3	3	3–0	27	16	7	2.33	2	29	1	1
E. Klaerner	2	1	0–0	4	6	4	9.00	1	7	0	0
Sanders	1	1	1–0	10	5	3	2.70	6	7	0	0
Schneider	1	0	0–0	0 ⅔	0	0	0.00	0	0	0	0
Langerhans	1	0	0–0	0 ⅓	2	2	54.00	2	1	1	0
Total	**15**	**15**	**14–1**	**137**	**96**	**41**	**2.69**	**35**	**124**	**4**	**3**

*These statistics include only 15 (of 16) Mountain League regular season games. Statistics were compiled from the published box scores available from newspaper accounts. Some box scores were either not published or not available. These statistics do not include the championship series against Boerne.

1934 Kerrville Braves (2–13)*										**Manager Jake Goss**	
Player	**POS**	**G**	**AB**	**R**	**H**	**2B**	**3B**	**HR**	**BA**	**SP**	**SB**
Warren	p-of	13	44	0	8	1	0	0	.181	.204	0
McBryde	rf	12	46	6	10	0	1	0	.217	.261	4
B. Brown	ss-2b	12	39	3	7	1	0	0	.179	.205	1
Fisher (Fischer)	cf-rf	11	36	1	7	0	1	0	.194	.250	3
Myers	1b-of	11	36	3	5	1	0	0	.139	.167	0
Toler	p-1b	11	30	2	4	0	0	0	.133	.133	1
Hughes	c-2b	11	34	1	3	0	0	0	.088	.088	0
Goss	lf-rf	10	39	5	11	0	0	0	.282	.282	1
Riley	2b-of	9	26	6	4	0	0	0	.154	.154	4
Crooks	3b-ss	8	24	0	6	3	0	0	.250	.375	1
Larrimore	3b-rf	8	17	1	3	1	0	0	.176	.235	0
C. Gray	2b-ss	5	19	0	6	1	1	0	.316	.474	0
Colbath	2b-3b	5	9	1	1	0	0	0	.111	.111	0
G. Brown	c-3b	2	3	0	1	0	0	0	.333	.333	1
Grantham	c-p	2	8	1	2	0	0	0	.250	.250	0
Howry	c	2	5	0	1	1	0	0	.200	.400	0
Dixon**	2b-lf	2	2	0	0	0	0	0	.000	.000	0
Mast	1b	1	4	0	0	0	0	0	.000	.000	0
Gowen	p	1	1	0	0	0	0	0	.000	.000	0
Morgan	ss	1	4	0	0	0	0	0	.000	.000	0
Storms**	c	1	1	0	0	0	0	0	.000	.000	0
Morris	2b	1	2	2	0	0	0	0	.000	.000	0
Sturins**	1b	1	1	0	0	0	0	0	.000	.000	0
Dickson**	ph	1	0	1	0	0	0	0	.000	.000	1
Total		**13**	**430**	**33**	**79**	**9**	**3**	**0**	**.184**	**.219**	**17**

Pitcher	G	GS	W/L	IP	H	R	TRA	BB	SO	HBP	WP
Toler	11	9	2–6	73⅔	92	88	10.75	42	52	6	2
Warren	6	3	0–3	26⅔	46	37	12.49	7	11	0	1
Grantham	1	0	0–1	3	5	5	15.00	2	2	0	0
Gowen	1	1	0–1	2	5	5	22.50	1	1	0	0
Myers	1	0	0–0	1⅔	1	3	16.20	3	0	1	0
Hughes	1	0	0–0	1	4	6	54.00	1	1	0	0
Crooks	1	0	0–0	1	1	2	18.00	1	0	1	1
Colbath	1	0	0–0	1	2	3	27.00	1	0	0	1
Total	**13**	**13**	**2–11**	**110**	**156**	**149**	**12.19**	**58**	**67**	**8**	**5**

*These statistics include only 13 (of 15) Mountain League regular season games. Statistics were taken from the published box scores available from newspaper accounts. Some box scores were either not published or not available.

** Due to inaccurate spellings and discrepancies in various box scores, it is possible that "Dixon" and "Dickson" are the same player and that "Storms" and "Sturins" are the same player.

APPENDIX F: MOUNTAIN LEAGUE STANDINGS AND TEAM STATISTICS, 1935

1935 Mountain League Standings

Team	W	L	GB	Pct.
Fredericksburg	15	2	---	.882
Legion	10	7	5	.588
Comfort	9	8	6	.529
Kerrville	4	14	11½	.222
Bandera	2	16	13½	.111

Second-Place vs. Third-Place Playoff: Comfort defeated Legion, 12–5, to advance to the championship series vs. Fredericksburg.

Championship Series: Fredericksburg defeated Comfort, two games to none.

NOTE: Boerne withdrew from the league on July 12. Boerne's record was 11–1 at the time of withdrawal. The records of Legion and Comfort were adjusted to eliminate two games each with Boerne. See chapter 15. Due to Boerne's withdrawal, the total wins and losses in the above standings are not equal.

1935 Bandera Cowboys (2–16)*									**Manager unknown**		
Player	**POS**	**G**	**AB**	**R**	**H**	**2B**	**3B**	**HR**	**BA**	**SP**	**SB**
Dugosh	cf	12	47	0	6	0	0	0	.128	.128	1
Click	3b-ss	12	39	1	4	0	0	0	.103	.103	3
Knibbe	rf	11	41	1	6	1	1	0	.146	.220	1
Adamietz	c	11	41	2	5	0	0	0	.122	.122	1
Billings	1b-c	9	14	1	2	0	0	0	.143	.143	1
Rugh	ss-2b	9	30	0	4	0	0	0	.133	.133	0
Hamilton	2b-p	8	32	0	9	0	1	0	.281	.344	0
C. Gray	p-2b	8	26	2	6	1	0	0	.231	.269	3
Short	if-of	7	26	4	6	0	1	0	.231	.308	3
Davenport	lf-p	7	17	0	3	1	0	0	.176	.235	0

Player	POS	G	AB	R	H	2B	3B	HR	BA	SP	SB
M. Gray	1b	7	21	2	3	1	0	0	.143	.190	1
Anderwald	3b-p	7	14	0	1	0	0	0	.071	.071	0
V. Kalka	of-c	5	13	2	2	0	0	0	.154	.154	2
O'Bryant	p	5	9	0	0	0	0	0	.000	.000	0
E. Jenschke	lf	4	10	0	0	0	0	0	.000	.000	0
Pierce	ss-2b	2	6	0	2	0	1	0	.333	.667	1
T. Kalka	1b	2	9	1	3	1	0	0	.333	.444	1
Thallman**	1b	2	2	0	0	0	0	0	.000	.000	0
Mazurek	rf	1	3	0	0	0	0	0	.000	.000	0
Total		**14**	**400**	**16**	**62**	**5**	**4**	**0**	**.155**	**.188**	**18**

Pitcher	G	GS	W/L	IP	H	R	TRA	BB	SO	HBP	WP
C. Gray	8	8	2–6	61	56?	47?	6.93?	?	?	3	0
O'Bryant	5	4	0–4	18	18	11?	5.50?	?	13	0	0
Anderwald	3	1	0–1	7⅓	16	10	12.27	3	0	0	0
Davenport	2	1	0–1	10⅔	16	7	5.90	?	5	0	2
Short	2	0	0–0	6	8	5	7.50	?	3?	0	0
Hamilton	2	0	0–0	5	10	13	23.40	?	?	1	0
V. Kalka	1	1	0–0	5	8	9	16.20	?	5	0	0
Total	**14**	**14**	**2–12**	**113**	**132?**	**102?**	**8.12?**	**?**	**?**	**4**	**2**

*These statistics include only 14 (of 18) Mountain League regular season games. Statistics were taken from the published box scores available from newspaper accounts.

** "Thallman" was sometimes spelled "Thalman" or "Thalmann."

1935 Boerne White Sox (11–1)*						**Manager Clarence Holkamp**					
Player	**POS**	**G**	**AB**	**R**	**H**	**2B**	**3B**	**HR**	**BA**	**SP**	**SB**
R. Leidl	2b	12	53	19	22	3	0	1	.415	.528	4
Schweppe	lf	12	51	7	18	0	0	1	.353	.412	3
Bourgeois	cf	12	47	7	14	1	1	2	.298	.489	2
Phillip	c	12	40	7	12	0	1	0	.300	.350	4
J. Uecker	3b	12	46	12	12	5	1	0	.261	.413	0
Nagel	ss	11	52	16	22	3	2	0	.423	.558	4
Pfeiffer	rf-ss	11	48	14	19	5	1	0	.396	.542	2
Wendler	1b	11	46	10	12	1	1	0	.261	.326	1
E. Bergmann	p	10	32	4	7	0	1	0	.219	.281	1

Lawhorn	rf-1b	4	12	1	3	0	0	0	.250	.250	1
J. Bergmann	of	4	7	0	0	0	0	0	.000	.000	0
Schultz**	p	3	3	0	0	0	0	0	.000	.000	0
W. Bergmann	p	2	5	0	0	0	0	0	.000	.000	0
Holekamp	1b	1	1	0	0	0	0	0	.000	000	0
T. Bergmann***	c	1	1	0	0	0	0	0	.000	.000	0
A. Bergmann***	c	1?	0	0	0	0	0	0	.000	.000	0
Total		**12**	**444**	**97**	**141**	**18**	**8**	**4**	**.318**	**.421**	**22**

Pitcher	**G**	**GS**	**W/L**	**IP**	**H**	**R**	**TRA**	**BB**	**SO**	**HB**	**WP**
E. Bergmann	10?	10	9–1?	82?	54?	23?	2.52?	?	37?	?	?
Schultz**	2	1	1–0	4	0	0	0.00	?	3?	0	0
W. Bergmann	1	1	1–0	8	3	0	0.00	1	7	0	0
Total	**12**	**12**	**11–1**	**94?**	**57?**	**23?**	**2.20?**	**?**	**47?**	**?**	**?**

* These statistics include the 12 Mountain League regular season games before Boerne's withdrawal from the league on July 12 but do not include any games with independent teams after the withdrawal. Statistics were taken from the published box scores available from newspaper accounts. Some box scores were either not published or not available.

** "Schultz" may be "Schulze."

*** "A. Bergmann" is Anton Bergmann. Since Tony is a nickname for Anton, T. Bergmann and A. Bergmann may be the same person, especially since T. Bergmann and A. Bergmann were behind the plate in their only games. If so, the statistics of "T. Bergmann" and "A. Bergmann" should be combined.

1935 Comfort Broncos (9–8)*									**Manager unknown**		
Player	**POS**	**G**	**AB**	**R**	**H**	**2B**	**3B**	**HR**	**BA**	**SP**	**SB**
S. Pankratz	3b	16	67	9	20	1	1	0	.299	.343	0
J. Pankratz	ss	16	61	14	16	2	0	0	.263	.295	1
A. Bergmann**	c	15	55	9	13	2	0	2	.236	.272	0
Goforth	1b	14	57	5	14	1	0	0	.246	.263	0
Spenrath	rf-c	14	56	10	11	0	1	1	.196	.286	0
Lindemann	lf-if	14	59	9	11	2	0	0	.186	.220	1
Lindner	2b	13	54	5	19	3	0	0	.351	.407	0
Krauter	p	13	43	5	7	0	0	0	.163	.163	0
Meyer	cf	10	34	4	7	2	0	0	.206	.265	1
Kutzer	cf-2b	6	26	3	3	0	0	1	.115	.231	0

Player	POS	G	AB	R	H	2B	3B	HR	BA	SP	SB
H. Stieler	p-of	6	15	0	1	0	0	0	.066	.066	0
Thomas	2b-cf	4	12	1	4	1	0	0	.333	.417	0
Weiss	if-of	4	6	1	1	1	0	0	.167	.333	0
Boerner	rf	3	4	0	0	0	0	0	.000	.000	0
Faust	rf	1	4	1	1	0	0	0	.250	.250	0
A. Pankratz***	rf	1	3	0	0	0	0	0	.000	.000	0
T. Stieler?	cf-p	1	4	0	0	0	0	0	.000	.000	0
Total		**16**	**560**	**76**	**128**	**15**	**2**	**4**	**.229**	**.284**	**3**

Pitcher	G	GS	W/L	IP	H	R	TRA	BB	SO	HBP	WP
Krauter	12	11	7–4	102	112	48	4.23	?	?	2	0
H. Stieler	5	5	0–4	25	40	28	10.08	?	?	1	0
T. Stieler?	1	0	0–0	5	9	8	14.40	2	2	1	0
J. Pankratz	1	0	0–0	1	0	0	0.00	2	?	0	0
Total	**16**	**16**	**7–8***	**133**	**161**	**84**	**5.68**	**?**	**?**	**4**	**0**

*These statistics include only 15 (of 17) Mountain League regular season games plus the game against Boerne on July 7 which the HCL later eliminated after Boerne withdrew from the league on July 12. Thus, the statistics above include 16 games, except for pitchers' records which do not reflect the eliminated July 12 game. Statistics were taken from the published box scores available from newspaper accounts. Some box scores were either not published or not available. These statistics do not include the championship series against Fredericksburg or the second-place playoff game against Legion.

** "A. Bergmann" is Arthur Bergmann.

*** "A. Pankratz" is August "Manny" Pankratz, younger brother of Joe and Skeeter Pankratz.

1935 Fredericksburg Giants (15–2)*						Manager Felix Saenger/ Andy Andrews					
Player	**POS**	**G**	**AB**	**R**	**H**	**2B**	**3B**	**HR**	**BA**	**SP**	**SB**
Klett	lf	17	69	21	30	6	3	1	.435	.652	6
E. Klaerner	cf-p	17	71	16	23	3	2	0	.324	.451	5
Andrews	c	16	46	10	17	3	1	1	.370	.543	1
P. Klaerner	p-3b	16	58	8	18	5	1	0	.310	.431	2
Ransleben	ss	16	60	13	11	2	0	0	.183	.217	1
Schnerr	rf	15	65	16	23	8	2	0	.354	.538	7

Weise	2b-ss	14	56	11	17	4	1	0	.304	.411	4
Stahl	1b	14	36	6	10	0	0	0	.278	.278	1
A. Klaerner	3b-p	14	56	13	12	4	0	0	.214	.286	0
Langerhans	2b-1b	12	43	12	15	2	0	2	.349	.535	1
Hahn	c-1b	7	19	4	5	1	0	0	.263	.316	0
Henke	cf-lf	7	17	3	2	1	0	0	.118	.176	0
Icke	c	3	9	1	2	0	0	0	.222	.222	0
Johnson	c-2b	2	2	6	1	0	0	0	.167	.167	0
Schneider	ss	1	5	0	2	0	0	0	.400	.400	0
Peterman	lf	1	2	0	0	0	0	0	.000	.000	0
Total		**17**	**614**	**140**	**188**	**39**	**10**	**4**	**.306**	**.422**	**28**

Pitcher	**G**	**GS**	**W/L**	**IP**	**H**	**R**	**TRA**	**BB**	**SO**	**HBP**	**WP**
P. Klaerner	13	13	10–2	97?	84?	34?	3.15?	?	?	3	1
E. Klaerner	4	2	3–0	27	9	2	0.67	?	?	0	0
A. Klaerner[**]	3	2	2–0	18?	12?	5	2.50?	?	?	1	1
Total	**17**	**17**	**15–2**	**142?**	**105?**	**41?**	**2.60?**	**?**	**?**	**4**	**2**

[*] These statistics include all 17 Mountain League regular season games. Statistics were taken from the published box scores available from newspaper accounts. These statistics do not include the championship series against Comfort.

[**] A. Klaerner also had one balk.

The following are 1935 Mountain League hitting statistics for the Fredericksburg Giants as published in the *Fredericksburg Standard*.[*]

Player	**AB**	**H**	**RBI**	**SB**	**BA**
Klett	69	31	21	7	.450
Andrews	45	18	18	3	.400
Langerhans	40	14	17	2	.350
Schnerr	69	24	14	13	.347
Weise	54	18	13	5	.333
Hahn	15	5	2	0	.333
P. Klaerner	58	18	16	1	.310
E. Klaerner	65	20	13	4	.307
Icke	11	3	2	0	.273
Henke	17	4	2	1	.235

Player	AB	H	RBI	SB	BA
A. Klaerner	60	14	12	3	.233
Ransleben	59	11	4	2	.200**

* *Fredericksburg Standard*, August 29, 1935, 2.

** Ransleben's batting average should be .186, not .200.

1935 Kerrville Braves (4–14)*									Manager Ben Grantham		
Player	**POS**	**G**	**AB**	**R**	**H**	**2B**	**3B**	**HR**	**BA**	**SP**	**SB**
Grantham	2b-c	15	60	10	18	2	0	1	.300	.383	2
Warren	cf	13	48	7	9	0	0	0	.188	.188	7
Toler	p-1b	13	34	2	2	1	0	0	.088	.118	2
Goss	rf-cf	12	38	1	7	0	0	0	.184	.184	3
J. Hollimon	c	12	44	3	7	3	0	1	.159	.295	1
C. Gray	ss-2b	11	38	4	5	0	0	1	.132	.211	1
Esbeck	p	10	18	0	0	0	0	0	.000	.000	0
Maybeaux	1b	9	34	4	10	2	1	0	.294	.412	1
B. Brown	3b-lf	9	33	3	7	0	0	0	.212	.212	0
Fisher (Fischer)	lf-cf	6	22	1	7	2	0	0	.318	.409	1
Morris	3b	5	21	4	5	2	0	0	.238	.333	2
Childress?	1b	4	17	2	4	1	0	1	.235	.471	3
Redman	p-rf	4	8	1	1	0	0	0	.125	.125	0
Troutner	rf-1b	4	4	1	0	0	0	0	.000	.000	0
Lowe	ss-lf	3	13	2	7	0	0	0	.538	.538	3
McBryde	lf	3	11	0	2	0	0	0	.181	.181	0
Hughes	2b-cf	3	12	0	2	0	0	0	.167	.167	0
T. Reed	3b-p	3	9	0	1	1	0	0	.111	.222	0
Jones	cf	2	9	1	2	0	1	0	.222	.444	0
Hartmann	rf	2	3	0	0	0	0	0	.000	.000	0
Dawson	ss-2b	2	6	1	0	0	0	0	.000	.000	0
Bourland	3b-ss	2	6	0	0	0	0	0	.000	.000	0
Clebowski	p	1	3	0	1	0	0	0	.333	.333	0
Morgan	rf	1	3	0	1	0	0	0	.333	.333	0
C. Hollimon**	rf	1	4	0	1	0	0	0	.250	.250	0
Crooks	3b	1	4	0	0	0	0	0	.000	.000	0
Total		**15**	**502**	**47**	**99**	**14**	**2**	**4**	**.197**	**.257**	**26**

Pitcher	G	GS	W/L	IP	H	R	TRA	BB	SO	HBP	WP
Toler	12	9	1–8	64⅔	68	62	8.62	?	?	5	8
Esbeck	10	5	1–4	43	54	35	7.33	?	?	3	1
T. Reed	2	0	0–0	7	3	0	0.00	?	14	0	0
Clebowski	1	1	0–1	9	8	6	6.00	4	4	0	1
Redman	1	0	0–0	3⅓	2	5	13.50	?	3	0	0
Total	**15**	**15**	**2–13**	**127**	**135**	**108**	**7.65**	**?**	**?**	**8**	**10**

* These statistics include only 15 (of 18) Mountain League regular season games. Statistics were taken from the published box scores available from newspaper accounts. Some box scores were either not published or not available.

** Clergy Hollimon played 12 games for Legion.

1935 Legion Cubs (10–7)*								**Manager Bob Barry**			
Player	**POS**	**G**	**AB**	**R**	**H**	**2B**	**3B**	**HR**	**BA**	**SP**	**SB**
H. Kaiser	3b-ss	17	70	10	13	1	0	0	.186	.200	5
Baker	lf-2b	17	62	12	16	1	0	1	.258	.323	1
Wootton	ss-cf	16	65	19	20	3	0	2	.308	.446	1
Powell	ss-2b	16	72	10	16	3	0	0	.222	.264	0
Archer	of-p	15	63	11	20	3	0	1	.317	.413	1
Gotthardt	c-2b	15	57	13	14	1	0	0	.246	.263	3
C. Hollimon**	1b-2b	12	53	11	17	1	1	1	.321	.434	1
McDonald	1b-rf	12	31	3	7	1	1	0	.226	.323	1
Foster	of	11	25	3	6	1	0	0	.240	.280	2
Wood (Woods)	p-rf	9	18	1	5	1	0	1	.277	.500	1
Allsbrook	rf	8	31	2	10	2	0	0	.323	.387	0
Beaver	c-1b	8	24	2	6	2	1	0	.250	.417	4
Dickey	p	7	11	1	1	0	0	0	.091	.091	1
Garard	of-2b	6	20	0	5	0	0	0	.250	.250	0
Crooks	lf-rf	5	9	0	0	0	0	0	.000	.000	0
Albrecht	p	4	9	0	1	0	0	0	.111	.111	0
Barry	p	3	4	0	1	0	0	0	.250	.250	0
McElroy	rf-cf	2	5	1	1	0	0	0	.200	.200	0
Burton	p	1	5	1	2	1	0	0	.400	.600	0
Sowers	1b	1	4	0	1	1	0	0	.250	.500	0
Hughes	2b	1	4	0	0	0	0	0	.000	.000	0
Brown	ss	1	2	0	0	0	0	0	.000	.000	0

Player	POS	G	AB	R	H	2B	3B	HR	BA	SP	SB
Gray	2b	1	1	0	0	0	0	0	.000	.000	0
Witt	p	1	1	0	0	0	0	0	.000	.000	0
O. Kaiser	rf	1	1	0	0	0	0	0	.000	.000	0
Osborne	cf	1	1	0	0	0	0	0	.000	.000	0
Total		**17**	**648**	**100**	**162**	**22**	**3**	**6**	**.250**	**.321**	**21**

Pitcher	G	GS	W/L	IP	H	R	TRA	BB	SO	HBP	WP
Archer	9	3	6–0?	37⅓?	30?	11?	?	?	30?	0	0
Dickey	8	5	0–3	44⅓?	23?	25?	?	?	20	0	0
Albrecht	4	3	0–3	25	32	22	7.92	7	13	2	0
Wood (Woods)	4	3	0–0	11⅔	11	5?	?	7	11	1	0
Wootton	3	3	2–1	25	22	15	5.40	6	21	0	0
Barry	3	0	0–0	8⅓	14	11	1.88	5	10	1	2
Burton	1	1	1–0	9	9	7	7.00	0	8	0	0
Witt	1	0	0–0	1⅓	0	0	.00	3	1	0	0
Total	**18**	**18**	**9–7***	**162**	**141?**	**96?**	**5.33?**	**?**	**114?**	**4**	**2**

* These statistics are based on box scores from 16 (of 17) Mountain League regular season games plus the two games against Boerne on June 23 and June 30 which the HCL later eliminated after Boerne withdrew from the league on July 12. Thus, the statistics above include 18 games, except for pitchers' records which do not reflect the two eliminated games. Statistics were taken from the published box scores available from newspaper accounts. Some box scores were either not published or not available. These statistics do not include the second-place playoff game against Comfort.

** Clergy Hollimon played one game for Kerrville.

APPENDIX G: HILL COUNTRY LEAGUE STANDINGS, 1933–1936

1933 Hill Country League Standings – First Half

Team	W	L	GB	Pct.
Llano	9	3	---	.750
Fredericksburg*	9	3	---	.750
Brady	8	5	1½	.615
Mason	6	7	3½	.462
San Saba	5	8	4½	.385
Junction**	1	12	8½	.077

* Fredericksburg withdrew on June 23.

** Junction was dropped on July 6.

1933 Hill Country League Standings – Second Half*

Team	W	L	GB	Pct.
Mason	8	3	---	.727
Llano	8	4	½	.667
Eden**	7	5	1½	.583
San Saba	6	5	2	.545
Brady	5	7	3½	.417
Richland Springs**	1	9	6½	.100

* These standings are shown as listed in the *Llano News*. It is not clear why total team wins do not equal total team losses. *Llano News*, September 7, 1933, 1.

** Eden and Richland Springs replaced Fredericksburg and Junction in the second half.

NOTE: Mason and San Saba played a tie game that was not replayed.

Championship Series: Llano defeated Mason, two games to one.

1934 Hill Country League Standings – First Half*

Team	W	L	GB	Pct.
Richland Springs	9	2	---	.818
Llano	7	4	2	.636
Bend	7	5	2½	.583
Pontotoc	6	6	3½	.500
Brady**	5	5	3½	.500
Goldthwaite	5	6	4	.455
Menard**	2	8	6½	.200
San Saba	2	9	7	.181

* These standings are shown as listed in the *Llano News*. It is not clear why the total team wins do not equal total team losses. *Llano News*, June 14, 1934, 1.

** According to the *Llano News*, Brady withdrew from the league on April 6 and Menard dropped out June 10. *Llano News*, June 14, 1934, 1. However, given that Brady played ten games, Brady likely withdrew in June rather than April 6.

1934 Hill Country League Standings – Second Half

Team	W	L	GB	Pct.
San Saba	8	2	---	.800
Richland Springs	6	4	2	.600
Pontotoc	5	5	3	.500
Llano	4	5	3½	.444
Bend	4	6	4	.400
Goldthwaite	2	7	5½	.222

Championship Series: San Saba defeated Richland Springs, two games to one.

1935 Hill Country League Standings – First Half

Team	W	L	GB	Pct.
Brownwood*	8	2	---	.800
Lometa	6	4	2	.600
Marble Falls	5	4	2½	.556
San Saba	4	4	3	.500
Richland Springs	4	6	4	.400
Llano	1	8	6½	.111

1935 Hill Country League Standings – Second Half*

Team	W	L	GB	Pct.
Richland Springs**	8	2	---	.800
San Saba**	8	2	---	.800
Brownwood	5	5	3	.500
Lometa	5	5	3	.500
Brady***	3	6	4½	.333
Llano	1	9	7	.100

* These standings are shown as listed in the *Llano News*. It is not clear why the total team wins do not equal total team losses. *Llano News*, August 22, 1935, 1.

** Richland Springs defeated San Saba, 2–0, to break the second-half tie and advance to the championship series against Brownwood.

*** Brady replaced Marble Falls in the second half.

Championship Series: Brownwood beat Richland Springs, three games to two, winning Game 5, 6–1.

1936 Hill Country League Standings*

Team	W	L	GB	Pct.
Fredericksburg	16	3	---	.842
Richland Springs	11	8	5	.579
Llano	11	9	5½	.550
Brady	10	10	6½	.500
Junction	4	4	6½	.500
Mason**	4	8	8½	.333
Lampasas**	2	7	9	.222
Legion	1	9	10½	.100

* These standings are shown as listed in the *Llano News*. It is not clear why the total team wins do not equal total team losses. *Llano News*, August 20, 1936, 1.

** Mason and Lampasas did not finish the season; Junction replaced Mason while Legion replaced Lampasas.

Semifinal Series: Fredericksburg defeated Llano, two games to one; Richland Springs defeated Brady, two games to one.

Championship Series: Fredericksburg defeated Richland Springs, two games to none, winning the decisive game, 8–3.

NOTES

PREFACE

1. Jacques Barzan, *God's Country and Mine* (Boston: Little, Brown, 1954), 159.
2. Harold Seymour and Dorothy Seymour Mills, *Baseball: The People's Game* (New York: Oxford University Press, 1990), 11.
3. Ibid., 287.
4. *Comfort News*, May 20, 1926, 1.

AUTHOR'S NOTE

1. Sabermetrics has found that ERA may not be the best pitching statistic, but it is preferable to TRA. However, the limited information in most box scores in the 1930s does not allow the calculation of ERA.

CHAPTER 1

1. Clay Coppedge, *Texas Baseball: A Lone Star Diamond History from Town Teams to the Big Leagues* (Charleston: History Press, 2012), 6.
2. David Vaught, *The Farmer's Game: Baseball in Rural America* (Baltimore: Johns Hopkins University Press, 2013), 52.
3. Ibid.
4. Ibid.
5. Mark Gustafson, *A Naturalist's Guide to the Texas Hill Country* (College Station: Texas A&M University Press, 2015), 1.
6. Jefferson Morgenthaler, *The German Settlement of the Texas Hill Country* (Boerne, TX: Mockingbird Books, 2007), first page of intro.
7. Gustafson, *A Naturalist's Guide to the Texas Hill Country*, 1.
8. Hal K. Rothman, *LBJ's Texas White House* (College Station: Texas A&M University Press, 2001), 9.
9. Glen E. Lich, *The German Texans* (San Antonio: University of Texas Institute of Texan Cultures at San Antonio, 1981), 22.
10. Ibid., 64.
11. Ibid., 23–31.
12. Terry G. Jordan, "The German Influence in Texas: History and Cultural Impact," *Handbook of Texas Online*, accessed March 9, 2026, https://www.

tshaonline.org/handbook/entries/germans.

13. Morgenthaler, *The German Settlement of the Texas Hill Country*, 31, 53–73.
14. Lich, *The German Texans*, 16; Morgenthaler, *The German Settlement of the Texas Hill Country*, 89.
15. Lich, *The German Texans*, 16.
16. Morgenthaler, *The German Settlement of the Texas Hill Country*, 4, 90.
17. Ibid., 4.
18. Rudolph Leopold Biesele, *The History of the German Settlements in Texas, 1831–1861* (Austin: Eakin Press, 1930), 149.
19. Martin Donell Kohout, "History of Fredericksburg, Texas: A German Settlement," *Handbook of Texas Online*, accessed April 14, 2026.https://www.tshaonline.org/handbook/entries/fredericksburg-tx.
20. Biesele, *The History of the German Settlements in Texas*, 149.
21. Ibid.
22. Ibid.
23. Kohout, "History of Fredericksburg, Texas."
24. Ibid.
25. Ibid.
26. Ibid.
27. Gillespie County Historical Society, *Gillespie County*, Images of America (n.p.: Arcadia Publishing, 2013), 9.
28. Morgenthaler, *The German Settlement of the Texas Hill Country*, 106.
29. Ibid.
30. Ibid.
31. Ibid.
32. In fact, the Heart of the Hills Heritage Center is a nonprofit organization operating today to foster and preserve the history of Kerrville and Kerr County.
33. Morgenthaler, *The German Settlement of the Texas Hill Country*, 115.
34. Ibid., 110–11. For many years, historians believed that the name of this utopian settlement was "Tusculum." However, recent research by Boerne historian Bryden Moon Jr. has determined this claim to be unfounded. Moon concluded that in 1894, historian Adolf Paul Weber referred in his book to the Boerne-region property of Dr. Ferdinand Herff as a "friendly Tusculum." Even though the utopian settlement was on land separate from Dr. Herff's property, historians mistakenly attributed the term "Tusculum" to the utopian settlement. Moon has determined instead that Weber was making only a metaphorical reference to the Tusculum area in Italy—a hilly region where wealthy Romans visited their villas, not unlike Dr.

Herff visiting his Hill Country during the summer months. Contrary to later interpretations of his work, Weber's application of "Tusculum" was *exclusively* used to describe Dr. Herff's landholdings, not the separate land where the utopian community was located. When Weber addressed the pre-Boerne settlement, he ascribed no nickname to the young settlers' commune. Thus, it is not accurate to refer to the pre-Boerne settlement as Tusculum. Bryden Moon Jr., "The Pre-Boerne Settlement, Part I," *Echoes from the Archives* (Patrick Heath Public Library) 35 (Winter 2021–2022): 1–3.

35. Morgenthaler, *The German Settlement of the Texas Hill Country*, 112.
36. Ibid., 116.
37. Ibid., 112.
38. Ibid., 172. See chapter 6 for Kendall's enduring legacy of sheep farms in the Hill Country.
39. Ibid., 128.
40. Ibid., 125.
41. Ibid. It is interesting to note that one of the historic buildings in Comfort is named Bolshevik Hall.
42. Lich, *The German Texans*, 91, 94; Don H. Biggers, *German Pioneers in Texas* (Austin: Fredericksburg Publishing, 1983), 57. On February 23, 1861, Texans voted on secession. In Gillespie County where Fredericksburg is the county seat, only 3.8 percent voted in favor of secession (16 yes, 398 no). A. Ray Stephens, *Texas: A Historical Atlas* (Norman: University of Oklahoma Press, 2010), 170. Morgenthaler, *The German Settlement of the Texas Hill Country*, 141.
43. Morgenthaler, *The German Settlement of the Texas Hill Country*, 138.
44. Ibid., 139.
45. In the 1861 popular vote on secession, the Comfort precinct in Kerr County voted against secession, 53–34. Morgenthaler, *The German Settlement of the Texas Hill Country*, 141.
46. Ibid., 57–61.
47. Some historical accounts claim that a total of 36 Union loyalists were killed. Since there are 35 names on the Treue der Union monument, we have used 35 as the correct figure.
48. Morgenthaler, *The German Settlement of the Texas Hill Country*, 167.
49. Ibid., 125.
50. Ibid., 106–7.
51. Ibid. Upper Silesia is located mostly in Poland today.
52. Morgenthaler, *The German Settlement of the Texas Hill Country*, 106.

53. Due to the rugged nearby hills, the *Bandera Bulletin* advertised Bandera as the "Swiss Alps of Texas" in the 1930s.
54. Rudolph L. Biesele, "Fisher-Miller Land Grant," *Handbook of Texas Online*, accessed October 25, 2024, https://www.tshaonline.org/handbook/entries/fisher-miller-land-grant.
55. Ibid.
56. Cornelia Marschall Smith and Otto W. Tetzlaff, "Meusebach, John O.," *Handbook of Texas Online*, accessed October 25, 2024, https://www.thsa-online.org/handkbook/entries/meusebach-john-o.
57. Daniel J. Gelo and Christopher J. Wickham, *The German Texas Frontier in 1953, Ferdinand Lindheimer's Newspaper Accounts of the Environment, Gold, and Indians* (Denton: University of North Texas Press, 2024), 145.
58. Vivian Elizabeth Smyrl, "McCulloch County," *Handbook of Texas Online*, accessed October 25, 2024, https://www.thsaonline.org/handbook/entries/mcculloch-county.
59. Vaught, *The Farmer's Game*, 54.
60. Glen E. Lich, *The Federal Republic of Germany and Texas* (Bonn: Inter Nationes Bonn, 1986), 19.
61. Lich, *The German Texans*, 162, 166.
62. The names of specific clubs were often anglicized by splitting the applicable German word into two words. For example, the *Turnverein* in Boerne is known as the Boerne Turn Verein. Similarly, the name of the *Schuetzenverein* in Boerne is the Boerne Schuetzen Verein (although this was later changed to the Boerne Shooting Club).
63. Vaught, *The Farmer's Game*, 55.
64. Jerrold I. Casway, *The Culture and Ethnicity of Nineteenth-Century Baseball* (Jefferson, NC: McFarland & Company, 2017), 18.
65. Vaught, *The Farmer's Game*, 54.
66. Ibid.
67. Coppedge, *Texas Baseball*, 8.
68. J. Marvin Hunter, *One Hundred Years in Bandera, 1853–1953: A Story of Sturdy Pioneers, Their Struggles and Hardships, and Their Heroic Achievements* (Salem, MA: Higginson Book Company, 1953), 45.
69. Ibid.
70. Ibid.
71. Ibid. The Bandera roster consisted of the following players: George H. Rice, captain and first base; John Davenport, pitcher; Anton Pyka, catcher; Loss Carmichael, shortstop; John Gersdorff, center field; Frank Gersdorff, left field; John Zimmerman, right field; John Montague, third base; and

Will Hay, second base.

72. Ibid.

CHAPTER 2

1. The Deadball Era is generally regarded as 1901–1919, before Babe Ruth transformed baseball into a game emphasizing the home run ball.
2. *Fredericksburg Standard*, August 17, 1933, 3. Falk played in the major leagues from 1920 to 1931 and had a career batting average of .314. "Bibb Falk," Baseball-Reference.com-Major League Statistics and Information, accessed October 11, 2025, https://www.baseball-reference.com/players/f/falkbi01.shtml. After Falk retired from the major leagues, he managed in the minor leagues then served as baseball coach at the University of Texas. Joseph Wancho, "Bibb Falk," SABR Baseball Biography Project, accessed October 11, 2025, https://sabr.org/bioproj/person/bibb-falk/.
3. Garland Perry, *Historic Images of Boerne and Kendall County, Texas, Sesquicentennial Edition* (Boerne, TX: Perry Publications, 1998), 184.
4. Uniforms bearing the "Sox" logo are shown in the 1932 team photograph of the Boerne White Sox in chapter 8 and in the photo of White Sox pitcher Edgar Bergmann in chapter 16.
5. *Comfort News*, February 2, 1995, 8, quoting from *Comfort News*, May 13, 1904.
6. *Comfort News*, April 3, 1908, 2.
7. The 1922 photograph is found in "Comfort Broncos, 1922–1958," a wonderful history of the team (compiled in 2002 and revised 2003 and 2004) by Shirley Pankratz Solis, daughter of Comfort player Joe Pankratz. A copy of the volume is maintained at the Comfort Heritage Foundation.
8. *Kerrville Mountain Sun*, April 15, 1917, 1.
9. *Kerrville Mountain Sun*, March 17, 1984, 5.
10. The Bandera County History Book Committee, *History of Bandera County Texas* (Bandera, TX: Bandera County History Book Committee 1986), 57.
11. Charles Montague coached the team to the 94–0 loss to Kerrville in 1891 mentioned in chapter 1.
12. The Bandera County History Book Committee, *History of Bandera County Texas*, 28.
13. Ibid.
14. Ibid.
15. *Llano News*, May 22, 1913, 5.
16. See chapter 12 for more information on the ballpark in Robinson State

Park in Llano.

17. *Llano News*, June 23, 1914, 1. See chapter 12 for more information on Llano's ballpark.
18. *Llano News*, January 27, 1916, 1.
19. Ibid.
20. Seymour and Mills, *Baseball*, 265–66.
21. Ibid.
22. Ibid., 286.
23. Ibid., 267.
24. *Comfort News*, May 20, 1926, 1.
25. Seymour and Mills, *Baseball*, 280.
26. Gillespie County Historical Society, *Fredericksburg, Texas: The Second Fifty Years* (Fredericksburg, TX: Gillespie County Historical Society, 2022), 5. Fredericksburg is the county seat of Gillespie County.
27. United States Fifteenth Census, 1930, Texas, Table 5, Population of Incorporated Places, 1930 and 1920, National Archives, Washington, DC, accessed January 7, 2025, https://www2.census.gov/library/publications/decennial/1930/population-volume-1/03815512v1ch10.pdf. Since Comfort was unincorporated, we do not have a separate population figure for it. Kendall County, which includes both Boerne and Comfort, had a 1930 population of 4,976. United States Fifteenth Census (1930), Texas, Table 3.-Area and Population of Counties: 1890 to 1930, National Archives, Washington, DC, accessed January 7, 2025, https://www2.census.gov/library/publications/decennial/1930/population-volume-1/03815512v1ch10.pdf.
28. Fredericksburg even had five members of the Klaerner family on the club briefly in 1932 when teenager Alfons Klaerner joined his older brothers, Hugo and Chester, and their cousins, Phillip and Elias. See chapter 8.
29. The name "Uecker" is pronounced "ECK-er" in the Hill Country which is more faithful to the German pronunciation than the Americanized "YOO-ker" familiar from the name of Bob Uecker, the Hall of Fame broadcaster and former major league catcher.
30. According to his niece, Shirley Pankratz Solis, Skeeter's nickname originated when it was said that he was so speedy, he could catch a mosquito in midair. Also, August "Manny" Pankratz, younger brother of Joe and Skeeter, later starred for the Broncos.
31. In the late 1940s, the Pankratz family fielded a team entirely of Pankratz family members known as the Pankratz Panthercats. Team members included Julius, Hilton, Melvin, August ("Manny"), Skeeter, Eugene,

Werner, Bobby, Joe, and Albert Pankratz. Shirely Pankratz Solis, "Comfort Broncos, 1922–1958" (compiled in 2002 and revised 2003 and 2004). A copy of this volume is maintained at the Comfort Heritage Foundation in Comfort, Texas.

32. Michael Barr, "All-Brother Hye Baseball Team," *Blanco County News*, June 19, 2019, accessed October 21, 2025, https://www.hillcountrypassport.com/blanco/article/26403/all-brother-hye-baseball-team.
33. Ibid. In 1935, the Deike brothers were Victor, age 15, outfielder; Emil, 17, third base; Ernest, 21, first base; Clarence, 21, second base; Levi, 23, shortstop (Levi played with the Fredericksburg Giants in 1935); Red, 25, pitcher; Marvin, 28, pitcher-outfielder; Herman, 30, catcher; and Edwin, 33, outfielder. *Fredericksburg Standard*, July 18, 1935, 2.
34. Ibid.
35. Lich, *The German Texans*, 162.
36. Bill Nowlin, "July 3, 1932: Yankees beat Red Sox in first Sunday game in Fenway Park," Society for American Baseball Research (SABR), accessed December 10, 2024, https://sabr.org/gamesproj/game/july-3–1932-yankees-beat-red-sox-in-first-sunday-baseball-game-at-fenway-park/; Albert J. Menendez, "The Battle for Sunday Baseball," *Liberty Magazine*, September–October 2007, accessed September 27, 2025, https://www.libertymagazine.org/article/the-battle-for-sunday-baseball. Sunday baseball was permitted in Boston in 1929 but only if the ballpark was not near a church. As a result, Sunday games were permitted at Braves Field in 1929, but they were not permitted at Fenway Park until 1932 when the church restriction was lifted.
37. It should be noted that blue laws did not always apply to semipro or town baseball even in places like Boston. Seymour and Mills, *Baseball*, 369.
38. *Llano News*, June 30, 1921, 1, 5.
39. Ibid.
40. Major league baseball outlawed the spitball in 1920 but 17 spitball pitchers, including Burleigh Grimes, were exempt from the ban for the remainder of their career. Grimes pitched until 1934.
41. *Llano News*, June 30, 1921, 1, 5.
42. Ibid.
43. *Fredericksburg Standard*, July 2, 1921, 8.
44. U.S. Bureau of Labor Statistics, Annual Unemployment Data, 1929–1939, accessed December 21, 2024, https://data.bls.gov/timeseries/LFU21000100&series_id=LFU22000100&from_year=1929&to_year=1939&periods_option=specific_periods&periods=Annual+Data.

45. Gillespie County Historical Society, *Fredericksburg, Texas*, 5.
46. Ibid., 31.
47. Ibid., 5–6.
48. Before the post–World War II rise of professional football and basketball, the only sports besides baseball that received much coverage were boxing, golf, and horse racing. Even so, San Antonio sports pages were not focused solely on baseball at the major league level. Sports editors also devoted copy to minor league teams such as the San Antonio Missions as well as semiprofessional and city league teams. Occasionally, San Antonio newspapers would even cover town teams in the Hill Country, especially if they were playing San Antonio clubs.
49. Michael Barr, "All-Brother Hye Baseball Team," *Blanco County News*, June 19, 2019, accessed October 21, 2025, https://www.hillcountrypassport.com/blanco/article/26403/all-brother-hye-baseball-team.
50. Ibid.

CHAPTER 3

1. Alan H. Levy, *Rube Waddell* (Jefferson, NC: McFarland & Company, 2000), 21–23.
2. Ibid., 38.
3. "Rube Waddell," Baseball-Reference.com-Major League Statistics and Information, accessed September 27, 2025, https://www.baseball-reference.com/players/w/wadderu01.shtml.
4. Ibid.
5. Ibid.
6. Levy, *Rube Waddell*, 285–94.
7. Ibid.
8. Ibid., 297.
9. Ibid.
10. Ibid., 298, 301.
11. Ibid., 301.
12. *Comfort News*, October 2, 1958, 1; *Comfort News*, August 18, 1977, 6; *Comfort News*, June 23, 1977, 9; *Comfort News*, June 15, 1995, 6.
13. The author has examined other photographs in Dean's teenage years, including a photograph of an 18-year-old Dizzy in Robert Gregory's biography, Robert Gregory, *Diz: The Story of Dizzy Dean and Baseball During the Great Depression* (New York: Viking, 1992). Based on these examinations, the author concludes that the player in the photograph is

not Dizzy Dean. Instead, the man in the photograph appears to be much older than 15, Dean's age in 1925. However, the error in ascribing the player's identity to Dean does not mean that Dean did not pitch for the Broncos. Several Broncos players recalled Dean pitching for Comfort, including catcher Buck Nowlin, as discussed in this chapter.

14. *Comfort News*, October 2, 1958, 1.
15. *Comfort News*, August 18, 1977, 6.
16. Ibid.
17. *Comfort News*, June 23, 1977, 9.
18. Shirley Pankratz Solis, daughter of Joe Pankratz, shared that her father told this story about Dizzy Dean's motorcycle antics.
19. *Comfort News*, April 9, 1925, 1.
20. Ibid.
21. See chapter 12 for more on Kerrville's ballpark. This game was one of the first played in the new ballpark on the north side of town.
22. *Kerrville Mountain Sun*, April 16, 1925, 6.
23. Ibid.
24. Ibid.
25. *Comfort News*, April 30, 1925, 1. See chapter 12 for more on Faltin Field.
26. Ibid.
27. *Comfort News*, May 21, 1925, 1.
28. Ibid.
29. Ibid.
30. *Comfort News*, May 28, 1925, 1.
31. Ibid.
32. Ibid.
33. It is not clear if "Van Biber" was the player's surname or if "Van" was his given name and "Biber" was his surname.
34. *San Antonio Light*, June 9, 1925, 10.
35. Joseph Wancho, "Dizzy Dean," SABR Baseball Biography Project, accessed December 13, 2024, https://sabr.org/bioproj/person/dizzy-dean/.
36. Vince Staten, *Ol' Diz: A Biography of Dizzy Dean* (New York: HarperCollins, 1992), 26–27; Gregory, *Diz*, 29.
37. Ibid.
38. For example, Staten says that the Deans moved from Arkansas to Oklahoma in 1923, while Gregory concludes that they did not move to Oklahoma until 1925. Staten, *Ol' Diz*, 21; Gregory, *Diz*, 25–26. Staten states that Dean left school in Oklahoma in March 1926 when he went to Houston to live with his stepbrother, Claude Parham, who persuaded him

to join the army at Fort Sam Houston. Staten, *Ol' Diz*, 26–27. Gregory finds that he took a train to Fort Sam Houston on November 15, 1926. Gregory, *Diz*, 29.

39. Gregory, *Diz*, 33.
40. Ibid.
41. Ibid.
42. Ibid.
43. *Comfort News*, September 8, 1927, 1.
44. The record of "Van Biber" pitching for Comfort is a bit odd in that he pitched well except for his last effort against the San Antonio Aztecs, who rocked him for eight runs in less than four innings. Perhaps this suggests that the real "Van Biber" made the first two starts for Comfort, but Dean was slipped in as "Van Biber" against the Aztecs. This supposition is supported by the fact that the real "Van Biber" signed a professional contract about two weeks later and left the army for the Three-I League, suggesting that the loss to the Aztecs was uncharacteristic of the real "Van Biber."
45. Wancho, "Dizzy Dean."
46. "Dizzy Dean," Baseball-Reference.com-Major League Statistics and Information, accessed December 10, 2024, https://www.baseball-reference.com/players/d/deandi01.shtml.
47. Ibid.
48. Ibid.

CHAPTER 4

1. *San Antonio Light*, April 2, 1933, 47.
2. *Kerrville Mountain Sun*, February 6, 1930, 1.
3. *Comfort News*, February 27, 1930, 1.
4. *Kerrville Mountain Sun*, April 25, 1929, 1. The house still stands today at the corner of West Main Street and Jackson Road.
5. *Kerrville Daily Times, A Pictorial History of Kerr County, Texas* (Marceline, MO: D-Books Publishing, 1994), 97.
6. *San Antonio Light*, April 2, 1933, 47.
7. See the map of the Hill Country in chapter 1.
8. *San Antonio Light*, April 2, 1933, 47.
9. *Kerrville Mountain Sun*, April 3, 1930, 1, 10. The 26-game schedule included doubleheaders on July 4 that were not listed on the schedule but counted in the standings. The July 4 doubleheaders were Boerne at Kerrville, Comfort at Fredericksburg, and Llano at Mason.

10. *Fredericksburg Standard*, April 4, 1930, 1.
11. *Comfort News*, March 13, 1930, 1, 8. There is some indication this rule was not strictly followed by all clubs, leading to occasional suspicion. See, e.g., *Fredericksburg Standard*, April 7, 1933, 6, in which the *Standard* expressed doubt that all those not listed by clubs as paid players were truly rendering their services gratis.
12. Hugo Klaerner of Fredericksburg and Edgar Bergmann of Boerne are the best examples of players who later became community leaders. See chapters 14 and 16.
13. See chapter 8 for more on Vernon Taylor's sojourns in the Hill Country League.
14. *Fredericksburg Standard*, June 27, 1935, 1.
15. See photos in chapter 2.
16. For more on Adler, see chapter 9.
17. *Kerrville Mountain Sun*, March 27, 1930, 1; *Kerrville Mountain Sun*, March 12, 1931, 1; *Kerrville Mountain Sun*, January 21, 1932, 1, 12; *Kerrville Mountain Sun*, March 2, 1933, 1.
18. *Kerrville Mountain Sun,* February 28, 1935, 1; *Kerrville Mountain Sun,* March 7, 1935, 1. See chapter 13 for more on Kerrville's 1934 season.
19. The archives of the Pioneer Museum in Fredericksburg include the constitution and bylaws of the Fredericksburg Giants.
20. *Kerrville Mountain Sun*, March 20, 1930, 11. The game was played at the Kerrville ballpark at the northeast corner of McFarland and Paschal, where Kerrville's team played from 1925 through 1935. See chapter 12 for more information on the Kerrville ballpark.
21. A player named "Fisher" did not appear for the Giants in the 1930 regular season. Moreover, a search of Baseball Reference did not find a major league player named "Fisher" who played anywhere in the major leagues during this time frame. Fisher probably never appeared in a regular season major league game.
22. "Blackerby" was probably outfielder George Blackerby, who played briefly for the White Sox in 1928 but did not play for them in the 1930 major league regular season.
23. *Kerrville Mountain Sun*, March 20, 1930, 11. As an aside, Moe Berg, whom Casey Stengel called "the strangest man ever to play baseball" and who later worked for the agency that preceded the CIA during World War II, started the game at catcher for the White Sox. Ralph Berger, "Moe Berg," SABR Baseball Biography Project, accessed December 10, 2024, http://sabr.org/bioproj/person/Moe-Berg/.

24. *Kerrville Mountain Sun*, March 13, 1930, 1.
25. *Fredericksburg Standard*, March 28, 1930, 1.
26. Ibid.
27. *Fredericksburg Standard*, April 4, 1930, 1.
28. *Comfort News*, April 3, 1930, 1.
29. Felix Saenger managed the Giants between 1924 and 1937 but for unknown reasons, Hollmig served as player-manager in 1930.
30. "C. L. Taylor," Baseball-Reference.com. Major League Statistics and Information, accessed December 21, 2024, https://www.baseball-reference.com/players/t/tayloch01.shtml. In 1929, Taylor played for Houston of the Class A Texas League and Chattanooga of the Class A Southern Association.
31. Darren Gibson, "C. L. Taylor," SABR Baseball Biography Project, accessed December 21, 2024, https://sabr.org/bioproj/person/c-l-taylor/. "C. L. Taylor," Baseball-Reference.com. Minor League Statistics, accessed December 21, 2024, https://www.baseball-reference.com/register/player.fcgi?id=taylor003c—. Taylor later purchased a Magnolia Petroleum filling station.
32. Leidl's first name is sometimes spelled "Rudie" in newspaper articles but in most US census reports, his name is spelled "Rudy," so we use "Rudy" throughout the book. "Rudy" is an abbreviated version of his given name, Rudolph. Leidl's niece, Janet D'Spain, confirmed that "Rudy" is correct.
33. *Kerrville Mountain Sun*, April 3, 1930, 1. We note that some newspaper reports identified the player as "Woods Thornberry." For consistency, we refer to him as "Wood Thornberry."
34. Ibid.
35. We note that the surnames of Clergy Hollimon and his brother, Jess Hollimon, are frequently misspelled in box scores as "Holloman," even in the *Kerrville Mountain Sun*, their hometown newspaper.
36. *Kerrville Mountain Sun*, April 9, 1925, 1.
37. See chapter 12 for more on Fair Park as the home diamond of the Giants.
38. *Fredericksburg Standard*, April 11, 1930, 6.
39. A player named "William Saenger" played for the Kerrville club and is shown in a photograph of the 1925 Kerrville Athletics. It seems likely that the Kerrville second baseman was William Saenger although in 1925, William Saenger was a pitcher. It is unknown if William Saenger was related to Felix Saenger, who served as manager of the Fredericksburg Giants for many years.
40. *Comfort News*, April 10, 1930, 1.

41. *Llano News*, April 10, 1930, 1. It is not clear why, but Llano used a makeshift lineup for the opening game. Four players who started the game (Brown, Hammontree, McDougal, and Shankel) never appeared again in a Cowboys uniform in 1930.
42. *Kerrville Mountain Sun*, May 1, 1930, 6.
43. *Kerrville Mountain Sun*, May 1, 1930, 1.
44. "Frank Watt," Baseball-Reference.com-Minor League Statistics, accessed December 10, 2024, https://www.baseball-reference.com/register/player.fcgi?id=watt—001fra.
45. *Kerrville Mountain Sun,* May 8, 1930, 1, 12.
46. *Kerrville Mountain Sun*, May 22, 1930, 1.
47. Ibid.
48. *Kerrville Mountain Sun*, May 29, 1930, 1, 12.
49. *Kerrville Mountain Sun*, June 5, 1930, 1, 12.
50. *Kerrville Mountain Sun*, May 29, 1930, 12. The newspaper article reported the three wild pitches, but the box score recorded only one wild pitch by Thornberry.
51. Ibid.
52. *Llano News*, April 17, 1930, 1.
53. *Kerrville Mountain Sun*, May 8, 1930, 12.
54. *Llano News*, May 15, 1930, 1.
55. *Llano News*, May 29, 1930, 1.
56. *Llano News*, June 5, 1930, 1.
57. Ibid.
58. *Fredericksburg Standard*, May 30, 1930, 12. The reference to manager "Schuch" is puzzling. In 1930, player-manager Al Hollmig served as manager of the Giants. Perhaps "Schuch" was filling in for Hollmig that day. However, we have found no other references to a player or manager named "Schuch."
59. Ibid.
60. *Comfort News*, June 5, 1930, 1.
61. Ibid.
62. *Comfort News*, May 22, 1930, 1, 8. See chapter 5 for a dispute between the editorial writers of the *Comfort News* and two players regarding the Broncos' play early in the season.
63. *Comfort News*, June 5, 1930, 1.
64. *Llano News*, May 22, 1930, 1.
65. *Llano News*, June 5, 1930, 4.
66. Ibid.

67. Chester Klaerner is sometimes referred to as "Smokey" and other times as "Smoky." For consistency, we refer to him only as "Smokey."
68. Now Rice University.
69. *Fredericksburg Standard*, July 4, 1930, 12.
70. *Kerrville Mountain Sun*, July 3, 1930, 1.
71. This would not be the last time that a member of the Klaerner family would pitch for Kerrville. In 1931, Hugo Klaerner pitched for Kerrville for most of the 1931 season after a dispute with the Giants' management; see chapter 6.
72. *Kerrville Mountain Sun*, July 10, 1930, 1, 4.
73. Ibid.
74. *Fredericksburg Standard*, August 1, 1930, 12.
75. *Llano News*, July 10, 1930, 1.
76. Llano had played two fewer games than Fredericksburg due to rainouts on June 8 and June 15 and the 2–2 tie with Kerrville on April 27 that was called on account of darkness after 15 innings. Fredericksburg had just one rainout, on June 15.
77. Gregory, *Diz*, 34. English later played in the major leagues.
78. *Kerrville Mountain Sun*, July 31, 1930, 1, 8.
79. *Fredericksburg Standard*, July 4, 1930, 12. No box score was found for this game, but a line score appeared in the *Fredericksburg Standard*.
80. *Fredericksburg Standard*, July 18, 1930, 9.
81. *Kerrville Mountain Sun*, June 5, 1930, 12.
82. *Kerrville Mountain Sun*, July 24, 1930, 1, 12.
83. *Kerrville Mountain Sun*, July 31, 1930, 1, 8.
84. *Kerrville Mountain Sun*, August 7, 1930, 1, 8. It is not clear if the reference to Llano "Lambs" was derogatory or a secondary nickname for the Llano club.
85. Ibid.
86. Anton Leidl was occasionally referred to as "Tony" Leidl. For consistency, we will use his full name, Anton Leidl.
87. Ibid.
88. *Fredericksburg Standard*, August 8, 1930, 4.
89. Ibid.
90. *Llano News*, August 14, 1930, 1.
91. *Fredericksburg Standard*, August 15, 1930, 6.
92. *Fredericksburg Standard*, August 22, 1930, 7.
93. *Fredericksburg Standard*, August 29, 1930, 5.
94. *Llano News*, August 28, 1930, 1.

95. Ibid.
96. No box score was published for this game but the Boerne scorebook for the 1929–34 seasons contains the scoresheet for this game. The scorebook survives in the Dietert Historical Archives of the Patrick Heath Public Library in Boerne. English hit .328 (22 for 67) for the 1930 White Sox. English later played in the major leagues for parts of four seasons.
97. Robinson State Park is now Robinson City Park in Llano. See chapter 12 for more info on the diamond in Llano.
98. *Fredericksburg Standard*, September 5, 1930, 5.
99. Ibid.
100. Ibid.
101. *Llano News*, September 4, 1930, 1.
102. Ibid.
103. *Kerrville Mountain Sun*, September 4, 1930, 1, 12.
104. *Fredericksburg Standard*, September 12, 1930, 19. By agreement, the clubs planned to play only a seven-inning game, but the game went eight innings before the Giants tallied the winning run.
105. See chapter 12 for more info on Boerne's diamond at the Kendall County Fairgrounds.
106. *Llano News*, September 11, 1930, 1, 4.
107. Ibid.
108. Ibid. See later in chapter 4 regarding payments made to Hargrove and Myler for the doubleheader, as shown by the Boerne White Sox ledger for 1930.
109. *Fredericksburg Standard*, September 12, 1930, 19.
110. *Comfort News*, September 18, 1930, 1.
111. *Kerrville Mountain Sun*, September 18, 1930, 12.
112. Ibid., 1.
113. Ibid.
114. *Llano News*, September 25, 1930, 1.
115. Ibid.
116. It is not known why Lefty Draper was not available to pitch in the championship series. Since he was young, he may have returned to college. The fact that he did not start a game until the fourth game of the season on April 27 supports this hypothesis.
117. *Llano News*, October 2, 1930, 1.
118. *Fredericksburg Standard*, October 10, 1930, 1. It is not clear why the October 12 game was played in Fredericksburg rather than Llano as originally scheduled.

119. *Fredericksburg Standard*, October 17, 1930, 1, 7.
120. Ibid.
121. *Fredericksburg Standard*, September 19, 1930, 1.
122. Ibid., 2.
123. Ibid. See earlier in this chapter regarding Fredericksburg's distribution of surplus revenues to players at the end of the season.
124. The ledger is part of the Dietert Historical Archives of the Patrick Heath Public Library in Boerne. The ledger includes the years 1927 through 1935.
125. The statistics in Appendix A reflect only the regular season games for which box scores were found.
126. *Fredericksburg Standard*, February 20, 1931, 2.
127. *Fredericksburg Standard*, January 30, 1931, 2.
128. The statistics published by the *Fredericksburg Standard* were season statistics provided by the Giants. Since the statistics in Appendix A include only those games for which box scores were found in newspapers, the *Fredericksburg Standard* statistics are different from those in Appendix A.
129. For all teams other than Fredericksburg, the statistics cited for 1930 are taken from Appendix A, reflecting only games for which box scores were found.
130. As stated in the Author's Note preceding chapter 1, total run average (TRA) is calculated the same way as earned run average (ERA), except that TRA uses total runs (earned and unearned), not just earned runs, since most box scores do not identify earned runs. See also Notes on Team Statistics Compiled from Box Scores following the acknowledgments.

CHAPTER 5

1. Many thanks to Shirley Pankratz Solis for her book, *Comfort Broncos, 1922–1958*, a history of the Comfort team (compiled in 2002 and revised 2003 and 2004). Her book alerted the author to this contretemps between the *Comfort News* and two Broncos players which included her father, Joe Pankratz, captain of the Broncos.
2. *Comfort News*, May 1, 1930, 2.
3. *Comfort News*, May 8, 1930, 1, 10.
4. Ibid.
5. *Comfort News*, May 8, 1930, 1. See chapter 4 regarding Kerrville's protest of the game based on Comfort's use of Watt.
6. *Comfort News*, May 8, 1930, 2.
7. *Comfort News*, May 15, 1930, 2.

CHAPTER 6

1. For more information on George Kendall, see Morgenthaler, *The German Settlement of the Texas Hill Country*, 172.
2. *Kerrville Mountain Sun*, February 18, 1932, 1.
3. Mohair prices for the spring clip were expected to be 30 cents per pound for grown hair and 40 cents per pound for kid hair. *Kerrville Mountain Sun*, January 15, 1931, 1, 12.
4. *Kerrville Mountain Sun*, January 15, 1931, 1, 12.
5. W. Eugene Holland, "Charles A. Schreiner, *Handbook of Texas Online*, accessed October 25, 2024, https://www.tshaonline.org/handbook/entries/schreiner-charles-armand.
6. *Kerrville Mountain Sun*, January 8, 1931, 1.
7. Ibid.
8. *Kerrville Mountain Sun*, February 19, 1931, 1, 12. Louis A. Schreiner and A. C. Schreiner were the sons of Captain Charles Schreiner who came to Texas in 1852 and joined the Texas Rangers. He opened a general store, Faltin & Schreiner, in 1869, later buying out his business partner. His general store in Kerrville grew to a vast business empire that included banking and ranching. *Kerrville Daily Times*, *A Pictorial History of Kerr County, Texas,* 11.
9. Ibid.
10. Ibid.
11. Ibid.
12. *Fredericksburg Standard*, March 20, 1931;*Kerrville Mountain Sun*, March 26, 1931, 1.
13. *Kerrville Mountain Sun*, March 26, 1931, 1.
14. Junction is located 53 miles northwest of Kerrville.
15. Ibid.
16. Ibid.
17. Ibid. In a final order of business at the meeting, the league voted to allow clubs to set their own admission prices, likely in response to the effects of the Depression.
18. The distance from Boerne to Junction is about 83 miles, only slightly farther than the distance from Boerne to Llano.
19. *Kerrville Mountain Sun*, April 2, 1931, 1.
20. *Fredericksburg Standard*, March 27, 1931, 1.
21. Ibid.
22. Ibid.

23. *Kerrville Mountain Sun*, March 19, 1931, 1.
24. Ibid. Sometime during the first half of the 1931 season, Nelson Davis took over as manager for reasons that are not clear. Davis returned as manager in 1932.
25. The Junction team may have also been known as the Jaguars. Several articles in the *Kerrville Mountain Sun* refer to them as the Jaguars rather than the Firemen. *Kerrville Mountain Sun*, June 25, 1931, 12; *Kerrville Mountain Sun*, August 6, 1931, 1.
26. *Fredericksburg Standard*, April 10, 1931, 2; *Kerrville Mountain Sun*, April 16, 1931, 12.
27. *Fredericksburg Standard*, April 17, 1931, 1.
28. *Fredericksburg Standard*, April 24, 1931, 4.
29. *Fredericksburg Standard*, April 10, 1931, 12.
30. *Kerrville Mountain Sun*, April 16, 1931, 12.
31. *Fredericksburg Standard*, May 1, 1931, 1.
32. *Kerrville Mountain Sun*, May 21, 1931, 1.
33. Ibid.
34. *Fredericksburg Standard*, May 1, 1931, 1.
35. Ibid., 1, 12.
36. Ibid.
37. *Fredericksburg Standard*, May 29, 1931, 1, 3.
38. Ibid.
39. Little is known about pitcher McDonald. This was the only game that he started, which is not surprising given his shaky debut.
40. *Llano News*, June 11, 1931, 1.
41. *Fredericksburg Standard*, June 5, 1931, 3. Melvin Durst doubled in the winning run in the bottom of the 12th inning.
42. *Kerrville Mountain Sun*, June 18, 1931, 1, 12.
43. Ibid., 12.
44. Ibid.
45. Ibid.
46. Ibid.
47. *Comfort News*, June 25, 1931, 1.
48. *Kerrville Mountain Sun*, June 25, 1931, 1, 12.
49. Ibid.
50. Ibid.
51. *Kerrville Mountain Sun*, July 9, 1931, 1, 12.
52. It is unknown if William Saenger was related to Felix Saenger who managed the Fredericksburg Giants for many years.

53. *Kerrville Mountain Sun*, July 9, 1, 12.
54. *Kerrville Mountain Sun*, July 23, 1931, 1.
55. Ibid.
56. Ibid.
57. *Fredericksburg Standard*, July 31, 1931, 3.
58. *Comfort News*, July 9, 1931, 1.
59. *Llano News*, July 23, 1931, 1.
60. *Llano News*, August 6, 1931, 1.
61. Ibid.
62. *Kerrville Mountain Sun*, August 20, 1931, 1, 8.
63. Ibid.
64. No box scores were found for these games. Only the scores were reported.
65. *Fredericksburg Standard*, September 4, 1931, 3.
66. *Fredericksburg Standard*, September 18, 1931, 1, 6.
67. *Kerrville Mountain Sun*, September 10, 1931, 1, 12; *Kerrville Mountain Sun*, September 17, 1931, 1, 12.
68. *Kerrville Mountain Sun*, September 10, 1931, 1, 12.
69. *Fredericksburg Standard*, September 18, 1931, 1, 6.
70. *Llano News*, September 3, 1931, 1.
71. Ibid.
72. *Fredericksburg Standard*, September 18, 1931, 6.
73. *Fredericksburg Standard*, September 18, 1931, 6. Bell Mountain has an elevation of 1,956 feet.
74. Ibid. These batting averages are full season statistics listed in the *Fredericksburg Standard*. They vary from the statistics shown in Appendix B because Appendix B does not reflect all games but only those games for which box scores were found.
75. Ibid.
76. *Fredericksburg Standard*, September 25, 1931, 1.
77. The *Fredericksburg Standard* lists the player's name as "Collins," while the *Llano News* lists his name as "Collings." Since Harold Collings played for Llano in these years, we presume that "Collings" is correct.
78. *Fredericksburg Standard*, September 25, 1931, 1, 3.
79. *Fredericksburg Standard*, October 2, 1931, 3.
80. Ibid., 1, 3.
81. *Llano News*, October 8, 1931, 1.
82. Ibid.
83. *Fredericksburg Standard*, October 9, 1931, 3.
84. The statistics cited here are taken from Appendix B and include only those

games for which the author found box scores in newspapers. Thus, these batting averages differ from those listed earlier in the chapter which were based on statistics reported by the *Fredericksburg Standard* for all games of the season.

85. See Author's Note preceding chapter 1 regarding total run average (TRA). See also Notes on Team Statistics Compiled from Box Scores following the acknowledgments.
86. The Giants' batting averages referenced here were taken from the article in the *Fredericksburg Standard* on September 18, 1931. Those statistics, provided by the Giants, included all games. The statistics in Appendix B include only those games for which box scores were found in newspapers. Thus, the batting averages in Appendix B differ from those cited here.
87. *Comfort News*, August 6, 1931, 1.
88. *Comfort News*, August 20, 1931, 8.
89. *Comfort News*, September 3, 1931, 1, 8.
90. *Comfort News*, September 17, 1931, 1, 8.

CHAPTER 7

1. *Comfort News*, June 9, 1995, 4.
2. See chapter 12 for more information on Faltin Field.
3. Ibid.
4. *Comfort News*, March 2, 1995, 5.
5. Ibid.

CHAPTER 8

1. *Kerrville Mountain Sun*, February 25, 1932, 1.
2. Ibid.
3. *Fredericksburg Standard*, April 1, 1932, 1.
4. *Fredericksburg Standard*, March 4, 1932, 1.
5. Ibid.
6. *Fredericksburg Standard*, April 15, 1932, 1.
7. *Kerrville Mountain Sun*, July 7, 1932, 1, 10. Some areas near Kerrville received 10–19 inches of rain within 48 hours.
8. *Kerrville Mountain Sun*, July 7, 1932, 1, 10. On July 4, 2025, Kerrville and nearby areas suffered a sudden and calamitous rise in the Guadalupe River, resulting in a horrific flood that killed at least 137 persons. Until the 2025 flood, the 1932 flood held the record for the highest flood elevation of the Guadalupe River at Hunt, Texas, west of Kerrville. KHOU,

July 7, 2025, accessed October 4, 2025, https://www.khou.com/article/news/state/texas-news/texas-flood/texas-flooding-guadalupe-river-all-time-record-hunt-kerrville/285-b1782b91-d2e6–439e-8664–7de2c5efb8bf. At Kerrville, the 1932 flood's elevation at 39.0 feet was higher than the flood elevation of 34.29 feet for the 2025 flood. Ibid.

9. Ibid.
10. Ibid.
11. Ibid.
12. Ibid.
13. *Fredericksburg Standard*, September 18, 1931, 6.
14. *Comfort News*, April 14, 1932, 1.
15. *Comfort News*, May 19, 1932, 1.
16. Ibid.
17. *Comfort News*, August 25, 1932, 1. On occasion, Boerne and Comfort also played industrial teams. For example, Comfort drubbed Dibble Sports, 3–0, on July 10 and shut out the Merchants Poultry Hawks, 10–0, on July 24. *Comfort News*, July 14, 1932, 1; *Comfort News*, July 28, 1932, 1.
18. Most newspaper articles refer to Brady's club as the "Turks." There is some indication that "Turks" was short for "Turkeys" since the team was occasionally referred to as the "Gobblers." For consistency, we refer to the team as the "Turks,'" the most common nickname for the club.
19. Peel's .451 average is his full season average taken from the *Fredericksburg Standard*. This figure varies from Appendix B which reflects only those games for which box scores were found in newspapers.
20. It was later reported that Memphis released Leidl in May, but he then pitched in the Memphis city league. *Kerrville Mountain Sun*, May 19, 1932, 12.
21. Kott played with Fredericksburg before the Hill Country League was formed in 1930.
22. *Fredericksburg, Standard*, January 15, 1932, 3; *Kerrville Mountain Sun*, March 10, 1932, 10; *Fredericksburg Standard*, January 29, 1932, 3; *Fredericksburg, Standard*, February 5, 1932, 3.
23. *Fredericksburg, Standard*, March 25, 1932, 3.
24. *Fredericksburg, Standard*, April 1, 1932, 3.
25. *Fredericksburg, Standard*, April 8, 1932, 3.
26. *Fredericksburg, Standard*, March 18, 1932, 3.
27. Ibid.
28. Ibid.
29. Ibid.

30. *Kerrville Mountain Sun*, April 7, 1932, 1, 12.
31. *Kerrville Mountain Sun*, March 10, 1932, 10.
32. *Kerrville Mountain Sun*, January 21, 1932, 10. Nelson Davis took over the managing duties from Dick Bischofhausen sometime during the 1931 season.
33. Only Hardy's last name was reported in the available newspaper articles for games in which he pitched in 1932. However, his pitching prowess in 1932 makes it likely that this pitcher was Harvey Hardy, a fine hurler who pitched well for Kerrville in 1933. Accordingly, we refer to him as Harvey Hardy when pitching for Mason in 1932.
34. Although the *Kerrville Mountain Sun* and the *Llano News* referred to the team as the "Mountaineers," the *Fredericksburg Standard* still referred to them as the "Firemen" in 1932. For consistency, we refer to them as the Mountaineers in 1932.
35. *Junction Eagle*, April 21, 1932, 1.
36. *Fredericksburg Standard*, April 8, 1932, 1.
37. Ibid.
38. *Fredericksburg Standard*, April 8, 1932, 1, 3.
39. Wendler's given name is not mentioned in the *Fredericksburg Standard*, but it is likely that "Wendler" was Gus Wendler, who later played for the Boerne White Sox.
40. It is likely that Harvey Hardy pitched the shutout for the Mavericks, but no box score was found for this game.
41. *Fredericksburg Standard*, May 6, 1932, 3.
42. Ibid. Hugo Klaerner's time in El Paso was short. He returned to the Giants by June 12, resuming his pitching duties.
43. *Fredericksburg, Standard*, May 13, 1932, 3.
44. Ibid. However, Hollmig did return to Fredericksburg for two games near the end of the 1932 season.
45. *Llano News*, April 14, 1932, 1.
46. Ibid.
47. *Fredericksburg, Standard*, April 22, 1932, 1, 3.
48. Ibid.
49. Ibid.
50. *Fredericksburg, Standard*, May 27, 1932, 3.
51. *Fredericksburg, Standard*, June 3, 1932, 3.
52. Ibid.
53. *Fredericksburg Standard*, June 24, 1932, 3.
54. *Kerrville Mountain Sun*, May 26, 1932, 12.

55. *Llano News*, June 30, 1932, 1.
56. *Fredericksburg Standard*, June 3, 1932, 3.
57. *Llano News*, June 9, 1932, 1.
58. *Fredericksburg Standard*, June 17, 1932, 1, 3.
59. *Llano News*, June 30, 1932, 1.
60. Ibid.
61. *Fredericksburg Standard*, July 1, 1932, 3.
62. Archer may have been Haskell Archer, who later pitched for Kerrville, Comfort, and Legion.
63. *Fredericksburg Standard*, June 3, 1932, 1, 3.
64. *Llano News*, June 9, 1932, 1.
65. *Kerrville Mountain Sun*, August 18, 1932, 10.
66. Ibid.
67. *Kerrville Mountain Sun*, July 7, 1932, 6.
68. Ibid.
69. Ibid.
70. Sanders was signed by the St. Louis Cardinals in November 1931 and assigned to Springfield of the Western Association. *The Sporting News*, November 12, 1931, 6. However, we could find no record of Sanders appearing for Springfield in the 1932 season. According to a brief reference in the *Fredericksburg Standard*, Sanders returned from Mobile in May 1932. However, we could find no record of Sanders pitching for the Mobile Red Warriors, a Class B affiliate of the Cardinals. In any event, after he returned to the Hill Country, Sanders made two starts for Fredericksburg in 1932 before leaving for Kerrville.
71. Ibid.
72. *Fredericksburg Standard*, July 8, 1932, 1, 3.
73. Ibid.
74. *Fredericksburg Standard*, June 24, 1932, 3.
75. *Fredericksburg Standard*, July 8, 1932, 1, 3
76. Ibid.
77. *Llano News*, July 14, 1932, 1.
78. *Llano News*, July 7, 1932, 1.
79. *Fredericksburg Standard*, July 29, 1932, 1, 3.
80. *Fredericksburg Standard*, August 5, 1932, 1, 3.
81. *Fredericksburg Standard*, August 12, 1932, 1, 3.
82. Ibid.
83. Ibid.
84. Ibid.

85. *Fredericksburg Standard*, July 29, 1932, 1, 3.
86. *Llano News*, August 18, 1932, 1.
87. *Llano News*, August 25, 1932, 1.
88. *Llano News*, September 1, 1932, 1.
89. *Llano News*, September 8, 1932, 1.
90. Ibid.
91. Ibid.
92. Ibid.
93. Ibid. Despite the assumed name, fans must have known the true identity of "Bradley" since it was reported in the *Fredericksburg Standard*.
94. *Llano News*, September 15, 1932, 1.
95. Ibid. Kygar's name is sometimes spelled "Kyger" in other newspaper reports. For consistency, we refer to him as "Kygar."
96. The game account in the *Llano News* refers only to "Falk." However, a later article in the *Llano News* (September 22, 1932, 8) refers to a player named "Spot" Falk. Thus, we conclude that "Falk" is Spot Falk. It is unknown if Spot Falk was related to Austin native Bibb Falk, who played briefly with the Fredericksburg Giants in 1918 before beginning a 12-year major league career. See chapter 2.
97. *Llano News*, September 15, 1932, 1.
98. *Fredericksburg Standard*, September 16, 1932, 3.
99. *Llano News*, September 22, 1932, 1. See chapter 4 for an occasion when the ground rules for balls hit into the automobile parking lot affected the outcome of a game at Robinson State Park.
100. Ibid.
101. *Llano News*, September 22, 1932, 8.
102. *Llano News*, September 29, 1932, 1.
103. Of course, the "F. H." in "F. H. Bradley" may have stood for "Flop Harris."
104. Ibid.
105. *Llano News*, October 6, 1932, 1.
106. *Kerrville Mountain Sun*, October 6, 1932, 10. The distribution of revenues was presumably based on the overall standings, but it is unknown why Kerrville did not receive a share of the net revenues. Kerrville finished in fifth place but ahead of Junction, which received a small share.
107. Starting in 1934, Taylor pitched in the minor leagues for four years. Taylor spent most of his career bouncing from one level to another. In 1935, Taylor went 1–5 with Houston of the Class A Texas League but managed a respectable 3.14 ERA. In 1936, he enjoyed his best season record with a 16–9 mark in 227 innings for New Iberia of the Class D Evangeline

League. He served as player-manager for both New Iberia in 1936 and Kinston of the Class D Coastal Plain League in 1937, his last season in the minors. "Vern Taylor," Baseball-reference.com. Minor League Statistics, accessed December 20, 2024, https://www.baseball-reference.com/register/player.fcgi?id=taylor001ver.

108. *Fredericksburg Standard*, September 9, 1932, 3. In games for which box scores were found, Taylor posted a 4–4 record, as shown in Appendix C. Taylor's 8–5 record reflects all games as published in the *Fredericksburg Standard*.
109. *Kerrville Mountain Sun*, August 4, 1932, 10.
110. Goat Gardner hit .361 but played in only nine games before leaving to play for Brady the rest of the season.
111. "Charlie English," Baseball-reference.com. Minor League Statistics, accessed December 19, 2024, https://www.baseball-reference.com/register/player.fcgi?id=englis001cha.
112. Ibid.
113. Ibid.
114. Ibid.
115. Ibid.
116. Ibid. The Boerne White Sox scorebook for the 1929–34 seasons contains a handwritten note stating that "Charley English-shortstop, later went to Houston, Tex league (St. Louis Cardinals chain) & then played regularly with St. Louis Cardinals-National League." This note is incorrect on several points. First, Charlie's first name is misspelled. Second, no player with the surname "English" has played for the St. Louis Cardinals. Third, English never played for the Houston minor league club (although he did play for Galveston and Fort Worth). At first blush, one might assume that the scorebook was simply mistaken that the "Charley English" who played for Boerne in 1930 later became a major leaguer, especially since English was born in South Carolina with no apparent connection to Texas. However, one of the biographies of Dizzy Dean helps to solve the scorebook's cryptic reference to "Charley English." In *Diz*, author Robert Gregory refers to Charlie English as a "top player for the 15th Field Artillery who moonlighted on the same semipro lots as Diz and who made it to the Chicago White Sox in 1932." Gregory, *Diz*, 34. As a result, Charlie English, like Dizzy Dean, played for Hill Country teams and other clubs while playing for the Fifteenth Field Artillery at Fort Sam Houston. Until we discovered Gregory's reference to Charlie English, there was little to tie Charlie English to Texas, much less the Hill Country. However,

Gregory places Charlie English at Fort Sam Houston in the proper time frame to play for the 1930 Boerne White Sox. In addition, when English made it to the major leagues in 1932, the *San Antonio Express* noted that he had been teammates with Dizzy Dean at Fort Sam Houston before English left the army in 1930, thus confirming English's availability to play for Boerne in 1930. *San Antonio Express*, July 26, 1932, 8. As a result, even though the scorebook misspells "Charlie" and English never played for St. Louis, it is reasonable to conclude that the "Charley English" in the Boerne scorebook was in fact Charlie English who later played shortstop with three teams in the major leagues.

117. *Kerrville Mountain Sun*, September 15, 1932, 10. See chapter 18 regarding the "badly depleted treasury of the Braves" following the 1932 season, which resulted in the Braves playing a game against Kerrville's Black team, the All-Stars, to recoup their losses.
118. *San Antonio Light*, April 2, 1933, 47; *Kerrville Mountain Sun*, February 16, 1933, 1; *Comfort News*, January 19, 1933, 1.
119. *Fredericksburg Standard*, January 20, 1933, 4.
120. *Kerrville Mountain Sun*, February 16, 1933, 1.
121. *Comfort News*, July 28, 1932, 1.
122. *Kerrville Mountain Sun*, February 16, 1933, 1.
123. Ibid. Kerrville's withdrawal must have been especially painful for Kerrville sportswriter Bob Bennett, who was instrumental in forming the league and was then serving as honorary league president. *San Antonio Light*, April 2, 1933, 47.
124. *Kerrville Mountain Sun*, February 16, 1933, 1.
125. Ibid.
126. *San Antonio Light*, October 3, 1933, 16.

CHAPTER 9

1. Perry, *Historic Images of Boerne and Kendall County, Texas*, 90.
2. Ibid.
3. Ibid.
4. *Comfort News*, February 13, 1930, 4.
5. *San Antonio Express*, August 29, 1926, 2.
6. Adler's tenure as Mountain League president ended when Boerne withdrew from the league in July 1935. See chapter 15.
7. *Boerne Star*, July 15, 1954, 1.
8. Ibid.

9. Ibid.
10. Perry, *Historic Images of Boerne and Kendall County, Texas*, 90.
11. *Boerne Star*, July 15, 1954, 1.
12. Perry, *Historic Images of Boerne and Kendall County, Texas*, 79. See chapter 16 for more information on Edgar Bergmann and the Bergmann Lumber Company.

CHAPTER 10

1. *Fredericksburg Standard*, March 3, 1933, 1; *Kerrville Mountain Sun*, March 9, 1933, 1.
2. *Kerrville Mountain Sun*, March 9, 1933, 1.
3. *Fredericksburg Standard*, March 10, 1933, 1.
4. *Fredericksburg Standard*, March 17, 1933, 1, 2.
5. *Fredericksburg Standard*, February 3, 1933, 1. According to Christopher J. Wickham, professor emeritus of German at the University of Texas at San Antonio, *Diezurzeitherrschendeschreckendegeldknappheit* is not a single word but instead is a phrase consisting of six combined words that mean "the-at-the-(present) time-prevailing-terrifying-money-shortage." Apparently, the words were combined for humorous effect. The German term for the Depression is actually "*die Weltwirtschaftskrise*," which translated literally means "the world economic crisis."
6. *Comfort News*, March 9, 1933, 8.
7. Ibid.
8. In fact, the Heart of the Hills Heritage Center is a nonprofit organization operating today to foster and preserve the history of Kerrville and Kerr County.
9. *San Antonio Light*, April 2, 1933, 47; *Kerrville Daily Times*, March 16, 1933, 8. Apparently, Kerrville's efforts to obtain a second San Antonio club failed.
10. However, after losing 14 of 15 games, Junction dropped out of the league on July 6. *Llano News*, September 7, 1933, 1.
11. *San Antonio Light*, April 2, 1933, 47.
12. Ibid.
13. *Kerrville Daily Times*, March 30, 1933, 8.
14. *Fredericksburg Standard*, March 31, 1933, 6.
15. Approximately $4.50 in 2026 dollars.
16. *Kerrville Mountain Sun*, February 23, 1933, 1.
17. Ibid.

18. *Comfort News*, March 30, 1933, 1, 8.
19. Uecker is sometimes referred to in newspaper articles as "Johnnie." For consistency, we refer to him as "Johnny" throughout the book.
20. Holekamp was the brother-in-law of White Sox business manager Udo Harz. Holekamp married Harz's younger sister, Selma.
21. Rudy Leidl played for Comfort in 1931 when Boerne dropped out of the Hill Country League to play independently. Leidl returned to the White Sox for the 1932 season.
22. *Kerrville Mountain Sun*, March 2, 1933, 1.
23. *Comfort News*, July 14, 1932, 1; *Comfort News*, September 22, 1932, 8.
24. For more information on Faltin Field, see chapter 12.
25. *Comfort News*, April 6, 1933, 1.
26. Ibid.
27. *Kerrville Mountain Sun*, April 6, 1933, 1, 10.
28. Ibid.
29. *Kerrville Mountain Sun*, April 20, 1933, 8.
30. *Kerrville Mountain Sun*, April 27, 1933, 10. We found no box score for this game; only the score was reported in the *Kerrville Mountain Sun.*
31. *Comfort News*, May 4, 1933, 1.
32. Ibid.
33. *Kerrville Mountain Sun*, May 18, 1933, 10. We found no box score for this game; only the score was reported in the *Kerrville Mountain Sun*.
34. *San Antonio Light*, May 29, 1933, 7-A. The HCL rules apparently did not prohibit a player under professional contract from playing under these circumstances.
35. Ibid.
36. Ibid.
37. *Comfort News*, April 6, 1933, 1.
38. *Comfort News*, April 13, 1933, 1.
39. On the off day, Comfort played an exhibition game, defeating the Richter Bakery, 3–2. *Comfort News*, April 20, 1933, 1. Joe Pankratz took the mound, holding the opponents to seven hits.
40. *Kerrville Mountain Sun*, April 27, 1933, 1, 10.
41. *Comfort News*, May 4, 1933, 1.
42. Ibid.
43. *Comfort News*, April 20, 1933, 1.
44. *Comfort News*, May 11, 1933, 1.
45. Ibid.
46. *Kerrville Mountain Sun*, June 1, 1933, 10.

47. Kerrville's loss to Comfort, 3–2, on May 28 dropped them to 3–4, ahead of Boerne (3–5) and Bandera (2–5).
48. *Comfort News*, June 15, 1933, 1.
49. *Kerrville Mountain Sun*, June 8, 1933, 12.
50. *Kerrville Mountain Sun*, June 15, 1933, 10. Unfortunately, we found no box score for this abbreviated game.
51. *Comfort News*, June 15, 1933, 1.
52. *Kerrville Mountain Sun*, June 15, 1933, 1.
53. Due to rainouts, these standings were not published by a newspaper but are imputed from earlier published standings.
54. See Author's Note preceding chapter 1 regarding total run average (TRA). See also Notes on Team Statistics Compiled from Box Scores following the acknowledgments.
55. *Kerrville Mountain Sun*, June 29, 1933, 1.
56. *Fredericksburg Standard*, April 28, 1933, 6.
57. *Comfort News*, June 22, 1933, 1.
58. Ibid.
59. In addition to Comfort's 9–3 win over Boerne on June 18, Alamo Heights defeated Bandera, 6–3, on the same day. *Kerrville Daily Times*, June 22, 1933, 11. No box score was found for the latter game.
60. *Kerrville Mountain Sun*, June 29, 1933, 10.
61. *Kerrville Mountain Sun*, July 6, 1933, 1, 9.
62. Ibid. In the other game, Comfort defeated Boerne, 6–1, in an exhibition that did not count in the league standings.
63. Ibid.
64. *Comfort News*, July 13, 1933, 1.
65. Kerrville defeated the Legion Cubs, 14–2, in an exhibition game on July 23. *Kerrville Mountain Sun*, July 27, 1933, 10.
66. *Comfort News*, July 27, 1933, 1.
67. *Kerrville Mountain Sun*, August 3, 1933, 10.
68. *Comfort News*, August 2, 1933, 1.
69. *San Antonio Light*, August 7, 1933, 5-B.
70. *Comfort News*, August 17, 1933, 1.
71. *Kerrville Mountain Sun*, August 17, 1933, 10.
72. *Comfort News*, August 17, 1933, 1.
73. *Comfort News*, August 24, 1933, 1, 5.
74. *Kerrville Mountain Sun*, August 17, 1933, 1.
75. *Kerrville Mountain Sun*, August 24, 1933, 10.
76. Ibid.

77. *Kerrville Mountain Sun,* August 24, 1933, 10. On August 27, a league off day for Kerrville, Hardy and the Braves defeated the Fredericksburg Giants, 2–1, now playing independently after withdrawing from the Hill Country League. *Kerrville Mountain Sun*, August 31, 1933, 10.
78. Ibid. The *Kerrville Mountain Sun* account refers to Hardy's record as 8–1 but that included an exhibition victory over Legion on July 23. He was 7–1 at that point in league play.
79. *Kerrville Mountain Sun*, August 24, 1933, 10.
80. Ibid.
81. *Comfort News*, August 24, 1933, 1.
82. *San Antonio Light*, August 28, 1933, 5-B.
83. *Comfort News*, August 31, 1933, 1.
84. Ibid.
85. Hardy's 9–1 record cited here includes an exhibition win over Legion on July 23 and an exhibition victory over Fredericksburg, 2–1, on August 27. *Kerrville Mountain Sun*, August 31, 1933, 10. Hardy was 7–1 in league games at this point in the season.
86. *Kerrville Mountain Sun*, August 31, 1933, 1. We note that Beaumont manager Bob Coleman is likely the same Bob Coleman who played for Kerrville in 1930 and 1933. See Appendices A and D for his statistics.
87. *Kerrville Mountain Sun*, September 7, 1933, 1.
88. Ibid.
89. *Kerrville Mountain Sun*, September 14, 1933, 1, 12.
90. Ibid.
91. Ibid.
92. Ibid.
93. *Kerrville Mountain Sun*, September 14, 1933, 1, 12.
94. Ibid.
95. Ibid. See Appendix D for team and individual statistics for 1933.
96. *Kerrville Mountain Sun*, September 21, 1933, 1.
97. *Fredericksburg Standard*, September 21, 1933, 3.
98. *Kerrville Mountain Sun*, September 21, 1933, 10.
99. Ibid.
100. Ibid.
101. Ibid.
102. Ibid.
103. *Kerrville Mountain Sun*, September 21, 1933, 1.
104. *San Antonio Light*, September 28, 1933, 16.
105. Ibid.

106. Ibid.
107. Ibid.
108. *Kerrville Mountain Sun*, October 5, 1933, 1, 6.
109. Ibid., 6.
110. *San Antonio Light*, October 3, 1933, 16.
111. Hardy's ineffective outing in the first game of the series may have resulted from arm fatigue after he dominated opponents for most of the season.
112. *Kerrville Mountain Sun*, October 12, 1933, 6.
113. Ibid. The report in the *Kerrville Mountain Sun* stated that the Alamo Heights stole a "dozen bases" but the box score showed only six.
114. *San Antonio Light*, October 9, 1933, 7-A.
115. Ibid.
116. Bandera scored 58 runs in 18 games. The statistics in Appendix D reflect only games for which box scores were found.
117. To pick just one example of the team's fielding difficulties, two catchers, F. Hamilton and Zumwalt, accounted for five passed balls in a single game. *San Antonio Light*, July 24, 1933, 12.
118. Thornberry's falloff in effectiveness is reminiscent of the 1930 season when he pitched well for Kerrville in the first two months of the season, including a 15-inning tie when he struck out 28 batters, but did not pitch after June 1 in 1930.
119. *Fredericksburg Standard*, April 21, 1933, 6.
120. Ibid. Regarding Goodman, the *Fredericksburg Standard* commented that the Cowboys would "very likely have released [him] anyway since he hasn't shown anything that would warrant him as a first class starting pitcher." Ibid. Goodman may have been the high school pitcher who pitched for Junction in 1932. See chapter 8.
121. *Fredericksburg Standard*, June 15, 1933, 2.
122. *Llano News*, April 20, 1933, 1; *Llano News*, April 27, 1933, 1.
123. In Fredericksburg's 12 games, Hugo Klaerner led the team with a .464 average. Among Klaerner's 26 hits were five doubles, four triples, and two home runs for a .732 slugging percentage. *Fredericksburg Standard*, June 29, 1933, 3. Klaerner scored 17 runs and accounted for 19 RBIs. He recorded a 7–3 mark on the mound. Ibid.
124. *Fredericksburg Standard*, June 15, 1933, 2.
125. *Fredericksburg Standard*, July 7, 1933, 3.
126. Ibid.
127. *Fredericksburg Standard*, September 7, 1933, 3.
128. *Fredericksburg Standard*, September 28, 1933, 3.

129. Ibid. Hugo Klaerner played for the Giants after he ended his minor league season with Waco/Pine Bluff. He also pitched for Llano in the 1933 HCL championship series. See chapter 10.
130. *Llano News*, September 7, 1933, 1.
131. Ibid.
132. *Fredericksburg Standard*, April 28, 1933, 6.
133. *Llano News*, June 29, 1933, 1.
134. *Llano News*, September 7, 1933, 1.
135. Ibid.
136. *Fredericksburg Standard*, September 21, 1933, 3.
137. Ibid. We found no newspaper report on the outcome of the scheduled series between Llano and the Texon Oilers.

CHAPTER 11

1. Cranes Mill no longer exists. Its location is now under Canyon Lake, which was created by a dam the construction of which was completed in 1964. KSAT.com, February 18, 2019, updated October 21, 2021, accessed December 31, 2024, https://www.ksat.com/news/2019/02/18/under-canyon-lake-how-cranes-mill-and-the-original-hancock-got-erased-from-the-map/.
2. *San Antonio Light*, May 29, 1933, 7-A.
3. In 1936, Suche had a combined 6–12 record with a 6.01 ERA pitching for New Orleans (Southern Association) and Zanesville (Middle Atlantic League). In 1937, Suche fashioned a combined 3–7 mark for Fargo-Moorhead and Montgomery (Southeastern League). "Charley Suche," Baseball Reference.com-Minor League Statistics, accessed December 10, 2024, https://www, abaseball-reference.com/register/player.fcgi?id=suche-001cha.
4. "Charley Suche," Baseball-Reference.com-Minor League Statistics, accessed December 10, 2024, https://www.baseball-reference.com/register/player.fcgi?id=suche-001cha; "Charley Suche," Baseball-Reference.com-Major League Statistics and Information, accessed December 10, 2024, https://www.baseball-reference.com/players/s/suchech01.shtml.
5. *Philadelphia Inquirer*, September 19, 1938, 17, 19.
6. Ibid.
7. Baseball-reference.com, Philadelphia Athletics vs. Cleveland Indians Box Score, September 18, 1938, accessed January 3, 2025, https://www.baseball-reference.com/boxes/CLE/CLE193809182.shtmlid.

8. Ibid.
9. Ibid.
10. Baseball-reference.com, Philadelphia Athletics vs. Cleveland Indians Box Score, September 18, 1938, accessed January 3, 2025, https://www.baseball-reference.com/boxes/CLE/CLE193809182.shtmlid.
11. *Philadelphia Inquirer*, September 19, 1938, 17, 19.
12. Ibid.
13. "Charley Suche," Baseball-Reference.com-Minor League Statistics, accessed January 3, 2025, https://www.baseball-reference.com/register/player.fcgi?id=suche-001cha.
14. Ibid.
15. Ibid.
16. "Charley Suche," Baseball-Reference.com-B-R Bullpen, accessed January 3, 2025, https://www.baseball-reference.com/bullpen/Charley_Suche.
17. United States Seventeenth Census, 1950, National Archives, Washington, DC, accessed December 10, 2024, https://1950census.archives.gov/search/?county=Bandera&name=Suche&page=1&state=TX.
18. "Charley Suche," Baseball-Reference.com-B-R Bullpen, accessed January 3, 2025, https://www.baseball-reference.com/bullpen/Charley_Suche.

CHAPTER 12

1. Philip J. Lowry, *Green Cathedrals: The Ultimate Celebration of All 271 Major League and Negro League Ballparks* (Reading, MA: Addison-Wesley Pub. Co., 1992). The book describes every ballpark used for a major league (including Negro League games), adding wonderful anecdotes and arcane facts to boot.
2. This conclusion is supported by a note in the Dietert Historical Archives of the Patrick Heath Public Library in Boerne. The note contains the recollections of Louis Bourgeois, who states that the White Sox played on the "high school grounds" before moving to the Kendall County Fairgrounds. The site at North School Street and Johns Road is the former location of Boerne High School.
3. *Fredericksburg Standard*, May 31, 1934, 3.
4. Joe Herring Jr., *Kerrville Stories: Historic Photographs and Newspaper Columns* (Kerrville, TX: Herring Printing Company, 2012), 140.
5. *Fredericksburg Standard*, September 5, 1935, 2. Despite this comment, Faltin Field did in fact host one of the games in the 1935 championship series. See chapter 15.

6. Joe Herring Jr. Blog, August 6, 2017, accessed December 21, 2024, https://joeherringjr.blogspot.com/2017/08/kerrvilles-west-texas-fair.html. See chapter 18 regarding Kerrville's Black team.
7. Ibid.
8. *Kerrville Mountain Sun*, February 21, 1924, 1.
9. Ibid.
10. *Kerrville Mountain Sun*, July 19, 1923, 1.
11. *Kerrville Mountain Sun*, January 29, 1925, 1.
12. *Kerrville Mountain Sun*, March 19, 1925, 1. While most of the stands were new, the grandstand from the old ballpark at Broadway and G Avenue was moved to the new ballpark for use as the "colored grandstand."
13. *Kerrville Mountain Sun*, March 19, 1925, 1.
14. *Kerrville Mountain Sun*, April 9, 1925, 1.
15. Ibid.
16. See chapter 4 for more information on this game.
17. *Kerrville Mountain Sun*, May 6, 1937, 1. The warehouse was designed to hold two million pounds of wool.
18. Interview of Clifton Fifer Jr., son of player and manager, Clifton Fifer Sr., December 4, 2023 (interview notes in possession of author).
19. See chapter 15 on the 1935 season for more information on the Legion Cubs and their home diamond.
20. *Llano News*, April 7, 2010, 7.
21. Ibid.
22. Ibid.
23. Ibid.
24. *Llano News*, April 7, 2010, 7.
25. Ibid.

CHAPTER 13

1. *Kerrville Mountain Sun*, March 8, 1934, 1.
2. Ibid.
3. On March 7, 1934, Huntsville prison officers thwarted an escape attempt by five prisoners. One of the prisoners, Roy Thornton, was motivated to escape because he was "crazy" about Bonnie Parker, to whom he was married at the time. *Fredericksburg Standard*, March 8, 1934, 8. Several months later, Bonnie and Clyde were killed after Texas Ranger Frank Hamer laid a trap for them in rural Louisiana, ending their murderous spree, which ranged from Missouri to Louisiana.

4. *Fredericksburg Standard*, February 8, 1934, 1, 2.
5. Ibid.
6. Ibid.
7. Ibid.
8. *Fredericksburg Standard*, April 5, 1934, 1.
9. *Fredericksburg Standard*, March 15, 1934, 1, 2.
10. *San Antonio Express*, April 3, 1934, 9.
11. *Fredericksburg Standard*, February 1, 1934, 2.
12. Ibid., 1.
13. *Fredericksburg Standard*, March 8, 1934, 3. Hondo is located 30 miles south of Bandera. Based on cursory research on the etymology of "broncho" and "bronco," the terms are interchangeable although "broncho" appears to be the English version of the Spanish word, "bronco."
14. Ibid.
15. Chicago assigned Klaerner to its minor league affiliate, the Waco Cubs/ Pine Bluff Judges, where he starred in 1933. He returned to the Judges in 1934. See chapter 14 for more on Hugo Klaerner.
16. Alfons was occasionally referred to as "Elmer," perhaps after Elmer Fudd, the Warner Brothers cartoon character. *Fredericksburg Standard*, June 27, 1935, 2.
17. *Fredericksburg Standard*, March 22, 1934, 4.
18. *Boerne Star*, September 24, 1964, 6.
19. The fact that Wootton, Jess Hollimon, and Clergy Hollimon played for Legion in 1934 is confirmed by the box score for an exhibition game between Legion and Kerrville on April 22. *Kerrville Mountain Sun*, April 26, 1934, 7.
20. The young pitcher's age was initially given as 17, but it was later reported that Toler was only 15 years old. *Fredericksburg Standard*, April 19, 1934, 3.
21. *Kerrville Mountain Sun*, April 12, 1934, 10.
22. Arthur Bergmann and Harry Bergmann were second cousins to Edgar and Walter Bergmann of the Boerne White Sox—all descended from their great-grandfather, Christian Bergmann (1817–88) who brought his family from Germany to Texas in 1854. See chapter 16 for more on the Bergmann family. Christian's son Carl was the grandfather of Edgar and Walter Bergmann. Christian's son Christoph was the grandfather of Arthur and Harry Bergmann.
23. *Fredericksburg Standard*, April 5, 1934, 1, 8.
24. *Fredericksburg Standard*, May 10, 1934, 1, 5.

25. *Fredericksburg Standard,* May 17, 1934, 1, 2.
26. *Comfort News,* May 17, 1934, 1.
27. Ibid.
28. *Fredericksburg Standard,* May 24, 1934, 3.
29. Ibid.
30. *Kerrville Mountain Sun,* May 24, 1934, 1, 12.
31. Fisher's last name may have been spelled Fischer.
32. *Kerrville Mountain Sun,* May 31, 1934, 10.
33. Ibid.
34. *Fredericksburg Standard,* June 14, 1934, 3.
35. *Comfort News,* June 7, 1934, 1.
36. *Fredericksburg Standard,* May 31, 1934, 3.
37. Ibid.
38. *Fredericksburg Standard,* June 7, 1934, 3.
39. Ibid.
40. Ibid.
41. *Fredericksburg Standard,* July 5, 1934, 3.
42. *Fredericksburg Standard,* July 12, 1934, 5.
43. *Kerrville Mountain Sun,* July 12, 1934, 12.
44. *Comfort News,* June 21, 1934, 1.
45. *Fredericksburg Standard,* July 19, 1934, 1.
46. Ibid.,1, 3.
47. The box score does not give Pfeiffer errors on the two misplays, but the article in the *Fredericksburg Standard* on July 19, 1934, reported that the plays should have been made.
48. Ibid.
49. *Kerrville Mountain Sun,* July 19, 1934, 1.
50. Ibid.
51. *Kerrville Mountain Sun,* July 26, 1934, 1, 10.
52. *Fredericksburg Standard,* July 26, 1934, 1, 2.
53. *Fredericksburg Standard,* August 2, 1934, 3.
54. *Fredericksburg Standard,* August 9, 1934, 3.
55. Ibid.
56. *San Antonio Express,* August 8, 1934, 10.
57. It is not clear why Boerne played only 15 of the 16 scheduled games but it appears that the games scheduled for the final Sunday of the season on August 12 were cancelled. The scheduled games (Bandera at Comfort and Boerne at Kerrville) could not affect Boerne's second-place finish so perhaps the league decided to proceed directly to the championship

series between Fredericksburg and Boerne without playing these final games. This is suggested by the fact that the first postseason game between Fredericksburg and Boerne was played on August 12 rather than August 19 as originally scheduled. This also explains why Comfort, Bandera, and Kerrville ended the season with less than 16 games played. See Appendix E for team and individual statistics for 1934.

58. *Fredericksburg Standard*, August 9, 1934, 3. The standings published in the *Fredericksburg Standard* show Comfort with a 7–7 record but based on a review of each game, Comfort's actual season record was 6–8. The standings do not balance (total wins equal to total losses) with a 7–7 record for Comfort.
59. *Fredericksburg Standard*, August 2, 1934, 3.
60. It is likely that "Deike" was either Levi Deike or Marvin Deike of the famous all-brother Deike team from Hye.
61. *Fredericksburg Standard*, August 16, 1934, 2.
62. Ibid.
63. Ibid.
64. *Fredericksburg Standard*, August 23, 1934, 1.
65. Ibid., 1, 2.
66. *Fredericksburg Standard*, August 30, 1934, 1, 3.
67. Ibid. The Farmer Boys League, which consisted of teams from rural communities near Fredericksburg, included teams from Luckenbach, Cain City, Meusebach, Stonewall, Gold, and Grapetown. *Fredericksburg Standard*, May 23, 1933, 2. Sisterdale in Kendall County played in the league in 1934. *Fredericksburg Standard*, June 14, 1934, 3. A similar league of smaller towns, the Granite League, played in 1933 with teams in Burnet, Johnson City, Blanco, Marble Falls, Dripping Springs, and Kingsland. *Fredericksburg Standard*, June 15, 1933, 2.
68. Ibid.
69. *Fredericksburg Standard*, August 30, 1934, 3.
70. Ibid. Handwritten records at the Pioneer Museum in Fredericksburg indicate that Felix Saenger managed the Giants from 1924 to 1937. His obituary states that he managed the club from 1924 to 1939. *Fredericksburg Standard*, September 22, 1976, 1, 4. However, Saenger's tenure as manager was interrupted by player-manager Al Hollmig in 1930 and player-manager Andy Andrews, who took over after Saenger resigned midway through the 1935 season. See chapter 15 regarding the 1935 season.
71. See Author's Note regarding total run average (TRA). See also Notes on Team Statistics Compiled from Box Scores.

72. *Fredericksburg Standard*, March 29, 1934, 3.
73. The eight clubs were Llano, Bend, Richland Springs, Goldthwaite, Pontotoc, San Saba, Brady and Menard.
74. Richland Springs is located 15 miles northwest of San Saba.
75. *Llano News*, August 23, 1934, 1.
76. Ibid.
77. *Llano News*, September 13, 1934, 1.
78. *Llano News*, August 23, 1934, 1.
79. Ibid.
80. *Brady Standard*, October 23, 1934, 1; *Fredericksburg Radio Post*, October 26, 1934, 1; *Fredericksburg Standard*, October 25, 1934, 1.
81. Ibid.
82. *The Sporting News*, November 12, 1931, 6.
83. As stated in an endnote in chapter 8, we could find no record of Sanders appearing for Springfield in the 1932 season. An obituary for Sanders noted that he pitched for Tyler in the East Texas League, but we could find no record of him playing for Tyler. The Tyler Trojans played in the East Texas League in the late 1920s and briefly in 1931. His obituary also noted that Sanders had a tryout with Houston of the Texas League.
84. *Fredericksburg Standard*, April 5, 1934, 8.
85. See Appendix G for the 1934 Hill Country League standings.
86. *Brady Standard*, May 8, 1934, 1.
87. *Brady Standard*, May 15, 1934, 1, 4.
88. *Llano News*, July 12, 1934, 1.
89. *Llano News*, August 16, 1934, 1.
90. Pontotoc lost the last game of the season to Richland Springs, 8–4, on August 19. *Llano News*, August 23, 1934, 1. Since no box score could be found, we could not determine if Sanders pitched in that game.

CHAPTER 14

1. *Fredericksburg Radio Post*, October 22, 1978, 9-A.
2. *Fredericksburg Standard*, October 17, 1930, 7.
3. *Kerrville Mountain Sun*, April 2, 1931, 1.
4. *Fredericksburg Standard*, October 2, 1931, 1.
5. "Hugo Klaerner," Baseball-Reference.com-Minor League Statistics, accessed December 17, 2024, https://www.baseball-reference.com/register/player.fcgi?id=klaern001hug.
6. *Fredericksburg Standard*, September 21, 1933, 3. See chapter 10.

7. *Fredericksburg Standard*, March 8, 1934, 3.
8. "Hugo Klaerner," Baseball-Reference.com-Minor League Statistics, accessed December 17, 2024, https://www.baseball-reference.com/register/player.fcgi?id=klaern001hug.
9. *Chicago Tribune*, September 11, 1934, 19.
10. *Chicago Tribune*, September 18, 1934, 23.
11. *Chicago Tribune*, September 23, 1934, 25.
12. "Hugo Klaerner," Baseball-Reference.com-Major League Statistics and Information.com, accessed December 10, 2024, https://www.baseball-reference.com/players/k/klaerhu01.shtml.
13. *Fredericksburg Standard*, August 22, 1935, 2.
14. *The Sporting News*, January 16, 1936, 6.
15. "Hugo Klaerner," Baseball-Reference.com-Minor League Statistics, accessed December 10, 2024, https://www.baseball-reference.com/register/player.fcgi?id=klaern001hug.
16. *Harper Herald*, February 12, 1982, 2.
17. Alfred's nickname was "Smokey." Chester Klaerner, brother of Hugo and Alfred's son, was also known as "Smokey." Alfred's nickname may have derived from his position of county sheriff, while Chester's likely had more to do with his fastball.
18. *Fredericksburg, Texas: The Second Fifty Years*, 53.
19. *Harper Herald*, February 12, 1982, 2, 5.
20. *Fredericksburg, Texas: The Second Fifty Years*, 53.
21. *Fredericksburg Standard*, September 29, 1971, 1, 3.
22. *Harper Herald*, February 12, 1982, 2, 5.
23. Ibid.
24. Ibid.
25. Ibid.
26. Ibid.
27. Ibid.

CHAPTER 15

1. *Comfort News*, January 24, 1935, 1.
2. *Kerrville Mountain Sun*, January 10, 1935, 1.
3. *Kerrville Mountain Sun*, January 17, 1935, 1.
4. *Fredericksburg Standard*, January 24, 1935, 1, 3; *Comfort News*, January 24, 1935, 8. The Nimitz Hotel was originally built and operated by Charles Nimitz Sr., grandfather of Admiral Chester W. Nimitz, the commander

in chief of the US Pacific Fleet in World War II. Today the site of the former hotel is home to the Pacific War Museum. A statue of Chester Nimitz stands outside the museum.

5. *Fredericksburg Standard*, January 24, 1935, 1, 3. Luther served as ambassador to the United States until 1937.
6. See chapter 1 for discussion of the "Massacre on the Nueces."
7. *Comfort News*, January 24, 1935, 8.
8. *Fredericksburg Standard*, April 11, 1935, 2.
9. Ibid.
10. Rebecca J. Herring, "Legion, TX," *Handbook of Texas Online*, accessed April 7, 2024, https://www.tshaonline.org/handbook/entries/legion-tx.
11. Ibid.
12. Ibid.
13. *Kerrville Mountain Sun*, April 25, 1933, 10.
14. *Kerrville Mountain Sun*, April 11, 1935, 1.
15. *Fredericksburg Standard*, August 29, 1935, 2.
16. *Fredericksburg Standard*, April 18, 1935, 2.
17. It is unknown if Perry Winkle was the columnist's actual name or a play on the word "periwinkle" as his nom de plume.
18. *San Antonio News*, April 1, 1935, 10. We note that it is unlikely that Clarence Holekamp had been managing the White Sox since 1923. Holekamp was born in 1905 so he would have been only 18 years old in 1923, younger than most players on the roster. Moreover, Ed Kaiser was known as the White Sox manager in the 1920s.
19. Chester fashioned an 18–9 record and 3.94 ERA in 27 starts for the Tyler Trojans of the Class C West Dixie League in 1935. Stats Crew, 1935 Tyler Trojans Statistics, accessed January 4, 2025, https://www.statscrew.com/minorbaseball/stats/t-tt15084/y-1935. In 1936, Chester went 15–9 in 225 innings with the Longview Cannibals of the Class C East Texas League, but his ERA rose to 5.03. Baseball-Reference.com, 1936 Longview Cannibals, accessed January 4, 2025, https://www.baseball-reference.com/register/team.cgi?id=111f2623. Chester was promoted to the Class A-1 Dallas Steers in 1936, but he went 0–3 in 25 innings with a 6.48 ERA. Baseball-Reference.com, 1936 Dallas Steers, accessed January 4, 2025, https://www.baseball-reference.com/register/team.cgi?id=f7f3e1f0.
20. *San Antonio News*, April 1, 1935, 10.
21. Ibid.
22. *San Antonio News*, April 9, 1935, 15.
23. The extra-base hits cited for Elias Klaerner are not correct. Based on box

scores of 15 of the 16 Mountain League games in 1934, Elias Klaerner had just nine extra-base hits in 1934. See Appendix E. In addition, there is some variation between the statistics listed here by Perry Winkle for other Giants and the compiled statistics in Appendix E. It is likely, however, that the statistics cited by Winkle include the Giants' two games in the championship series in addition to the 16 regular season games. The statistics compiled in Appendix E reflect only the 15 of 16 regular season games for which box scores are available.

24. The reference to "Alford Klaerner" presumably refers to Alfons Klaerner, younger brother of Hugo and Chester Klaerner.
25. *San Antonio News*, April 9, 1935, 15.
26. *San Antonio News*, April 13, 1935, 8.
27. Nagel hit .339 for Comfort in 1933 but for unknown reasons, he batted only four times in 1934.
28. *Kerrville Mountain Sun*, February 28, 1935, 1; *Kerrville Mountain Sun*, March 7, 1935, 1.
29. *Kerrville Mountain Sun*, March 28, 1935, 10. Esbeck formerly played with Brady in the Hill Country League. In the *Kerrville Mountain Sun* article, his name is misspelled as "Espect."
30. Ibid.
31. Infielder C. Gray on Kerrville and pitcher Charlie Gray on Bandera are two separate players since both played for their respective teams on the same day. It is unknown if they were related.
32. *Kerrville Mountain Sun*, April 18, 1935, 1, 10.
33. *Kerrville Mountain Sun*, April 25, 1935, 1, 10.
34. *Comfort News*, May 2, 1935, 1.
35. *Fredericksburg Standard*, April 18, 1935, 1, 2.
36. *Fredericksburg Standard*, April 25, 1935, 1, 2.
37. *Fredericksburg Standard*, May 2, 1935, 1, 2.
38. *San Antonio Evening News*, May 11, 1935, 8.
39. *Fredericksburg Standard*, May 16, 1935, 1, 2.
40. *Fredericksburg Standard*, May 23, 1935, 1, 2.
41. *San Antonio Express*, April 30, 1935, 13.
42. *Fredericksburg Standard*, May 30, 1935, 1, 2.
43. *Kerrville Mountain Sun*, May 30, 1935, 1, 12.
44. *Fredericksburg Standard*, May 30, 1935, 1, 2.
45. Ibid.
46. *Fredericksburg Standard*, June 13, 1935, 2.
47. *Kerrville Mountain Sun*, June 6, 1935, 1, 10.

48. *Kerrville Mountain Sun*, May 9, 1935, 10.
49. *Kerrville Mountain Sun*, June 6, 1935, 10.
50. *Kerrville Mountain Sun*, May 23, 1935, 1, 10.
51. *Kerrville Mountain Sun*, May 30, 1935, 1, 12.
52. *Kerrville Mountain Sun*, June 6, 1935, 1, 10.
53. *Kerrville Mountain Sun*, May 16, 1935, 1, 10.
54. *Kerrville Mountain Sun*, May 23, 1935, 1, 10.
55. *Kerrville Mountain Sun*, May 30, 1935, 1, 12.
56. *Kerrville Mountain Sun*, June 6, 1935, 1, 10.
57. Ibid.
58. *Fredericksburg News*, June 13, 1935, 2.
59. *San Antonio Express*, June 18, 1935, 10.
60. *San Antonio Express*, June 25, 1935, 12.
61. *Kerrville Mountain Sun*, July 4, 1935, 10.
62. *Fredericksburg Standard*, June 13, 1935, 1, 2.
63. *Fredericksburg Standard*, June 20, 1935, 1, 2.
64. *Fredericksburg Standard*, June 27, 1935, 1, 2.
65. *Fredericksburg Standard*, July 4, 1935, 1, 2.
66. *Kerrville Mountain Sun*, June 13, 1935, 10.
67. *Kerrville Mountain Sun*, June 20, 1935, 1, 10.
68. *Kerrville Mountain Sun*, June 27, 1935, 12.
69. *Kerrville Mountain Sun*, July 4, 1935, 10.
70. *Fredericksburg Standard*, July 4, 1935, 2.
71. *Fredericksburg Standard*, July 11, 1935, 1, 2.
72. *Comfort News*, July 11, 1935, 1.
73. Ibid.
74. *Kerrville Mountain Sun*, July 18, 1935, 10.
75. It is not clear why the umpires ruled the batter-runner out at first. It may have been that after the batted ball struck the runner, the ball caromed to the second baseman, who threw to first base and beat the batter-runner to the bag. If so, the umpires were wrong to rule the runner out at first. When the ball struck the runner, the ball was dead. The batter-runner should have been awarded first base on the runner's interference.
76. *Fredericksburg Standard*, July 18, 1935, 2.
77. *Kerrville Mountain Sun*, July 18, 1935, 10. The *Fredericksburg Standard* reported the meeting as occurring on Thursday, July 11. *Fredericksburg Standard*, July 18, 1935, 2.
78. *Kerrville Mountain Sun*, July 18, 1935, 10.
79. *Fredericksburg Standard*, July 18, 1935, 2.

80. Ibid.
81. *Kerrville Mountain Sun*, July 18, 1935, 10.
82. Ibid.
83. *Fredericksburg Standard*, July 18, 1935, 2.
84. Ibid.
85. *San Antonio Evening News*, July 17, 1935, 14.
86. *Fredericksburg Standard*, July 18, 2.
87. Ibid.
88. Another significant consequence of Boerne's withdrawal was that it created holes in the league schedule. For example, instead of meeting Boerne on July 21 and July 28, Fredericksburg would be idle on those dates unless they found non-league opponents to play. The Giants did in fact find opponents on those dates, Bear Creek on July 21 and the Dittlinger Millers of New Braunfels on July 28. The Giants lost the latter game to the Millers, 6–5. *Fredericksburg Standard*, August 1, 1935, 1, 2.
89. *Kerrville Mountain Sun*, July 25, 1935, 1, 10.
90. *Kerrville Mountain Sun*, August 1, 1935, 1, 10.
91. *Comfort News*, July 25, 1935, 1.
92. *Bandera New Era*, August 1, 1935, 1.
93. *Fredericksburg Standard*, August 8, 1935, 1, 2.
94. *Fredericksburg Standard*, August 15, 1935, 1, 2.
95. Ibid.
96. *Kerrville Mountain Sun*, August 8, 1935, 10.
97. *Kerrville Mountain Sun*, August 15, 1935, 10.
98. *Kerrville Mountain Sun*, August 22, 1935, 10.
99. *Kerrville Mountain* Sun, August 22, 1935, 10. The *Kerrville Mountain Sun* reported that Comfort was 10–8 while Legion was 9–7, creating a virtual tie. However, Comfort's record was 10–8 only if the loss to Boerne on July 7 and Boerne's forfeit on July 14 were counted in the standings. In addition, Legion's record was 9–7 only if its two losses to Boerne on June 30 and July 7 did *not* count. Since the league did not count the Boerne games, Comfort and Legion were both 9–7, contrary to the report in the *Kerrville Mountain Sun*. After Legion defeated Comfort, 18–4, on August 25, the *Fredericksburg Standard* correctly reported that Legion had finished second, one game ahead of Comfort. *Fredericksburg Standard*, August 29, 1935, 2. Legion ended 10–7 and Comfort finished 9–8.
100. In box scores, the player's name is sometimes listed as "Woods" and other times as "Wood."
101. *Kerrville Mountain Sun*, August 29, 1935, 1, 5.

102. *Fredericksburg Standard*, August 22, 1935, 2.
103. *Fredericksburg Standard*, August 29, 1935, 2.
104. *Kerrville Mountain Sun*, July 11, 1935, 1, 10.
105. *Kerrville Mountain Sun*, July 18, 1935, 10.
106. *Bandera New Era*, August 1, 1935, 1.
107. The author found no published final standings. As a result, these standings are imputed from prior standings and game results recounted in various newspaper accounts. See Appendix F for team and individual statistics for 1935.
108. *Kerrville Mountain Sun*, September 5, 1935, 1, 10. Legion's decision to play at Kerrville's ballpark rather than the grounds of the VA Hospital may have been influenced by the fact that VA regulations prohibited admission fees. If the game were held on the VA grounds, revenues could be generated only by voluntary donations. See chapter 12.
109. *Kerrville Mountain Sun*, September 5, 1935, 10.
110. Ibid., 1, 10.
111. *Fredericksburg Standard*, September 5, 1935, 1, 2.
112. Ibid.
113. *Fredericksburg Standard*, September 12, 1935, 1, 2.
114. *Fredericksburg Standard*, September 19, 1935, 1, 2.
115. Ibid.
116. *Fredericksburg Standard*, September 26, 1935, 1, 2.
117. Since the eighth inning was not completed, the game reverted to the end of the seventh inning as the official game.
118. *Fredericksburg Standard*, September 26, 1935, 1, 2.
119. Ibid.
120. Ibid.
121. *Fredericksburg Standard*, October 3, 1935, 2.
122. *Fredericksburg Standard*, October 10, 1935, 2.
123. Ibid.
124. See Appendix F for the full statistics of the Giants in 1935.
125. Archer's 6–0 record is based on games for which box scores exist. However, even some of those box scores do not provide complete information, leaving some statistics incomplete.
126. For unknown reasons, Archer did not play in the Mountain League in 1934. Archer pitched for Kerrville in 1931 and for Brady in 1932 in the Hill Country League. In 1933, Archer pitched for Kerrville and Comfort in the Mountain League before pitching for Legion in 1935.
127. *Kerrville Mountain Sun*, July 18, 1935, 10.

128. *Bandera New Era*, August 1, 1935, 1.
129. *San Antonio News*, July 23, 1935, 16.
130. *San Antonio Express*, July 22, 1935, 7.
131. *San Antonio News*, August 13, 1935, 12.
132. *San Antonio News*, August 20, 1935, 17.
133. *San Antonio Light*, September 3, 1935, 12-A.
134. *San Antonio Express*, September 24, 1935, 9.
135. See Appendix F for the statistics of the White Sox in Mountain League play before their withdrawal. The statistics do not include games played independently after the White Sox withdrawal from the league.
136. Brownwood, Llano, Lometa, Marble Falls, Richland Springs, and San Saba began the 1935 season in the HCL. Brownwood, Lometa, and Marble Falls replaced Pontotoc, Bend, and Goldthwaite from the 1934 campaign. Halfway through the 1935 season, Brady replaced Marble Falls.
137. *Llano News*, June 13, 1935, 1; *Llano News*, August 22, 1935, 1. For unknown reasons, only a few of the players from the 1931–33 HCL championship teams were still playing for the Cowboys in 1935. Llano defeated Richland Springs in the opening game of the season, 16–8, then proceeded to lose 17 of its next 18 games. *Llano News*, April 11, 1935, 1.
138. Ibid.
139. *Llano News*, August 22, 1935, 5.
140. *Llano News*, September 26, 1935, 1. Former Mason and Kerrville star pitcher Harvey Hardy pitched for Richland Springs in 1935, winning the fourth game of the championship series, 3–1, in "one of the best pitched games of his career." *Llano News*, September 19, 1935, 1. Apparently, Hardy failed to stick in his minor league stint with the Beaumont Exporters of the Texas League in 1934.

CHAPTER 16

1. *Founding Families: Christian Friedrich Bergmann and Johanna Dressler Bergmann* (Boerne, TX: Genealogical Society of Kendall County, 2013), 11:7–8 (this work is compiled and maintained by the Genealogical Society of Kendall County, Boerne, Texas). Interestingly, Christian Bergmann supported the Union in the Civil War, hiding Confederate deserters on his land. Many of the deserters were sons of German families who were conscripted into joining the Confederate Army. *Fifty First Families of Kendall County, Texas* (Boerne, TX: Genealogical Society of Kendall County, 2023), 2:17.

2. Bergman's record is based on available box scores as noted in the appendices. Box scores were not available for all games. See Appendices D through F for 1933–35 statistics.
3. *San Antonio Express*, August 12, 1940, 9.
4. Perry, *Historic Images of Boerne and Kendall County, Texas*, 184.
5. Ibid.
6. *Boerne Star*, July 19, 1951, 1.
7. Perry, *Historic Images of Boerne and Kendall County, Texas*, 184.
8. Ibid.
9. Perry, *Historic Images of Boerne and Kendall County, Texas*, 90.
10. Ibid. For more on H. O. Adler, see chapter 9.
11. The former Boerne Public Library is now the Patrick Heath Public Library.

CHAPTER 17

1. *Kerrville Mountain Sun*, February 20, 1936, 1.
2. Ibid.
3. *Fredericksburg Standard*, March 5, 1936, 2.
4. Ibid.
5. Ibid.
6. *Fredericksburg Standard*, March 26, 1936, 2.
7. *Fredericksburg Standard*, April 16, 1936, 2.
8. *San Antonio Evening News*, March 27, 1936, 27.
9. Ibid.
10. *San Antonio Evening News*, March 14, 1936, 20.
11. Ibid.
12. *Comfort News*, May 7, 1936, 8. The box score lists only "Bergmann" as the White Sox pitcher. Since Walter Bergmann was now starting regularly for Boerne, we have presumed that "Bergmann" in this game refers to Walter Bergmann, not his brother Edgar Bergmann.
13. *Comfort News*, May 14, 1936, 1.
14. The Seguin Pale Hose may have been known as the Seguin White Sox. If so, the *Comfort News* denoted Seguin as the Pale Hose to distinguish them from their opponent that day, the Boerne White Sox.
15. *Comfort News*, May 21, 1936, 1.
16. *San Antonio Express*, July 21, 1936, 11.
17. *Fredericksburg Standard*, July 9, 1936, 1, 2.
18. *Fredericksburg Standard*, September 3, 1936, 2.
19. *Kerrville Daily Times*, March 26, 1936, 1.

20. Ibid.
21. *Fredericksburg Standard*, August 13, 1936, 8.
22. *Fredericksburg Standard*, August 20, 1936, 8.
23. *Bandera New Era*, April 16, 1936, 1.
24. A list of former Giants players on file at the Pioneer Museum in Fredericksburg lists Walter Pfeil and Clarence Pfeil. Thus, it is likely that "Pfeil" is either Walter or Clarence Pfeil.
25. *Fredericksburg Standard*, August 27, 1936, 10.
26. The player listed as "Pankratz" in several box scores played third base. Since third base was Skeeter Pankratz's primary position in 1935, it is likely that this was Skeeter Pankratz rather than his brother, Joe Pankratz, although Joe Pankratz played on the infield (mostly shortstop) as well.
27. *Fredericksburg Standard*, August 27, 1936, 10.
28. *Llano News*, August 20, 1936, 1.
29. *San Antonio Express*, August 25, 1936, 8.
30. Ibid; *Llano News*, August 20, 1936, 1.
31. Ibid. Three teams failed to finish the HCL season: Mason (4–8), Lampasas (2–7), and Legion (1–9).
32. *Llano News*, August 27, 1936, 1.
33. *Fredericksburg Standard*, September 3, 1936, 2; *Llano News*, August 27, 1936, 1. The *Llano News* listed the score of the first game in the Brady-Richland Springs series as both 7–0 and 7–3.
34. "Pfeil" is likely either Walter Pfeil or Clarence Pfeil. See the prior endnote in this chapter regarding the player named "Pfeil."
35. *Fredericksburg Standard*, September 10, 1936, 2.
36. *Fredericksburg Standard*, September 17, 1936, 2.
37. *Fredericksburg Standard*, March 11, 1937, 3.
38. Ibid.
39. Ibid.; *Fredericksburg Standard*, April 15, 1937, 3.
40. The league's other division, the Southern Division, consisted of four teams: Luling, Seguin, Gonzales, and Yoakum. *Fredericksburg Standard*, April 22, 1937, 3. Later in 1937, it appears that another division was added, the Western Division, consisting of four teams: Alamo Heights, San Antonio Rangers, Lakeview, and Macdona. *Fredericksburg Standard*, August 5, 1937, 3.
41. *Fredericksburg Standard*, April 8, 1937, 1, 3. Perry Winkle's team, the San Antonio Rangers, dropped out of the Northern Division after one game and was replaced by the Pearsall Rangers for the remainder of the season. *Fredericksburg Standard*, April 22, 1937, 3.

42. *Fredericksburg Standard*, April 8, 1937, 1, 3. The Hondo Bronchos and the D'Hanis Pirates competed as separate teams in the Highway 90 League in 1934. The Bronchos were managed by former Fredericksburg player Al Hollmig. *Fredericksburg Standard*, August 30, 1934, 3.
43. *Fredericksburg Standard*, April 1, 1937, 3.
44. Former Comfort third baseman Skeeter Pankratz, brother of Joe Pankratz, also played for the Giants in 1937, but he had joined the club in 1936.
45. *Fredericksburg Standard*, July 29, 1937, 3.
46. *Fredericksburg Standard*, August 5, 1937, 3.
47. *Fredericksburg Standard*, July 29, 1937, 3.
48. Ibid.
49. *Fredericksburg Standard*, August 12, 1937, 1, 3.
50. *Fredericksburg Standard*, August 14, 1941, 7.
51. *Fredericksburg Standard*, August 24, 1949, 7; *Boerne Star*, July 23, 1953, 5. In 1952 and 1953, Boerne and Comfort also fielded teams in the Farmer Boys League. In 1952, the Farmer Boys League consisted of teams in Boerne, Comfort, Sisterdale, Enderlin, Harper, Stonewall, Doss, and Center Point. *Harper Herald*, March 28, 1952, 4. In 1953, Medina and Albert replaced Stonewall and Center Point while the other teams remained the same. *Harper Herald*, April 3, 1953, 4.
52. *Fredericksburg Standard*, July 10, 1963, 7. See chapter 18 for more on the Kerrville Black team.
53. *Fredericksburg Standard*, July 6, 1966, 6.
54. *Fredericksburg Standard*, May 24, 1967, 6.
55. *Fredericksburg Standard*, July 31, 1963, 7. The Fredericksburg Cubs played in the Cosmopolitan League in 1966 and the Metropolitan League in 1967.

CHAPTER 18

1. T. R. Fehrenbach, *Lone Star: A History of Texas and the Texans* (New York: Da Capo Press, 2000), 680.
2. Ibid., 681.
3. Alwyn Barr, *Black Texans: A History of African Americans in Texas, 1528–1995* (Norman: University of Oklahoma Press, 1995), 136.
4. Ibid., 137.
5. Tom Odzer, "Rube Foster," SABR Baseball Biography Project, accessed July 7, 2024, https://sabr.org/bioproj/person/andrew-rube-foster/.
6. Ibid.
7. "Joe Williams," Baseball-Reference.com-Major League Statistics and

Information, accessed July 7, 2024, https://www.baseball-reference.com/players/w/willijo99.shtml.

8. Mackey's birthplace is not definite. Some historians believe he was born in Eagle Pass, Texas, but Mackey's World War I and II draft registrations list Caldwell County (near Luling) as his birthplace. Either way, Mackey was born in Texas. Chris Rainey, "Biz Mackey," SABR Baseball Biography Project, accessed July 7, 2024, https://sabr.org/bioproj/person/biz-mackey/.
9. "Biz Mackey," Baseball-Reference.com-Major League Statistics and Information, accessed July 7, 2024, https://baseballreference.com/players/m/mackebi99.shtml.
10. Rainey, "Biz Mackey."
11. "Willie Wells," Baseball-Reference.com-Major League Statistics and Information, accessed July 7, 2024, https://www.baseball-reference.com/players/w/wellswi99.shtml.
12. Rob Fink, *Playing in Shadows: Texas and Negro League Baseball* (Lubbock: Texas Tech University Press, 2010), 20.
13. Ibid., 21
14. Ibid., 22.
15. Ibid., 23.
16. Ibid., 23–24.
17. Ibid., 26.
18. Ibid., 26.
19. Ibid., 75.
20. During its three-year existence, TOL teams played in Austin, Dallas, Fort Worth, Galveston, Houston, Monroe, New Orleans, Oklahoma City, Port Arthur, San Antonio, Shreveport, Tulsa, Waco, and Wichita Falls.
21. Fink, *Playing in Shadows*, 28.
22. Ibid., 84–85.
23. Ibid., 85.
24. Ibid., 88.
25. The Cincinnati Reds played the first Major League night game under the lights in 1935.
26. Ibid., 88.
27. Ibid., 90.
28. Mark Odintz, "Kerr County," *Handbook of Texas Online*, accessed October 2, 2025, https://www.tshaonline.org/handbook/entries/kerr-county.
29. United States Ninth Census, 1870, Vol. 1, Part 6, Table II-Population by Counties-1790–1870-State of Texas, 65, National Archives, Washington,

DC, accessed November 2, 2025https://www2.census.gov/library/publications/decennial/1870/population/1870a-10.pdf.

30. Raymond Hardee, who played for the All-Stars in the 1960s, personifies the community-minded legacy of his ancestors, receiving a Kerrville Kindness award from the City of Kerrville in 2026 for his work with special needs students, among many other civic activities.
31. *Hill Country Community Journal*, February 23, 2018, accessed December 19, 2024, https://www.hccommunityjournal.com/article_d563b3c6–1859–11e8–9b1e-831da449bb52.html.
32. By comparison, other nearby counties had the following percentages of Black residents in 1930: Gillespie County (Fredericksburg), 1.1 percent (about 128 residents); Kendall County (Boerne and Comfort), 1.3 percent (about 66 residents); and Bandera County 0.3 percent (about 11 residents). United States Fifteenth Census (1930), Vol. 3, Part 2, Table 21-Population by Sex, Color, Age, Etc. for Counties by Minor Civil Divisions: 1930, 1059, 1065, 1069, National Archives, Washington, DC, accessed November 2, 2025, https://www2.census.gov/library/publications/decennial/1930/population-volume-3/10612982v3p2ch09.pdf.
33. United States Fifteenth Census (1930), Vol. 3, Part 2, Table 21-Population by Sex, Color, Age, Etc. for Counties by Minor Civil Divisions: 1930,1069, National Archives, Washington, DC, accessed November 2, 2025, https://www2.census.gov/library/publications/decennial/1930/population-volume-3/10612982v3p2ch09.pdf.
34. At that time, Kerrville's White team was known as the Athletics.
35. *Kerrville Mountain Sun*, July 7, 1922, 1.
36. *Kerrville Mountain Sun*, August 18, 1922, 2.
37. Joe Herring Jr. Blog, August 6, 2017, accessed December 21, 2024, https://joeherringjr.blogspot.com/2017/08/kerrvilles-west-texas-fair.html. The site was on the river side of the intersection of Water Street and Junction Highway, called Five Points. Ibid. See chapter 12 for more details on ballparks in Kerrville.
38. Lester Fifer is the father of Clifton Fifer Sr., who both played for and managed the All-Stars, and the grandfather of Clifton Fifer Jr., who generously provided to the author a wealth of information about Kerrville's Black team.
39. *Kerrville Mountain Sun*, August 7, 1924, 2.
40. *Kerrville Mountain Sun*, April 9, 1925, 1. See chapter 12 for more on Kerrville's ballpark.
41. Ibid.

42. *Kerrville Mountain Sun*, May 7, 1925, 10.
43. Ibid.
44. Ibid.
45. Later that month, the Black Athletics played the Van Cortland Social Club of San Antonio, also immediately after White teams played on the same diamond. With Butler on the mound, the Black Athletics prevailed in a five-inning game, 3–2. *Kerrville Mountain Sun*, April 16, 1925, 6.
46. *Kerrville Mountain Sun*, May 7, 1925, 10.
47. *Kerrville Mountain Sun*, June 23, 1927, 1.
48. *Kerrville Mountain Sun*, May 24, 1928, 9; *Kerrville Mountain Sun*, July 19, 1928, 12.
49. *Kerrville Mountain Sun*, May 24, 1928, 9. The newspaper article refers to Kerrville's opponents as the "San Antonio Red Sox," but later the same season, Kerrville played the San Antonio "Black Sox," also according to the *Kerrville Mountain Sun.* Given the practice of using the term "Black" to describe Black teams, we assume that "San Antonio Black Sox" is correct rather than San Antonio Red Sox, and so we use it here.
50. *Kerrville Mountain Sun*, May 24, 1928, 9.
51. Ibid.
52. *Kerrville Mountain Sun*, July 19, 1928, 12.
53. *Kerrville Mountain Sun*, August 23, 1928, 5.
54. *Kerrville Mountain Sun*, August 30, 1928, 5.
55. *Kerrville Mountain Sun*, April 11, 1929, 1.
56. Ibid., 12.
57. *Kerrville Mountain Sun*, July 4, 1929, 3.
58. *Kerrville Mountain Sun*, April 10, 1930, 12.
59. *Junction Eagle*, May 26, 1932, 1.
60. Ibid.
61. Ibid.
62. Ibid.
63. Email interview of Clifton Fifer Jr., son of player and manager, Clifton Fifer Sr., September 27, 2024 (printed copy in possession of author).
64. Ibid.
65. The Colored School was later named for Anna W. Doyle, who was the head teacher for nearly two decades. Texas Historical Marker no. 18323, Texas Historical Commission, accessed November 1, 2025, https://atlas.thc.texas.gov/. Doyle School is now the Doyle Community Center. *Voices of Doyle* by Kerrville videographer Alyson Amestoy is a wonderful documentary about the Doyle School.

66. Texas Historical Marker no. 18779 and Texas Historical Marker no. 17312, Texas Historical Commission, accessed November 1, 2025, https://atlas.thc.texas.gov/.
67. Ibid.
68. Ibid.
69. Doyle Music Trail Historical Marker, accessed November 1, 2025, https://www.facebook.com/kerrvilleurbantrails/posts/621807626796604/.
70. Interview of Clifton Fifer Jr., son of player and manager, Clifton Fifer Sr., December 4, 2023 (interview notes in possession of author).
71. Interview of Sylvia Lewis, widow of player Joe Lewis, December 4, 2023 (interview notes in possession of author).
72. Interview of Clifton Fifer Jr., son of player and manager, Clifton Fifer Sr., December 4, 2023 (interview notes in possession of author).
73. Interview of Clifton Fifer Jr., son of player and manager, Clifton Fifer Sr., December 4, 2023 (interview notes in possession of author).
74. Ibid.
75. Interview of Sylvia Lewis, widow of player Joe Lewis, December 4, 2023 (interview notes in possession of author).
76. Email interview of Clifton Fifer Jr., son of player and manager, Clifton Fifer Sr., September 27, 2024 (printed copy in possession of author).
77. Interview of Clifton Fifer Jr., son of player and manager, Clifton Fifer Sr., December 4, 2023 (interview notes in possession of author).
78. Interview of Sylvia Lewis, widow of player Joe Lewis, December 4, 2023 (interview notes in possession of author).
79. *Kerrville Mountain Sun*, September 15, 1932, 10. We note that the deficit in the Braves' bank account may have been a factor in Kerrville's decision to propose the formation of the Mountain League in early 1933 after the Hill Country League rejected Kerrville's plan for a southern circuit to reduce travel expenses. See chapter 8.
80. Ibid.
81. "Colander" was probably Charley Callander, who pitched for the All-Stars in 1933 and 1934, and later served as manager in 1937.
82. *Kerrville Mountain Sun*, September 22, 1932, 1, 10.
83. Ibid., 10. We have printed the box score as it appeared in the *Kerrville Mountain Sun*. However, several totals in the published box score do not add up. For example, the box score shows five errors by the Braves but lists only four players committing one error each. Similar discrepancies are found in the total at-bats for the Braves and the total outs for the All-Stars. In addition, the number of innings pitched by All-Stars pitchers

Colander and Overton are missing. Finally, the All-Stars are shown as the home team in the box score, but the Braves scored the winning run in the bottom of the ninth with one out, ending the game.

84. *Comfort News*, June 15, 1995, 6.
85. Ibid. Later, in the 1940s, Frost served as the manager of the Kerrville All-Stars. See the team photograph in this chapter.
86. *Kerrville Mountain Sun*, March 30, 1933, 1.
87. *Kerrville Mountain Sun*, June 15, 1933, 1.
88. *Kerrville Mountain Sun*, June 22, 1933, 10.
89. *Kerrville Daily Times*, June 22, 1933, 11.
90. In August 1936, a notice in the *Kerrville Mountain Sun* indicated that the Black Braves were scheduled to play the Fredericksburg Giants—a White team and champions of the Mountain League in 1934 and 1935. *Kerrville Mountain Sun*, August 13, 1936, 3. However, the author found no published report that this game was played. At that time, the Giants were finishing the HCL regular season before starting the playoffs on their way to the 1936 HCL championship.
91. "Calander" was probably Charley Callander, who played for the team in 1933 and 1934, and served later as manager in 1937.
92. *Kerrville Mountain Sun*, October 12, 1933, 7.
93. The Kerrville Athletics had changed their name to the Kerrville Braves.
94. In 1953 and 1954, the team was known as the Giants but then returned to the All-Stars moniker.
95. *Kerrville Mountain Sun*, March 29, 1934, 3.
96. *Kerrville Mountain Sun*, April 5, 1934, 6.
97. Ibid.
98. Ibid.
99. The newspaper article in the *Kerrville Mountain Sun* identifies the pitcher only as "Callander" but we presume it was Charley Callander.
100. *Kerrville Mountain Sun*, July 12, 1934, 7.
101. Ibid.
102. *Kerrville Mountain Sun*, May 2, 1935, 9.
103. Ibid.
104. *Kerrville Mountain Sun*, April 25, 1935, 1. The brief newspaper report of the game does not indicate whether the Center Point team was a White or Black team.
105. *Kerrville Times*, March 19, 1936, 1.
106. *Kerrville Times*, March 26, 1936, 1.
107. *Kerrville Times*, April 2, 1936, 10.

108. This gimmick may have been patterned after a similar promotion by Gus Greenlee, owner of the Pittsburgh Crawfords in 1933. Fink, *Playing in Shadows*, 96–97.
109. *Kerrville Times*, April 16, 1936, 15.
110. Ibid. We could find no report of the game with the Black Tigers.
111. *Kerrville Times*, April 30, 1936, 1; *Kerrville Times*, May 10, 1936, 12.
112. *Kerrville Times*, May 21, 1936, 8.
113. Ibid. We note that Dimery's name is spelled "Demry" in the newspaper report. However, the proper spelling of the player's name was probably "Dimery."
114. *Kerrville Times*, April 22, 1937, 8.
115. *Kerrville Times*, March 17, 1960, 6.
116. *Kerrville Times*, April 5, 1960, 6.
117. *Kerrville Times*, April 12, 1960, 6.
118. *Kerrville Times*, May 22, 1960, 8.
119. *Boerne Star*, August 9, 1962, 4.
120. *Kerrville Daily Times*, March 10, 1964, 7.
121. Interview of Clifton Fifer Jr., son of player and manager, Clifton Fifer Sr., December 4, 2023 (interview notes in possession of author).

EPILOGUE

1. The only exception to this is New Braunfels, the first planned German settlement. New Braunfels did not field a team in the Hill Country League or the Mountain League.
2. Bandera was settled by Polish sawmill workers. See chapter 1.
3. In 1935, Legion, now a part of the City of Kerrville, also played in the Mountain League. At the same time, Llano dominated the Hill Country League, winning three consecutive league titles in 1933–35.
4. However, Boerne was sent into a frenzy when the Boerne Little League team played for the US Championship at the 2024 Little League World Series.
5. We note that Fredericksburg did not play in the Mountain League in 1933.

SELECTED BIBLIOGRAPHY

Bandera County History Book Committee. *History of Bandera County Texas.* Bandera, TX: Bandera County History Book Committee, 1986.

Barr, Alwyn. *Black Texans: A History of African Americans in Texas, 1528–1995.* Norman: University of Oklahoma Press, 1995.

Biesele, Rudolph Leopold. *The History of the German Settlements in Texas, 1831–1861.* Austin: Eakin Press, 1930.

Biggers, Don H. *German Pioneers in Texas.* Austin: Fredericksburg Publishing, 1983.

Casway, Jerrold I. *The Culture and Ethnicity of Nineteenth-Century Baseball.* Jefferson, NC: McFarland & Company, 2017.

Coppedge, Clay. *Texas Baseball: A Lone Star Diamond History from Town Teams to the Big Leagues.* Charleston, SC: History Press, 2012.

Fehrenbach, T. R. *Lone Star: A History of Texas and the Texans.* Updated edition. New York: Da Capo Press, 2000.

Fink, Rob. *Playing in Shadows: Texas and Negro League Baseball.* Lubbock: Texas Tech University Press, 2010.

Gelo, Daniel J., and Christopher J. Wickham. *The German Texas Frontier in 1953: Ferdinand Lindheimer's Newspaper Accounts of the Environment, Gold, and Indians.* Denton: University of North Texas Press, 2024.

Gillespie County Historical Society. *Fredericksburg, Texas: The Second Fifty Years.* Fredericksburg, TX: Gillespie County Historical Society, 2022.

———. Gillespie County Historical Society. *Gillespie County.* Charleston, SC: Arcadia Publishing, 2013.

Gregory, Robert. *Diz: The Story of Dizzy Dean and Baseball During the Great Depression.* New York: Viking, 1992.

Gustafson, Mark. *A Naturalist's Guide to the Texas Hill Country.* College Station: Texas A&M University Press, 2015.

Herring, Joe, Jr. *Kerrville Stories: Historic Photographs and Newspaper Columns.* Kerrville, TX: Herring Printing Company, 2012.

Hunter, J. Marvin. *One Hundred Years in Bandera, 1853–1953: A Story of Sturdy*

Pioneers, Their Struggles and Hardship, and Their Heroic Achievements. Salem, MA: Higginson Book Company, 1953.

Kerrville Daily Times. A Pictorial History of Kerr County, Texas. Marceline, MO: D-Books Publishing, 1994.

Levy, Alan H. *Rube Waddell.* Jefferson, NC: McFarland & Company, 2000.

Lich, Glen E. *The Federal Republic of Germany and Texas.* Bonn, Germany: Inter Nationes Bonn, 1986.

———. *The German Texans.* San Antonio: University of Texas Institute of Texan Cultures at San Antonio, 1981.

Morgenthaler, Jefferson. *The German Settlement of the Texas Hill Country.* Boerne, TX: Mockingbird Books, 2007.

Perry, Garland. *Historic Images of Boerne and Kendall County, Texas.* Sesquicentennial Edition. Boerne, TX: Perry Publications, 1998.

Rothman, Hal K. *LBJ's Texas White House.* College Station: Texas A&M University Press, 2001.

Seymour, Harold, and Dorothy Seymour Mills. *Baseball: The People's Game.* New York: Oxford University Press, 1990.

Staten, Vince. *Ol' Diz: A Biography of Dizzy Dean.* New York: HarperCollins, 1992.

Stephens, A. Ray. *Texas: A Historical Atlas.* Norman: University of Oklahoma Press, 2010.

Vaught, David. *The Farmer's Game: Baseball in Rural America.* Baltimore: Johns Hopkins University Press, 2013.

INDEX

Page numbers in italics refer to images. Note that some players are identified by last name only.

ABOUT THE AUTHOR

Richard W. Butler Jr. is a lifelong baseball fan and a retired local government attorney who practiced in Michigan for thirty-six years. After moving to the Texas Hill Country in 2022, Butler became fascinated with the history of baseball in the region. A member of the Society for American Baseball Research (SABR) since 1983 and a member of the Kendall County Historical Commission, Butler employed his analytical skills and baseball knowledge to research the story of Hill Country baseball. He has published several works in *Turnstyle*, a SABR publication. *Hill Country Ball* is his first book. He lives with his wife in Boerne, Texas.

www.ingramcontent.com/pod-product-compliance
Lightning Source LLC
LaVergne TN
LVHW050910220826
846195LV00026B/131